Enlightenment
East and West

Enlightenment
East and West

by
Leonard Angel

STATE UNIVERSITY OF NEW YORK PRESS

Published by
State University of New York Press, Albany

For information, address the State University of New York Press,
State University Plaza, Albany, NY 12246

Production by Christine Lynch
Marketing by Fran Keneston

Library of Congress Cataloging-in-Publication Data

Angel, Leonard, 1945-
    Enlightenment East and West / by Leonard Angel.
        p.   cm.
    Includes bibliographical references and index.
    ISBN 0-7914-2053-1 (alk. paper). — ISBN 0-7914-2054-X (pbk. :
alk. paper)
    1. Mysticism. 2. East and West. I. Title.
BL625.A52 1994
291.4′22—dc20   93-39936
                                                                    CIP

10 9 8 7 6 5 4 3 2 1

Contents

Preface

This book is written for both specialists and nonspecialists: It's written for students of religion and culture who assume, as I do, that where there are widely differing values, there must be a way, somehow, of establishing fruitful dialogue between their exponents. It's written for the postmodernist who thinks it's foolish to hope for any syntheses across widely divergent value systems; for my colleagues trained in analytic philosophy who would like to have mysticism made accessible; for theological students and religious practitioners of all traditions and backgrounds concerned about integrating social humanism with intuitions of sacralism and Divine Mystery; for the existentialist who is at the point of wanting more than freedom; for the student of paranormal psychology; for the cultural theorist interested in understanding the broad shape of history; and, finally, it's written for mystics who are looking for an account of mysticism, its content, its values, and its implications for human community, which pays more than lip service to the desire for clarity.

There are many topics swirling through this book, and it may be easy to get lost in the currents. Consequently, it will be useful to highlight some main theses I am advancing (one for each chapter):

1. Those who think that mysticism and scientific and social rationalism should be easy to accommodate to each other probably have not listened closely to the rumors of the many apparent irreconcilables.

2. Contrary to the tale told by postmodernist and relativist authors, a comprehensive framework of value can be articulated whose vocabulary and basic concepts are immediately recognizable to people of all cultures, and, which is sufficiently detailed to enable fruitful dialogue to take place between people no matter how divergent their backgrounds and values. This framework is the relational ethical framework presented in chapter 2.

3. It is widely agreed that in order to develop ethics completely one must engage in value theory. What is not recognized is that mysticism's primary thrust is in value theory. The mystic holds that mystical experience is of supreme value. Consequently, the ethicist must

undertake to become familiar with mysticism and mystical experience, or else admit that there is a central claim within value theory that she or he cannot address.

4. Mysticism can be understood by the non-mystic. Its claims can be articulated in a way that does no violence to the laws of logic or clear thinking, and a set of clear practices can be presented which enable the non-mystic to grasp, and practice if desired, the central elements of mystical training, and the six (or seven, depending how you count) main mystical standpoints.

5. Because mystical standpoints are in the first instance ways of experiencing the world, or ways of maintaining one's consciousness, and because each mystical standpoint has a corresponding, distinct metaphysical interpretation, mystical experience is of virtually no *evidential* value for mystical metaphysics. Nonetheless, acquiring mystical standpoints is of real aid for the philosopher: it informs philosophical psychology, and it reawakens the quest for speculative metaphysical understanding.

6. The most important point of contact between religion and ethics is not on the issue of Divine Command theory, but on the question of cultivating the intuition of the sacred as a crucial element of one's experience. The sacralist ethics is distinct from a secularist ethics; it doesn't involve any dogma or Divine Command component, and needs to be taken seriously by moral philosophers and cultural theorists.

7. Mysticism is not otherworldly, and can be fully integrated with the most worldly of social visions.

8. Examination of the evidence for paranormal occurrences such as clairvoyance, materializations, spontaneous past-life memories, and so on, leads to conclusions on the validity of these phenomena which are sure to startle many assumptions frequently made concerning the relations between science, mysticism, and the paranormal.

9. Without supplementation by a mystical vision, the western Enlightenment project cannot complete itself. Progress depends on the integration of mysticism into liberalism.

I am deeply indebted to more people than I can thank here. During the last few months I have been reworking many details, and comments by my philosophy colleagues at Douglas College have been most helpful. Robert Fahrnkopf gave me excellent responses to a recent draft. Brian Davies and Doug Simak have stimulated my thinking in many areas and provided helpful remarks.

For roughly a year, Dr. Shotaro Iida and I had weekly meetings, at which conversation ranged over an enormously wide variety of topics and projects. I'm deeply in his debt for his insights and his vibrant and indomitable approach to problems both practical and theoretical. Kurt Preinspurg was the official commenter when the first draft of what is now chapter four was presented at a U.B.C. colloquium some years ago. His helpful comments resulted in improvements to the chapter, and over the years we have had many fruitful conversations, on politics, history, metaphysics, and freedom. Verena Huber Dyson helped me clarify my thoughts on several topics over the years, and some of the discussions found in the book would have been much weaker were it not for her responses to some early versions of the arguments. Since the days when Mark Glouberman and I "measured the speed of light," I have been trying to keep up with the speed of his wit. I'm most grateful to him for his feedback on many ideas in so many areas, and his genuinely stimulating approach and comments. During the course of some pleasant and productive exchanges, Sol Kort urged me to read Charlene Spretnak's work, and I'm grateful for that lead. He has also provided many others, which have also proved useful. Ken Hertz gave me some important feedback on modes of identification given his excruciating (and unfortunately ongoing) experience as a victim of a severe form of almost total Parkinsonian paralysis. I thank Earl Winkler at U.B.C. for inviting me to make a presentation at the 1990 Centre For Applied Ethics Conference. The presentation was the initial draft of what has become chapter 2.

I'm equally indebted to many others who read portions of the manuscript, sent me articles, provided sources or advice, or conversed at length on various topics covered herein over the years, including: Ronald de Sousa, Alan Drengson, Ali Kazmi, Dale Beyerstein, Spencer Carr, Eileen Sowerby, Barry Beyerstein, Don Evans, Shia Moser, Rhoda Friedrichs, Michael Feld, Sam Coval, Chris Friedrichs, Steve Slutsky, Don LePan, Sue Wendell, Frank Leonard, Hugo Meynell, Howard Horsburgh, Vidjut Aklujkar, Ken Dangerfield, Louise Schmidt, and Bob Hadley. My students have tested the ideas in this book, and helped form them at every turn. I want to thank Barbara Sefran for her references, queries, and thorough work on the index. I'm also indebted to the anonymous readers for SUNY whose reports contained invaluable suggestions and comments, and to Lois Patton, Christine Lynch, Nancy Ellegate, and the other members of the SUNY editorial, production and marketing team for their superb suggestions and advice on the project. This work has been inspired, guided, aided, and reshaped by many. Its errors, however, are my responsibility alone; I would very much appreciate it if readers respond, pointing out errors and difficulties in lines of reasoning, so that I may improve my thinking on those matters.

Scholarship is always a pleasure, but within an atmosphere of serenity it has been blissful. I'm deeply grateful to my wife Susan for her serenity, wisdom, and constant support. Thanks also to Naomi, T'ai, and Ken for help with the ideas of chapters 2 and 3.

I wish to thank the editors of *Skeptical Inquirer* for permission to incorporate the material of my article "Is There Empirical Evidence for Reincarnation?" into chapter 8. Finally, I am most grateful for Social Sciences and Humanities Research Council of Canada grant No. 410-85-0132, which funded time for the development of this book.

New Westminster, B. C.
August 3, 1993

One

The Two Faces of Enlightenment

If we speak of 'enlightenment' in the context of the history of ideas in the western world, we are referring to that strand of thought beginning in Europe around the seventeenth century that centrally values the pursuit of scientific, objectively verifiable knowledge, individual autonomy, social progress, and justice. If we speak of 'enlightenment' in the context of eastern thought, we are referring to *satori*, or the mystically awakened mind. Accordingly, we may speak of an Enlightenment West perspective that revolves around the acquisition of scientific knowledge, increasing social justice and maximizing human happiness. And we can refer to an Enlightenment East perspective that values the practices held to be conducive towards mystical self-realization, or *moksha*, spiritual liberation, or *satori*.

Of course there is no intention to suggest by reference to Enlightenment East that the east is entirely or even predominantly mystical, nor is the term 'Enlightenment West' intended to suggest that the west is predominantly rational or anti-mystical. Our nomenclature, quite simply, derives from the different meanings the term 'enlightenment' acquires in the context of western compared with eastern philosophy and history of ideas. Indeed, neither 'Enlightenment East' nor 'Enlightenment West', on this usage, designates a perspective whose exponent is geographically located. Obviously, western thinkers can espouse a perspective or value system dominated by what the word 'enlightenment' means in eastern thought and vice versa. It is the perspectives, or value systems, we are referring to. 'Enlightenment West', then, means, roughly, humanistic and scientific rationalism, and 'Enlightenment East' means, roughly, mysticism.

To be more contextually precise, I will offer a list of some main sources one can look to in an effort to locate elements of Enlightenment East and West. The terms 'mysticism' and 'scientific and social rationalism' are sufficiently subject to interpretation that the concepts would be too open-ended without a set of paradigm texts

1

and sources. The list is not intended to be an exhaustive anchoring but merely suggestive.

Among sources within which to find expositions of Enlightenment East ethics and metaphysics, one could look to *(a)* Yoga philosophy as expounded by Patanjali, *(b)* Advaita Vedanta as systematized by Shankara, *(c)* Theravada Buddhism, *(d)* Madhyamika Buddhism, *(e)* Zen Buddhism, *(f)* philosophical Taoism, as in the writings attributed to Lao Tzu and Chuang Tzu, *(g)* the writings of Parmenides, where these are interpreted as asserting a strong form of monism, *(h)* the *Enneads* of Plotinus, and *(i)* the *Ethics* of Spinoza. We should also include *(j)* Jewish *devekut* mysticism, *(k)* Christian mysticism as found, for example, in Meister Eckhart, as well as *(l)* Islamic esoteric mysticism including Sufi texts and practices, as sources for some Enlightenment East notions, even though the encasement of the mystical teachings in theistic systems sometimes makes the classifications problematic. It should also be noted that the term 'Enlightenment East' as we're using it does not centrally include bhakti (i.e., devotional) forms of Hinduism, nor Dvaita (dualist) Vedanta texts, nor Pure Land Buddhism in its standard or exoteric interpretation, nor Carvakin materialism, nor much of Confucianism, each of which plays an important role in the history of eastern thought and culture.

To find sources for Enlightenment West notions, one might look to *(a)* foundationalist approaches to the theory of knowledge from the seventeenth century and on, *(b)* the French Encyclopedist movement, *(c)* social contractarian theory from Hobbes through Rousseau and on, *(d)* Kantian deontology, *(e)* utilitarianism from Bentham through Mill and Russell, *(f)* progressivism in the philosophy of history, *(g)* various utopian socialist movements, *(h)* Comtian humanism, and *(i)* many aspects of Confucian humanism, to name some prominent branches of the humanist tree. Enlightenment West does not include any of the prophetic authoritarian versions of Judaism, Christianity, and Islam, each of which is of immense importance in the history of western thought and consciousness. Nor does it include Parmenidean monism, nor neo-Platonic forms of mystical metaphysics, nor the esoteric mysticisms such as Kabbalah and Sufism associated with western religious traditions. Nor does Enlightenment West include radical subjectivism, radical existentialism, or radical postmodernism, each of which has been of crucial importance in recent thought in the west.

In sum, 'Enlightenment East' refers to a style of thought, wherever it may be found historically and culturally expressed, in which the central doctrine is the belief in the possibility of mystical experience, and in which the pursuit of mystical awakening is centrally valued. By mystical awakening or mystical experience we mean, roughly, the experience of dissolution of the ego, or oneness with the Absolute Ground of Being. 'Enlightenment West' refers to a style of thought, wherever it may be found historically and culturally expressed, in which the central value is the humanistic pursuit of social and individual well-being, justice, and scientific rationalism.

Our primary interest in what follows is to explore the relationship between these two value systems. Plainly, there is an important contrast of some sort between Enlightenment East and Enlightenment West values as thus articulated. And wherever there is a contrast between two sets of values, the question is immediately raised as to their consistency in relation to one another. It may be that there are serious practical or theoretical obstacles in the path of one who would wish to live in accordance with both Enlightenment West and Enlightenment East values. Indeed, there are many who have argued just that. In our times, we have the weight of the Anglo-American philosophical tradition heaving against any justification and, even, intelligibility, of the cognitive claims of the mystic; and there are social and religious thinkers who argue the irreconcilability of the Enlightenment East and Enlightenment West values. On the other hand, there are those who would like to think that Enlightenment East and Enlightenment West values can meet.

There are, however, two ways in which one might envision a meeting of these values. The values might be discovered to be broadly consistent, so that one can espouse both. One's task, then, would be to work out a schedule that reflects one's priorities of implementing them. (That's right, a schedule, in the literal sense: One spends so much of one's time emptying the mind of thought, and so much of one's time thinking; so much time sitting in the lotus posture, and so much time making sandwiches at free food outlets.) In such a case one might say that Enlightenment East and Enlightenment West values meet and shake hands. On the other hand, one might hope for more. One might hope to find that the values not only meet and shake hands, but date, become engaged, and married.

The theme of this book is that Enlightenment East and Enlightenment West traditions have come of age. They have gone through their puberty agonies, and are now ready for the nuptials. Enlightenment East and Enlightenment West values are not only minimally consistent, but also mutually required. Unless and until one integrates mysticism with scientific and social rationalism, one has an incomplete understanding of the cosmos, and incomplete ethics. The Enlightenment West project of making scientific and social progress must be informed by Enlightenment East mysticism. And developing Enlightenment East mystical doctrines, practices and institutions must be informed by Enlightenment West values of clarity in thought, scientific knowledge, and awareness of social justice.

Of course there is a problem for anyone who wants to argue not only the meeting but also the marriage of East and West Enlightenment perspectives. The problem is that there are apparent irreconcilables in the way the traditions either have worked themselves out or have appeared to work themselves out. Accordingly, our first task is to have a good hard look at the apparent obstacles to any marriage of Enlightenment East and West values. These apparent obstacles will provide us, in effect, with our table of contents for discussion.

The problem, in a nutshell, is that Enlightenment East traditions are, or sometimes appear to be, world-devaluing, whereas Enlightenment West traditions are wholeheartedly and devotedly worldly. Moreover, Enlightenment West traditions seem to some to objectify everything, to be based fundamentally on it-ification of world, self, and happiness, so that the very basis of the Enlightenment East approach, namely, dissolution of the ego, appears to be undermined. If the aim of Enlightenment West is to maximize ego happiness, and the aim of Enlightenment East is to dissolve the ego, then the aims are, or appear to be, irreconcilable.

Let us now look at the alleged irreconcilability in more specific terms. At this stage, we are not concerned about the accuracy of the charges leveled. Rather, our task here is to lay on the table the apparent irreconcilables, as they are taken to exist within recent currents of thought. Later we will assess the accuracy of the descriptions on which the appearances of irreconcilability are based, as well as the justification of the charges. Since the apparent problems are pure hearsay at this stage, we would do well to entitle our allegations the "Catalogue of Rumors."

CATALOGUE OF RUMORS PART I:
ALLEGED FLAWS OF THE
ENLIGHTENMENT EAST TRADITIONS

Rumor 1

Renunciation is the spiritual ideal of Enlightenment East. In the traditional Indian social system, it is alleged, anyone might at any time, despite objections from family members, decide to become a *sanyasin*, a renunciate. In some cases, the sanyasin might even decide to abandon wife and children in order to pursue mystical self-realization, as the founder of Buddhism is reported to have done. (See Kalupahana & Kalupahana, 1982, pp. 73f, for a contemporary conjecture concerning the social issues involved in such a decision as they would have been perceived in ancient times.) For the exponent of Enlightenment West, even the issue of financial responsibility for the welfare of the abandoned family is not ultimately determinative of the ethics of renunciation. Rather the objectionable fact is that the life of the sanyasin, which is devoted completely to the goal of liberation or moksha, is held to be the spiritual life par excellence, the following of the highest calling. The sanyasin has no social ties or obligations. The sanyasin does not go about instituting beneficial social changes, and goodness knows, says the critic of Enlightenment East, there were surely many such changes which would have been appropriately introduced. Thus, there is sanctioning in the mystical traditions of what to the Enlightenment West modernist appears to be social irresponsibility in the pursuit of the mystical goals.

As A. C. Bouquet writes, ". . . the world-renouncing ascetic is the type universally admired, and his renunciation is in no sense altruistic or philanthropic, but is purely self-regarding, since it is every man's business and license to look after his eternal welfare; and to be concerned with delivering oneself from the generally accepted chain of rebirth, and from the cycle of biological existence is not considered to be a blemish upon one's character" (Bouquet 1956, p. 147).

Rumor 2

Celibacy is an ideal. Within mystical traditions, according to the critic, it is often held that the person most fully suited to religious contemplation, mystical realization, or spiritual attainment is the celibate. The critic of Enlightenment East would not find it difficult to point to texts which support such claims. For instance, the well-known twentieth-century teacher of yoga, Sivananda, writes that "Celibacy . . . is of vital importance. It is the gateway to liberation or eternal bliss, it bestows super-human strength and supreme bliss, and it is the basis for morality. Absolute celibacy is the sine qua non of divine life or spiritual higher life. The door to nirvana or perfection is complete celibacy" (Sivananda, 1985, p. 286). The celibate may or may not be a forest dweller, but there appears to be a significant amount of world-devaluing in the ideal of celibacy. Furthermore, from the standpoint of Enlightenment West, it might be held, marriage and family life constitute the ideal spiritual training ground.

Rumor 3

The best one can attain is cessation of the cycle of rebirths. Mystical systems often teach that re-birth in this world is something to escape from. As Swami Nikhilananda puts it, ". . . from the relative standpoint, the Vedanta philosophy admits the existence of a multitude of individual souls, called jivatmas, and distinguishes them from the supreme soul. Attached to the body, the individual soul is a victim of the pairs of opposites. Entangled in the world, it seeks deliverance from the eternal round of birth and death, and with that end in view studies the scriptures and practices spiritual disciplines under the guidance of a qualified teacher" (Nikhilananda, 1968, p. 49). This too seems to be world-devaluing.

Rumor 4

According to the Enlightenment East doctrine as it is often presented, *one's station in life is fixed by the karma associated with one's past lives.* Hence, charges the critic, incredible suffering is ignored or rationalized. Instead of being eliminated, it is tolerated on the grounds that it is karmically fitting, and we need not exert ourselves unduly to alter the situation. Indeed the rigid and oppressive caste system as it has actually been practiced (not the theoretical meritocracy it has sometimes been touted as) has been justified along these lines. A. C. Danto forcefully articulates this criticism of Enlightenment East traditions: "Respect for life as a whole is consistent with a not especially edifying attitude towards one's fellowmen, who, for all that they may be one essentially, nevertheless remain lodged at different stations on the surfaces of the world. That they should be where they are is, as *karma* teaches, very much a matter of just desert: they are there because they deserve to be there. Our *karma* has brought each of us to whatever pass we are at. Indians tend to invoke *karma*, and hence their past wickedness, to justify the evils that befall them, much as Christians invoke their sins. As each man gets what he deserves, there seems to be no special reason to help one another. Men have only themselves to blame for what they are. Had they been better, they would be better off now. It is up to them to try for a better life next time. Present felicity, likewise, is the mark of having done well before. With a row of lifetimes in which to improve one's karmic station stretching endlessly before one, there seems very little urgency in doing very much in this brief moment" (Danto, 1973, p. 38f).

Scriptural authority for the theory of karmic justice is to be found in very ancient materials. Chandogya Upanishad, (5:10,7) states, "Those whose conduct has been good will quickly attain a good birth, the birth of either a Brahmin, or a Kshatriya, or a Vaishya. But those whose conduct has been stinking will attain a stinking birth, the birth of either a dog, or a swine, or an outcaste [Chandala]" (Kaufmann, 1976, p. 221). Facing a similar problem, Agehananda Bharati writes ". . . the second canto of the Gita teaches, 'Do not abandon such actions as are born with you. It is better to perform these actions, even though they be bad, than to perform others' actions', where 'others' actions' mean[s] actions. to which you are not entitled by your birth, actions, that is, to which persons of different birth are entitled. This passage, of course, is crass theological casteism; it goes without saying that the representatives of the Hindu Renaissance, which rejects innate rights belonging to any particular social group, cannot accept it at its face-value. On the other hand, it is such clear and unambiguous Sanskrit that esoteric interpretation would look too artificial even to those who are impressed by metaphorical verbosity" (Bharati, 1976, p. 133).

Rumor 5

In Taoism, the ideal individual, the Taoist sage, is one who realizes and cleaves to the ineffable, mysterious way. According to some critics, this implies that the Taoist sage lies low, follows nature, doesn't interfere, doesn't intrude a particular, private point of view on the world. *The ideal individual in Taoism is more or less socially invisible,* according to these critics. The justification for such criticism may be held to be found lurking even in such sympathetic expositions as Huston Smith's, for example, "The Taoists' refusal to clamber for position sprang from a profound disinterest in the things the world prizes. The point comes out in the story of Chuang Tzu's visit to the minister of a neighboring state. Someone told the minister that Chuang Tzu was coming in the hope of replacing him. The minister was severely alarmed. But when Chuang Tzu heard of the rumor he said to the minister: 'In the South there is a bird. It is called *yuan-ch'u.* Have you heard of it? This yuan-ch'u starts from the southern ocean and flies to the northern ocean. During its whole journey it perches on no tree save the sacred Wo-tung, eats no fruit save that of the Persian Lilac, drinks only at the Magic Well. It happened that an owl that had got hold of the rotting carcass of a rat looked up as this bird flew by, and terrified lest the yuan-ch'u should stop and snatch at the succulent morsel, it screamed, "Shoo! Shoo!" And now I am told that you are trying to "Shoo" me off from this precious Ministry of yours.' So it is with most of the world's prizes. They are not the true values they are thought to be" (Smith, 1958 p. 208). It seems that Taoist ideals run contrary to the grain of Enlightenment West valuation of highly visible, even heroic activities on behalf of society.

Rumor 6

In Taoism, Hinduism, and Buddhism, *the individual is encouraged to give up ego-ideation*. The giving up of ego-ideation seems to be diametrically opposed to the central value found in Enlightenment West conceptions of moral living as autonomous thought and activity. Giving up the ego-ideation expresses itself institutionally in Enlightenment East systems as the requirement in the guru-disciple relationship that the student demonstrate ego-lessness by serving the guru, the living embodiment of wisdom, in complete selfless obedience. "The student had to remain strictly celibate, constantly to guard against falling into ritual impurity, and to subordinate himself to his guru's every dictate while following a course of study which, for a Brahmin, might last twelve years or longer" (Parrinder, 1971, p. 198). "He who can appreciate the blessing of being taken into the fold of the Satguru . . . will forever sing of his Grace, beauty and perfect love. . . . He will never question the actions of his Master, even if he fails to understand them. . . . He will have to develop the faith of a child, who, having trusted himself to a loving hand, moves as directed, never questioning anything" (Kirpal Singh, *The Crown Of Life*, p. 181).

Rumor 7

Moreover a particular consequence of this selfless obedience is the tradition of not questioning, and therefore not properly investigating teachings. *The practice of serving the guru in perfect obedience tends to become a training in repressing of one's natural curiosity.* And this seems to be contrary to the scientism of the Enlightenment West system of thought. Agehananda Bharati writes, "There is in the Indian tradition the notion that guru-ninda 'criticizing the guru' is a thing that the disciples must not tolerate, and they don't" (Bharati, 1976 p. 103). A further consequence of the educational method, or method of training of people in mysticism found prevalent in the Enlightenment East systems, revolving around authoritarian patterns of teacher student relationship, is that the student is required to accept systems of thought which, according to the exponent of Enlightenment West, centering on analytic clarity and philosophic rigor, turn out to be fuzzy-minded, and philosophically unintelligible. In short, the conclusions of Enlightenment East values and their doctrinal expressions are often regarded as inevitably paradoxical, antilogical, and hence, as far as the exponent of Enlightenment West values are concerned, philosophically nonsensical. Indeed, even western exponents of Enlightenment East are willing to acknowledge that Enlightenment East experience cannot be described without abandonment of the laws of logic. Walter Stace, for instance, concludes that ". . . although the laws of logic are the laws of our everyday consciousness and experience, they have no application to mystical experience" (Stace, 1960, p. 270). Few exponents of analytic clarity will be able to accept Stace's, and the mystic's, advocacy of the notion that there are noetic experiences which are not themselves, or whose descriptions are not, subject to the laws of logic.

Rumor 8

Further still along these lines, Enlightenment East values tend to express themselves in paranormal and occult theories. The *locus classicus* of paranormal claims in Indian systems of thought is the Yoga Sutras of Patanjali, Chapter III, entitled, "Powers." In this chapter, it is stated that the yogi can learn to levitate, become invisible, and cultivate other powers over nature of a rather incredible kind. Contemporary rationalist investigators such as Paul Kurtz, James Randi, Abraham Kovoor, and the Indian scientist-magician, B. Premanand, suggest that no claimant to such paranormal powers has ever been able to demonstrate the claimed powers to pre-agreed standards when scientists and magicians are around to inspect. The conclusion of such rationalist exponents of Enlightenment West values of scientific rigor and clarity, is: *Belief in the genuineness of the paranormal effects is unjustified, and the methods which mystics use to convince people of the reality of these effects are anti-scientific.* Hence, there appears to be an unbridgable gulf between Enlightenment East and Enlightenment West values and practices. Enlightenment East values and practices induce the practitioner to give up on too many features of what Paul Kurtz calls "critical intelligence" (Kurtz, 1986, pp. 60-69).

Rumor 9

And again, a social consequence of the authoritarian patterns of student teacher relations in the Enlightenment East traditions, according to the critics, is a *prevailing political conservatism.* As we've seen, the charge is that the sociopolitical status quo is taken to be an expression of karmic necessity. If the response to suffering is escape of the cycle of rebirth, and the suffering is an expression of karmic justice, then the sociopolitical causes of the injustices are, in effect, endorsed. Even worse, the critic claims, there is a distinctly antinomian or amoralist aspect to Enlightenment East otherworldly teachings. The liberated being is all too often described in language which suggests that liberation is liberation from the constraints of moral behavior. Thus, for instance, the Brihad-aranyaka Upanishad, (4:4, 22) states, "This eternal greatness of a Brahmin is not increased by deed, nor diminished. One should be familiar with it. By knowing it, one is not stained by evil action." And later, (5:14), "Even so, although he commits very much evil, one who knows this, consumes it all and becomes clean and pure, ageless and immortal." Such language does nothing to assuage Enlightenment West exponents' concern that mysticism's otherworldliness conduces to amoralist attitudes.

Rumor 10

Finally, it is suggested that history is conceived in cyclical terms by exponents of Enlightenment East. Societies come and go. Political orders come and go. The round of existence, the wheel of karma keeps turning, never getting anywhere, but turning, turning anyway. That's how it is, and *no thought of a progressive march through history* enters the picture. "The logic of Hinduism and Buddhism is of a different sort from that of the Mediterranean creeds. There is no potential for progress in the Indian core tradition" (Bharati, 1976, p. 156). By contrast, the Enlightenment West vision posits at its center the potential for progress, and the need for decisive action to bring about such progress. Belief in the potential for progressive gains in happiness and social well being through worldly restructuring is one of the definitive elements of Enlightenment West. Once again, the Enlightenment East and Enlightenment West world views appear to be diametrically opposed and irreconcilable.

These criticisms of Enlightenment East traditions may be grouped into three: Enlightenment East traditions are thought by exponents of Enlightenment West values to be:

1. World devaluing
2. Philosophically unintelligible
3. Anti-scientific

CATALOGUE OF RUMORS PART II:
THE ALLEGED FLAWS OF ENLIGHTENMENT WEST

From the other side there is an Enlightenment East critique of Enlightenment West traditions, revolving around the alleged entrenchment of objectifying attitudes within the Enlightenment West program. This criticism may be elaborated in the following way, again, subject to the cautionary note that the allegations are being presented without critical scrutiny. Our assessments of accuracy we reserve for later:

Rumor 1

According to some mystically minded critics, the Enlightenment West tradition is, to its detriment, *excessively trusting of discursive language* and the capacity of discursive language to capture the important features of consciousness and ethics, whereas exponents of Enlightenment East tradition tend, quite properly, to be mistrustful of ordinary discursive language and its capacities in these regards. "The way that can be followed is not the eternal way. The name that can be named is not the eternal name," begins the Tao Te Ching. Consequently the very framework within which Enlightenment East and Enlightenment West attitudes are to be reconciled does not seem to exist. The Enlightenment West proponent will try to do the reconciling in an abstract theoretical language, whereas the Enlightenment East proponent is not interested in theoretical reconciliations, and doesn't think theories can express the Enlightenment East experiences in any case. Then where is a common framework within which reconciliation can take place?

Rumor 2

The Enlightenment West tradition expresses its political program in lists of rights, and its moral program in lists of principles. This incessant *centering of consciousness on principles and explicit laws and statutes* seems to be fundamentally distorted from the Enlightenment East perspective. According to some Enlightenment East critiques, Enlightenment West rationalism leads to a mind set in which one finds it ever more difficult to detach from the ego and to plumb the depths of consciousness or of simple, compassionate wisdom. Instead, one becomes more and more attached to the laws, the rules, the procedures, the principles, accumulating rigidities rather than abandoning them. The Tao Te Ching, once again, speaks eloquently about the gap between a principle centered consciousness and a consciousness which is directly, immediately, and intuitively, in harmony with nature or Tao. "The great Way declines: We have humanity and justice; Prudence and wisdom appear; There is cultivation of behaviour. When the six family relationships are out of accord, there is filial piety, and parental affection. When state and dynasty are disordered, there is loyal trust." (#18) And within a strictly western contrast, William Earle in *Mystical Reason* notes the association between abandonment of wonder and reverence and the modernist program of Enlightenment West: ". . . there still remained within the supremely philosophical Plato a sense of reverence and awe before the transcendental form of the Good. Not so, of course with the Enlightenment thinkers and their present-day descendents, still searching for a *formula* of the good and its justification" (Earle, 1980, p. 84, emphasis added).

Rumor 3

The Enlightenment West tradition centers on the development of the healthy ego. The Enlightenment East tradition regards ego-consciousness as the very problem itself. Thus, the effort of Enlightenment West traditions seems to be aiming at the very worst goal. Instead of eliminating, or, at least, softening the ego perspective, *Enlightenment West traditions strengthen the ego experience*, which is the cause of our problems. As Walter Stace expresses the point: "The basis of the mystical theory of ethics is that the separateness of individual selves produces that egoism which is the source of conflict, grasping, aggressiveness, selfishness, hatred, cruelty, malice, and other forms of evil; and that this separateness is abolished in the mystical consciousness in which all distinctions are annulled. The inevitable emotional counterpart of the separateness of selves is the basic hostility which gives rise to Hobbes' war of all against all. The natural emotional counterpart of the mystical awareness that there is, in that reality which the mystic believes himself to perceive, no separateness of I from you, or of you from he, and that we are all one in the Universal Self—the emotional counterpart of this is love" (Stace, 1960, p. 324). However, the foundational metaphysics of Enlightenment West includes the notion of an objective world in which there is a plurality of separate individuals. Moral, social, and political health are conceived in terms of the proper regulation of the relations among these separate selves. Many writers, moreover, see the ego-strengthening effects of the Enlightenment West epistemologies as inevitable. Morris Berman, for instance, writes, "Since the Cartesian or Newtonian personality sees only duality, only subject/object distinction, the stage of unity . . . is permanently inaccessible to him or her. But . . . this unity is the primary reality of all human being and cognition, and to be out of touch with it is to be suffering from severe internal distortion" (Berman, 1984, p. 171).

Rumor 4

According to the Enlightenment East tradition, the rampant scientism, which is the child of the Enlightenment West program, has resulted in a thorough, unpleasant, *self-alienating objectification* of everything. Because of the Enlightenment West program people have lost the experiential treasures of mystic participation and subject-object unity. In place of mystic participation and subject-object unity is an inescapable I-it relation with self and world. Accordingly, the Enlightenment West tradition seems to lead to one's being cut off from one's body, living up in the head, instead of the heart, and out of touch with one's intimate senses. Thus, Jeremy Rifkin summarizes recent research on the modern loss of the senses of touch, smell, and even sound in favor of allowing for a complete dominance of vision and mechanistic, control-minded thinking: "The balanced relationship that had long existed among sight, sound, taste, smell, and touch was abandoned during the early modern era to make room for a worldview immersed in visual imagery. The eye helped modern man become an individual. It fostered analytical thinking and rational thought. . . . Sight is the least participatory and the most isolated of the senses. It is also the most willed of the senses and is always projected outward onto the world. Its stance is largely aggressive and expropriating. In a world increasingly mediated by sight, autonomy is inevitably pursued at the expense of relationship. . . . The separation of human beings from nature and the parallel detachment of human consciousness from the human body has transformed Western man into an alien on his own planet" (Rifkin, 1991, pp. 235-236).

Rumor 5

Finally, scientism and its consequent I-it relation with the world, according to some Enlightenment East proponents, leads one inevitably to aggrandize all forms of control. The center of the Enlightenment West program is the myth of control, and the myth of control ultimately leads to rampant, unchecked, and possibly even uncheckable militarization. The forward march of history towards universal happiness sought by Enlightenment West seems instead to be veering towards *despoilation of the environment* through rampant technologization, and possible despoilation of humanity. These negative effects are but the more or less inevitable consequences of the Enlightenment West attitudes towards individuality and nature. As Fritjof Capra expresses this point, "Our progress, then, has been largely a rational and intellectual affair, and this one-sided evolution has now reached a highly alarming stage, a situation so paradoxical that it borders insanity. We can control the soft landings of space craft on distant planets, but we are unable to control the polluting fumes emanating from our cars and factories. We propose Utopian communities in gigantic space colonies, but cannot manage our cities. The business world makes us believe that huge industries producing pet foods and cosmetics are a sign of our high standard of living, while economists try to tell us that we cannot "afford" adequate health care, education, or public transport. Medical science and pharmacology are endangering our health, and the Defense Department has become the greatest threat to our national security. Those are the results of overemphasizing our yang, or masculine side—rational knowledge, analysis, expansion—and neglecting our yin, or feminine side—intuitive wisdom, synthesis, and ecological awareness" (Capra, 1982, p. 42).

Thus, to proponents of Enlightenment East, the Enlightenment West tradition seems to be:

1. Unduly trusting of language and discursive thought
2. Committed to a program that results in unhealthy objectifications of self and world
3. Based upon a control-minded mentality, which threatens the very survival of human population and the planet.

The agenda

These mutual criticisms, accurate, or inaccurate, provide us with our agenda. Enlightenment East and Enlightenment West traditions posit not only divergent but apparently irreconcilable central values. Furthermore, as we've seen, there appears to be no common framework of value within which these sorts of questions can be discussed. Accordingly our first task must be to address the question of whether there is a framework of valuation which is intelligible and appropriate to exponents of both Enlightenment West and East.

Our search is for what we may call, somewhat tendentiously, no doubt, a "universal ethical problematic." An ethical problematic is an expression of the questions one must answer in order to gain insight into one's situation. A universal ethical problematic is a set of questions which knowingly or unknowingly everyone is answering by the choices one is making in life. In less tendentious terms, we need an understanding of values at a level sufficiently rich and deep that exponents of both Enlightenment East and Enlightenment West can identify with these values, and proceed on to the clarification of the problems. We begin our exploration, then, with an examination of ethics, and particularly value theory, from the broadest possible perspective.

Candidate approaches

Aristotle tended to approach his topics by surveying the best thought on the subject among his predecessors and contemporaries, and I hope it will not be thought unduly rationalistic to adopt this strategy. Let us canvas the most general approaches to valuational questions which are available to us. Of course we are interested in both Enlightenment East and Enlightenment West approaches. However, in our exposition we will attempt to present them in the most universal possible manner. In addition, we will be interested in comparing these two traditions with approaches to value that cannot be identified either with Enlightenment East or Enlightenment West traditions.

(a) The Eudaimonian Approach to value. "Eudaimonia" is the Greek word for happiness, and so a eudaimonian approach to value is one which holds that the central value is human happiness. According to this approach, whether one is meditating in the lotus posture, bringing food to the food bank for the needy, or going to the theater with one's friends, one is attempting to increase happiness and decrease unhappiness. Thus, the eudaimonian approach to value would require that meditation practice be happiness making. If meditating in the lotus posture doesn't make you happy, to put it crassly, it's not to be ultimately valued. Bringing food to the food bank for the needy serves the ultimate value of happiness because it is very likely indeed to help make the recipients happy. It may also increase the donor's happiness to know that he or she has brought happiness to others. But without having brought happiness to others that knowledge would never occur. So it is the bringing of happiness to the recipients which is the primary way in which food donations serve the value of happiness. And of course going out to the theater with one's friends can serve the value of happiness insofar as one is likely to enjoy the experience of the outing even if one pans the performance. The eudaimonian approach, then, regards the universal happiness as the ultimate goal of each person, and each activity is seen as positively

contributing to the ultimate goal to the extent that it brings about an increase in overall happiness.

Now there is a paradox associated with this approach which we must immediately mention. The paradox is this: if one puts front and center in one's consciousness the search for happiness, one is bound not to find it. If one were, for example, to constantly ask oneself while out with one's friends at the theatre, "Are we having a good time now?" "Are we increasing our happiness this way?" one would be bound to have a much less enjoyable time than if one forgot utterly about whether one was having a good time, and concentrated instead on experiencing the play, discussing its merits or demerits over tea and dessert afterwards, and so on. Happiness is not sought, but it is nonetheless found. We find it when we seek more specific things, the things which seem to us to be constitutive of happiness. Happiness is empty as a concept, but it collects other things which are constitutive of it or the vehicles of it. Health, enjoyment, feelings of well being, sensory, social, and intellectual pleasures, knowledge for its own sake, these are the vehicles of happiness. And these vehicles of happiness we may go out in search of to a much greater degree. We go to the hot tub because we know we will feel good afterwards. We set a date to meet and socialize because we know or believe we will enjoy the social interaction for its own sake. While we are interacting, of course, we do not focus on the interaction as a vehicle of happiness. We focus on the interaction: agreeing or disagreeing with what's been said, recounting an anecdote or incident which occurred, speculating on the future of some political movement, and so on. We study because we believe or may believe that breadth of knowledge is itself a happiness-constituting thing. "Happiness has a way of sneaking up on persons when they are preoccupied with other things," is the way Joel Feinberg has put it (1958, p. 493). But these other things are not entirely other. They are the elements which are constitutive *of* happiness, or vehicles for those elements which are constitutive of happiness.

We make note of the happiness paradox in order to defuse a potential criticism of the eudaimonian approach to value which might come from either the Enlightenment East or Enlightenment West camp. If the eudaimonian approach were misunderstood as recommending a constant conscious obsession with happiness, eudaimonianism would be contrary to the psychology of happiness. But that would be to misread eudaimonianism. Eudaimonianism seeks to understand the fundamental value of human activity. We only consciously dwell on happiness as the central value when our activity is the attempt to clarify our fundamental values!

There is, however, a criticism of the typical eudaimonian, or happiness-based approach to value which renders it unsuitable for our purposes. The typical happiness-based approach appears to be settled in favor of the idea of the positive evaluation of ego-based experience. We do not in practice find articulations of happiness-based ethics at a level of generality which will do for us. Rather the most general statements of happiness-based ethics are given as explicitly Enlightenment West articulations in which the ego experience, and the desirability of enhancing the ego experience, are taken for granted. Consequently the happiness-based approach will often appear to the exponent of Enlightenment East as tainted or at least biased.

Consider, for instance, the most influential articulation of happiness-based ethics in circulation today, that of John Stuart Mill, in *Utilitarianism:* "If by happiness be meant a continuity of highly pleasurable excitement, it is evident enough that this is impossible. A state of exalted pleasure lasts only moments, or in some cases, and with some intermissions, hours or days, and is the occasional brilliant flash of enjoyment, not its permanent and steady flame . . . [H]appiness . . . is not a life of rapture, but moments of such, in an existence made up of few and transitory pains, many and various pleasures, with a decided predominance of the active over the passive, and having, as the foundation of the whole, not to expect more from life than it is capable of bestowing. A life thus composed, to those who have been fortunate enough to obtain it, has always appeared worthy of the name 'happiness.' And such an existence is even now the lot of many, during some considerable portion of their lives. The present wretched education and wretched social arrangements are the only real hindrance to its being attainable by almost all" (John Stuart Mill, *Utilitarianism*, chapter 2).

In this famous summary of what can be hoped for, the proponent of Enlightenment East finds explicitly denied the central value of his or her program, namely, the life of bliss transcendent through extinction of the self in *nirvana*, liberation from the cycle of desire or reincarnation, or Taoist uninterrupted immersion in the ineffable source of nature. Compare what Mill suggests is the best one can hope for, with the hopes the ninth century Hindu monist, Shankara, feeds: "Master your mind, and the sense of ego will be dissolved. In this manner, the yogi achieves an unbroken realization of the joy of Brahman. . . . When the mind achieves perfect union with Brahman, the wise man realizes Brahman entirely within his own heart. Brahman is beyond speech or thought. It is the pure, eternal consciousness. It is absolute bliss. . . . To taste, within his own heart and in the external world, the endless bliss of the Atman—such is the reward obtained by the yogi who has reached perfection and liberation in this life" (Shankara, 1963, p. 297).

Moreover, this value, ego-less experience of bliss transcendent as expressed in the various Enlightenment East systems, does not seem to accept the nomenclature of "happiness" too readily. Although Buddhist materials sometimes refer to mystical liberation as "the highest happiness," the vision of happiness in Enlightenment West is of the fulfillment of the egoic individual, whereas Enlightenment East liberation is liberation *from* the ego. The two notions of happiness seem fundamentally different.

We cannot, then, accept the Enlightenment West eudaimonianism as adequate to our purposes. This should not be taken as indicating any necessary defect in the eudaimonian approach. Rather, there is no articulation of it that it will be seen at the outset of the inquiry as an acceptable approach by all concerned. We need a specific articulation of ethical life which is not only unbiased in the final analysis, but is seen to be unbiased at the outset.

(b) The deontological approach. Deontology is usually presented as offering a theory of right action; as such it may be contrasted with the utilitarian theory of right action. But we may also construe deontology as a value theory in order to contrast it with the happiness-based value theory associated with utilitarianism. According to such a construal, the deontological approach posits as the central value, the value of justice. According to this approach, an action has ultimate value just in those cases where the action is intended to express respect for the recipient of the action. "Act towards every person as an end, and not merely as a means" is the fundamental principle of this approach.

Immanual Kant, in his classic formulation of this approach, puts it as follows: ". . . [M]an, and in general, every rational being exists as an end in himself and not merely as a means to be arbitrarily used by this or that will. In all his actions, whether they are directed to himself or to other rational beings, he must always be regarded at the same time as an end. All objects of inclinations have only a conditional worth, for if the inclinations and the needs founded on them did not exist, their object would be without worth. The inclinations themselves as the sources of needs, however, are so lacking in absolute worth that the universal wish of every rational being must be indeed to free himself completely from them. Therefore, the worth of any objects to be obtained by our actions is at all times conditional. Beings whose existence does not depend on our will but on nature, if they are not rational beings, have only a relative worth as means and are therefore called 'things'. On the other hand, rational beings are designated 'persons' because their nature indicates that they are ends in themselves, i.e., things which may not be used merely as means. Such a being is thus an object of respect. . . . [W]ithout them nothing of absolute worth could be found." (Immanuel Kant, *Foundations of the Metaphysics of Morals*).

In other words, if satisfying desires (which Kant refers to as achieving objects of our inclination) were all there were to value, then every value would be conditional on one's having that desire, and there would be no absolute value. If there is to be an absolute value, it must come from the nature of a person as person, (a rational being, in Kant's terminology), who is deserving of respect as a person. This deservingness as it were is a kind of justice, and so the fundamental value of deontological ethics is justice.

The deontological approach to value has an austere glory, and its merits are manifest from many points of view. However, for our purposes, to find an approach to value which is seen to be neutral with respect to the fundamental controversies splitting the Enlightenment East and Enlightenment West vision, the deontological approach is not satisfactory. The goal of extinction of desire or extinction of attachment to desire which is frequently found in the Enlightenment East traditions would seem to be consistent with the Kantian dismissal of desire satisfaction as a central feature of ethics. However, the philosophical psychology of the Kantian realm of ends is as ego-bound as is that of the happiness-based ethic. In other words, the only value for the deontological scheme arises outside of the context of the individual acting for himself or herself, and only in the context of two agents, one acting for the other. Even where the individual is acting in a self-regarding way, Kant's analysis requires that the individual abstract herself from herself and treat the act more or less as though it were one person acting upon another. The subjective placement of the agent is irrelevant. But the Enlightenment East value is the release of the agent from a narrow or partial or incomplete relationship with the Absolute Ground of Being. The fulfilling of this project can be undertaken in hermitude, and, indeed, is apparently aided by hermitude. Thus, the central value of deontology appears to be incommensurate with the central value of Enlightenment East.

Once again, this does not indicate an ultimate flaw with the deontological approach to value, but only that the deontological approach will not serve us at the outset as a framework within which to discover whether there can be a meeting ground for our discussion of Enlightenment East and Enlightenment West values.

(c) The Complex approach. The complex approach to ethics has been developed as a response to various problems with respect to the completeness of the eudaimonian and deontological approaches. Many western philosophers have regarded each of these approaches as incomplete, even for the purposes of the Enlightenment West program. For instance, if all we were interested in were increasing happiness, then one could conceive of a situation in which it would serve happiness to find an innocent person guilty. Consider a case in which we have a marginal individual, a hapless waif, with no family, who is ill, malnourished, suicidal, and so forth, and whose personal position is improved through imprisonment, in a situation in which finding someone, anyone, guilty of some unsolved crime, will increase respect for law in society, and so will increase order, stability, and thus happiness. In such a case, the pure eudaimonian, it is argued, has no way to represent the intuition that it would be wrong to deliberately frame the hapless waif and find her or him guilty of the crime.

Thus, justice appears to some to be an absolute value that is not included within the purview of the eudaimonian approach. On the other hand, if the only value we have is justice, then our ethics is incomplete in that it cannot establish priorities in pleasures or in happiness-making features. However, once we recognize happiness and justice as ultimate, but distinct values we will have a complex ethical theory. Perforce there will be the potential for dilemmas, situations in which justice and happiness cannot both be achieved, so that a priority must be established between them. Yet there is no apparent way to commensurate the values involved, as they are fundamentally distinct. Then only a very subtle discriminative wisdom can negotiate such situations. If one held that the only two fundamental values were happiness and justice, then one would express one's approach this way: "Increase happiness, and practice justice. And when the two come into conflict, do the best you can." In this case, the injunctions, "increase happiness" and "practice justice" are conditional or hedged. An action might increase happiness, but be unjust. Since they are conditional, or hedged, they are merely prima facie injunctions, injunctions one unhesitatingly tries to fulfill, all other things being equal. Other things not being equal, one does the best one can under the circumstances.

The leading exponent of the complex approach to ethics is W. D. Ross. In fact Ross holds that there are six independent prima facie injunctions: (1-a) To be faithful to one's promises, and in one's speech to be honest; (1-b) to make restitution for damage one has caused; (2) to manifest one's gratitude appropriately in circumstances in which one has received benefit; (3) to be just in the distribution of goods; (4) to help others whom one is in a position to help; (5) to improve oneself; (6) to refrain from harming others (W. D. Ross, *The Right And The Good*, p. 21).

However, once again we find that there is nothing in this list which corresponds or even opens the door to what appears to be the supreme value within the Enlightenment East tradition, namely, a certain kind of experience, *satori*, or awakening to the fundamental Void character of all things, or *moksha*, liberation from the cycle of rebirth. In the end we may well come round to something that has the form of a complex approach to ethics, but at the outset we cannot accept the complex ethical systems which have been articulated within the western philosophical tradition as providing us with a valuational common ground.

(d) Postmodern approaches to value. Until now we have been assuming that our reconciliation project essentially involves only exponents of Enlightenment East and exponents of Enlightenment West. But what about that important third stream, the postmodernist tradition which rejects the Enlightenment West approach to metaphysics, epistemology, ethics, and politics, and yet by no stretch of the imagination can be taken as directly reintroducing an Enlightenment East system or approach?

We want to consider postmodernist approaches to value theory for two reasons. First, we may find something of use in our search for a meeting ground in an approach whose final outcome rejects both of the traditions whose reconciliation we're seeking. The fact that postmodernism rejects both Enlightenment East and Enlightenment West approaches does not indicate that within it we won't be able to find useful and potentially important points.

Second, and more importantly, we do not want merely to assume that our debate is constrained by the dynamics of Enlightenment East and Enlightenment West, as though the only proper approach to value theory and metaphysics-epistemology *must* be through either the Enlightenment West tradition or that of Enlightenment East! We want to consider the postmodernist approach or approaches, then, because if rejection of Enlightenment West values of rationalism, individualism, and historical progress is justified, we will not continue to seek for a reconciliation of Enlightenment West and Enlightenment East. Rather we will abandon Enlightenment West values if that is what seems warranted.

Postmodernist and anti-modernist approaches

Postmodernism is a complex phenomenon and it is difficult to summarize briefly so variegated an intellectual movement. For our purposes, I propose to distinguish five strains of postmodernism. In two cases—egoism and skepticism—the label "postmodernism" is stretching the usual terminology. According to usual conventions, these might be called "anti-modernist." In what follows, I won't continue to distinguish anti- from post-modernity, however, but will rather include the anti- strands within the rubric "postmodernism." I've decided to include them under the postmodernism rubric for the reason that the label "postmodernism" is meant to convey the idea that the exponent has rejected and in fact gone beyond modernism. And modernism is the rationalist (and foundationalist) individualist belief in human perfectibility, social progress and scientific, and perhaps metaphysical, knowledge of an objectively existing, language independent reality, which we've been calling "Enlightenment West." By such a gloss, all five streams to be considered emerge as forms of postmodernism, even if skepticism and egoism precede modernity by roughly two millenia.

The five streams of broadly postmodernist thought are: neo-Marxist, eco-feminist, deconstructionist, skeptical, and egoist. I'll briefly describe the salient features of each, and then critique them together, as the main limitation of each, for our purposes, applies to them all, although in somewhat different ways.

Neo-Marxism embraces several diverse views, ranging from the effort to interpret Marx' thought in a Hegelian light, which is a rather modernist neo-Marxism, to Marxism-Leninism, and to the New Left of the sixties and seventies which are, or may be, postmodernist. What the postmodernist Neo-Marxist views have in common is, first, a tendency to look at the economic underpinnings of any particular intellectual exercise for critical socioeconomic analysis; and second, the tendency to hold that there is no need, nor is it advisable to enter the debate with liberal individualists within the principles and vocabulary under which liberal individualism finds its meaning. The Enlightenment West tradition calls for justifications of social, ethical, and political programs, and these justifications are paradigmatically of a certain sort. There is an attempt to characterize as accurately and sensitively as possible the objective circumstances in which the question arises. And there is the application of a purportedly well justified value theory to the situation as thus described. A purportedly well justified value theory is an ethical, social, or political theory which sees itself as justified ultimately along utilitarian, deontological, or complex lines, as we've been seeing. Rationality is understood as moral rationality, and moral rationality is conceived as branching forth from these three trunks, as it were. The neo-Marxist postmodernist doesn't register pressure to enter the debate in this way. Rather the neo-Marxist postmodernist regards the typical methods of justification as being themselves expressions of the liberal bourgeois individualist standpoint, and, thus, better abandoned than joined. Herbert Marcuse in *One-Dimensional Man*, though a modernist Marxist himself, incisively described the processes whereby liberal individualist regimes swallow up opposition through a process he called "repressive toleration." By smiling benignly on dissent, the dissent is absorbed and co-opted. Hence the need, as some New Left postmodernist Marxists saw it, to abandon the discourse of the liberal individualist modernists altogether. Economic relations are, au fond, power relations, and one's intellectual activities are themselves essentially economic and political, not theoretical. The Enlightenment West, or modernist justifications are thereby undercut. Louis Althusser is a Marxist theorist who holds that it is a mistake to think of ideological systems as being justifiable or demonstrable along straightforward, objective lines. This has led to a form of Marxist anti-humanism, espousing a radical divorce between the realm of scientific knowledge and the realm of social practice. Given such an isolation of these realms, any effort to articulate humanism in the modernist vein is seen as a mere illusion. (Althusser, 1977, 1984, 1990; for a refutation of the view that Marx abandoned the notion of an objective human nature, see Norman Geras' succinct *Marx and Human Nature*.)

Feminist post-modernism comes in two varieties, only one of which needs specific consideration here. On the one hand, there is post-modernist feminism that seeks to replace the defectively patriarchal elements and assumptions of the modernist, or Enlightenment West tradition as it has in fact come down to us. Such defective elements will be replaced with appropriately egalitarian and gender sensitive elements. An eloquent spokesperson of this variety of postmodernism is Charlene Spretnak. Spretnak does not view patriarchal injustices and cultural biases as infections at the very core of the Enlightenment West project. Rather, her effort as a postmodernist is, in her words, "to create a passage beyond the failed assumptions of modernity and a radical reorientation that preserves the positive advances of the liberal tradition and technological capabilities but is rooted in ecological sanity and meaningful human participation in the unfolding story of the Earth community and the universe" (Spretnak, 1991, p. 4). This eco-feminist postmodernism inherits the mantle of Enlightenment West and itself seeks an integration with first peoples' spirituality, and wisdom paths akin to and including Enlightenment East traditions. The project we are engaged in here parallels that of Spretnak, but seeks to accomplish the integration paying full attention not only to the broadly social and attitudinally philosophical issues, but also to the specific and sometimes technical issues in philosophical value theory, epistemology, metaphysics, and some of the more traditionally framed and, again, sometimes technical issues in social and political theory. In our sense, then, Spretnak's vision is essentially modernist in style; it does not undercut the search for universal discourse.

On the other hand, the eco-feminist postmodernism, which radically rejects the basic assumptions of Enlightenment West thinking, holds that the legal and moral doctrines that are at the center of liberal modernism are after the fact rationalizations of patriarchal systems of power. The very notions of principles of substantive and procedural justice, systems of justification, and even rationality as it has developed within the Enlightenment West tradition are irremediably tainted with patriarchal biases, and need jettisoning. Mary Daly's *Gyn/Ecology* is a good example of radical feminist thought. Robin West, (1988) provides an overview of radical feminism vis à vis the law. Moira Gatens in *Feminism & Philosophy* supplies a critique of radical feminism.

We may also note that just as feminism comes in various degrees of radicalness, ecophilosophy can range from essentially modernist to radically postmodernist. Ecophilosophy which assumes that only sentient beings have intrinsic value is essentially modernist. On the other hand, Arne Naess's (1988) attribution of intrinsic value to non-sentient entities is decisively postmodernist. Perspectives at various points on the spectrum from modernist to postmodernist ecophilosophy can be found described and articulated in Alan Drengson's *Beyond Environmental Crisis*, Henryk Skolimowski's *Living Philosophy*, and Robert Carter's *Becoming Bamboo*.

The deconstructionist brand of post-modernism presents as global a challenge to modernism and Enlightenment West as can be imagined. For according to the deconstructionist, (and the deconstructionist's allies, the pragmatists, relativists, and ethical nihilists) the notion of an objective, language-independent reality is an illusion. Every metaphysics, science, religion, or ideology is an imposition of order, the valorization of a meta-narrative, which constitutes an illusion, a piece of self-deception, or an attempt at domination. As John Caputo puts it, the task of the intellectual is to be a Socratic gadfly deconstructing the meta-narrational fictions of the ideologues, metaphysicians, and other hierophants of the day (1987, p. 197).

Deconstructionism as thus presented embraces or is at least allied with relativism and non-representationalism in the theory of knowledge and the theory of language. There are non-representationalist or relativist ingredients in American pragmatism, the philosophy of the later Wittgenstein, and in such contemporary philosophers as Thomas Kuhn, Nelson Goodman, Richard Rorty, and W. V. O. Quine. A prominent and influential critic of the modernist, Enlightenment West perspective is Michel Foucault, who argued vigorously in *The Order of Things*, in *The Archeology of Knowledge*, and in other works, against the notion that there are discourse independent truths. Rather, it is the discourse of a discipline which makes for truth. Thus, truth becomes radically relativized.

In addition to non-representationalism and holistic relativism, we should probably also include the views known as cultural relativism, ethical relativism, and ethical nihilism within this general heading. Cultural relativism is the view that there are many fundamentally different world views and the standards of belief justification are so different from one to the next that one can't effectively ever get outside of one's own world view enough to be able to assess the contents of another world view. Ethical relativism is the view that all one need think about in ethics is tailoring one's actions to the moral code of the society one is living in. "When in Rome, do as the Romans do," is the practical injunction of this view.

Ethical nihilism is the view that the search for intrinsic value is delusional or fruitless. Nothing has intrinsic value, and ethical injunctions are merely conditional. "If you want this, do that" is the ultimate content of "That is the right thing to do." As far as justifying that "this is good" is concerned, any attempt to provide such a justification is misguided, according to the ethical nihilist. (See Moser 1968 for an extensive treatment of these positions.)

The ethical nihilist perspective sometimes results from a certain attitude towards nature. If nature just is as it is, then, it seems to some people, nothing can be added to nature of the right kind to yield intrinsic value. Nature just is as it is, and values are nowhere to be found. I react favorably to some outcomes and unfavorably to other outcomes. I prefer certain things to others. And I have hopes, fears and so on. But there is nothing in nature, or in my reactions, and my emotions, which entitles me to think that one outcome is genuinely or objectively *better* than another. It is preferable to me, but that's all. Thus, values are strictly relativized to those who hold them. There's no sense in which an action can be right except in that it is the right action for me, or preferable to me.

Another avenue into the ethical nihilist perspective is that of determinism. If one thinks that every action a person makes is the result of functional causal antecedents (the neurons in the brain firing because they were stimulated in certain ways, and so on) then it may seem as though there is no room for free choice. And if there is no possibility of free choice, then the sphere in which ethics and values are to arise suddenly disappears. Hence ethical judgments are delusional. (This source of ethical nihilism is decidedly modernist in epistemology, however. Once again, though, the conclusions are anti-Enlightenment West in ethics.)

Skepticism and non-representationalism are philosophical cousins. The skeptic accepts the view that language has a representational function, so that the pursuit of knowledge is a proper pursuit. The trouble is, according to the skeptic, that this pursuit has, does, and always will fall short of achieving its goal. The non-representationalist, as we've seen, abandons the pursuit altogether, rejecting the very idea that language has representationalist functions, or that the world is an objective, cognizer-independent and language-independent system. Skepticism and non-representationalism are philosophical cousins, then, in that both result in the view that knowledge of an objectively existing, language-independent world, is impossible. In the ancient world, skepticism was a thriving philosophical world view. In our day, it is mostly conceived of as a theoretical springboard. Nonetheless it is not entirely without its principled defenders, such as Peter Unger in *Ignorance* (1974), although he has since shifted his focus to the issue of philosophical relativism (1984).

And finally, egoism is the view that one need take no account of the welfare of others except insofar as they are means towards the fulfillment of one's own overall interest. Traditionally, one distinguishes between psychological egoism and ethical egoism. Psychological egoism is the thesis that everyone always acts, consciously or subconsciously, exclusively to secure his or her own overall greatest good, regarding the goods of others always as instrumental goods, and never as intrinsic goods. Ethical egoism is the view that one *ought* to regard everyone else's good as merely instrumental to one's own fulfillment.

Thus, ethical egoism contrasts sharply with deontology, which requires that we never regard another merely as a means. It is important to note that egoism in either variety here is distinct from what is sometimes called "rational egoism," or "egoist utilitarianism." Egoist utilitarianism is the view that the strategy to bring about the greatest happiness for the greatest number is for everyone to act *as though* he or she were ignoring everyone else's good as intrinsic good, and only taking account of others' good if it is regarded as instrumental towards his or her own. The best way to bring about the general happiness is for everyone to look out for *numero uno*. Through such competitive living, strong, healthy, ego-satisfying individuals generally result, and so the general happiness results. But this egoist utilitarian view sets its sights on the general happiness. If one were to become persuaded that the strategy doesn't work in certain circumstances one would not, or should not, according to the theory, act egoistically in those circumstances. Ethical egoism, on the other hand, never sets aim at the general happiness. Its ultimate aim is egoist. Hence, egoist utilitarianism is not genuinely ethical egoist. The egoist utilitarian ultimately does recognize others as bearing intrinsic value. The ethical egoist does not.

In one way or another, then, each of these five strains of postmodernist thinking rejects one or another of the key elements of Enlightenment West: the belief in a language-independent reality, the belief in the possibility of knowledge, the belief in systems of moral evaluation which are rationally justifiable, and, thus, the belief in the possibility of progress in history through application of reason and the idea of justice to social process and goals. On the one side, then, postmodernism rejects objectivity in grounds for belief. On the other side, postmodernism rejects objectivity in ethical judgment. In a word, postmodernism rejects objectivity.

It is this anti-objectivist feature that allows for a general response to postmodernism. For our ultimate purposes it will suffice if we can see why postmodernism in any of its forms will not do for us as a starting framework. Our concern is to understand the relationship between Enlightenment East and Enlightenment West, and to mediate the apparent conflicts and inconsistencies between the two. If postmodernism can neither convince us that such a mediation is impossible or fruitless, nor provide us with an initial framework within which to conduct our inquiry, then we need not consider it further in this context. But merely to canvas these two points of potential relevance of postmodernism for us may be to ignore an opportunity. For by seeing where shortcomings may lie in the very attack mounted by postmodernism on objectivity we may be helped in our search for a sufficiently broad framework within which to conduct the inquiry. Accordingly we will try to indicate briefly some lines along which the postmodern methods or conclusions may be found to be unsatisfactory.

Obviously, the remarks on this subject will be mere indications. They are not likely to convince the confirmed postmodernist of one variety or another. But merely to proceed without any form of direct confrontation with postmodernist content would not serve us either. I will try to indicate the problems inherent in radical postmodernism with reference to two phenomena: first, the practice of corrections, not only in details, but also at fundamental levels both moral and cognitive; second, the legitimacy of a presumption of universality, and hence of the rationality of dialogue.

First, then, let us consider the distinction between *a change in one's view*, whether descriptive or evaluative, and *a correction, or improvement*, in one's view. For instance, suppose that you replace the image you have of your boss as a tough, stubborn, cruel martinet, and in its place you substitute the image of one who has been treated harshly, who reacts irrationally, who has a hidden heart of gold. It may be this replacement of one image by another occurs without any particular external justification. The boss's behavior doesn't seem to you changed, but rather, you consciously decide to alter your image of the boss. Perhaps what motivates the change is the desire to *accept* the boss' idiosyncrasies, and be able to work under her supervision with greater comfort than one would under the old image. This is an instance of a mere change of image or view.

Contrast such a change with a substitution in which it appears to you that you are correcting the old image. Suppose your company survives while all the competitors fold. And suppose you read some old directors' meetings minutes in which the boss astutely predicted the tough times which have, in fact, come. Suppose you also come to believe that had it not been for the tough measures taken, your position would have been unsavable. Furthermore, with the other companies out of the way, the company is prospering and the boss generously gives out raises and bonuses. No longer does she insist on the tough measures she had earlier implemented. Rather, she shifts her focus from mere survival of the company to ethical investment reviews and so on. Now it seems to you that your previous image of the boss was inaccurate. No cruel martinet, the boss was a rational visionary. In this case, you regard the new image under whose light you see the boss as a correction of the old.

We are not interested in whether or not you might be mistaken even now, as you were, apparently, before, in your appraisal of the situation. What we are interested in is that you distinguish between a mere change of image and an apparent correction, or, more generally, an improvement. On the one hand, you can decide in the absence of evidence to act under a different image of the boss, or the world, than the image you previously acted under. On the other hand, you can come to see your boss, or the world, differently, under the pressure of what seems to you to be new evidence.

And the same distinction between change and improvement which we've just made in a descriptive matter, can also be made for the moral sphere. Sometimes we change our practices for essentially non-moral reasons. We may change our practices for aesthetic reasons, for instance. But sometimes we change a practice because we understand, or at least take it that we understand, why this new practice is a better practice: it keeps everyone happy, it has fewer harmful consequences, it embodies an intrinsically right practice, and so on. Now given that the contents of every cognitive scheme and of every evaluative scheme are subject to apparent corrections and improvements, it follows that the assumption of rationality is an inevitable accompaniment to our cognitive and moral practices. Yes, we are always interpreting reality. And yes, we alter, shift, change our interpretations. But some of our shifts, changes, alterations in interpretation and recommendation are regarded by us as improvements on the old interpretations and/or recommendations. Yet we cannot very well regard them as improvements unless we accept the assumption of some form of *objectivity* within which they are regarded as improvements. An improvement can be a relative improvement in relation to an objective standard. But without an objective framework even the aspiration towards relative improvement becomes ultimately fruitless or unintelligible. Why consider anything better than anything else if what is better is only better relative to x, and worse relative to y? Thus, practical and epistemic reasoning commits one to the methodological assumption of objectivity.

According to this argument, it is not merely some of the details which are amenable to correction under the pressure of evidence. Rather the foundational strategies themselves, the procedures whereby we assess matters for our moral approbation or cognitive assent, are not insulated from rational consideration. Suppose you form a belief, and it seems to you that your belief-forming strategies inevitably lead to the very conclusion you have come to. But then someone comes along and claims to have identified a slip up or an error in your fundamental procedures. Of course you may choose to ignore altogether this claim. But you need not. You are capable of recognizing that there is no a priori bar upon your becoming persuaded that something was wrong with your conclusion, or perhaps even your procedure. There is no insulating layer which makes procedures and methods immune from rational investigation and potential improvement. But as soon as we can conceive of a story, if you like, in which someone comes and persuades us that something ought to be changed in our manner of forming beliefs or in our manner of choosing courses of action, we have conceived of a rationalistic correction at the foundation. And this seems to point to a fundamental assumption of rationality at the base. And what, further, is a commitment to rationality at the base, if not a commitment to a maximally sensible perspective? A commitment to rationality at fundamental levels is thus a commitment to a theoretical perspective of objectivity. This objectivity may be a horizon ever vanishing in our pursuit of it, but it is a horizon whose pursuit we are methodologically committed to.

Thus, the modernist catechism: interpretation and evaluation, practically speaking, presuppose occasional correction; correction, even occasional, can occur anywhere down the cognitive or moral levels; so correction presupposes not only rationality, but fundamental rationality; and fundamental rationality presupposes objectivity.

The objectivity, moreover, which rationality points to need not be regarded as the limited, small *o* objectivity encapsulated in our own particular viewpoints. Rather, the objectivity which rationality points to may well be the always vanishing horizon as we move in whatever direction along the plains of truth seeking. But the horizon of objectivity is there. It guides us when we compare beliefs and attempt to assess them. It is presupposed even within the postmodernist rejections of objectivity or foundationalism, for it lurks within the very notions of intersubjectivity, pragmatism, or communitarianism. Whenever we reason about the better course of action we presuppose a framework of objectivity of the very sort critiqued by the postmodernist. Obviously, it is not necessary to claim that every shift of perspective, every act of reinterpretation is a correction. But for anyone who participates in the practices of justice-seeking, dialogue, harmonization and mediation in conflict, and assessment of rival views, the central principles of rationalist modernism are to be found alive and thriving. Distinguishing, then, between radical postmodernism that seeks to undermine all forms of cognition based upon which cognitive and moral corrections can be practiced, and non-radical postmodernism that seeks to reform various versions of the modernist program, we see that radical postmodernism will serve neither as a mediating platform for Enlightenment East and West to meet, nor as a platform for any moral or cognitive practice to advance. Non-radical postmodernisms provide in each individual instance a critique of one or another element of Enlightenment West, but no comprehensive critique of fundamental provisions of that tradition.

The skeptic may still object that the cognitive and moral practices we engage in are nonetheless groundless. We have practices which require rationality, but we are not entitled to take the availability of that rationality for granted. For instance, standard moral practices require that there is a plurality of sentient beings, that solipsism in one or another of its stronger forms is false. But according to the cognitive skeptic, we are not entitled to regard ourselves as knowing that there are indeed many independent sentient beings. This is an unfortunate predicament to be in, but we're saddled with it, according to the skeptic.

To this point we may respond in different ways. Few are positively persuaded by skepticism, and Alvin Goldman, Paul Moser, and others have recently been busy countering both skepticism and antifoundationalist theories of belief. But what if one is positively persuaded by skepticism? One may carry on one's moral practices offenselessly like the Pyrrhonians, or like Descartes at the outset of his inquiry, and one may also take note of the beliefs presupposed by those practices. In other words, one may hold that unless the skepticism attacks not only attributions of knowledge to one's cognitive states but also attributions of justified belief to one's cognitive states, the moral and cognitive practices presupposing rationality and objectivity survive. And even if one holds that skepticism about knowledge properly implies the impossibility of justified fundamental beliefs, it would still be necessary to regard the practices which survive, or apparently survive, as embodying mythologies or images of the world. These images of the world can still be assessed for rationality of adoption, which is quite a different matter compared to justification of belief. Only one who (i) abandons the idea that knowledge claims are justified, (ii) holds that where knowledge claims are not justified, and one is aware that knowledge claims are not justified, one has no justified beliefs, and (iii) holds that without justified beliefs one is not even entitled to select rationalistically between convictionless images of the world, can defeat this response. But whereas there might be skeptics who hold both (i) and (ii), there are no skeptics I'm aware of who hold (iii) in addition. The most severe skeptical challenge leaves rationality of adoption of mytho-ideological stances intact, and that is all we need for our enterprise. In particular, all we need is the rationality of the adoption of a mytho-ideological stance which sees the world as calling forth apparent cognitive and moral corrections. In other words, all we need for our purposes is the reasonableness of a *tradition* of rationalism, the reasonableness of a tradition which seeks and actively pursues mediating dialogues between rival conceptions of the good life.

Let us review the point from another, more technical, angle. The modernist, characteristically, wants to identify some beliefs as justified. If so, there should be a way to tell the justified from the unjustified beliefs. A criterion for justified belief will relate a modality of belief (e.g., 'probable,' or 'certain') to belief justification. For example, the criterion might say that just so long as it would be unreasonable to doubt a belief, would one be justified to believe it. (Here 'beyond reasonable doubt' would be the modality.) The skeptic asks for an assessment of the modality of the criterion itself. Is it not reasonable to doubt the correctness of the criterion? If so, the criterion fails its own demands. Suppose you say "The criterion is itself beyond reasonable doubt." Then the skeptic asks, "Is that assignment of modality itself beyond reasonable doubt?" Here you'd surely have some doubts! Or if not here then soon enough. So sooner or later you will discover yourself to be working with an epistemic principle which has a weaker modality than the principle itself requires in order that one be justified in believing it. This, and similar arguments, weaken the entire structure, and the skeptic has a field day from the first point of doubt on.

To reply to this it is not necessary, as some would-be contemporary foundationalists have thought, to find a direct way through the tumbling inferential regresses and eddying vicious circles of epistemic reasoning so as to yield a bedrock of justified belief. Rather, it suffices to distinguish between beliefs and hypotheses, and to show that although skepticism may have its way with justified belief, skepticism cannot have its way with weak, or even with strong rational hypothesis adoption. We will explore some of these issues further in chapter six, but for our purposes here perhaps the following sketch will suffice.

A hypothesis is a convictionless image which one adopts or does not adopt as a guide for one's actions. For example, suppose a friend has been accused of a crime, and the evidence seems 50-50 for his having done it. Then one might (and William James would say there are circumstances such that one must) choose whether or not to adopt the hypothesis of innocence. To adopt the hypothesis of innocence is to act as you would if you believed the man was innocent. But to adopt the hypothesis, then, is distinct from holding the belief. The image is convictionless, since you keep in mind that your assessment of the evidence is 50-50.

Next let us say that it is strongly rational to adopt a hypothesis just in those circumstances in which it would be irrational not to adopt it. And it is weakly rational to adopt a hypothesis just in those circumstances in which it would not be irrational to adopt it. Now the principle that if a proposition appears to be true beyond reasonable doubt, then it is strongly rational to adopt that proposition as a hypothesis, is itself beyond reasonable doubt. Then no matter how large a wedge the skeptic drives between even weak rationality and justified belief, the skeptic is powerless to wreak the same havoc over the relation between apparent justified belief and even strongly rational hypothesis adoption. It may be true that an apparently justified belief is neither true, nor even justified despite the appearances. It may be true as well that apparent justified belief does not allow us to make any claims as to our being justified in our beliefs. Nonetheless, it is surely rational to adopt that hypothesis whose proposition one would appear to be justified in believing; it would, indeed, be irrational to adopt any other hypothesis. And since Enlightenment West modernity at worst only needs the notion of strongly rational hypothesis adoption, skepticism has been thereby disarmed for all practical purposes. The epistemic cornerstones on which our Enlightenment East and Enlightenment West dialogue takes place, at worst, are those of strongly rational hypothesis adoption. This phenomenological epistemology is sufficient for our purposes.

The skeptical challenge to our first response to postmodernism has thus been neutralized. And this brings us to the second way in which we might seek to point out the limitations of the postmodernisms. The postmodernisms hope to cut off dialogue between apparently irreconcilable traditions for theoretical reasons, right from the start. We cannot hope to translate from one mind-set to another, says the postmodernist. Or, the idea of a mediating dialogue is fruitless because there is no possibility of a common language within which both traditions may be adequately articulated. Thus, for example, Richard Rorty holds that "the quest for a universal human community will be self-defeating if it tries to preserve the elements of every intellectual tradition, all the 'deep' intuitions everybody has ever had. It is not to be achieved by an attempt at commensuration, at a common vocabulary that isolates the common human essence of Achilles and the Buddha, Lavoisier and Derrida" (1987, p. 46).

In response to this it might be said that the postmodernist insistence on incommensurability and/or tradition-relativism is at odds with what is actually managing to take place, and has managed to take place again and again. Again and again throughout history there have been encounters of rival conceptions both within a single culture and across cultures, and yet commensurating dialogue has apparently taken place. For instance, it is fruitful to regard Plato as a brilliant synthesizer of the rival perspectives he encountered within his own culture. Hegel, too, was a synthesizer. Moreover, commensurating movements exist across cultures as well. Egyptian culture influenced Greek culture; Greek culture and Hebraic culture had a fruitful interaction; likewise first exilic Jewish culture and Babylonian culture; Islamic and Hindu cosmic conceptions came into necessary contact with each other during the Islamic expansion into India, and so on. Out of all these interactions various synthetic projects resulted. And in each case to effect the synthesis required a commensuration or a discovery of commonality of sorts. We are witnessing the transformation of the world into an interlocking network if not a global village. Now it appears to be the postmodernists' insistence on impossibility of commensurating dialogue which is out of touch with the practical realities of world interrelationality and independent cultural parallelisms.

Moreover, to think that Enlightenment East and West traditions are in the first instance geographically distinct traditions, or that the main divisions in thought occur *across* cultural lines, is mistaken. Spinoza and Sankara advocated a mystical monism; Confucius and Protagoras were humanists. Mo Tzu had a utilitarian frame of mind. Mencius opposed the utilitarian levelling somewhat in the spirit that Alisdair MacIntyre opposes utilitarian levelling from Bentham through Mill. Descartes wondered if he was being deceived by an evil demon into mistaking a dream for a reality. Chuang Tzu wondered if he was a butterfly dreaming he was a human. In the Middle Ages, each of Jewish, Christian, and Islamic theologies was internally split into a Platonist and an Aristotelian faction. And so it goes. Rorty holds that if there is to be a world community it will come about not through synthesis of elements eastern and western, but rather through transcending both traditions altogether in "acts of making rather than of finding—by poetic rather than Philosophical achievement. The culture that will transcend, and thus unite, East and West, or the Earthlings and the Galactics, is not likely to be one that does equal justice to each, but one that looks back on both with the amused condescension typical of later generations looking back at their ancestors." *(Ibid.)* This seems to constitute intellectual slipperiness of the first order. For when we consider our relations with our ancestors, we find not amused condescension on the whole but appreciation of circumstances, including epistemic circumstances, in which viewpoints developed made sense and contributed to the ongoing syntheses which resulted in the perspectives found today. There is nothing in the cave paintings at Lascaux to look back on with amused detachment, nor is there anything in shamanic wisdom to be condescending about. Indeed, does it not rather seem that Rorty's hope for a world community born of condescending Transcendence is an expression of his desire to skip the synthetic work, to skip the hard task of participating in the commensurating dialogue which is as much between the rival conceptions within a culture as it is across geographically isolated cultures? It is hard work, yes, the search for a comprehensive framework within which to conduct these dialogues. And sometimes it may seem as though there is no path to mediating apparently irreconcilable traditions within and across cultures. But if intellectual history holds any lesson for us it is that syntheses manage in some cases at least to emerge. We can find ourselves at a stage at which it's tempting to throw up our hands at the difficulties. But we need not. We can participate actively in the synthetic efforts in the understanding that where human beings interact, mediating dialogues may, and at some level, must be possible. If postmodernists hope to nip the dialogue in the bud by a priori means, it is they who are out of touch with both the historical and contemporary realities of human interaction and dialogue within single cultures and across disparate cultures.

These two considerations may not suffice to persuade the confirmed postmodernist of whatever variety to join us in our search for mediating dialogue, but perhaps they will suffice to indicate reasons why we need not rule out our project from the start.

Radical postmodernism, it thus appears, does not succeed in its critique of modernism, and certainly will not do for us in our search for an initial framework within which to conduct our inquiry. But then Enlightenment West modernism itself is inadequate to our Enlightenment East/West comparative task. Neither modernism nor radical postmodernism, then, will do for us in our current situation. What we are looking for is a universalistic system of value which is sufficiently neutral with respect to the contentious issues so as to provide us with a vocabulary and language of analysis in attempting to bridge the apparent irreconcilables between Enlightenment East and West. Can we find such a system outside of the recent western philosophical analyses?

(e) Divine Voluntarism. Enlightenment West approaches were developed largely as a reaction against Divine Voluntarism, of Jewish, Christian, or Islamic type. Divine Voluntarism is the view that the fundamental value is the will of God, the Supreme Personal Being. What God wants is constitutive of the good. Most simply, Divine Voluntarism states that whatever action is good is good solely because it is God's wish that the action be done; it is not the case that whatever action is good is good for some reason which provides the ground based on which God wants the action to be done. There are several presuppositions of the Divine Voluntarist conception as thus expressed. The first presupposition is that there is a personal Supreme Being, a Being who has knowledge, power, and volition. The second presupposition is that the personal Supreme Being has wishes for human beings. The third is that the Supreme Being has communicated these wishes to humanity.

Many people assume that believers in the Supreme Personal Being will tend to be Divine Voluntarists in ethics. Whether this is true outside of philosophical circles I do not know, but there are few philosophers who espouse Divine Voluntarist ethics, even if they are believers in a Supreme Personal Being. To be a Divine Voluntarist one must not only believe that there is a Commanding God, but also that there is nothing else to the rightness of an action but that God commanded it. Most sophisticated theists hold that if God commands an action it is because God, being omniscient, knows the right-making feature of action, and knows that that action embodies it. In chapter six we will examine some modified forms of Divine Voluntarism in detail.

In any case, it is clear that Divine Voluntarism will not do for us as a sufficiently neutral framework for our purposes, since Enlightenment East traditions include prominent elements which are either Impersonalist, or reject the centrality of the question of the existence of a Supreme Personal Being for the Enlightenment quest, for example, Advaita Vedanta, and Theravada Buddhism, respectively.

(f) The Eightfold Path of Buddhism. The central value in Buddhism is the extinction of suffering. The core teachings of the Buddha are the four noble truths: *(a)* there is suffering; *(b)* there is a cause of suffering; *(c)* the elimination of the cause of suffering results in the elimination of the suffering; and *(d)* there is a way to eliminate the cause of suffering, namely, by following the eightfold path. The eightfold path consists of: right understanding, right thought, right speech, right action, right livelihood, right effort, right mindfulness, and right meditation.

As a system of blanks to be filled in as we wish, the Buddhist approach holds some promise for us. The happiness-based theory seems to be put negatively, at least in the four noble truths. Where the eudaimonian says, "Pursue happiness", the Buddhist says, "Eliminate suffering." The one can acknowledge the perspective of the other. However, when we realize that there is a specific content to the categories, we see that the Buddhist approach is not a set of blanks to be filled in as we wish. For example, right understanding, the key to the eightfold path, consists in the grasping of three basic truths: nothing has any fixed self-nature; the world is a vast co-dependent system, which in effect amounts to a denial of a primary reality or God as usually conceived; and all things are impermanent. The realization of these truths is held to be the sine qua non of the other elements of the eightfold path. Thus, apparently, a very particular metaphysical view is entrenched within the central valuational expression of the Buddhist approach. And it is not clear to the exponent of Enlightenment West that there is any room left for what the Enlightenment West project holds to be central. For instance, the individual person is a sacrosanct locus of value in Enlightenment West. In characteristic expressions of Buddhism, the person is seen as a bundle of matter, sensations, perceptions, thoughts, and consciousness, without any ultimate identity. The preciousness of the individual self which is the foundation of Enlightenment West ethics presupposes or seems to presuppose a metaphysics which is denied by, or seems to be denied by the metaphysics implicit in the first step of the noble eightfold path. Whether extended analysis can resolve this apparent irreconcilability is an open question. But Buddhism does not provide the framework we are looking for at the outset.

(g) Eightfold (Ashtanga) Yoga. The eightfold ashtanga yoga system posits as its central practices the *yamas*: nonviolence, truthfulness, non-theft, chastity, and non-greed; the *niyamas*: cleanliness, contentment, discipline, self-awareness, surrender to God; the *asanas*, bodily postures which stretch the muscles, render supple the body, and prepare the aspirant for meditation practice; *pranayama*, or breathing exercises; *pratyahara*, or sense withdrawal; *dharana*, or uninterrupted concentration of the mind; *dhyana* or fusion of the mind with the object of concentration; and *samadhi*, the sustained absorption in the Absolute, whether in stillness or engaged in motion. Once again as a neutral system of value this will hardly do. Although there are many elements of the *yamas* and *niyamas* which

are familiar and acceptable to the Enlightenment West proponent, the content of the last three of the eight is simply not accessible or intelligible as fundamental values to the typical Enlightenment West proponent. Yet these are the culminating practices and values of the system.

(h) The Taoist hierarchy of value. In many places within the primary literature of philosophical Taoism, we find a hierarchy of value presented. Harmony or accord with the Tao, or the ineffable Way of nature, is always given central place in the valuational schema. For example, "When Tao is lost, there is virtue. When virtue is lost, there is kindness. When kindness is lost, there is justice. When justice is lost, there is ritual" (*Tao Te Ching* #38). Awareness of the good is itself a defect, a lack of harmony with the Way. "When the great Way is forgotten, kindness and justice arise. When cleverness is born, pretense begins. When there is no peace within the family, filial piety arises. When the country is confused and in chaos, loyal ministers appear"(*Ibid.*, #18). This approach certainly won't provide a common framework within which the Enlightenment West exponent can comfortably explore the relationship between science, social progress on the one hand, and the mystical quest on the other.

We've canvassed the central valuational systems of Enlightenment West, western systems other than Enlightenment West, and some paradigmatic systematic expositions of Enlightenment East values as well. It should be no great surprise to us that none of them provides us with what we need, since if there were an obvious choice which did, we probably wouldn't be facing the apparent irreconcilability in the first place.

There is, however, a framework which I suggest will provide us with what we need. The framework is the relational ethical framework. It has something of the characteristics of W. D. Ross's complex ethical theory. But it is even more closely related to the foundational framework of Confucian thinking. Accordingly, we may think of it as a modern Confucianism. In chapter two, I will expose the relational ethical framework, and, beginning with chapter three, I will apply it.

Two

Relational Ethics: A Modern Confucianism

I. THE RELATIONAL APPROACH TO ETHICS

The phrase 'relational ethics' may be recent, but the concept of relational ethics is not recent, having been employed not only by the Confucians, but also, in one form or another, and to one degree or another, by many ancient thinkers, including Aristotle, Augustine, the prophetic author(s) of the Mosaic law, the author of the Laws of Manu, and the Buddha or disciples of the Buddha. In this chapter, I will be developing both a framework for any systematic relational ethics, and a particular implementation of this framework for our assessment of Enlightenment East and West.

Some examples

Rather than define the term 'relational ethics' at the outset, we'll begin informally by sampling ethical thought which explicitly or implicitly relies on a characterization of fundamental relational types and modes of conduct or virtues appropriate to them.

We'll begin with ancient Chinese thought because it explicitly refers to various enumerated sets of relational categories. In the *Tao Te Ching*, #18, reference is made to "the six relations." "When the six relations go awry, there are devoted children." D. C. Lau notes that the third century C. E. philosophical commentator Wang Pi interprets these relations as between "father and son, elder and younger brother, and husband and wife" (*Tao Te Ching*, 1963, p. 74). In the *Tao Te Ching*, though, emphasis is not placed on cultivation through virtues appropriate to each relation. Rather, the reverse: "Do away with wisdom and sagacity, and the people will benefit a hundredfold. Do away with kindness and eject righteousness, and the people will rediscover filial piety and affection" (#19).

A relatively explicit dichotomy of relational types is at work in the *Chuang Tzu* materials. For instance, the text attributes to Confucius a distinction between those relations governed by nature, and those relations governed by duty. "In the affairs of the world, two universal principles may be observed; one is the natural order and the other is duty. It is natural for a son to love his parents; this cannot be erased from his heart. It is duty for a man to serve his sovereign; everywhere he goes there will be a sovereign" (*Chuang Tsu*, 1974, p. 73). This dichotomy is shortly afterwards synthesized by the remark, "To serve one's own mind, unmoved by sadness or joy, accepting whatever happens, is the true virtue" (Ibid.). What results, then, is a threefold distinction between intimate relations governed by natural feeling, distant relations governed by obligation; and the self-relation, governed by the practice of equanimity. A still richer articulation of role related fulfillment, however, is provided by the Confucian literature itself.

Because the Confucian literature evolved in the first few centuries following the death of Confucius, it is often difficult to determine what belongs to Confucius proper, and what is later accretion. But for our purposes we need not distinguish between views demonstrably held by Confucius, and views expressed in the ancient Confucian materials, just as we have not concerned ourselves with the problems of attribution concerning the Taoist materials. Allowing ourselves the latitude of referring to Confucian thought rather than to Confucius' thought, we may say that the Confucian approach is founded in what the tradition takes to be the fundamental or cardinal human relationships, and the proper character or conduct for each one. In Confucian literature, there are at least five cardinal relations: child and parent, subject and sovereign, junior and senior (as in younger and elder siblings), husband and wife, and friends. (Notice that this would have been called eleven, or perhaps twelve relations following Wang Pi's way of counting relations.) There are, in any case, somewhat different enumerations of fundamental relations in Confucian works, and many expressions of the virtues appropriate to each relation. Thus, for example, "There are five activities of high importance under heaven, and they are practiced with three virtues. I mean there are the obligations between prince and minister; between father and son; between husband and wife; between elder and younger brothers; and between friends. Those are the five obligations that have great effects under heaven. The three efficient virtues are: knowledge, humanity and energy; and they are to be united in practice, do not attempt to split them apart one from the other" (*Chung Yung*, 1928, XX: 8).

"The ethics of the man of true breed contains four things, and I have not been able to perform one of them. I have not been able to serve my father as I would have a son serve me; nor my prince as I would have a minister serve me; nor to treat my elder brother as I would have a younger treat me; nor a friend as I would have a friend treat me. No. These things I have not attained to. The honest man looks into himself and in his daily acts maintains constant respect to his given word that his deeds fall not below it. If he have failed in something, he dare not slacken in the attempt toward it; if he have erred, he dare not carry the error to the extreme; his words accord with his acts and his conduct with his words as of one who turns to compare them with scruple. The essence of honesty is that it springs from the heart" (Ibid., XIII: 4).

And, "Filial piety and fraternal deference, these are the roots of becoming a person" (*Analects*, I: 2, Hall and Ames, 1987, p. 229).

We want to call attention here not only to the enumerations of the cardinal relations, but also to the suggestions as to the appropriate modes of conduct, or virtues, specifically appertaining to the different relations. It is such a role-based articulation of virtues which makes for full-fledged relational ethical thinking. Thus, to sample some further materials which focus on the virtues specific to the relations:

"Meng Yi Tzu asked about being filial. The Master answered, 'Never fail to comply'" (*Analects*, 1974, II:5).

"Tseng Tzu said, 'A gentlemen makes friends through being cultivated, but looks to friends for support in benevolence'" (Ibid., XII: 24).

"Tzu-lu said, 'If the Lord of Wei left the administration of his state to you, what would you put first?' The Master said, 'If something has to be put first, it is perhaps, the rectification of names'" (Ibid., XIII:3).

"The Master said, 'Rule over [the common people] with dignity and they will be reverent; treat them with kindness and they will do their best; raise the good and instruct those who are backward and they will be imbued with enthusiasm'" (Ibid., II: 20).

"There are nine standards by which to administer the empire, its states, and the families. They are: cultivating the personal life, honoring the worthy, being affectionate to relatives, being respectful toward the great ministers, identifying oneself with the welfare of the whole body of officers, treating the common people as one's own children, attracting the various artisans, showing tenderness to strangers from far countries, and extending kindly and awesome influence on the feudal lords. If the ruler cultivates his personal life, the Way will be established. If he honors the worthy, he will not be perplexed. If he is affectionate to his relatives, there will be no grumbling among his uncles and brothers. If he respects the great ministers, he will not be deceived. If he identifies himself with the welfare of the whole body of officers, then the officers will repay him heavily for his courtesies. If he treats the common people as his own children, then the masses will exhort one another [to do good]. If he attracts the various artisans, there will be sufficiency of wealth and resources in the country. If he shows tenderness to strangers from far countries, people from all quarters of the world will flock to him. And if he extends kindly and awesome influence over the feudal lords, then the world will stand in awe of him" *(Chung Yung*, Wing-Tsit Chan trans. p. 105).

And not only do particular roles have their associated virtues and modes of conduct, but also there are ways of understanding key virtues, virtues which conduce to the others. For instance in the Confucian vision filiality can constitute a form of participating in the government of society (*Analects*, II: 21). This places a primacy on self-cultivation in the intimate relations based on which more distant relations are also positively touched. Self cultivation allows for filial devotion, which makes the self-relation a key role in the Confucian vision. As we'll shortly see from consideration of Aristotle, a relational ethic can have a quite different vision of the key or prototypic relation. But first we'll glance at Hebraic Law.

The author(s) of the Mosaic law were implicitly relational in the presentation of the Ten Commandments. The first four of the Ten Commandments present key elements of the human relation to the Divine Person, namely, to acknowledge God, the liberator from bondage, to worship God without graven images, to refrain from using the Divine Name in vain, and to observe the Divinely appointed Sabbath day. The fifth commandment, "honour your father and mother" is the filial commandment. The seventh commandment, "do not commit adultery" is the spousal command. The sixth, eighth, and ninth are commands governing the social relation, namely, not to kill, steal, or bear false witness. And the tenth commandment governs one's mastery of oneself and one's desires: "Do not covet." In many other ways as well, one can discover underlying relational frameworks in the Mosaic myths and ethos.

Aristotle uses a rather explicit relational framework when he classifies friendship according to the equality or inequality of the relation, and, in particular, when he discusses those relations which he regards as friendships in which there is inequality: ". . . [T]here is another kind of friendship, viz., that which involves an inequality between the parties, e.g., that of father to son and in general of elder to younger, that of man to wife, and in general that of ruler to subject. And these friendships differ also from each other; for it is not the same that exists between parents and children and between rulers and subjects, nor is even that of father to son the same as that of son to father, nor that of husband to wife the same as that of wife to husband. For the virtue and the function of each of these is different, and so are the reasons for which they love; the love and the friendship are therefore different also. Each party, then, neither gets the same from the other, nor ought to seek it; but when children render to parents what they ought to render to those who brought them into the world, and parents render what they should to their children, the friendship of such persons will be abiding and excellent" (*Nicomachean Ethics*, VIII. 7, Ross trans., 1980, p. 203).

For Aristotle, then, friendship appears to be the key or prototypic relation through which specific forms of relation are to be understood; but many specific forms of relation have virtues and modes of conduct specific to them.

The Hindu *ashramas*, or stages of life, as articulated in the *Laws of Manu*, imply a dynamic framework of relational ethics. The dominant relation of the first stage of life is the student to teacher relation, and the virtue is skillful learning and continent conduct. The dominant relation of the second stage of life is that of family member to the others in the family, and the virtues are those of responsible cultivation of familial prosperity, affection, and relations with those outside the family. The dominant relation of the third stage of life is the forest dweller or retirement stage, which spouses may undertake together, in which the virtue is simplifying to the bare minimum one's home life, if a forest dwelling is a home, so that one may more fully engage in holy pursuits; and the final stage is that of the homeless, propertyless wanderer, or renunciate, whose goal is the achievement of *moksha*, liberation. These ashramas, however, are articulated together with a promulgation of caste relations. The overall relational vision includes modes of social identification which will have little use for a modern relational ethic.

One more example of this sort, and then we will consider relational ethics in more general terms. In the Buddhist *Sigala-sutta*, (N. 31 of the *Digha-Nikaya*) the story is told of a young man named Sigala who used to worship the six cardinal points of space, namely, east, south, west, north, nadir, and zenith. The Buddha told him that in the noble discipline of his teaching, the six directions were understood in reference to the fundamental relations: east for the relation of children to parents; south for the relation of student to teacher; west for the relation of husband to family members; north for the relations between friends, relatives and neighbors; nadir to the relation of employer to servants, workers, and employees; and zenith, the relation of religious practitioners to their sages. The *Sigala-sutta* text then goes on to discuss in detailed terms the behaviors and attitudes appropriate to each of the six relations, and their inverse relations, for example, wife to husband. (For an overview of the organization of the Buddhist canon, see Sthavira Sangharakshita, 1985.)

Thus, there seems to be something deeply natural about thinking things through based on an articulation of fundamental relations.

Relational ethics: A definition

What, then, is relational ethics?

Relational ethics, as I will be using the term, is the approach to ethics which holds that both from a methodological point of view and a substantial point of view the articulation of appropriate role related activity and experience is the key to having a comprehensive understanding of ethics, which is to say, the practice of living well.

The term 'role-related activity,' as will become quickly clear, is meant in a maximally broad manner. I have a role as parent, say, or as husband, or as worker, or as teacher, or as child to my parents. But I also have a role as monadic self, the person I am without regard to my relationships with others, the person I am when alone in nature, or alone with my thoughts and experiences. In fact, the monadic self is a dimension of my experience of myself and the world which may be called out during the life of personal interrelatedness as well.

For many people the self relationship seems so fundamental that it cannot be brought under the concept of role. For many people, the very idea of role implies a separation, a masking, an inhabiting a costume which is exterior to one's self. However, essential to what follows is the notion that identifying under a role is not occupying a mask or a costume. To identify under the role of father is to *be* a father. To identify under the role of adult child to one's parents is to *be* an adult child to one's parents. And so, similarly, to identify under the role of monadic individual is to *be* a person in nature. Plainly, then, we occupy many roles at once. Relational ethics is the approach to ethics which holds that the key to living well lies in disentangling and understanding the multiplicity of our roles in this broad sense. Having said this much we are ready to proceed with the framework.

THE FRAMEWORK OF A RELATIONAL ETHICS

1. The fundamental problematic

There are three types of practical moral questions, and three basic types of problems we have, or may have, in life. These are:

a. Should I occupy role X? (For example, should I be a hermit or should I live in society? Should I get married or remain single? Should I try to have children?)

b. Given that I do occupy role X, how do I realize or fulfill or consummate this role? (For example, given that I am a parent, how do I fulfill my parenthood? What is it to be a good parent?) When one asks a question of this sort, one wants to understand the requirements of the fulfillment of this particular role without reference to all the complicating factors which arise from occupying more roles than this one.

c. Given that I occupy roles X, Y, Z, and so forth, how do I establish priorities between them? (For example, given that I am a parent and also a worker, how do I decide between conflicting demands, for example, helping out extra at work or helping out extra with my children?)

2. Possible roles

In different cultures the range of available basic roles is different. And there is an important area of theory concerning the way in which the roles are or may be conceived within any given cultural context. For example, in our culture at this time, it will appear that one has, or may have, a basic relationship or concern with:

- oneself
- one's parents (and aunts, uncles, and grandparents)
- one's siblings (and cousins)
- one's friends
- one's fellow workers, both colleagues and clients
- one's romantic partner
- one's domestic partner
- one's spouse
- one's children (and nieces, nephews, and grandchildren)
- one's fellow citizens
- strangers
- a disembodied spirit, a deity, or The Deity

- nature at large
- non-human animals, especially vertebrates and particularly mammals
- the atemporal order

It will be noted that some of these roles may overlap. For example, one's domestic partner may well be one's spouse as well. When one is a child, one's parents, that is, one's adult primary nurturers, are almost certain to be one's domestic partners. One's spouse may, perhaps, be one's colleague at work.

And of course, the very reality of some of the entities through which some of the roles are defined is controversial. For instance whether there are any disembodied spirits, and whether there is a Deity, are controversial issues. So whether anyone has a relation with such a being is as controversial as the existence of that being. More on such controversies later.

Further, this list is not intended to be definitive. Some might hold that 'enemy' designates a fundamental role. Others might hold that one's spiritual mentor or guru is not adequately represented even as the combination of several of these roles. Others might reject the notion that there can be a fundamental relationship with cats for instance. And some might hold that more fundamental than the "task-oriented" relational roles of the sort listed above are what we'll call "personality roles." Thus, for instance, one might hold that appropriate articulation of the following sorts of roles is more pertinent to central ethical concerns than those in the first list:

- one-who-goes-by-the-book
- the star
- the devotee
- the party animal
- the survivor
- the homebody
- the dreamer-poet-prophet
- the adventurer
- the eccentric
- the loner
- the catalyzer
- the rebel
- the saint
- the leader

Of course the theoretical articulation of the personality roles is as controversial and difficult as is the articulation of the task-oriented roles. The personality roles given above are adapted from John Oldham and Lois B. Morris' useful categorization of healthy personality types which is itself based on the DSM III classification of personality disorders (Oldham & Morris, 1990). Robert Solomon's *The Passions* (1977) might provide one with an alternate classification of personality types based on dominant passional stances. Again, archetypal personality classifications such as are attempted in Peter Lemesurier's *The Healing of the Gods* (1988), Anthony Stevens' *Archetypes* (1982), and Jean Bolen's *Goddesses in Everywoman*, and *Gods in Everyman* (1984, 1989), all of which are inspired by Jungian archetype analysis, would provide one with still another sort of classification system, one based on mythic archetypes. There would probably be ways to translate the main terms of any good personality classification into those of another, and, similarly, to translate the main terms of any good personality classification into those of a good archetypal classification system. The mythic archetypes, after all, are intended to be expressions of fundamental personality dynamics.

But the intention of the task-oriented role classification is fundamentally different from that of the personality classification. Only rarely would it be possible to translate or regard as common the elements of the one and the elements of the other. For instance, whether someone is one's sibling or not has to do with the accidents of family life. This is independent of the personality style one brings to one's relationships in general and to one's siblings in particular. If one is an adventurous type, then one is likely to go off and be unconcerned with one's siblings. If one is a leader type, one is likely to lead one's siblings. If one is largely governed by the archetypes of Demeter, the mother, and Athena the skillful, one is more likely than not to be nurturing towards one's sibling, and clever in providing for their means of sustenance as well. At least, such is the "character is destiny" view of human relations implicit in the personality classifications and archetypal classifications. (And one should also mention, at this point, that any application of personality and archetypal classifications to individual persons worth its salt regards each person as dominated not by just one but by several personality styles or mythic archetypes. It is the selection and proportioning of the salient personality styles or archetypes from a much larger range of possibilities which makes for the endless variety in personality complexions.) Thus, the personality-archetype roles cut across and are not but another version of the task-oriented or situational roles listed in the first instance.

It seems to me, however, that the personality-archetype roles cannot be of interest in ethical analysis in quite the way that the task-oriented, situationally defined roles such as domestic partner, spouse, parent-child, coworker, fellow citizen, can be. An easy way to see this is to attempt to apply the personality-archetype roles to the three basic questions given above. We can begin by recognizing that ethics is fundamentally centered on our choices in life. Now when we ask ourselves whether we should try to become parents, for example, we are asking ourselves a concrete and simple question which is of fundamental importance to the shape of our lives. However, if we ask ourselves whether we should try to become governed by the archetype of Athena, the goddess of craft and skill, rather than that of Aphrodite, goddess of erotic love, we are into much murkier territory. Some will hold that all the archetypes are in each of us, and our task in life is to bring them all into consciousness. If so, the first of our three basic questions is not a matter of choice or direction in life, but rather of bringing what is subconscious into consciousness. Others will hold that each of us is dominated by a constellation of archetypes, and that we had better make good use of the archetypes we have by disposition. For there are, according to such an approach, ways to be abused by our archetypal tendencies, and ways to harness our archetypal tendencies towards creativity and harmonious, self-realizing living.

At the deeper level then, we allow that the situational roles need addressing first. Personality and archetypal self-fashioning will emerge as being of importance within a task-oriented role analysis. For instance, it may be that if one properly regards oneself as pretty much stuck in an antisocial, or loner personality role, this must be counted as a factor in one's determination of whether or not to attempt to start a family. Similarly, once one is able to identify one's task-oriented roles, the task-oriented roles one sees oneself as occupying, and properly occupying, one will want to raise issues of personality in the relevant way. One will allow one's archetypal proclivities to influence the priorities balance amongst the various roles one occupies. A saintly personality may find that it makes sense to disengage citizenship activities from remunerative considerations. A leader personality may find that it makes sense to combine her citizenship activities with the worker role.

Having distinguished between situational or task-oriented roles on the one hand, and personality roles on the other hand, we should now distinguish between a variegated relational ethical analysis such as we are embarking on here, and a relational analysis based on a single fundamental ethical relational intuition. Recently, Nel Noddings in

Caring (1984) has provided an ethical analysis based on the nurturing relation with which women particularly are intimately familiar. Rodger Beehler in *Moral Life*, (1978) has also argued that without the human capacity for caring, no ethical analysis can be undertaken. One might regard Martin Buber's *I and Thou* as articulating a religious ethical analysis based on the contrast between I-thou stances and I-it stances. Stretching the point, perhaps, one might say that Kant's ethics calls to our attention the relational value implicit in respect for persons, and Hume's ethics calls to our attention the relational value implicit in the attitude of sympathy. In each of these cases, a claim could be made that a relational ethical analysis is being provided based on a central positively evaluated relational stance, attitude, or emotion. Yet surely there is an important difference between a variegated ethical analysis launched by a task-centered role analysis and that of the promotion of a single attitude or stance, however important that attitude or stance may be.

It is possible of course for there to be a full-fledged uni-valued relational ethic. For instance, a full-fledged agapism might be such a uni-valued relational ethic. Agapism in this sense would be the ethical system which holds that so long as one connects with the intuition of love and caring in one's relations with others and oneself, and acts in that consciousness, one will be doing the best one can do.

By contrast with such a uni-valued relational ethic is the relational analysis that holds that the variety of task-centered roles needs to be analyzed in order for one to determine what to do, and what particular form loving-kindness may or should take in a given circumstance. If a man has proposed marriage to you, and you are the sole caregiver of your invalid mother, and to marry the man requires living in a different city, and no longer being able to provide anything like the same level of care for your mother, is it enough to "act in the consciousness of love?" If your problem is a dilemma of love, love pulling in two worthy directions, then you need a method of analysis which enables you to prioritize the situational relations. In this case, many people in our culture would say that it may make sense to temporarily postpone a marriage for the sake of an invalid mother, but it does not make sense to put one's marital life indefinitely and potentially forever on hold for her sake. It is precisely such a prioritization which is made possible by an analysis that articulates fundamental situational relations and then raises the three questions of occupation, fulfillment in each individual role case, and prioritization. It is one thing to point to caring as an attitude that infuses ethical thinking and analysis, and another to hold that ethical analysis, and in particular, role prioritizations, can be dispensed with by an ethics of caring. Nodding's ethics of caring, for instance, has been criticized for its incapacity to guide ethical functioning in the public sphere, and also for its inherent tendency, as Eileen Sowerby puts it, towards "shrinkage" not only *to* the private sphere, but also *within* the private sphere (1993). In general, construing ethics in terms of a single stance will leave out too much.

I hope that this brief discussion has suggested some of the theoretical interest in the problems of articulating fundamental task-oriented roles, fundamental personality or archetypal roles, and the potential usefulness of both of them to ethical analysis. We will summarize the framework thus far presented with the following capsule: To live well is to choose well which of the basic task-oriented roles to occupy; to know how to fulfill the roles one does come to occupy through conscious choice or otherwise; and to know how to make priorities and establish balances between the demands of the various different roles. We'll now look at some basic issues arising with respect to the first of these concerns, the concern with choosing well which roles to occupy or attempt to occupy.

3. Choosing roles

Most people don't want to consciously choose their basic roles. If I have to wrestle with whether to be a hermit or not, I am wrestling with something I would prefer to flow naturally. The ideal condition to be in is the condition of one for whom the roles that one occupies or wants to occupy appear to be the only roles one would want to seriously consider. "*Of course* I will be a hermit. Who wants to bother with other people?" Or, "*Of course* I want to marry and have a family. This is basic."

On the other hand, there are issues of obligation and moral choice involved in role occupation. If one wants to live in a mountain cave contemplating the cosmos, one may have to leave aging, ill, poor, needy parents, or a spouse and children behind, to suffer one's absence. Is one's choice to abandon one's parents, or one's spouse and children, a morally unconstrained choice?

We observe, then, that occupying roles occurs through two very different processes: (a) those of social and personal destiny, that is, social and personal givens, as it were, and (b) those of reflective and conscious activities of choosing. In the first case, role occupation only becomes a problem if one discovers that one wants to drop out of a role. In the second case, role occupation can be a prospective problem as well as an exit problem. But in either case, there can be no aid to a decision which ignores considerations of role fulfillment and of role priorities.

More generally, we can see that there are four factors involved in making role occupation choices:

1. There is the purely self-creative factor: choosing one's destiny, forging one's personality, creating one's life story, deciding that, other things being equal, one's life would have this shape rather than that shape. This factor may also be called the "aesthetic factor" or the "existentialist factor" in ethics.

2. Making choices based on anticipated fulfillments, given a particular view of what particular role fulfillments consist in and what sort of prospects of satisfaction one has for them without regard to role priorities and role conflicts. In making these choices one regards oneself as having a personality or archetype of a more or less determined complexion or mix, and therefore one is thinking more on consequentialist lines than when making aesthetic or existentialist choices.

3. Making choices based on the effects of multiplicity of role fulfillment, role conflicts, and conflicting obligations, demands, needs, and interests, (including obligations to oneself, and one's own demands, needs, and interests). It is in this area that the traditional western problems requiring resolution of utilitarian, deontological, and existentialist approaches to ethics rise to the foreground.

4. Recognizing and accepting any non-defeasible roles. Candidates for non-defeasible roles are child to parent, monadic individual (the non-defeasibility of which might prohibit suicide), citizen, worshipper of Deity, and would-be-parent. To say that such and such is a non-defeasible role is to say that everyone ought to occupy it, or everyone ought to try as hard as possible to come to occupy it. For instance, to say that child to parent is a non-defeasible relation is to say that everyone ought to continue to regard themselves as falling under the role of children in respect to their parents. To hold the view that worshipper of Deity is a non-defeasible role is to say that everyone ought to be a worshipper of God, or a servant of God. To say that would-be parent is a non-defeasible role, is to say that everyone should hold it as a goal, at some degree of priority, to become a parent.

We can easily see that exiting from a role involves working through all four factors. Choosing whether to occupy a role involves at least the second factor, since choosing to occupy a role involves understanding the role. It also involves the fourth factor in the sense that it might be a role that one has no license to refrain from occupying. And it involves in addition the first, for that sheer self-creating existentialist factor is always present in our choices; and also the third, role conflict, factor. The only person deciding a role occupation question who is free of role conflicts is a friendless, orphaned, never married, unemployed hermit contemplating suicide. And even there the hermit's subjective identification might not tally with a proper moral calculus enjoining the citizenship role on everyone.

4. Fulfilling roles

Since the questions of role fulfillment are studied without reference to any conflict between the role in question and other roles, the questions of role fulfillment do not appear to be as difficult as the questions of role occupation and role prioritization.

One addresses the question of monadic fulfillment, that is, fulfillment of the self relation or the self role, by asking: If I were alone in the world, with no other person to interact with ever, how would I fulfill myself? How might anyone fulfill himself or herself in a similar position? What can be said in the most general way about such fulfillment?

One addresses the question of the fulfillment of the role of parent in relation to the child by asking: If I have no needs of my own, that is to say no monadic interests unfulfilled at the moment, and I am a parent, what does the fulfillment of my relationship with my child consist of?

One addresses the question of the fulfillment of the role of strangers who are members of a single large community by asking: Aside from my personal needs, and those of my family, and those of all other intimate relations, what does the fulfillment of my relationship with strangers, or my fellow citizens, consist of?

And so on for each of the fundamental relations.

At this stage we only need to call attention to these questions raised in this way, and to observe that these questions provide an excellent point of departure for ethical analysis. If we try to discuss role occupation questions or role prioritization questions without having first satisfied ourselves as to these role fulfillment questions, we will be building a moral theory on thin air. (It is a striking fact that so many of the happiness-based moral expositions have construed intrinsic value as intrinsic monadic value. As we will see later on, a good deal of unnecessary confusion and inadequacy has resulted.)

5. Establishing priorities

The important general point to note at this stage concerning establishing priorities is that it is in this area that we come to employ one or another of the Divine voluntarist, eudaimonian, deontological, or complex moral theoretic approaches. When we justify one or another prioritization, we will tend to do so with reference to happiness, justice, contract or quasi-contract, the divine will, or the cosmic order.

For example, a typical ethical question is that of the morality of adultery. Is it morally permissible for one partner in a marriage to have a sexual relation outside of the marriage, either secretly, or without the consent of, or even with the consent of, the other partner in the marriage? The relational ethics approach to the problem is to suggest that the question is one of prioritization. The prioritization is at least between the spouse relation and the romantic partner relation. The spouse who wants the sexual relation outside of the marriage has separated off the romantic relation from the spouse relation, and wants to maintain a separate romantic relation exclusive of, or in addition to, the spouse relation. Now (putting aside for the moment the question of the morality of adultery to which the other spouse consents, and putting aside as well complicating Divine voluntarist beliefs, and the like) suppose one holds that an established marital relationship takes priority over the desire for a romantic relation outside of the spouse relation. This prioritization may be justified using utilitarian reasoning ("Taking the marriage vows lightly inevitably leads to unhappiness all around"), or deontological reasoning, ("Contract keeping is a categorical imperative, and the marriage relation is founded in mutual promises"). Similarly, the opposite prioritization may be justified using utilitarian reasoning. ("Maintaining conventional obstacles to sexual fulfillment such as a past vow does not lead to overall happiness; rather, discreet affairs, despite marriage vows, do, in many cases, lead to more happiness than preserving the vows.") And the opposite prioritization may be justified using deontological reasoning. ("If promise keeping were a categorical imperative, then the individual now would not be an autonomous moral agent. The individual of twenty years ago would have authority over the individual twenty years later, and the individual's ethical stance would be fundamentally heteronomous. But the categorical imperative must be to respect individual autonomy. So it is proper for a partner in a marriage to expect the other partner to respect his or her absolute autonomy, and, essentially, his or her right to overturn the marriage vow made by what might as well be regarded as a different individual.")

As we will see in the next section, the fact that we employ a eudaimonian or a deontological approach, for example, in justifying or establishing a role prioritization does not entail that we must settle the controversy between eudaimonian and deontological ethics in order to establish role priorities. Rather, the role prioritizations may be expressed using the theoretical vocabularies of different theories, but the outcomes do not line up along the axes of differentiation of the different theories. This feature exhibits the particular usefulness of the relational ethic framework whenever practical ethics are the central focus.

II. THE ADVANTAGES OF THE RELATIONAL APPROACH TO ETHICS

There are two types of advantage or superiority we may be concerned with in assessing the relational approach to ethics. The first is an advantage or superiority which emerges in comparison with existing approaches to ethics, considering only the ability of the existing approach in question to satisfy its own internal goals and agendas. The second is an advantage or superiority of relational ethics as a framework within which we may discuss problems of value without presupposing Enlightenment West, postmodern, or Enlightenment East conclusions. I believe that the relational approach to ethics has important advantages of both types, and, indeed, that the superiority of relational ethical schemas to other approaches to ethics emerges with especial vividness when the various approaches to ethics are compared for their adequacy to our assessment of Enlightenment East and Enlightenment West values. Any approach to value which is capable of being neutral with respect to Enlightenment East and Enlightenment West, must have depth and breadth. The search for such an approach to value is simultaneously the search for an approach which inevitably will have advantages within the ethical enterprise as more narrowly conceived along western or eastern lines.

There will be some advantages of the first type to which we will call attention as the discussion progresses. Here, though, it is sufficient for us to exhibit the adequacy of relational ethics to our task.

1. Relational ethics is both comprehensive and yet practical

Moral philosophers are undoubtedly familiar with a certain nagging difficulty in ethics as it is usually practiced in the western philosophical tradition, namely, the tendency to lose the practical focus as one struggles to be comprehensive. It is very difficult to present a comprehensive normative ethical theory. The more comprehensive one gets, the less specificity there is in the result. For instance, the eudaimonian, or utilitarian, says, "Bring about as much happiness for as many people as you can." But this advice is the eudaimonian philosopher's equivalent of the stockbroker's advice, "Buy low, sell high." It's well nigh empty of specific content.

This doesn't mean that there are no differences between the eudaimonian on the one hand, and the deontologist on the other hand. There are important differences between a moral theory which holds that happiness is the only fundamental value and a moral theory which holds that justice is the only fundamental value, or the only value capable of producing a categorical imperative. But on any practical moral question (e.g., is adultery immoral?) there can be utilitarian reasoning for the pro answer, and utilitarian reasoning for the con answer; there can be, as well, a pro and con answer for deontological reasoning. Similarly, there can be a Rossian complex moral theorist who answers the question in the affirmative, and one who answers the question in the negative. Consequently, the many-sided debate between the deontologist, the utilitarian, and the proponent of a Rossian complex ethical theory is not a debate in which moral outcomes line up along the lines of the debate.

However, different answers to the fundamental questions posed by the relational ethical framework result in, nay, *constitute*, practical differences at the level of the moral outcomes themselves. We cannot answer the questions posed by the relational ethical framework without having a specific yet comprehensive moral theory. And the different answers are practical differences. On the other hand, we can answer the questions posed by utilitarianism, deontology, and complex moral theory as to the fundamental value or values, and be left without a specific practical moral theory, and the different specific practical moral theories do not line up along theoretical axes.

It may even be a mistaken assumption of western ethical theory that we need to resolve the debate between utilitarianism, deontology, and complex moral theory in order to satisfy our fundamental ethical questions. If answering the questions posed by the relational ethical framework can be done without resolving the debate between utilitarianism, deontology, and complex moral theory, then these debates are revealed as strictly metaethical in import. Two proponents of the same moral outcomes will have different ways of understanding their moral practices, but they do share them. Two opponents at the practical outcome level may share a moral theory.

2. Utilitarianism stands incomplete until one supplies principles of an intermediate nature

Yet it appears one cannot fully assess such intermediate principles without invoking a relational ethical framework.

Traditional utilitarian theory recognizes the need for intermediate principles. For instance, John Stuart Mill, in *Utilitarianism*, refers to them as "intermediate generalizations." "[O]n any hypothesis short of [universal idiocy] mankind by this time must have acquired positive beliefs as to the effect of some actions on their happiness, and the beliefs which have thus come down are the rules of morality for the multitude, and for the philosopher until he has succeeded in finding better. . . . But to consider the rules of morality as improvable is one thing; to pass over the intermediate generalizations entirely, and endeavor to test each individual action directly by the first principle, is another. It is a strange notion, that the acknowledgement of a first principle is inconsistent with the admission of secondary ones" (*Utilitarianism*, chapter 2). Mill does not himself supply the intermediate generalizations, but we are not at a loss as to what such intermediate generalizations might state. They might tell us to speak truthfully, to fulfill promises, to make restitution for damages, and so on. They might, moreover, include each of Ross' prima facie duties. At a slightly more abstract level, there might also be overarching intermediate generalizations. By contrast with the intermediate generalizations just stated, the overarching intermediate generalizations would in some cases be exclusive of each other. Indeed, what the student of philosophy expects from ethics is an analysis of methods by which these very different intermediate generalizations may be assessed. Four such generalizations (pairwise inconsistent except for some pairs including the fourth) are:

(*a*) The way to bring about maximum happiness is for everyone to act egoistically. That is, the way to bring about maximum happiness is for everyone to adopt the attitude that his or her own interest is the only interest that counts as an intrinsic interest. Such an attitude leads to vigorous competition. And when everyone competes vigorously in this way, overall happiness will tend, as a matter of fact, to increase. Everyone toughens up, as it were, and becomes adept at making sure that he or she gets what he or she needs. This view, as mentioned earlier, may be called "egoist utilitarianism."

(*b*) The best way to maximize happiness is for everyone to put his or her own interests second to the interest of some group of people. With everyone subordinating his or her interests to a group, everyone's interests tend to get served because everyone is serving many people, and everyone thus tends to be on the recipient end of many persons' actions. This view may be called "altruist ulilitarianism."

(*c*) The best way to maximize happiness is for everyone to sometimes be egoist, and sometimes altruist. This view may be called that of the "mixed egoist-altruist utilitarian." Of course the systematic mixed egoist-altruist utilitarian will need some supplementary guideline as to the situations in which happiness is increased by altruist conduct and the situations in which happiness is increased by egoist conduct.

(d) The best way to maximize happiness is to connect with the feeling of loving-kindness, and to act in the conscious experience of loving-kindness. When one acts out of the conscious experience of love for each human being affected by one's choices, one is more likely than by any other way to bring about the maximum happiness. This view may be called "agapistic utilitarianism."

But the utilitarian, or the complex moral theorist with a happiness component, will discover that when one tries to justify one or another of these overarching intermediate generalizations, one inevitably begins to think within the terms of role-related activity. For instance, altruist utilitarian strategies cannot be assessed without consideration of role specifics. Do we always increase happiness by expanding the group of primary moral identification? Should one participate in the feeding of every child on the globe in the same way that one participates in the feeding of one's own children? No, one might say, reasoning that not all relations are those of citizen to citizen. I am concerned with the feeding of a child, any child, the way I am concerned with the feeding of adults wherever they be. That is, I am concerned with the feeding of people as people. But I am concerned with the feeding of my own child insofar as I am the parent of that child. Thus, it is revealed that I have a duality of roles, and in thinking this way, I have begun to think within the framework of relational ethics. I may take it that there is a single all-embracing value being pursued in all the relations, namely, happiness, but this does not detract from the point that the implementation of the happiness monolith of the utilitarian needs sorting out with regard to role differentiation.

Similarly, both deontological and complex moral theories require a relational ethical framework before the substantial content can be extracted from the theoretical approach. The deontologist has no way to sort out hard cases, cases in which several imperatives, each of which has been deduced from the root categorical imperative, come into conflict with each other. Adequate characterization of such situations will result, as before, in the appearance of relational ethical terms. And the Rossian complex moral theorist will not capture the basic moral intuitions that the Rossian theorist hopes to capture without adverting to the relational ethical framework. For instance, Ross would say that my feeding of my child is an obligation arising from a past action of mine. By fathering the child I have implicitly promised to look after the child. Or, if I didn't feed the child, then I would be causing harm through neglect, and must make restitution. However, neither of these analyses captures the simple relational intuition that I feed the child *as* the parent of the child. It is my role (whether biological parent or not) to be the nurturer of the child. So if I see myself as the parent of the child, if I occupy the role of parent, I occupy the role of nurturer. To say that I have an obligation because of a past action is to miss the mark. This is as clear in the case of biological as non-biological parents. People who adopt children are not best described as contracting obligations and benefits in virtue of their adoptive acts. Rather, they are best described as choosing to occupy a role in relation to the child being adopted, that role being the role of parent or nurturer.

It is useful in this context to note that Ross himself invokes relational roles in criticizing utilitarianism. He says, "[T]he theory of 'ideal utilitarianism' if I may for brevity refer so to the theory of Professor Moore, seems to simplify unduly our relations to our fellows. It says, in effect, that the only morally significant relation in which my neighbours stand to me is that of being possible beneficiaries by my action. They do stand in this relation to me, and this relation is morally significant. But they may also stand to me in the relation of promisee to promiser, of creditor to debtor, of wife to husband, of child to parent, of friend to friend, of fellow countryman to fellow countryman, and the like; and each of these relations is the foundation of a prima facie duty, which is more or less incumbent on me according to the circumstances of the case" (Ross, 1930, p. 24). In this list of relations, Ross augments the six basic duties with role defined relations. Indeed, he seems to regard the role relations as prior to the duties. If he had followed through on the line of thought begun in this criticism, his theory might have had the full blown structure of the relational ethical theory.

The strong way of expressing this point is to say that what the relational ethicist represents as a role prioritization question will not be adequately represented except as a role prioritization question, and to do so requires articulation of a relational ethic in which the issue is so construed.

3. The relational ethical framework is a deeply natural framework for studying practical ethics

The relational ethical framework addresses questions and expresses dilemmas, difficulties, and problems at the level at which they present themselves to people who are not familiar with the intricacies of metaethical debate. Classic dilemmas, such as whether to stay home to care for invalid parents or go off to school to study violin, are easily, directly, and naturally expressed within the relational ethical framework. And any particular value finds its application conveniently and naturally expressed through canvassing the fundamental roles.

To take one of innumerable possible examples, when Augustine wishes to present his vision of peace he finds no better way to do so than by canvassing what peace is in the context of the fundamental roles as he sees them: "Peace between a mortal man and his Maker consists in ordered obedience, guided by faith, under God's eternal law; peace between man and man consists in regulated fellowship. The peace of a home lies in the ordered harmony of authority and obedience between the members of a family living together. The peace of the political community is an ordered harmony of authority and obedience between citizens" (*The City of God*, bk 19, chap. 13). The exposition of a value is very conveniently undertaken by studying its meaning in the context of each of the fundamental task-oriented relations, however one typologizes them. And when these relations and values pose problems of conflict, then the solutions of such conflicts themselves define new theories of value, values which are implicit prioritizations.

Thus, it is reasonable to expect that the relational ethical framework provides a natural and highly clarifying methodology for approaching any practical ethical question. The naturalness of the relational ethics is also evident in more technical and difficult areas. For instance in the theory of partial compliance, one deals with the question of the degree of one's obligations to the whole of the moral community when one can reasonably expect that many or most people will not be fulfilling their minimum obligations. The theory of partial compliance is very important in our age, because we have the capacity to causally interact with all people on the planet, and because so few people are doing as much as might minimally be done to help improve things. Traditional utilitarian analysis often leads to a conclusion many people find counterintuitively demanding. The relational analysis would suggest that the high standards of obligation attach to each citizen qua citizen of the world. But to determine one's obligations qua world citizen is not yet to determine one's final obligations. The relational ethical analysis thus has the capacity to represent both the intuition that one has an obligation to do an awful lot on behalf of strangers, and also the intuition that in the final analysis one's duties to strangers do not need to overwhelm one.

4. Most important of all, the relational ethical framework sets out an elaborate and comprehensive set of questions without presupposing any answers to these questions whatever

Thus, it serves us exactly at the point at which we need a theory. It is, in technical terms, a universal ethical problematic without a valuational bias of any kind, and certainly without a valuational bias with regard to the questions of socio-scientific rationalism in relation to mysticism.

To see that this last claim is true, one only needs to see that each of the ethical theories we had previously mentioned and rejected as unsuitable as frameworks for use in our analysis, will be able to reestablish itself, as appropriate, within a relational ethical analysis. This should be readily apparent for the western theories. And that this is also true in the case of the eastern moral theories emerges when we notice that the Enlightenment East systems are embodied in relational ethical schemas. Thus, traditional Buddhist instruction includes right livelihood as a fundamental element of the eightfold path, which implies the fundamental character of the work relation; it includes sexual propriety as one of the basic *silas*, or precepts, which implies the fundamental character of the romantic relation; it includes duties of a husband to wife, which implies the fundamental character of the spouse relation; and so on. Aside from somewhat systematic articulations of relational ethics as in the case of the *Sigala-sutta* (No. 31 of the *Digha-nikaya*) mentioned above, relational ethical elements permeate the foundational approach to Buddhism. We've already seen how the stages-of-life conception in Hinduism implies a relational ethics. And Yoga-Vedanta systems such as that of Patanjali make similar use of the components of the relational ethic schema. Thus, the relational ethics framework is eminently intelligible to the proponent of Enlightenment East.

Now it might be objected that the notion of monadic interests will be ultimately unintelligible to some Buddhist schools, in particular, those which emphasize the incoherence of the attribution of ultimate identity to any particular (apparent) thing. If no particular thing may be ascribed ultimate identity in a coherent manner, then, it might be asked, what sense is there in ascribing monadic values to individuals? In response to this objection, while it is true that the vocabulary of monadic value may be foreign, from one perspective, to Buddhist schools with leanings towards one or another form of ontological nihilism, the objection itself cannot be articulated easily unless any effort to express ethical analysis in a manner acceptable to the ultimate metaphysical position of the school is doomed to failure. There are, to put it simply, two possibilities. Either ethical discussion at the relative level (as it might be put) is to be tolerated, or it is not. If it is not, then there is no hope for a reconciliation of that branch of Enlightenment East with Enlightenment West ethical analysis. If it is to be tolerated, then it should be possible to consider a variety of vocabularies for discussion of things at the relative level in the hopes of finding one which does as little violence as possible to the direction the ontological analysis wishes to move in. Once it is seen from the analysis of chapters three, four, and five, how the relational analysis proceeds and in particular how the view of mystical value as monadic value ties in with the analysis of the logical, metaphysical, and epistemic issues surrounding the nature of mystical experience, it will be seen, I hope, that the relational ethical framework provides a vocabulary within which clarity can be brought to the very difficult relation between what have been called the "relative" and "absolute" levels of discourse, a relation which plagues the metaphysics of both Advaita (nondual) Vedanta, and Madhyamika Buddhism. In any case, to put it simply, any mystical system, which hopes to make sense of ethical relations, needs to be able to conceive of goods that can be regarded as intrinsic goods by a hermit. And that is all that is required for the terminology of monadic value, or the monadic relation to be intelligible.

The framework of relational ethics, it may be useful to note, helps call into question deconstructionist postmodernism. Obviously, postmodernists eat, drink, and work like everyone else, have families, more likely than not, like everyone else, and pay their bills and their income tax. Less obviously, it seems, these activities rely on accepting some set of relational categories of the sort that gives rise to the narratives supposedly to be deconstructed. Postmodernists, too, I'm suggesting, must understand what they're doing in relational terms. If a storm hits town, the postmodernist goes out to find his or her children, just as the modernist does. The utilitarian will explain such conduct one way: it would be chaos if everyone related to everyone else's child on the same basis as to his or her own. The deontologist will perhaps explain such conduct another way: there is intrinsic rightness in maintaining a special relation of parents to children. But whether explained one way or another, the valorization of the roles, as the postmodernist may put it, is not a limitation of the roles, but is intrinsic to them, and to the character of the dynamic interplay we are all engaged in. If the deconstruction of the narratives and myths is an intellectual exercise meant to allow the survival of the practices, conducing to a mere correction of attitudes, or a prevention of *excessive* valorization, then the postmodernism is more accurately regarded as an implementation of modernism.

5. Finally, the relational ethical framework clarifies the distinction between a theory of monadic value and a comprehensive moral theory

A theory of monadic value may have a strong mystical component without the structure of the overall moral theory being swallowed or submerged under the weight of the mystical monadic theory.

This latter point will be emphasized again as our inquiry progresses. Indeed, it will be one of the central themes of this account that mystical realization is a monadic value. It is important, then, to distinguish between assessing it as a monadic value and assessing it within an interrelational context. I will suggest that it is the failure to make this distinction that has led to the appearance of irreconcilability of Enlightenment East and Enlightenment West visions and traditions.

III. THE RECONCILIATION

Our next task, then, is to see how the clarification of the distinction between monadic values and overall value theory enables us to demonstrate the reconcilability of Enlightenment West and Enlightenment East values. In this section, I will present a sketch of the role-fulfillment component of the relational ethics scheme. It seems to me that what I am about to say about role fulfillment, that is, what the fulfillment of each role consists in apart from any questions of role occupation or role conflict, is not particularly controversial. The very fact that one can make relatively uncontroversial yet foundational normative remarks by using the relational ethical framework exhibits some of the clarifying capacity of the approach.

(I) Monadic Fulfillment

Everyone has a monadic aspect. This is the aspect of one's fulfillment that has nothing to do with any other person—not even a personal God if one exists. Monadic fulfillment is the fulfillment of the hermit in everyone. The fulfillment of one's monadic interests is the fulfillment of those interests which one has in virtue of being an agent in (an otherwise impersonal) nature. Thus, monadic interests are interests everyone has, and we may discover the content of monadic fulfillment by discovering what a hermit's intrinsic interests are or may be. To be precise, monadic interests are the interests which one might posit as intrinsic interests even if there were no other persons in the world, namely:

- Survival
- health
- joy in being: joy in seeing, hearing, touching, smelling, tasting, voluntary agency, and the exercise of the cognitive and agentive faculties; pleasure in eating, and other bodily functions
- emotional well being: serenity, optimism, cheerfulness; and intense emotional satisfactions such as thrilling to real or simulated dangers
- joy in the expansion of one's powers and abilities in planning and execution
- knowledge for its own sake

Thus, we begin our ethical investigation with an acknowledgment of a stunning fact: the list of monadic values is not particularly controversial. Indeed, to take the strongest challenge possible, the existentialist slogan "existence precedes essence" will provide a prima facie challenge to deontological ethical systems, and the other-regarding component of utilitarian systems, but it will bump up solidly against the uncontroversial status of most elements of this list.

The possibility of specific controversy arises when we begin to ask, which of these are apt to diminish the fulfillment of the others, and if so how does one make priorities between them? For example, coming to the conclusion that there is no personal God may disturb one's serenity and optimism. There is, then, a potential conflict between two monadic values: pursuing knowledge for its own sake, and cultivating serenity or optimism. Having to expose oneself to the elements to gain some knowledge may jeopardize one's health. In this case, pursuing knowledge for its own sake may have a consequence which is in conflict with other monadic goods. Pursuing a thrilling but dangerous pleasure such as hang gliding may jeopardize one's survival, and so on. How does one make priorities between the competing intrinsic monadic goods?

In chapter three, I will suggest that there is a general answer to such questions, and that this general answer is supplied to us by the proponent of mysticism or Enlightenment East. In this context, however, we need only observe that a theory of monadic fulfillment is a mystical theory, or, perhaps more accurately, that it has a mystical component, just in case it includes within the list of monadic values that of mystical experience. The uncontroversial list given above does not highlight its mystical component, but it has been drawn up at a sufficiently general level so as to accommodate the mystic. The mystic would include within knowledge for its own sake and joy in being a more particular description along the lines of the mysticism involved.

For instance, the Buddhist might say that the highest monadic value is the knowledge and clarification in one's experience of impermanence, the absence of fixed identity, and the mutual interrelatedness of all forms of existence. The non-dualist Hindu or Yoga-Vedantist might say that the highest monadic value is experiencing Sat-Chit-Ananda, or blissful knowledge of Being. The Taoist mystic along with Western extrovertive mystics might say that by actively deepening one's sense of the absoluteness, ineffability, and ultimacy of the present moment, one simultaneously acquires that knowledge of which other more specific objects of knowledge are models, and also the bliss of being which is shadowed in other desire-and-satisfaction forms of pleasure.

In general, the mystic is one who holds that the experience of sustained joy in being or continuous monadic fulfillment is produced by the continuous contemplation of the fundamental grounding of the life process that one is immersed in. If one holds that the fundamental grounding is recognition of emptiness of all forms of existence of inherent fixed identity, then one holds that sustained joy is produced by the contemplation of the emptiness of all things. If one holds that the metaphysical grounding is the Absolute Self, then one holds that sustained blissfulness is produced by the contemplation of the Absolute Self manifesting in this way at this moment. I have expressed the fundamental ethical tenet of mysticism in a hedonic vocabulary. But express hedonism might also be removed, just as a utilitarian theory need not be a hedonic theory. A non-hedonic expression of mysticism is this: the greatest monadic good is the continuous contemplation of and experience of the truest, deepest reality in which one's life process is grounded.

There is, to be sure, a contrast between a mystical and a non-mystical theory of monadic value, especially to the degree that the mysticism is expressed within a controversial metaphysical vocabulary. The non-mystical theory of monadic value does not agree with the mystic theory which states that there is any special mystical knowledge, or does not agree with the mystic theory that contemplation of the supposed metaphysical truths or realities is in any privileged position as a monadic value-realizing practice. According to the non-mystic, the contemplation of the mystical metaphysics, even if the metaphysics is justifiable, is a fine thing for those to whom it brings pleasure, but so is the practice of darts. There is no special value-realization relevance to the contemplation of arcane and dubious metaphysical concepts.

We leave the details of the mystic's theory of monadic value to the next chapter. Here it suffices us to recognize that as long as the mystic begins by presenting mystical experience as a component of a theory of monadic value, there will be no stubborn irreconcilability of Enlightenment East and Enlightenment West values. The proponent of Enlightenment West can accept, or ought to be capable of accepting, that, if a mystical component of monadic value can be established, this will not threaten the basic fabric of the Enlightenment West value scheme. If the having of mystical experience is a monadic end in itself, or can be a monadic end in itself for some people, then it should be entered as an element in the overall moral scheme. Just as knowledge of science, history, and so on, is standardly conceived of as an element of monadic value, so, too, would the cultivation of mystical knowledge, experience, or bliss, depending how one understands and characterizes it, be conceived of as an element of monadic value. But just as the fact that knowledge of science, history, and so on is conceived by some as an end in itself does not lead those who so conceive it to ignore or hold as irrelevant all the complex questions of role occupation or role prioritization, so, too, the fact, if it is a fact, that mystical knowledge, experience, or bliss, is an end in itself does not, or should not lead those who so conceive it to ignore, or hold as irrelevant all the complex questions of role occupation or role prioritization.

In other words, by distinguishing between mysticism as a component of a theory of monadic value, on the one hand, and, on the other hand, those comprehensive systems of thought which not only include mysticism as a component of the theory of monadic value, but also which have particular resolutions of role conflict between monadic and social roles, we allow both for a defense of mysticism as a component of the theory of monadic value, and also for a critique of the particular systems of prioritization which have emerged in those cultures which developed the monadic value of mysticism, should such a critique be necessary.

In simpler terms, if mysticism is a healthy practice, it is a healthy practice the same way that physical exercise is a healthy practice, or the study of human culture is a healthy practice. To say this is not to say how important the cultivation of mystical experience is in relation to the social fulfillments. Genial mysticism, then, should be perfectly intelligible to the exponent of Enlightenment West values. Genial mysticism holds that it is empirically possible for one to dramatically raise the hedonic level of everyday experience by attending as much as possible to one's current experience under the aspect of ultimacy. By attending to the indissoluble reality of the current moment, one tends to be filled with pleasure. The more one allows the flow experience, the experience of being immersed in a vast, ultimate process not of one's own making, but to which one is an active, absolute participant, to be highlighted and stabilized at the center of everyday consciousness, the more one experiences ultimate Joy in Being. Genial mysticism, thus, is an empirical or psychological theory of *monadic* value. It does not come saddled with exotic metaphysical or ontological presuppositions, and by degrees should be accepted readily by the exponent of Enlightenment West, so long as the psychology is accurate.

We will continue, then, with a particular account of interrelational fulfillments, both intimate and distant. My aim in this account is twofold. I hope to illustrate how the relational framework can be filled out so that the general character of a relational ethic can be better suggested. And, second, I aim to do so in such a way that the ground is prepared for our discussion in chapter six of monadic versus interrelational value, and, not unconnectedly, for our discussion in chapters seven, eight, and nine, of the integration of Enlightenment East and West values. I will present the account baldly, without justificatory digressions, given my hope that it will be judged as sound in the main lines relevant to our task without the need for such bolstering.

(II) Fulfillment of Intimate Relations

We can distinguish two kinds of interpersonal roles or relationships: our intimate and our distant interpersonal relationships. Relations between parents and children, siblings, friends, and romantic, domestic, and spouse partners, are intimate. On the other hand the relations between fellow citizens and between strangers are distant. The relations between fellow workers are sometimes felt to be intimate and sometimes felt to be distant.

Each intimate relation is both externally centered and internally centered, both functionally centered, and heart centered. The external tasks or activities central to the different intimate relations differ one from the other.

A parent provides food, warmth, shelter, affection, and education to the child. This is the parent's task in relation to the child.

Domestic partners cooperate in the management of the affairs of the household, the cleaning, the decorating, the financial upkeep and long-term planning.

Workers supply each other with various services or goods, typically with one providing the service or goods, and the other providing monetary reward.

However, the ultimate center of the internal focus of each relationship does not differ one from the other, for in each case it is the giving and receiving of love. But because the tasks and activities differ, the bridges leading from external to internal focus can be seen to differ.

It is these bridges, which we may refer to as the spiritual tasks of the various relationships, which characterize the uniqueness of each relationship. The term 'spiritual' is not meant to have any ontological connotation. It is, rather, meant to convey the sense of the moral in which the practice of love is regarded as the center of each interpersonal relation. Each relationship has a basic issue, a spiritual task of its own.

The parent-child relationship revolves around the issue of pure or absolute dependence and independence. The child begins in full dependency, grows to a position of absolute independence, and ends up having to be prepared for the dependency of the old and possibly infirm parent on the child.

Siblings have the task of learning cooperation, of converting competitive and aggressive feelings into feelings of wholesome competition and cooperation.

Friends fulfill the role of what may be called "other self," or "pure Other," and thus are available as healthy outlets from the frustrations and burdens of other areas of one's life. The friend's task is to share leisure time, to offer support and concrete assistance, as well as to model neutrality and pure otherness which enables friends to be perfect reflections of self to each other.

The task of the lover, or romantic partner, is to embody the ideal of the beloved. This form of embodiment is special. On the one hand, it is not a demanding requirement, for it is the lover who attributes the ideal to the beloved. On the other hand, allowing oneself to embody the ideal requires subtlety.

The external task of the spouse is fulfillment of the nesting activities, the provision for long-range domestic planning, emotional stability, and the raising of family. Because so many ethical systems—for quite different purported reasons, ranging from the fulfillment of the Divine Will to the disutility of anything other than monogamy—expect the extensional identity of the romantic relation and the spouse relation, there is a characteristic spiritual task associated with the combination of romance and spouse relation which is called "marriage." The spiritual task in marriage is to develop the capacity to see another human being both as ideal or archetypal beloved, and as real human being with individuality and idiosyncrasy, strength and weakness. The spiritual task in marriage is to develop the ability to see another human being both as perfect and as just another imperfect human being. It is this feature, which emerges so clearly in the parent-child relationship and in marriage, which makes the parent-child relationship and the marriage relationship prototypic vehicles of the development of the capacity to love in adult life.

The spiritual task of the work relation is to humanize every work and commercial encounter. When working, one has the potential to see each and every exchange as fulfilling a win-win relationship rather than a win-lose one. The spiritual task of the worker is to enfold the work relation, however commercial or exchange-of-goods oriented, within a human narrative, a human story which allows for the identification of both parties with each other's needs, interests, and aspirations. It is this transformation which enables the exchange of goods to be the vehicle for people to experience their interpersonal work lives as vehicles of the giving and receiving of love.

Thus, each intimate relation is a task-centered bridge to the giving and receiving of love. It is appropriate, moreover, to return continuously to the accessibility of the ideal experience through the actual people one is involved with so long as there has been no violation of the basic trusts of the relationship.

In a word, then, to summarize what has been said so far, the fulfillment of the self relation and the intimate relations depends on two things: the identification and fulfillment of the external tasks appropriate to each relationship; and the capacity of the person to idealize the other person in the relationship. Such idealization will be healthy so long as there has been no abuse, or fundamental violation of trust in the relationship, and so long as such idealization does not distract from the energetic attention to the external tasks.

(III) Fulfillment of Distant Relations

As has been implied, we may see strangers in two ways. We may see strangers as people with whom we have no relationship at all. On the other hand, we may see strangers as fellow citizens, as members of a single community, the community defined by participation in the same sovereign institutions, for example, the state, or the same ethnic or religious community, or as members of the world community of human beings, or as members of the community of sentient beings, which is to say, the moral community. The latter perception enables us to see animals as members of our larger moral community, and would enable us to see even extraterrestrials as fellow citizens of sorts if any such came into contact with us. In order to make maximum use of the distinction between 'stranger' and 'citizen,' then, we may say that the stranger, in our sense, is anyone to whom one is not related under a system of positive law, whereas a citizen is anyone to whom one is related under a system of positive law. We have moral obligations to strangers, and we have, in addition, positive legal obligations to fellow citizens.

The key difference between intimate relations and distant relations is that each intimate relation is founded in a relation between two parties. Thus, to take the most difficult cases with respect to this notion, even the parent-child relation is conceivable outside of the many-person family context, as is the relation between siblings. But the relation between fellow citizens is not similarly extractable from a members-of-a-group context. By contrast with any intimate relation, the citizen relation always implies a group of people relating to each other in such a manner as to create positive law.

The spiritual task of the relationship I have with my fellow citizens is to see the stranger as member of a single moral community, a single family of sentient beings, and to express this membership in a common moral family through appropriate institutions of justice.

Thus, the external task of the citizen relationship is to construct institutions which render justice amongst interacting citizens or strangers, or amongst interacting intimates who have become estranged through dispute. The activity of constructing institutions of justice is the primary form of activity which the kindness of strangers takes.

And the institution of justice is not a two-party institution. For there are three parties to the rendering of justice: the two disputants, and the judge. To understand my relation with the stranger, then, implies that I see both of us as existing in a single community in which any dispute between us of sufficient gravity is to be brought before a judge, in some cases whether we will it or not. And this in turn implies that there is a distinction between two types of conflict: those conflicts which may obtain between intimates without changing their relational status into that of disputing citizens, and those conflicts which do change their relational status into that of disputing citizens. For instance, a spouse who wants to move from Vancouver to Toronto to take up her new job may be in conflict with her husband who wants to stay in Vancouver because the quality of city life in Vancouver, he thinks, is better for raising their children. This is a conflict which may be serious. It may even be marriage threatening. But it is not a conflict which is appropriate to bring before a judge so that the judge may apply some theoretical objective perspective and make a resolution. It is appropriate for such a conflict to be brought before a counselor who will facilitate the parties' determination of their own deepest paths to resolution. And even in those societies in which any marriage-threatening problem of this kind is resolved by a judge when the spouses can't resolve it, one would still draw a line *somewhere* between those conflicts which are appropriately resolved by a judge and those which are appropriately resolved by the conflicted parties with the assistance, if necessary, of advice, or counsel.

We may say, then, that in each society there is conflict which is mediated through counsel, and there is conflict which is resolved through judgment, however variable the location of the distinction is from society to society. The latter sort of conflict, conflict which is appropriate to bring to judgment, may be called "dispute." There are, further, two sorts of dispute: those which the sovereign community has a duty to bring to judgment, such as the disputes implicit in armed robbery, kidnapping, murder, or attempted murder; and those disputes which are appropriately resolved through judgment, but only at the discretion of the plaintiff such as those which prompt actions for debt recovery, specific performance, and liability for damages arising from tortious actions. Once again, there is variability as to the location of the distinction, but once any society has reached a certain level of complexity it inevitably will develop such a distinction.

There is a tendency to think of disputes as occurring between atomic or monadic individuals whose desires and needs have come into conflict without these individuals having considered the desires and needs of the other. That is, there is a tendency to take it that insofar as two individuals are engaged in a dispute, they are not relating to each other within the context of mutuality. This tendency, however, is fundamentally misleading, I believe. For although it is true that the issue of a dispute is often the distribution of goods whose acquisition provides for monadic fulfillment, it does not follow that once the dispute has been engaged, the individuals are acting as atomic individuals without mutuality.

For example, two people are disputing over a well. The use of the well would provide each with monadic satisfaction. Further, they are not related to each other as spouse, parent-child, friend, co-worker, or sibling. On the contrary, they are, as we might put it, strangers in the ordinary sense. But the fact that they are engaged in dispute reduces their strangerhood, and creates the relationship of co-citizen. Their dispute places them inside the framework of objectivity which requires the possibility of judgment. Their dispute transforms their status as mutual strangers into the status of equal citizens in a framework of objectivity appearing before a judge.

Disputants, then, occupy the role of citizen with respect to each other. And just as each of the intimate roles has a spiritual issue associated with it, the role of citizen has a spiritual issue associated with its fulfillment. The spiritual challenge posed by the citizen role is the challenge of identifying in a primary way with the interests of one to whom one is not connected by the bonds of mutuality through one of the other roles—sibling, friend, spouse, parent-child, co-worker. The spiritual issue associated with the role of citizen is precisely the development of a relationship of mutuality and love with one to whom one has no intimate bond. And the task or functional role of the citizen, whether involved in a dispute or not, is the facilitation of the institutionalized resolution of disputes.

Similarly the task or functional role of the stranger is the facilitation of response to emergency as an expression of love.

The claims of citizenship on the individual in our time are, aside from considerations of role priorities, enormous. To be a citizen in our time, in my view, involves working towards the establishment of basic institutions of justice at the international level, and participating in the reduction of poverty, social oppression, racism, and inequities wherever they occur. We will have a good deal more to say about the citizenship relation, and about private and public spheres of life in the final chapter on mysticism and the philosophy of history.

(IV) Fulfillment of Worship, Contemplator of
      Nature and the Atemporal

The fulfillment of the worshipper is peculiar in being dependent on the truth of a controversial existential claim, namely, that a personal Deity exists. If no such being exists, then worship activities are monadically fulfilling activities which are mistakenly being conceived of as interpersonal. Similarly, the fulfillment of one's relationship with the atemporal, and with nature, depends on one's conception of the atemporal. Accordingly, we need to engage in metaphysics in order to determine what fulfillment is available through these relations, and this we will take up to the extent we need to in chapters four through six.

IV. THE ESTABLISHMENT OF PRIORITIES
AMONG ROLES

Our role fulfillments are relatively clear and easy to mark out on the assumption that no interferences exist from other roles. But, hermits aside, there always are interferences from other roles. For everyone else there is at least monadic fulfillment which is always to some mild degree, or more, in tension with the other roles. And anyone involved in work, marriage, family, citizenship—the whole catastrophe, as Zorba put it—knows well how many tensions and pulls of schedule exist between the endless demands of each of the roles.

Although, as mentioned earlier, it is not to our purposes to engage in the deeply controversial aspects of role occupation and role prioritization here, nonetheless, there are some useful but still not particularly controversial observations which may be made in this context.

Here the central focus of attitude is the reverse of that of role fulfillment considered in isolation. As monadic individual, I may reasonably expect to find overwhelmingly satisfying fulfillment through the pleasure of existence, the bliss of experiencing tastes, touch, sound, sight, thought, breathing, and so forth. As a husband, I may reasonably expect to experience deep, overwhelmingly satisfying fulfillment within the mutualism of marriage. As a parent, I may reasonably expect to find family life deeply fulfilling.

But it is not realistic to expect that the combination of friendships, marriage, work, social obligations will be neat and harmonious and deeply fulfilling qua combinations. It is not appropriate to idealize *the schedule* resulting from combining all our roles. Rather the opposite focus of attitude is appropriate. It is best to demystify and pragmatize the life process in trying to arrive at decent balances between the various endless claims of citizenship acitivity, monadic fulfillment, family life, friendship, play, and work life.

There is a particular form of idealization of schedule which may, however, be appropriate, and that is the idealization of schedule arising from the traditional religions. A religious tradition may enable one to establish some priorities based on mythic idealizations of Sabbath Day, Christmas Day and Easter, Ramadan, Buddha's enlightenment day, and so on. Even if such idealizations are appropriate, though, it remains the case that there are important role prioritizations unsolved thereby, and these need to be resolved through schedule pragmatization as opposed to idealization.

Thus, individual role fulfillment and role prioritizing lead us in psychologically opposing directions: idealization, mysticism, and task-anchored sentimentality on the one hand; pragmatism, demystification, acceptance of finitude, and accommodation on the other hand. In this way, Seneca's saw (often attributed in our day to Niebuhr), "let me have the courage to change the things that can be changed, the strength to accept the things that can't be changed, and the wisdom to know the difference," becomes, at least in part, interpretable in a concrete way. Here is a maxim which may contain the kernel of wisdom Seneca wished for: There will always be room for acceptance and compromise in the juggling of the many roles; there need never be room for compromise in accessing the ideals of each individual role fulfillment.

We do not hope in short order to resolve the more controversial aspects of role prioritization, but it may be useful to mention some of the methods one might attempt to bring to bear upon these difficult issues. Probably the first contrast which needs mentioning is the contrast between those who hold that there is, or at least it makes sense to adopt the practice of searching for, a single system which should be universally applicable, on the one hand, and those who hold that there is inevitably an irrationalist component in any given prioritization, on the other hand. For short we will call these two the rationalist and the irrationalist prioritization approaches.

Amongst rationalist approaches there is the application of deontological principles to role prioritization; there is the application of the principle of utility to role prioritization; and there is the application of both deontological and utility principles to role prioritization. These may be ultimately expressed in prioritized rules of conduct or in prioritized virtues. Virtues being dispositions towards forms of conduct, the two forms of expression of rationalistic role prioritization should be intertranslatable.

There is, however, a type of virtue based approach towards role prioritization which moves away from rationalism. The more one holds with Aristotle that the supreme virtue is discriminative wisdom, the more or less non-discursively statable ability to recognize the salient features of a situation, and find a line through the situation to a proper moral resolution, the more one is likely to hold that there is no fully expressible system of role prioritization. Discriminative wisdom being a form of wisdom, this type of role prioritization would stand anyway at the lower end of the rationalistic scale.

Among irrationalist approaches, there is, first, the traditionalist approach, which may in some cases, like a prioritization reliant on wisdom, straddle the border between rationalism and irrationalism. A traditionalist approach holds that a system of case analysis, or casuistry, as developed by tradition, is the proper way to analyze given circumstances. Because traditions tend to invoke deontological and utility principles at various junctures in case analysis, any traditionalist prioritization is amenable to some degree to reconstruction, modification, transformation, and evolution. But because there are also junctures in case analysis at which the traditionalist receives the tradition simpliciter, and appeals to the traditional method of prioritization, there is always a perspective from within which the traditionalist prioritization lacks ultimate rationale.

For instance, in rabbinic Judaism, the prioritization between duties to support the indigent and duties towards one's intimate circle is spelled out in a series of rulings concerning the obligation to make financial contributions towards those in need. A minimum figure of 10 percent of one's earnings is designated by the rabbis (*Yoreh Deah*: 249). Once this figure has been established, then, a form of prioritization has been rendered concrete. Subsequent analyses of observant Jews hearken back towards the original ruling as authoritative, and while it could not be said that the ruling is arbitrary, there is surely an important difference between one who prioritizes from scratch, and one who prioritizes based on tradition. The very identification that an observant Jew makes with a covenanted community indicates a prioritization in favor of a particular form of citizenship relation, and this identification is itself in large psychological measure traditionalist, and customary. While such traditionalist identifications, again, are not arbitrary, there are surely significant differences of practice, for example, between Jewish, Islamic, Shinto, and Hindu mandated prioritizations. The rationales one can give for a given traditionalist identification which in turn mandates a particular prioritization will be similar to the rationale one can give for a different traditionalist identification with its different particular prioritization. An observant Jew and an observant Hindu will give similar rationales for their respective identifications, but their practices and prioritizations are frequently significantly different.

Less rationalistic still is the existentialist approach to role prioritization. According to the Sartrian existentialist, anyone who relies on an external system of role prioritization is hiding from his or her own radical freedom, and living in bad faith. The only way to prioritize roles is to make decisions which issue from one's own freely willed self-creative direction. One forges one's destiny despite the lack of a fixed standard by which one does so.

Probably the most devastating challenge to existentialism in its strong Sartrian form is the question of autonomous ethical analysis. If an existentialist is presented with a mathematical proof, or a piece of causal analysis, surely the existentialist must be prepared to acknowledge the validity of the proof, or the cogency of the causal analysis to whatever degree is warranted. Only the most radical relativist in epistemology will challenge in principle every such reasoning, and the most radical relativist in epistemology will usually hold a position inconsistent with her own belief correction practices, as discussed in chapter 1. But given the availability of norms of reasoning, the question arises whether or not there can be analogously compelling moral reasoning. In relational ethical analysis, the question raised is whether or not there are non-defeasible roles. If there are non-defeasible roles, the Sartrian existentialist approach to role prioritization will not be justified. To put the matter more charitably, within self-creative activity one must acknowledge the possibility and even desirability of rational factor analysis. The existentialist, too, needs to make sense of the options. There may still be a vital element of self-creative voluntarism, and hence an important existentialist factor in role prioritization, but it will not be all-embracing. Rather it will occur within the very sort of putatively rationalistic analysis that Sartre would have had us jettison. (We will continue to develop a modified existentialism of this sort towards the end of chapter 7.)

V. RELATIONAL ETHICS AND THE QUESTION OF OBLIGATION. ARE THERE ANY NON-DEFEASIBLE ROLES?

We have seen that the understanding of individual role fulfillment and role prioritization, at least for intimate relations, and in broad outlines for the demands of citizenship, is reasonably approachable and straightforward. If I identify as a citizen, I know what sorts of things I would be doing if I had nothing to do but fulfill my citizenship. If I identify as a parent, I know what sorts of things to do in fulfillment of my parenthood. And if I identify as a parent, a spouse, a worker, a sibling, a friend, a citizen, I know both what each role involves considered individually, and roughly the sorts of compromises in focus occupying all of them will entail. But the questions of which roles to occupy, if they intrude on me, and do not flow naturally, are problematic in a different way, for they raise what is often considered the central moral question, the question of whether or not there are obligations to others apart from the fulfillment of role identities one happily occupies and wishes to continue occupying.

For instance, what if I don't want to see myself as a citizen? What if I only want to concern myself with my intimate role fulfillments? Am I ignoring some abstract obligation to others, others who are, in the ordinary sense, strangers to me? Is such a choice morally illegitimate? And if so, what makes it so?

Our role relational analysis now enables us to raise what is often regarded as the central question of ethics in the modern western tradition, the question of obligation over and above fulfillment, as follows: Is there any reason why one cannot be a hermit in society, which is to say, an egoist, a person who relates to people just as a hermit relates to stones and the earth? (Well, not quite *just as*. A hermit may love and respect the stones for their stoneness, the trees for the treeness, and so on, whereas the egoist does not love and respect persons for their sentient personal agency.)

To argue that everyone has to relate to people with due regard to their sentience and personal agency, is to think as the citizen thinks, to identify with one's citizenship or potential for citizenship. The egoist doesn't think that way, and the person struggling with selfish desires is someone who sometimes thinks as a citizen and sometimes as a hermit in society, that is, as an egoist. But is there *an obligation* to think one way rather than another?

Our answer can be phrased this way: It makes no more sense to think of people the same way one thinks of stones and vegetation, on an entirely egoist or monadic basis, than it would to think of stones and vegetation the same way one thinks of persons, that is, on an interpersonal basis. We all know that when a car breaks down just as one needs it for an important trip there is a tendency to become angry *at* the car. Some people even express such anger, directing it to their cars. "You good for nothing heap of garbage, deliberately breaking down at the worst time!" and so on. This may let off a little steam. The expression of anger at the car may even be healthy for the person getting angry. But in the very way that this is not a particularly enlightened way to think of the car and what has happened, the reverse attitude towards people which sees them only as, say, cars, as ways of getting from A to B, only as means to one's ends, is inconsistent. People either are sentient beings or they are not. Cars either are deliberately breaking down just when you need them or they are not. If it's okay for you to let off steam at the car, it's because you recognize (in the background) that the car doesn't hear you, and so is not taking undue offense. Similarly if it's okay for you to accept a benefit from a person, or use a person instrumentally, it's because you also recognize that person as acting within a particular form of mutuality, even if it's the maximally distant relationship of fellow citizenship. If you subsequently decide to drop that relationship of citizenship, unilaterally, thinking "What *obligation* do I have to continue to relate as citizen to that person? None. Obligation arises under the citizenship role, but doesn't precede it!" then this is done in one of two possible ways. First, one may, as it were, forget that the other person is a sentient being. One is focused so strongly on one's own experience of monadic goals that one forgets or ignores the other as an independent center of consciousness. "I am now a hermit among very complicated stones, as it were; the only concerns to take account of are mine alone." Alternatively, one may remember the other as an independent center of consciousness, but take it that one's own concerns count for more. "Their concerns, although thoroughly central to them, are not central to me."

The first approach to egoist consciousness is either solipsistic or sociopathic. It requires denying the sentience of others. Does one really believe that others are not sentient beings? If one does, one is a solipsist, and egoist conduct is thoroughly justified. "If solipsism is true, I have no more intrinsic obligation to those person-like things called persons than I do to the automata in store windows." But who believes that others are not sentient? Rather, the egoist of the first variety conveniently forgets or ignores the sentience of others, and as soon as this egoist is reminded of the sentience of others, the stranger-hood-cum-citizen relationship is back. Although it is true that obligation arises from citizenship and does not precede it, the recognition of sentience confers the citizenship relation on the recognizer and all who are so recognized.

The second sort of egoist recognizes the sentience of others but either derives pleasure from their suffering, or places their suffering in a very low priority compared to his or her gain. Either way this egoist recognizes or is acting under the experience of citizenship and mutuality. The (unilateral) sadist has a warped and ultimately internally inconsistent mutuality; the other may (for good or not so good reason) hold that everyone in the long run tends to be best off when everyone looks out for *numero uno*.

So either one is a solipsist, a sociopath unable to maintain awareness of the sentience of others, or one recognizes the role of citizenship. Discounting the first two, one sees citizenship as obligatory.

The point can also be set out in more formal terms:

1. To make sense of one's choices, or to make good choices, requires that one characterize one's options and the circumstances in

which one finds oneself, including desires and so on, as features of the circumstances.

2. To make a sensible, or good choice requires that one think of one's choice as optimific and/or commendable, the best choice, or at least a good choice, under the circumstances, and that one do so with regard to the characteristics or features of the circumstances.

3. For agent A to make sensible choice O in a circumstance of type C requires that A take it that any other person B who is acting in a circumstance of type C but who has no causal connection to A would be acting rightly, or at least acting well, by making choice O in that circumstance.

4. My own choices cannot be intelligible to me unless I understand them through the notion of my thinking of myself as a person or sentient being with intrinsic value.

5. Similarly, for agent A to judge that some other, causally unrelated person, B, would be right or acting well by making choice O in circumstance C requires that A attribute intrinsic value to a person (or sentient being) other than A.

6. For every person A, there is some other person B who is for all practical purposes causally unconnected to A, and who might be in a circumstance of similar type to a circumstance A is in.

7. Therefore, if a person A is to make sensible, or good choices, then A is epistemically obligated to attribute intrinsic value to some other person B.

8. If an agent A attributes intrinsic value to a causally unrelated person B then A is epistemically obligated to attribute intrinsic value to all persons.

9. Therefore for agent A to make sensible choices requires that A attributes intrinsic value to all persons.

10. If A attributes intrinsic value to all persons then, at the ultimate level of ethical analysis, A ought to consider the interests of all causally related persons in making choices, and should consider those interests as intrinsic interests.

11. Therefore for A to choose sensibly, or intelligibly, or well, A ought to consider the interests of all persons causally related to the choice, and should consider those interests as intrinsic interests.

12. A person should choose sensibly, or intelligibly, or well.

13. Therefore a person should, at the ultimate level of ethical analysis, consider the interests of all people causally related to his or her choices, and should consider them as intrinsic interests. This is the principle of universalism in ethics.

Once we see how rendering our own choice-making intelligible requires ethical universalism, we see that what remains, practically speaking, is a choice whether to be:

1. a true hermit, and live without intimate relations, and with only minimal fulfillment as citizen;
2. a citizen living in society with fulfillment as a citizen, but without much in the way of intimate relations; or
3. a citizen living in society and actively balancing and prioritizing all or many of the basic available roles.

Further, we see that all three options recognize citizenship, and differ only in prioritizations. Even the hermit's option (in times where there is no universal abundance) must be construed as a particular prioritizing of the two fulfillments of monadic interests and citizenship interests which places an extremely low priority on the latter. Citizenship is a non-defeasible role.

It is worth observing at this juncture that the way in which the nondefeasible role of citizenship provides the scaffolding for the articulation and exploration of the various non-defeasible and optional roles, finally giving rise to an articulation of a system of roles, practices and virtues, at once traditionalistic, self-creative, and yet supported by the modernist ethical perspectives, highlights some of the strengths and limitations of Alisdair MacIntyre's analysis of modernity vis à vis ethics in *After Virtue*. On the one hand, MacIntyre's analysis endorses the values inherent in role based identifications and traditionalist virtues; on the other hand, his analysis holds that there is an incompatibility between modernity and such identifications and virtues. Although the end points of the analyses share important features, the analyses themselves, and the placements of a relational ethic in the context of the history of western philosophy, are very different.

According to MacIntyre, the pre-modern modes of identification, ("I am brother, cousin and grandson, member of this household, that village, this tribe" p. 33) under which my life can be fulfilled and represent an achievement, and under which "death is the point at which someone can be judged happy or unhappy" give rise to a "conception of a whole human life." This conception, however, "ceases to be generally available at some point in the progress—if we can call it such—towards and into modernity" (p. 34). Furthermore, according to MacIntyre, the enlightenment project (in our terms the Enlightenment West project) of justifying morality had to fail because Protestant Reformation and secularization both had the effect of leading exponents of the enlightenment to abandon the notion that reason could specify the *telos* or end for human beings. But without this notion all that remains is a bifurcation between untutored-human-nature as it is, and the search for moral rules or principles, a search which, lacking the vision of a *telos* or end for human beings, must remain forever unconsummated (pp. 53-55). The missing vision of *telos* or end only occurs in a tradition in which "to be a man is to fill a set of roles each of which has its own point and purpose: member of a family, citizen, soldier, philosopher, servant of God. It is only when man is thought of as an individual prior to and apart from all roles that 'man' ceases to be a functional concept" (p. 59). The ultimate consequences of the failure of the enlightenment project of justifying morality are the development of a decline into emotivism, an exclusively managerial virtue, and a society in which "[t]he bureaucratic manager, the consuming aesthete, the therapist, the protester, and their numerous kindred occupy almost all the available culturally recognizable roles" (pp. 256-257).

The swift response to this historical and contemporary diagnosis is to note the conflation of the distinction between what we called "task-centered roles" and personality or archetypal myths, and, not unconnectedly, the extraordinary arbitrariness of the description of the roles available in our society. *Pace* MacIntyre, everyone in modern society knows what it is to have an identity as friend, as sharer of domestic space, as parent, as child, as sibling, as worker, as citizen in a community, and so on. If the fulfillment of such roles can constitute a *telos*—and MacIntyre relies on exactly such a notion—then the Enlightenment West project is perfectly consistent with what MacIntyre says it can never have, a vision of human teleology! The relational ethical framework is the surrounding environment for the Enlightenment West universalisms of utilitarianism, deontology, and Rossian complex moral theory, and by no means requires their rejection.

We continue, then, with a look at the possibility of non-defeasible roles other than citizenship. One possibility mentioned was that of child to parent.

The basic idea here is that consideration of the form of feeling of parenthood requires one to recognize that under normal circumstances (i.e., so long as the parent or parents have not abused fundamental features of the parent-child relation) one's childhood in relation to one's parents is a non-defeasible role. That is, although the adult child may experience what he or she takes to be a complete psychological independence from the parent, nonetheless, the parent's feelings dictate that the adult child too continue to express a special respect to the parents as parents.

The role of would-be parent was also mentioned as a candidate for non-defeasible role. Its candidacy arises in that some ethical systems include an obligation to take appropriate steps towards becoming a parent. Such an obligation is sometimes derived from an obligation to a Supreme Personal Being, who omnisciently and benevolently instructs people to be fruitful and multiply; sometimes the obligation to take steps towards parenthood is derived from a citizenship role. These, however, would be at most secondary non-defeasible roles.

Finally, along these lines, the only coherent rights based or intrinsicalist justification for allowing monadically motivated suicide (suicide the motive for which is not self-sacrifice for others) will be in cases in which it is reasonable to conclude that the person has no prospects for fulfillment of his or her main monadic interests. Whatever its legal implications, this is a fundamentally different moral position from the position which holds that a person has a basic or fundamental right to suicide, that is, a basic right to opt out of the role of monadic individual, or rational agent.

In conclusion, recognizing one's own sentience gives one monadic identity. Recognizing the sentience of others gives one citizenship. Maintaining one's awareness of the sentience of others is a kind of meditation supportive of the citizenship intuition. Recognizing the particular forms of feeling which govern being a parent makes one's childhood non-defeasible (under normal circumstances). In this way, we see that the only role occupation questions one can legitimately ask (under normal circumstances) are with regard to the voluntary intimate relations. And these intimate role occupation questions are fully and properly resolved by existential self-creation in the light of *(a)* the nature of the intimate role fulfillments, together with the prospects for their fulfillment in one's own case, given one's personality-mythic identities; and *(b)* the practicalities of role prioritization given the monadic, citizenship, and other roles one occupies.

We have not provided much guidance in the way of resolving the many complex issues of role prioritization. But to the extent that the mystical component of an Enlightenment East vision, in the first instance, will be expressed as an element of the theory of monadic value, it is not the case that there must forever be an irreconcilability between Enlightenment East and Enlightenment West. Enlightenment East and West have a common framework of valuation within which to meet. If genial mysticism has a genuine contribution to make to the theory of monadic value, then any theory of monadic value benefited by genial mysticism and supplemented by some other particulars on interrelational role fulfillment, role occupation and role prioritization, will already be a value theory in which Enlightenment East and Enlightenment West have met, shaken hands and begun to court each other.

Given this framework of relational value, we can now go on to consider more deeply the relevance of genial mysticism to ethics, and particularly to the theory and practice of monadic fulfillment.

Three

Monadic Fulfillment: The Mystic's Paradigm

I am a monadic being insofar as I have interests which have nothing to do with my personal interrelationships. As we put it earlier, the monadic dimension of existence is that dimension which I have in common with a hermit. Now, if the relational framework developed in chapter 2 is sound, then every problem of monadic fulfillment falls under one or more of these three questions:

A. Should I occupy the role of monadic being? That is, should I continue to exist? Are there any situations in which it might be permissible, or even rational, to deliberately end my life?

B. Given that I do occupy the role of monadic being, how do I realize or fulfill or consummate this role? That is, what are my monadic interests? Do they come into potential conflict with one another, and, to the extent that they do, what is the way to prioritize them?

C. Given that I am not only a monadic being, but also a (parent) (friend) (lover) (child) (worker) (citizen), and so forth, how do I establish priorities between them? How do I live well given that there is potential conflict between my monadic interests and my other interests?

In this discussion, we will focus on the second of these three questions. In any general treatment of monadic value, the second set of issues, the monadic role fulfillment issues, are methodologically central. Without answering them, neither of the other two can be broached. In any case, our enterprise of showing the contribution of mysticism to the theory of monadic value only requires discussion of the monadic role fulfillment issues. Our discussion of mysticism and morality in general (chapter 7) will require the other issues to be raised.

Monadic fulfillment

How may a hermit come to fulfillment? By definition a hermit does not have interpersonal relations. Note that we should include higher animals, ghosts, spirits, deities, and a God with personal attributes, if any such exist, in the class of persons. A hermit ceases to experience himself or herself as a hermit when taking it that he or she is in interaction with a personal Deity, a ghost, a spirit, a human being, or a higher animal. In any case, the elements of monadic fulfillment are those intrinsic goods or interests one might posit even if there were no other persons in the world. And these are:

1. survival
2. health
3. joy in ordinary seeing, hearing, touching, smelling, tasting, voluntary agency, and the exercise of the cognitive and agentive faculties; pleasure in eating, in sexual activity, in being massaged, and pleasures in other bodily functions.
4. emotional well-being: serenity, optimism, cheerfulness; and intense emotional satisfactions such as thrilling to real or simulated dangers.
5. the expansion of one's powers and abilities in planning and execution
6. knowledge for its own sake, including mystical knowledge if any such is available.

Controversies with regard to monadic fulfillment are:

A. Whether survival is a permanent monadic interest, or, alternatively, a defeasible monadic intrinsic interest.
B. Whether any of these is not an intrinsic monadic interest of some people.
C. Whether some of the elements of this list are to be valued more highly than the others as monadic goods, for example, whether knowledge is to be valued more highly than sensual pleasures, and whether such rankings are uniform for all people.
D. Whether there is any mystical knowledge, and if so, what its value is, if any.
E. How to achieve fulfillment in any particular element of the list. How can health be maximized? How can the pursuit of knowledge be furthered? And so on.

A. Is Survival Defeasible as a Monadic Interest?

With regard to A, it can be seen that survival is a permanent monadic interest. Although there are very real moral questions concerning the permissibility of suicide and the defeasibility of survival as an overall goal, these questions fall under the questions of whether or not to occupy the role of individual, that is, whether or not it is permissible to drop out of the world altogether; or whether or not some other person's welfare or some other group's welfare has higher value than one's own, and therefore whether or not one ought to, or is permitted to, sacrifice one's life for their good. Survival, however, is a necessary condition of monadic fulfillment, and is thus not defeasible as a monadic interest. To construe survival as a defeasible monadic interest is unintelligible. Survival could only be defeasible within the context of the role occupation question applied to the self relationship.

B. Are the Monadic Goods Universal Interests?

Our first question is whether or not survival belongs in a list of fundamental, or intrinsic, monadic interests at all. The ethical hedonist, who believes that only pleasures are worthy of adoption as intrinsic interests, may well hold that there is nothing inherently pleasurable in survival, and that therefore survival doesn't belong on the list. It seems to me that it is psychologically possible to identify survival as an intrinsic good. Given such a psychological identification, it seems to be difficult, if not impossible to explain the sense in which it will be held by the hedonist that survival is not worthy of this psychological identification. It is not so much that no such accounts of unworthiness can be given. For example, to choose survival without any consciousness for five years over survival with full consciousness and agency for one year would appear to be unintelligible. So long as 'survival' means conscious survival, then, it can be adopted as an intrinsic good. It is intelligible that someone would choose an extremely painful, even tortured, conscious survival, over the release from consciousness of death. This example seems to me to count as a counterexample against ethical hedonism, the view that only pleasures are worthy of being identified as intrinsic goods. There is a view called "logical hedonism" according to which whatever intuitions we have of intrinsic good should be used to define pleasure, so that if something is identified as intrinsically good it becomes analytic, or true by definition, that it is a pleasure. But so long as we allow our intuitions of pleasure to operate independently of our intuitions of intrinsic good it seems likely we will come to the conclusion that not all intrinsic monadic goods are pleasures.

Roughly the same story can be told for the expansion of agency powers and knowledge as intrinsic goods. The expansion of agency powers is held by hedonists, or at least some hedonists, as instrumental goods only. According to them we can only identify increased capacity to affect our environment as instrumentally good. Once again, though, it would seem that the expansion of one's volitional powers is identified by some as intrinsically good, and there is no good reason for the hedonist to object on grounds of unworthiness. There is a distinction between the pleasure of power, and the power itself. But there seems to be no good reason to insist that only the pleasure is worthy of identification as an intrinsic good.

Similarly, some hold that knowledge is a purely instrumental good, that is, it is held to be only worth obtaining for the sake of some other benefit which follows from having that knowledge. According to others, however, some or even all knowledge is worth having for its own sake, as well as instrumentally. The question of the worthiness of the pursuit of knowledge for its own sake leads us directly into questions central to our Enlightenment East and West assessment, and so it will be useful to consider knowledge as an intrinsic monadic value within a broad theory of monadic value, and particularly, within non-hedonistic monadic value theory.

The issue of the suitability of members of our list which are not obviously pleasures, namely, survival, expansion of agency powers, and knowledge, for intrinsic good status, is clarified with reference to the intrinsic desirability of having the attributes, or approximating the attributes, of the Personal God. It is surely a plausible view that being the Personal God, which is to say, being the eternal, omniscient, omnipotent, benevolent Creator, is intrinsically desirable. From this can be derived the proposition that it is intrinsically desirable to be as close as one can, or to have as many of the attributes as one can of the Personal God, whether or not a Personal God exists, and to identify the having of any contributing attribute (an attribute which if you didn't have it would count against your being God, and which if you did have it would contribute toward your being God) as being intrinsically desirable. It follows that survival, expansion of agency power, and knowledge are intrinsically desirable.

Indeed, it is odd that the attribute of perfect blissfulness is not as often included in the list of the attributes of the Personal God as the others. If we do include it, then the Personal God is the eternal, perfectly blissful, benevolent, omnipotent, and omniscient being who created everything. Benevolence is not really a monadic good as it requires interrelationship for its exercise. Subtracting benevolence, we see that what remain as intrinsic monadic goods, other things in each case being equal, are survival (to the point of being eternal, if possible), pleasure (to the point of being perfectly blissful, if possible), increasing agency powers (to the point of being omnipotent, if possible), and knowledge (to the point of being omniscient, if possible.)

Since, other things being equal, everyone would choose to be as God-like as possible, then every bit of knowledge, however trivial, is worthy of knowing for its own sake, regardless even of the pleasure that accompanies that knowledge. The only controversy remaining is the relative weighting to be assigned the different possible objects of knowledge given finite capacities, talents for knowledge of human beings, and time in which to master these subjects.

Our conclusion, thus, is that of normative universalism with regard to knowledge as an intrinsic good. All knowledge is worth pursuing purely for its own sake, by everyone, without regard either for such pleasure as accompanies it, or for further benefits which the knowledge brings. And the reason descriptive universalism with regard to knowledge does not hold, that is, the reason not all people take all knowledge to be an intrinsic good is that they are so immersed in the practicalities of choosing how to spend their limited amount of time and resources that they do not recognize or reflect on what their attitude would be towards knowledge were it not for such factors which require them to apportion and weigh the various intrinsic goods. It must also be acknowledged, however, that our reasoning here, based on the desirability of being as much like God, The Supreme Personal Being, as possible, has, in some respects, been sufficiently remote from the practical limitations and choices, as to verge on the meta-ethical. We have shifted the normative burden onto the weighting problems of controversy (C), that is, how to assign weights and priorities to the various monadic intrinsic goods. To this topic we now turn. The goal of being as God-like as possible, however, will inform our subsequent discussion of mystical knowledge and experience in monadic value theory.

C. Assigning Weights to the Various Monadic Goods

There are several main questions here: Can monadic pleasures, and goods in general, be ranked as superior versus inferior? Here the problems revolve around commensurating factors of duration, intensity, quality, and secondary utility or disutility. How do we compare dangerous but intensely thrilling pleasures against safe and more durable but milder pleasures? And how do we compare intellectual pleasures against sensual pleasures, and against the monadic pleasures of agency such as monadic sporting pleasures (e.g., mountain climbing)? Further, and most centrally, is there a summum bonum, or supreme good such that all other goods are but shadows, as it were, of this good?

We should also remind ourselves, before proceeding to answer these questions, that they may be given both a normative and a meta-ethical slant. To the extent that we are comparing pleasures in the abstract, we are considering these questions from a meta-ethical point of view. We are trying, that is, to understand what it is in virtue of which one pleasure or good may be superior to another. But to the extent that we are comparing pleasures the pursuit of which may come into conflict with each other, we are pursuing the questions from a normative ethical slant. And it is the latter focus we wish to maintain. Accordingly, we are considering the various weightings and evaluations given that there is only a finite amount of time to pursue the various goods, and we cannot simultaneously pursue them all.

We will approach these questions through the central question of the monadic summum bonum, the greatest good for the individual considered as a monadic unit, which, if any such can be properly identified, ought to be the goal or focus of everyone's awareness and endeavor within the dimension of solitude.

As sketched in chapter 2, I hold that there is a monadic summum bonum, and that it is the experience of joy conjoined with the understanding: "This is Real; this is Ultimate." In religious terms, the monadic summum bonum is the blissful contemplation of the current situation as an expression of the Ultimacy which is by some called "Godhead." (Even Buddhists, who may vigorously deny the ultimacy of any particular thing, may accept this sort of vocabulary for informal purposes. And some Buddhists will be able to regard the entire codependent nexus as itself Ultimate, so that contemplation of the world is a contemplation of Ultimacy. In chapter 5, we will deal with this issue further.)

Intuition of the truly real

Everyone is familiar with what might be called "the flipping of the Reality Switch." In the midst of the humdrum and the everyday, the individual (often suddenly) has a heightened awareness of self and surroundings as actually happening, and happening right now. Initiatory experiences are characteristically accompanied by such heightened awareness. For example, when one walks down the aisle during one's marriage, one feels: "this is real, and it is really happening to me." When a plain dweller goes on a voyage during the course of which she has an opportunity to look down from some mountaintop on a great vista, the experience "This is Real, this is Ultimate" is likely to occur. People describe these experiences in terms of feelings of absorption, clarity, attentiveness, spontaneity, flow, ultimacy, and significance.

There is nothing more motivating than having an opportunity to fire the reality trigger.

Arena preferences

It seems that different people tend to associate the Reality experience with different arenas of life. Some people, for example, feel that "it is really happening" when they are with friends—fishing with the gang, chatting over tea or coffee with the group of friends. But then others feel that everything else is shadowier than courtship-romance. Indeed, the experience of infatuation is the very experience: "when I am with him/her, the world is real; when we are apart, nothing is as real, except to think of him/her" and so forth. For still other people, it is family satisfaction, family association that is "really real." Such people may have very absorbing and satisfying careers, friendships, and so forth, yet still have the feeling deep down that it is family that really counts, and the fulfillment of family relations that is the "true context of reality." The reality sense is triggered more through family association than through work for such people. For others, again, it will be the reverse. Such people may have satisfying and responsible family lives, yet feel deep down that there is "more reality" in the status, advancement, and contribution to the world that one makes through the work arena.

Similarly, even the hermit or the individual outside interpersonal relations can have the monadic equivalent of arena preferencing. One hermit may find that making things gives him or her the feeling that something truly real has taken place, whereas another may feel that to go hiking in the wilderness is to connect with what is truly real, namely, the ultimacy of solitude in nature. Still another individual experiences sitting in stillness as the activity which most strongly enables him or her to experience heightening reality, the moment in all its distilled clarity and uniqueness.

And some people have little familiarity with intrinsic monadic fulfillment. For such people, the activities one does in solitude—such as bathing, self-beautification, and so forth, are not experienced as intrinsically satisfying so much as instrumental towards specific interpersonal relations to come, so that it is almost impossible for them to imagine happiness or fulfillment as a hermit.

Either way, however, whether one has a vehicle for the experience of happiness in solitude, or lacks one, monadic happiness consists in one's capacity to deeply enjoy and experience the embracing moment, however the moment is being spent. The fulfillment of the hermit, by which we mean here the monadic dimension of experience, consists in the capacity to experience chores as play, purposive activity as dance, and repose as blissful stillness. In religious terms, monadic fulfillment consists in the ability to experience agency as sacred ritual embodying Divine or Inexpressible mystery, and repose as an expression of pure consciousness.

The person for whom chores are sacred play, purposive activity is dance, and repose is pure, blissful awareness of the ultimacy of things, lives in grace. The monadic summum bonum is immersion in grace.

And it is with reference to immersion in grace that we can answer our question of the weighings of the various monadic intrinsic goods. Since the fulfillment of the hermit or monadic individual consists in the deepening of the enjoyment and blissful experience of ultimacy of the current life, we will have no need to impose a particular hierarchy of pleasures or intrinsic goods, holding, for instance, that the hermit is better off accumulating knowledge of astronomy and physics than making skis and perfecting the art of skiing. Rather the hermit is fulfilled by discovering a vehicle of deep satisfaction in solitude and learning to expand the kind of satisfaction obtained thereby into other areas of monadic life. If one enjoys bathing but detests cooking, one wants to clarify the pleasure of bathing, and learn to experience something of the same pleasure while cooking. To be sure, there is a particular knowledge which is superior to all other forms of knowledge and all other goods or specific pleasures: the knowledge of how to enjoy the current moment under its aspect of Ultimacy and preciousness or sacredness. But its superiority consists in its extraordinary applicability and universal availability.

Higher and lower monadic goods and pleasures

A consequence of this view of the monadic summum bonum is that the traditional treatment of higher and lower pleasures has been deeply flawed. Western philosophers in the past from Aristotle, through Epicurus, and on to John Stuart Mill have overwhelmingly tended to identify the pleasures of the senses as the lower pleasures, and the intellectual pleasures as the higher pleasures. (See Mill's *Utilitarianism*, Chapter 2, for example, for an emphatic insistence on the cogency of the ancient approach to the distinction.) But this conceptual framework is distorted. If it is proper to make a distinction between higher and lower pleasures, that distinction should be associated with the distinction between universal and specific pleasures respectively.

Specific and universal pleasures

Specific pleasures are those pleasures which arise through the satisfaction of specific desire: the pleasure of eating when hungry, sexual pleasure, the massage of aching muscles, the pleasure attendant upon the solving of an intellectual puzzle or problem, the experience of victory in a competition, and so on. Specific pleasures, then, are desire-reduction pleasures; and specific pleasures may be sensory or intellectual. On the other hand, there is universal pleasure, pleasure which may be experienced in all circumstances, or all normal circumstances, certainly, through attention to the quality of experience both sensory and intellectual, and to the function of agency as dance, or grace in agency. It is the attention to universal pleasure which is properly identified as contemplative activity. Thus, contemplative activity may properly be identified as higher pleasure, but this contemplative activity is as much contemplation applied to the realm of the senses as it is contemplation of intellectual matters. It is not to be identified with the desire-reducing aspect of these activities, but the attention to the joy of being an experiencer, and an agent, more or less regardless of the content of the experience or the doing.

Universal pleasure is pleasure that is experienced throughout normal activity, even in desire. The universal or contemplative pleasures are higher than the specific pleasures because attention to them is ongoing and produces a permanent change in our psychological modality. By deeply fulfilling our monadic identity to the point of overflowing with the pleasure base of sheer experience we are capable of entering into our other relationships (should we not be hermits in the ordinary sense) more fully and deeply. In any case, attention to the specific pleasures and satisfactions of desire reduction is an ongoing process; but if unaccompanied by universal pleasure-contemplation, it is a mere round of desire and pleasure.

The hermit astronomer, the hermit physicist, and the hermit metaphysician then, do not have a superior monadic fulfillment as compared with the hermit mountain-climber, the hermit skier, or the hermit incense maker. Indeed, qua monadic individual, the hermit Einstein cannot be said to be fulfilling solitude in a manner superior to the hermit idler and berry-picker, so long as the hermit idler and berry-picker experiences the joyous ultimacy of the idling and the berry-picking. This is the essence of the monadic summum bonum: being pure (entirely nondogmatic and nondoctrinal) religious contemplation it can and should be applied equally to each moment of experience, and does not require cognitive content of any more particularity than that connected with the intuition "THIS really is!"

We now turn to consider the seemingly intractable problems of weighing of quantity, quality, duration, intensity, certainty, and secondary utilities or disutilities. I will briefly suggest that these problems may well be intractable at the meta-ethical level of analysis, but are perhaps surprisingly resolvable at the normative or practical ethical level. For although it is difficult to say what would make specific goods and pleasures of different types and qualities, intensity and duration commensurable, we do not need to provide an answer to this question in order to have a comprehensive understanding of the practice of monadic ethics.

For if each person's fulfillment qua monadic individual consists in the deepening of the experience of grace, universal pleasure, or joy in being, then the main focus of monadic ethics is on the method (if there is any) whereby such deepening occurs, which falls under the last in our list of the main controversies in monadic ethics. It need not be assumed, nor is it in fact the case, that there is general counsel to be given on weighing the various specific pleasures with regard to quality, duration, intensity and so on. Rather, the counsel here is rather more procedural or methodological: everyone should remember that specific monadic goods are valued differently by different individuals, and that specific monadic goods are valued differently by the one individual at different times. Accordingly what people need to be reminded of is the need for robust experimentation and attentiveness to one's experience of these specific goods. In any case, each specific monadic good is now seen as a vehicle for the cultivation of the monadic summum bonum.

If there are any remaining problems under our current question, it will be because achieving health may come into conflict with experiencing intense but dangerous sensual pleasures, or because acquiring certain sorts of knowledge will interfere with one's capacity for pleasure, or because maximizing one's chances for survival conflicts with expanding one's powers of agency. The degree to which there are such conflicts, however, one would be in a better position to assess after a discussion of the means of maximizing these various monadic goods, for one would then have a firmer grasp on the practices and courses of conduct which lead to monadic fulfillment.

D. Is There Any Mystical Knowledge, and
   What Would its Value Be, if Any?

Mysticism is understood in many different ways. For our purposes at this stage we will take as genial and metaphysically uncontroversial an approach to mystical knowledge as one can. Mystical knowledge, for our purposes here, is knowledge by acquaintance of the ultimacy of THIS. One is a mystic to the degree that one is continuously aware of THIS as ultimate. By 'THIS' we mean whatever is present to everyone, always, no matter how distant in space and time one person is from another. What further can be said about THIS is not relevant to our present concerns, for here we merely want to know whether mystical knowledge constitutes a special kind of intrinsic monadic good. And that THIS is, it seems, can only be controversial to a dyed in the wool global skeptic, solipsist, or ontological nihilist. For such a person, the entire enterprise of ethics must seem empty anyway. Since we are doing ethics, we need not be worried that our reflections have some metaphysical presuppositions, so long as these presuppositions are not controversial amongst the ethicists. To put the matter another way, all that is required is that orientation towards THIS is understood as occurring at the phenomenal or relative level. Even the Madhyamika exponent is willing to acknowledge the process as understood thus. As Tenzin Gyatso, the Dalai Lama, put it recently, "[Although] there is an absolute level of truth, as expressed in Chandrakirti's interpretation of Nagarjuna's teachings . . . according to which there is nothing which has no parts, and thus nothing which has fully independent identity, . . . [nonetheless], this doesn't mean that the phenomena don't exist. There is the danger of a shallow understanding which is nihilistic, and is a profound misunderstanding of the doctrine of emptiness. Rather a profound understanding of codependence increases one's appreciation for phenomena and interdependence."(From the author's notes taken during the Dalai Lama's lecture on the discipline of the mind, BC Place, Vancouver, June 27 1993.)

We may say, then, that a person is a mystic to the degree that she or he continuously and directly experiences the wholeness and ultimacy of the current moment grasped under the largest possible frame of reference. This sort of intuition is widely known. There is hardly anyone who does not awaken from time to time to the final mystery of this very moment seen within the stream of the vastness of eternity.

Mysticism as an "ism" is the view that the cultivation of this intuition, the incorporation of it into one's daily life and the stabilization of it is of unique, and in some sense supreme, value to the individual as monadic individual. If this is a sound view, it will be so for two reasons: first, because the intuition is an intuition of the mystery of the union of contingency and timelessness, and as such is a direct experience of what is ultimately true; second, because the intuition is accompanied with a special pleasure and joy, the pleasure and joy of acknowledging the mystery of being. Accordingly, we can see the mystic as one who wants to fire the Reality trigger as continuously as possible, and who holds that the stabilization of the Reality sense, the joyous intuition of the ultimacy of THIS, moment after moment, is indeed possible and practical to a high degree.

Seen thus, mystical knowledge is not a monadic good of a fundamentally different character than the universal joy in being which we have been discussing. To be sure, the mysticism which has just been defined is a garden variety mysticism. Hence, its geniality. By contrast, there are varieties of mysticism which receive arcane and intensely puzzling doctrinal expression, and we will return to discuss the coherence of these in chapter 4, and their relevance to metaphysics and philosophy of mind in chapter 5. But the point which we will be stressing here is that mysticism in its simplest form combines a simple metaphysical thesis, an empirical psychological thesis, and an ethical thesis. The metaphysical thesis is that something ultimate is manifesting now, or that what is happening now is, or can be appropriately seen as, manifesting what is ultimate. The psychological thesis is the practicability of maintaining awareness of the ultimacy of the present moment. The ethical thesis is that such stable awareness produces blissful, full consciousness which is the monadic summum bonum.

E. Fulfillment of Monadic Interests

At this stage we come as close to being scientists as it is possible for the practical ethicist to be. Our questions are: how do we maximize survival, physical and emotional well being, joyousness, expansion of agency powers, intellectual achievement and (to whatever extent it is a refinement of the experience of joy in being) mystical realization? We are primarily interested in the contribution of mystical realization to monadic fulfillment, but we will briefly work our way through the questions of survival maximization.

The obstacles to survival are few in type, and all too many in number: natural disasters, political or social persecution, enmity of intimates, disease, accidents, the effects of aging on the body. Some of these one has little control over. Natural disasters, for instance, are hard to predict, and aside from moving to an area which supposedly has few hazard indicators, all one can do is educate oneself, and ensure that minimum standards of safety and shelter in case of earthquake, tornado, hurricane, flood, and so forth are met as best one can. Similarly it is not clear what can be said in a useful but general way with regard to maximizing one's chance of survival pitted against racially or ethnically motivated persecution. It is clear that groups may stop at nothing when motivated by racial, ethnic, religious, or nationalist prejudice. Monadic interests are best served by avoidance of such circumstances. On the other hand, the communal interests may well be best served by either coercive or pacific active struggle against the oppressors. Accordingly the tradeoff between social roles on the one hand, and monadic interests or the self relationship, on the other hand, needs to be considered within the context of a general discussion of role prioritization.

Similarly, the maximization of monadic pleasures or fulfillments attendant upon fulfillment of interrelational roles must be covered simultaneously with a discussion of the maximization of these roles themselves. There is no special method to maximize the monadic aspect without considering the fulfillment of the relations themselves.

There is, however, considerably more that needs to be considered concerning the way to maximize physical, emotional, and intellectual monadic interests, and these discussions are directly relevant to our assessment of Enlightenment East and West.

It is a curious fact that the more ancient, and the more religious the foundation of an ethical system is, the more the system tends to provide discussions of the path to fulfillment of monadic interests. For instance, we are not surprised to find in Maimonides' *Mishneh Torah* (vol. I., Hilchot Deot, chap. IV) all sorts of details about what foods one may eat and what foods one should not eat, how much to eat and so on. Some of these prescriptions arise from Jewish dietary law. Some, however, do not. The latter are simply the counsel of Maimonides the physician-philosopher about how to eat healthily. We are not surprised to find in the *Yoga Sutras* of Patanjali the recommendation to practice yoga *asanas*, and *pranayama*, bodily postures, which are supposed to be conducive to physical, mental, and spiritual well being, and breathing techniques. We would be rather surprised to find a contemporary western philosopher recommending specifics of diet or *asanas* or breathing methods, in a discussion of practical ethics. Peter Singer, (1979) for instance, will advise us of our moral obligations to animals, and this may have implications for our diet. He will advise us of the degree of obligations we owe to starving people on the planet, and this may have implications for our schedule and our pocket book. But would he advise us on whether we ought to arise early or late, or suggest that we practice some form of yoga, T'ai Chi, aerobics, or Zen? Would he advise us about what diet to have, obligations to other members of the moral community aside? On the other hand, disciplined postural meditation is central to the way of life recommended by Gautama Buddha, who suggested that the ideal life includes—in addition to the practice of right speech, right intellectual pursuits, right conduct, right choice of mode of livelihood, and right emotional attitude or effort—right practice of concentration, meditation, and *samadhi*. How many contemporary applied ethicists have been concerned to evaluate the practice of meditation in the context of monadic fulfillment?

There will be various explanations of the absence of these discussions in contemporary applied ethics. One factor is the assumption that people are already taking advantage of whatever techniques as are available to maximize the monadic interests in health, emotional and intellectual well being, and no particular comment is required, therefore, from the philosopher. Another is the lack of experience most westerners have with techniques such as disciplined postural meditation. Further, such experience as westerners may have is likely to be in the context of institutions which are relatively unsophisticated in their expression of the relation between philosophical and practical matters. This tends to create the atmosphere of hobby, and even the philosopher who has some experience of yoga, meditation, and so on is unlikely to think of them in much more than the hobby mode. Why should a philosopher recommend a particular hobby? Still another factor is cultural: western philosophers are unlikely to have any competence in eastern philosophical texts, for linguistic and other sociological reasons. This predisposes the western philosopher to stay away altogether from issues which might require such familiarity. Further still, the eastern techniques are often associated with miraculous or scientifically anomalous parapsychological claims which association makes them at least suspect to the western scientist and philosopher. The list of factors is large, and the ones mentioned above are but some of them. However, this being a treatise in ethics rather than the sociology of philosophy, we will drop the effort to explain the matter and pick up the substantive issue at hand.

The point is this: many if not all of the main religio-philosophical traditions of the world include injunctions to practice psycho-physical, that is, postural meditation-prayer, along with descriptions of sages' experience of dissolution of the ego, merging with Absolute Being, and of the special mystically blissful "Light," or "Sound Current" which, it is said, is awakened in conjunction with such practice. It is incumbent upon the *moral philosopher* to have some account of these claims. The usual interest of Western philosophers in mysticism is in the veridical content of the claims. In my view this approach to mysticism is unfortunately one-sided.

The primary thrust of mysticism is practical and, broadly speaking, moral, focusing on monadic fulfillment. Regardless of whether the doctrinal side of mysticism is intelligible, the value-claims of mystico-religious institutions and practices cannot be ignored. These value claims center on the notion that there is a special blissfulness awakened by meditation practice. Even if there is no special cognitive content delivered with the fruits of mystic contemplation, there is still the question of the psychological fruit of mysticism to be assessed: just what is the metaphoric reference to the kundalini serpent at the base of the spine, when understood in more literal psychophysiologic terms, and how does the bliss of its awakening compare with other blissful experiences? How does the bliss allegedly associated with its awakening relate to the neurochemistry of the hedonic base of consciousness, and how do those familiar with it compare this blissfulness with other pleasurable states? What does one make of the "circulation of the Light"or "ki" in the Chinese esoteric system, the blazing emptiness of Meister Eckhart, the *sukha*-bliss of *samadhi* realization in Buddhism, the *ananda*-bliss of yogic meditation, the Hidden Light revealed to the Tzaddik in Jewish Kabbalah, and to the God-realized Sufi? Are these wholly fake reports invented so as to justify a weak authority system? Are they genuine reports, but the bliss only comes to the individual spontaneously, unconnected with meditation and other postural practices? Are such experiences the genuine fruits of meditation practice, but the coming to fruition of the practices is insufficiently predictable, and the practices are themselves so arduous that the benefits are not worth the effort? Jewish, Christian, Islamic, Hindu, Buddhist, Sikh, Sant Mat, Taoist, and other traditions, hold that the ideal life includes a hefty proportion of time spent in formal or informal periods of meditation and prayer/contemplation. A comprehensive moral vision requires an inquiry into the highly significant evaluative claims with regard to monadic fulfillment made by mystics and the proponents of meditation and the like.

In dealing with questions such as these it must be confessed at the outset that we are still at a highly primitive stage in our ability to make anything like objective or scientific examinations of the matter, despite the best efforts of depth-dimension psychologists such as Abraham Maslow. Our knowledge of brain neurophysiology in relation to phenomenological reportage is still too undeveloped, our ability to separate out the various causes in the claims of individuals who purport to have awakened the "blissful Light" or "dazzling noncognitive Knowledge" is too uncertain to allow us to rely on anything other than primary exploration, often of a highly personal nature. But at the very least we should acknowledge that the subject is a vitally central one to moral philosophy insofar as the theory of monadic fulfillment is at the vital center of moral philosophy. Even a proponent of agapistic ethics, for whom the experience of loving interrelationship or I-Thou experience is held to be the *summum bonum*, will recognize that loving relationship needs to be manifested in concrete terms by the lover helping the beloved to be monadically fulfilled. Thus, monadic fulfillment remains at the vital center of ethics for everyone. If mystic bliss is the supreme monadic value, then anyone who has healthy self-regarding and other-regarding love will want the beloved to taste mystic bliss, and to taste mystic bliss himself or herself. And so the moral philosopher should be prepared to either make a personal investigation or admit that there is an issue central to moral philosophy which he or she is unable to discuss from an informed position.

It is instructive then, to note the degree to which what should be an obvious and central topic requiring analysis and assessment, the importance of mysticism for value theory, has been virtually ignored not only by ethical theorists, but also by the main philosophical analysts of mysticism. Rigorous philosophical analysis of mysticism, in the modern context, was more or less launched by William James in the *Varieties of Religious Experience*, Lectures 16 and 17. James stipulates that a mystical experience is one which is ineffable, and has a noetic quality, by which he means that it is regarded by the experiencer as conferring some form of knowledge. Two further quasi-defining features of the mystic experience are transiency and passivity. Thus, the analysis of mystic experience got off to a roaring start centered on the many questions surrounding the attempt to evaluate from the outside the possibility that an ineffable experience can nonetheless be in some sense a perceptual apprehension of the Transcendent object.

Bertrand Russell, in "Mysticism" is concerned to show the falsity of the view that there is a nonscientific, mystical avenue to the truth whose authority or plausibility ought to be recognized by the non-mystic. The doctrines he regards as definitively mystical are: "(1) That all division and separateness is unreal, and that the universe is a single indivisible unity; (2) that evil is illusory, and that the illusion arises through falsely regarding a part as self-subsistent; (3) that time is unreal, and that reality is eternal, not in the sense of being everlasting, but in the sense of being wholly outside time" (1961, p. 179).

Similarly, Russell's "Mysticism and Logic" is centrally concerned with assessing these doctrines associated with mystical experience, along with the mystic's championing of the notion that mystics can arrive at special knowledge as the result of "reflection upon the inarticulate experience gained in the moment of insight" (1959, p. 14). Although by no means unsympathetic to mysticism, Russell's preoccupation was almost entirely with an assessment of mystical doctrines concerning plurality and the spatiotemporal order. At the end of "Mysticism" he makes a brief remark about the value of a dedoctrinalized mysticism. However, having been so preoccupied with the metaphysical content of mysticism, he never concerned himself with assessing what amounts to the mystic's claim of the centrality of mystical experience for the theory of monadic value, and the concomitant importance of practices conducive to mystical experience for the theory of normative ethics.

Walter Stace's treatment of the relationship between mysticism and ethics in *Mysticism and Philosophy*, concerns itself with the relationship between mystical experience and *interrelational* value. Thus, he takes it that we will discover whether mysticism has a positive effect on living the good life by asking, "Does it make men more moral or less, more active in giving loving assistance to their fellow men or less? Does it tend to operate as an incentive to nobler living, or does it not rather serve mainly as an escape hatch from the responsibilities of life?" (1960, pp. 323, 324). From this we can see that Stace identifies moral value with interrelational moral value. Indeed, he goes on to suggest that the introvertive mystical experience is the source of everyone's experience of the love for children, friends, strangers or whomever, whether one has explicitly experienced the mystical state or not. Stace's focus in the study of mysticism as a whole is on the doctrines associated with the mystical state, and insofar as he treats of the connections of mysticism to moral theory, he does so in regard not to the theory of monadic value but to the theory of interrelational consciousness, impulses, and obligations.

Zaehner in *Mysticism Sacred and Profane* (1957) continues the tradition that regards evaluating mystical metaphysical doctrines as being at the very center of the philosophical study of mysticism. He champions theistic mysticism against monistic mysticism, but his championing of it is largely dependent on the attempt to analyze Christian and Advaita Vedanta texts in which both moral and doctrinal concerns have been subtly woven together. For example, he approves of Ruysbroeck's dismissal of non-theistic mystical emptiness. But Ruysbroeck's dismissal characterizes these mystics as maintaining "that they are free, and united with God without mean, and that they are advanced beyond all the exercises of Holy Church, and beyond the commandments of God, and beyond the law, and beyond all the virtuous works which one can in any way practise" (Ruysbroeck, quoted in Zaehner, 1957, p. 171). It is obvious that Ruysbroek's concern is with what he takes to be an ineluctable link between mystical rest and antinomianism. Without analysis of this link, the condemnation of the rest cannot be taken at face value. Further, since both Zaehner and Ruysbroeck do not employ the distinction between monadic and interrelational value, it is not surprising that their assessments of the relation between mystical experience and mystical doctrine conflate practical, doctrinal, and experiential concerns. In any case, Zaehner uncritically accepts a typology that prevents him from assessing blissful mystical experience as a central element of monadic value.

Ninian Smart, however, does present the centrality of the claims concerning mystical bliss and what amounts to monadic value. In the section on "What is mysticism?" in chapter 2 of *Reasons and Faiths*, Smart defines mysticism via mystics' self-disciplining methods and subsequent claims. He says, "The following are a few main points typically made by such men: that they have achieved unspeakable bliss; that this experience is timeless and other-worldly; that it is gained after a long course of self-mastery and meditation (referred to as 'the Path,' 'the Way,' etc.); that upon attaining it they acquire a new vision of the world" (p. 55). Thus, front and center of Smart's analysis is the claim of unspeakable bliss. In a note to this passage, Smart defends the vocabulary of 'bliss' against the charges that "bliss implies enjoyment and if the mystic seeks enjoyment he will not find it. Also 'bliss' like similar words has a tendency towards debasement in usage." Smart's response is that "'bliss' has the advantage of being the common translation of the Sanskrit *ananda*, frequently used of the mystical state (see e.g., Taittiriya Upan. II.8.1) and also used to describe an aspect of the nature of Brahman; and it is a reasonable word for the Pali sukha, used in connection with nirvana" (n. 1, p. 56). Later Smart explicates the mystic's doctrine of ineffability as expressive of the overwhelming character of the bliss, rather than as making a logical or semantic point about the experience. He says, ". . . the indescribability of mystical experience has two sides to it. First the intensity of the bliss is such that it is best, albeit inadequately, expressed by saying that it is 'indescribable,' 'ineffable,'" etc. Second, the mystical state does not involve having mental images or perceptions (and thus in the Upanisads is compared to dreamless sleep) and so there is nothing about it to describe (and thus it is unlike day-dreaming and visualization in general)" (p. 71).

Smart, then, cannot be saddled with the charge of ignoring the fundamental status of overwhelmingly blissful experience in descriptions of what mysticism consists in. However Smart's main task in *Reasons and Faiths* is to aid in "the description of the character of doctrinal schemes (and in general of religious discourse) in such a way as both to compare and contrast these with other language-frames and to show the differences and connections between logical strands within the religious frame" (p. 18). He is not there concerned with direct philosophical assessments of the doctrines themselves so much as with helping to prevent philosophical distortions in interpreting religious doctrines prior to assessing the doctrines. Nor in his many other works does he turn to the task of assessing the mystical claim with regard to the centrality of mystical experience for monadic ethics. The work in which he is most concerned to philosophically evaluate religious claims is *Philosophers and Religious Truth* (1964), and there his chapter on religious experience is particularly concerned with whether or not religious experience ought to be regarded as an encounter with transcendent Being or as pointing towards the truth.

Frits Staal's, *Exploring Mysticism* (1975) strikingly contrasts with much of the academic analysis of mysticism which precedes it. The thrust of Staal's argument is that mysticism has been distorted by academics who have unjustifiably assumed that mysticism is irrationalistic, and who have attempted to study mysticism as academic analysts of classic texts and of experiences as reported by mystics, without having attempted to acquire mystical states themselves. Staal attempts to distinguish the practices and rituals superstructurally associated with mysticism from those practices whose efficacy can be expected to be naturalistically explicable, at least in principle, such as fasting, meditation, and breathing exercises. Staal then encourages the academician to recognize that "(o)nce we abandon the armchair approach we need not be surprised that we may have to prepare an investigator of mysticism by means of an appropriate course of fasting, just as we may prepare an astronaut by an appropriate course of eating" (p. 136). Further, "meditation stands most in need of experiential or subjective study. But it is unlikely that meditation could be properly learned without what most of the traditional mystics consider essential: *viz.* without the guidance of a competent teacher" (p. 141). Staal concludes his exploration of easy and hard paths, of effortful activity directed towards mystical attainments versus graceful experiences, and of religious superstructural elements versus nonsuperstructural directives and naturalistically efficacious practices, by saying that "we can only make progress in the study of mysticism if we direct our attention to the experiences themselves" (p. 178). Whoever wishes to undertake a genuine examination of mysticism "will have to put a stop to speculation and start a real investigation. Paradoxically, his first action may have to be contemplation under the guidance of a guru. No harm there, even if it yields, in addition to scholarly results, what Nagarjuna called dhyanasukham 'the joy of contemplation'" (p. 186). Staal concludes with a call for investigation. But the book is a call to investigation, not an assessment subsequent to such a thorough experiential investigation as he is calling for. And in any case, the call is issued to academics who want to understand and present proper interpretations of mysticism. Staal canvasses dogmatic, philological and historical, phenomenological, physical, and psychological approaches to mysticism, but does not focus on any directly philosophical issues at all. To be precise, then, Staal does not raise the issue of the relevance of access to mystical experience to value theory even though he does emphasize the issue of access for other academics.

Ben-Ami Scharfstein undertakes a partial analysis of mystical value of roughly the kind I'm suggesting in "Personal and Pragmatic Defences of Mysticism" (chapter 3 of *Mystical Experience*, Penguin: Baltimore: 1973). However he directly reviews only two cases, that of al-Ghazali and William James. The inclusion of William James in this context is certainly peculiar. James himself denies having had mystical experiences, and Scharfstein even quotes the passage! "Whether my treatment of mystical states will shed more light or darkness I do not know, for my own constitution shuts me out from their enjoyment almost entirely, and I can speak of them only at second hand" (*Varieties*, Lecture 16, quoted in Scharfstein p. 38). Based, then, on the reports collected in *Varieties*, and on al-Ghazali's remarks, Scharfstein concludes: "I see no reason to believe that there should be a larger number of generous than selfish mystics, nor should I be surprised to find as many mystical scoundrels as mystical saints. As for peace of mind, the mystic finds it, but sometimes only fitfully, and always, I should think, after a depth of suffering that the non-mystic may never have to undergo" (p. 40). At least the assessment here is roughly of the right type. But what justifies the remark that the mystical peace only arrives after a depth of suffering that the non-mystic doesn't have to undergo? Surely even based on James' analysis, Scharfstein would have been in a position to recognize the distinction between the once born and the twice born religious type, and to realize that the once born type can as easily occur within a mystical religious tradition as within a devotional or worship centered religious tradition. Scharfstein's remarks, then, besides being impressionistic at best, skirt a key problem, and ignore an entire tradition. The key problem skirted is the assessment of the superlative bliss against the depth of suffering in cases where depth of suffering has indeed preceded the attainment of mystic release. Mystics seem to think the result was more than worth it, and would be found to be more than worth it by anyone else who passes through the dark night of the soul to the mystic peace. An attempt should be made to weigh the worthiness of the bliss even for those who must endure great suffering to realize it. Similarly an attempt should be made to weigh the worthiness of the goal given that some cases occur in which the dark night does not lead to dawn. And the entire tradition ignored is the tradition of mystical realization which is not preceded by abysmal suffering on its behalf. There are many Zen stories of sudden realization preceded by great effort and doubt, but not by nightmarish darkness. And there are many stories of Taoist sages who found the valley spirit naturally and instinctively as it were. Plainly, Scharfstein's assessment, though of the requisite type, is cursory, ill-informed, and, on balance, inadequate.

Subsequent treatments have returned to study the many problems of the relation between mystical experience and the interpretation of mystical experience, and the surrounding epistemological issues, for example, the contributions in Steven Katz' anthology, *Mysticism and Philosophical Analysis* (1978); and Wayne Proudfoot's "Mysticism" (chapter 4 of *Religious Experience*, 1985). James Horne's *The Moral Mystic* (1983) is centrally concerned with the relationship between mysticism and the moral life, but the focus of study is the interrelational moral life in relation to various forms of mysticism. Here too, there is little assessment of the claim that mystical experience is the monadic summum bonum. Probably the most ambitious analytic study of mysticism since Stace's *Mysticism and Philosophy* is William Wainwright's *Mysticism* (1981). However, as with Stace's analysis and with Horne's, the question of the relation of mysticism and morality for Wainwright is centered on the relationship between mystical pursuits and interrelational activities, not on monadic value. Consider the concluding remarks of the final chapter, "Mysticism and Morality": "Mysticism sometimes affects morality adversely. It does so when it makes a person indifferent to moral values and the importance of moral distinctions. On the other hand, mysticism often appears to have a positive and beneficial effect upon the moral lives of those who are touched by it. Mysticism strengthens morality both by strengthening those attitudes and dispositions which are moral or which have moral consequences (such as charity, equanimity and detachment) and by bringing certain truths home to us (such as, for example, the truth of the reality of the transcendent order and the fact that persons belong to that order as well as to nature.) What is not clear is that mysticism teaches any morally relevant truths which are not available to us apart from mystical experience, or that any moral ideal or norm depends upon mystical consciousness for its validity. . . . I therefore conclude that while there may be significant psychological or social connections between mysticism and morality, there are few significant logical or epistemic connections" (pp. 225-226). Thus, Wainwright effectively leaves the question of the monadic value of mystical experience out of consideration.

There is, then, little or no detailed examination of the claim that mystical experience is the monadic summum bonum. Once again, it is an understandable problem: you have to be a mystic, or have good access to mystics in situ, in order to be able to undertake such an assessment. Staal, working in a slightly different context, nonetheless identified both the cause and the remedy. Value theorists as well as philosophers of mind and metaphysics need to abandon the armchair pulled up to the reading desk approach and adopt the zafu-zabuton, or meditating upon cushions, approach or some reasonable substitute. Otherwise there will always be a crucial issue at the center of monadic value theory from which the value theorist will be more or less excluded.

In *Utilitarianism* chapter 2, Mill suggests that the only way to rank rival intrinsic goods is to trust to the judgment of the most widely experienced people. If you want to know how sensual pleasures stack up against intellectual pleasures, you had best consult neither the sensualists nor the eggheads, but rather those who are familiar with both the sensual pleasures and the intellectual pleasures. Mill therefore would ask that an assessment of mystical bliss be done by the active mystics, those familiar with mysticism by direct acquaintance, and for whom mysticism has not been a prescription for avoidance of the life of activity.

The difficulty is that so long as these active mystics are rather rare, it is hard to see how anything remotely resembling consensus can emerge among value theorists concerning the centrality or noncentrality of mystical experience in the theory of monadic value. It is unrealistic to expect most moral theorists to suddenly decide to spend fifteen, ten, or even five years in arduous training in meditation under the guidance of a guru or meditation teacher simply because without such training their assessment of monadic value is incomplete in a certain respect. Consequently, for the forseeable future theorists of monadic value will perforce have to rely on their own personal explorations where they are so motivated, or the accounts of others who have been sufficiently motivated towards the mystical pursuits. Anecdotal accounts of mystical bliss as the monadic summum bonum are hardly adequate for so many reasons. But for a long time to come, they will be the best we have.

Four

Mysticism and Logic: Is Mysticism Intelligible?

Towards the end of the last chapter, our focus began to shift somewhat. We began the chapter by clarifying the role of genial mysticism in value theory. But by the end of the discussion, we had waded into murkier waters. It is one thing to claim that the monadic summum bonum is sustained experience of the blissful ultimacy of being-here-now, it is another thing to refer to the experience of *"ki"* or *"prana"* or "diamond body," and to go on to express the content or non-content of such experience in the baffling, paradoxical expressions found within Enlightenment East traditions, such as "I became one with Absolute Being, yet everything remained the same as it was."

Having attempted to demonstrate the relevance of at least some Enlightenment East values for the understanding of monadic fulfillment, I now face the more formidable task of attempting to demonstrate the intelligibility of the typically arcane expressions of these values. The view that one can train oneself to the experience of joy in Ultimacy, moment after moment, is legitimately called "mysticism," (and specifically underlies much of what is called "extrovertive mysticism" in Stace's classification scheme, for example). But the mysticism which gets so many backs up is the mysticism which expresses itself in highly puzzling forms. Moreover, those who advocate the genial mysticism whose relevance for monadic ethics I've been attempting to demonstrate are often the very ones who also advocate one or another of the arcane, puzzling, mystical expressions. And, to be accurate, even extrovertive mysticism can receive rather esoteric expression.

Before introducing the more esoteric mysticisms, we should inspect briefly the connection between the genial mysticism and the arcane expressions. At first blush, there would seem to be no opportunity for connection between holding that one is capable of sustaining the experience of joy in Being and such claims as "All is without identity," or "You are the Cosmos." But the form of the connection is, after all, not as obscure as might at first appear. The mystic asserts that the experience of joy in Being can be sustained, moment after moment. How can this be done, asks the aspirant? Well, says the mystic, when you realize that You are the Cosmos, then you will be filled with the joy of Being, and this joy will be your constant form of experience. Or, when you discover firsthand that you have no identity, and that all is without identity, then you will be awakened and be transformed, and the mystical bliss will be yours.

In other words, the connection is an empirical, more specifically, a psychological one, dependent on a metaphysical or quasi-metaphysical putative insight. Earlier we referred to the empirical content of mysticism in that the mystic asserts the sustainability of the experience of joy in Being. Here we see a second element of empirical claim associated with mysticism. The ethical goods associated with genial mysticism, it is claimed, are achieved together with, or through, some realization about self and the world, which is held to be difficult if not impossible to express adequately, or which when expressed is expressed in the puzzling forms. The mystic approaches as an ethicist, emerges next as a psychologist, and finally appears to be driven to woolly metaphysics in order to account in a straightforward manner for the psychological phenomenon. It would be impractical, then, to defend genial mysticism, and divorce it from the puzzling, apparently unintelligible, mystical viewpoints, descriptions, and metaphysical doctrines.

Nor must we ignore the bewildering variety of formulations of these viewpoints, descriptions, and doctrines:

"I am the cosmos" and its variations, "I am the All," "I am God," "My me is God" (Saint Catherine of Genoa), or "I became that which I saw before and beheld from afar" (Saint Symeon the younger, A.D. 942-1022, quoted in Campbell, 1973, p. 39), are characteristic expressions of subject mysticism in its expansive mode. "There is no self" is the paradigmatic expression of subject mysticism in its negating mode. Then there are the characteristic varieties of mysticism concerning the world of objects, captured in such claims as "All this is One," or "There is only Oneness, unity," and "There is nothingness," or "There is no individuality," or "There is only emptiness."

Many, perhaps most, people have had glimmerings of some such mystical enlightenment at one time or another. And a substantial proportion of recent philosophers trained in the western mold have been curious about it. However, very early on in one's efforts to take mysticism seriously, one will be up against two brick walls.

(a) At the core of enlightenment doctrine concerning the Self is an apparent contradiction. If I am Leonard and you are Pat, and I am

the universe and you are the universe, then I am you, and Leonard is Pat. If Pat is charged with a crime, can Pat say "I am not guilty, because I am Leonard, and Leonard has a perfect alibi?"

(b) At the core of the enlightenment doctrine concerning the world of objects is apparent abandonment of the law of contradiction altogether: "At first you think rivers are rivers and mountains are mountains, then you discover rivers are mountains and mountains are rivers. . . ." Whoa! responds the analytic philosopher. It's little comfort to be told that when you really understand, you re-discover that rivers are rivers and mountains are mountains. The first task is supposed to be to discover that rivers are mountains and vice versa, and this is uninterpretable. And sometimes mystics enshrine the violation of logic in explicit general terms. Thus, for instance, we find in P. T. Raju's *Structural Depths of Indian Thought*, "Ramanuja's teacher was Yadavaprakasa, who held that the Brahman, the individual souls, and the world of matter are all real and yet they are both identical with and different from one another. He did not see that the same relation could not be both identity and difference, his reason being that it was natural and that our theory should accord with facts, but not facts with theory" (p. 438). For the mystic, then, logic may be regarded as mere theory, whereas mystical experience is factual, and logical theory must be revised even in its most fundamental principles in order to accommodate the mystical experience.

The situation, then, is something like this: We have had vague glimmerings that there might be something absolutely fundamental about consciousness that we haven't encountered yet, or come to terms with. Even if we haven't, there are mystics who have told us that if we only experience the true nature of consciousness we know a joy so supreme, so unutterable, a bliss so profound that words fail to convey its exalted blessedness. Either way we may want to know more. "Sounds good," we say. "How do we get there?" The mystics hand us their maps and point to a vehicle. On inspection, however, the vehicle appears to be missing an engine, and when we look at the maps we find the terrain described variously, and in any one map, in any case, there are some roads leading straight over the edge of apparent cliffs. Worse still, there are several sets of compass references, and they apparently contradict each other. Crestfallen, we return the map and the keys to the vehicle with a reluctant "No thanks."

This, then, is my enterprise in this chapter. It is addressed especially to the logically rigorous folk, to whom I say: I do not hope to transport you into the terrain whose map I'm showing you. But I do hope that this map will be intelligible and the vehicles provided will be apparently sturdy.

Should mystical states be subject to the laws of logic?

Probably the most influential account of the relationship between mysticism and logic has been that of Walter Stace, despite, or per-haps because of, its rather challenging conclusion on the subject of the relation of mysticism to logic. According to Stace's analysis, we should not expect that descriptions of mystical states, any more than mystical states themselves, should be subject to the laws of logic. Stace emphasizes the paradoxicality of mystical claims: "I need merely remind the reader of the pantheistic paradox that God and the world are both identical and non-identical or distinct; of the positive-negative or plenum-vacuum paradox with its three aspects, that the One or the Universal Mind is both qualified and unqualified, both personal and impersonal, both static and dynamic; of the paradox of the dissolution of individuality wherein I cease to be individual and yet retain my individuality; of the paradox that he who reaches nirvana neither exists nor does not exist; and of the paradox of the extrovertive mys-tical experience that the objects of the senses are both many and one, both identical and distinct. These paradoxes have not been foisted upon mysticism by the present writer but have been discov-ered and fully documented by the study of the utterances of the mys-tics themselves" (1960, p 253). Stace rejects the theory that these utterances are merely rhetorical devices, and that the mystical expe-riences could be "described and the same thoughts expressed without loss of content in nonparadoxical language." Rather, he holds that any attempt to eliminate the paradoxical character of mystical expres-sions and doctrines will strip away what is essential to mysticism. Mysticism just isn't commonsensical. And "There is nothing wrong with common sense or with everyday experience. But we cannot have it both ways. We cannot both believe that the mystical con-sciousness is unique, different in kind from our ordinary conscious-ness, and yet at the same time that there is nothing in it which cannot be 'reduced' to our ordinary consciousness" (p. 265). Stace's conclu-sion is that "[T]he laws of logic . . . have no application to mystical experience." Stace finds this acceptable because, according to his view, mystical experience is not of multiplicity, and laws of logic are rules for thinking of or dealing with a multiplicity of separate items. "But in the One there are no items to be kept distinct, and therefore logic has no meaning for it" (pp. 270-271).

The most sustained criticism of Stace's view of the relation between mystical states and logical principles is that of William Wainwright in *Mysticism*. Wainwright suggests that Stace was unduly short with the possibilities of metaphor, expressive exaggeration, and ambiguity in mystical language. Thus, for example, "Mystics typically distinguish between a person's true self (*nous*, Atman, *purusa*, etc.,) and his empirical self (soul, *jiva*, manas, etc.) This distinction can be used to explicate 'I cease to exist and yet continue to exist.' In its first occurrence 'I' refers to the empirical ego. In its second occurrence it refers to the pure ego. There is thus no contradiction" (p. 148). Most importantly, though, Wainwright takes Stace to task for holding, or appearing to hold, that paradoxical statements can be meant literally, and thus be contradictory, and yet appropriate or true. Moreover, according to Wainwright, Stace has not shown that the "mystical paradoxes are not about items in a multiple world, or that they are not in many cases about two or more items. . . . Since he has not shown this, he has not shown that logic does not apply to the statements in question, and . . . we must continue to suppose that they are false if they are logically impossible" (pp. 153, 154).

Wainwright is surely right in insisting that we do not take lightly the objection that mystical descriptions characteristically appear to be logically incoherent. Either we find ways to explicate the paradoxes, or we are left with incoherent defenses of mystical doctrines. Unfortunately, although Wainwright is correct in wishing to find a logically intelligible account of mystical states, the direction of his own account appears to be as subject to logical objection as the theories Stace mentions. Wainwright favors a cognitive account of mystical experience based on the perceptual model. According to Wainwright, there is good reason to think that mystical experience is perceptual experience, or analogous to perceptual experience, in that mystical experiences have an object (unlike pains, or feelings of depression); and the object of mystical apprehension is regarded by the mystic as being really there, and experimentally apprehended in mystical experience (See p. 83).

However, Wainwright's perceptual analysis appears merely to push the logical objections back one step. Assume that mystics sometimes experience the Transcendent One, or the Transcendent God. Is the object of such mystical experience multiplicitous or simple? If the One is composite, we have a contradiction. If the One is simple, we have a paradox of a different flavor, for perceptual relations only appear to be coherent when the object of perception, supposedly something really there, as Wainwright puts it, has sufficient location in or around space-time to have a determinate identity of the usual worldly sort. Perhaps it will be suggested that mystical experience is not exactly perceptual experience. But this is the very issue: how to explicate what mystical experience is, how to account for the supposed fact that mystical experience can be of an object which is simple, and still be a sort of perceptual experience. Consider: if an object is simple, either it has location but no extension in space-time, or it has no location in space-time at all. If the former, the object is a mere spatial point, and cannot be the One. If the latter, then it would appear to be impossible to characterize it either as simple or composite, let alone as really there and open to something like perceptual apprehension. What has no space-time participation on its own cannot be described without a great deal of difficult metaphysical work as having real or objective, independent existence. Are we to think that such a contemporary account of the One will be any less troubled by logical objections than Plato's theory of forms? And how does perception of something really there, and really Transcendent of space-time enter into space-time sufficiently to be an object of experience? If we belong to a multiplicitous world, then the One is but one element of the multiplicitous order of things. Further, it follows that the Whole embraces the One. But then the One no longer transcends the many but is a mere part of the many. In these and many other ways, the usual paradoxes quickly reappear within the sort of analysis Wainwright is attempting to clear the way towards. There are at least as many logically disturbing issues raised by Wainwright's perceptual account as are cleared away by his rejection of Stace's arguments.

It should also be mentioned that Wainwright's analysis is presented more as a ground clearing enterprise than as a full explication of mysticism. It is probably the most ambitious account of mysticism since Stace's, but the majority of theses defended by Wainwright are either critical theses of analyses of others or tentatively phrased door-openers rather than positive claims. Thus, ". . . I shall argue that mystical experience is sufficiently similar to sense experience to create a presumption in favor of its cognitive validity." This indicates the modesty in the degree of strength that Wainwright's conclusion is meant to hold. Surprisingly—astoundingly, even—none of the resurfacing metaphysico-logical objections raised just now is brought forward by Wainwright in his section on objections to the perceptual account! Instead, he deals with more easily treatable objections trading on epistemic, psychological, and descriptive problems (pp. 102-125). Having ignored the salient metaphysico-logical problems, it is easy for him to take a rejection of *(a)* Stace's dismissal of the possibilities of expressive exaggeration, metaphor, ambiguity, and the like; and a rejection also of *(b)* Stace's explanations of why logic doesn't apply to descriptions of mystical states, to constitute sufficient ground to warrant the conclusion that "there is no reason to believe that mysticism transcends logic" (p. 138). But this abandonment of the logical worries would only have been warranted had he at least raised and somehow treated the many metaphysico-logical objections to the sort of cognitive perceptual account towards which he is attempting to pave the way.

In short, the logical problems associated with mysticism must be dealt with. This is one bull which must be grabbed by the horns, and not ignored. On the following point, however, we must agree with Wainwright's analysis: The usual view that mystical states involve obliteration of the distinction or gap between the subject and the object needs very cautious scrutiny indeed.

Subject and object: Some misconceptions

Mysticism is often presented as the teaching that it is possible for a person to experience the dissolution of the subject-object distinction. In mystical experience, it is said, there is no gap or separation between the perceiving subject and the perceived object. For example, Karl Jaspers says in *The Way To Wisdom*: ". . . we are in a position to understand the meaning of mysticism . . . man can transcend the subject-object dichotomy and achieve a total union of subject and object" (p. 33). Similarly, Toshihiku Izutsu says, in *Toward a Philosophy of Zen Buddhism*, "What Nan Chu'uan himself wants to convey by his statement ['The ordinary people see this flower as if they were in a dream'] is quite clear. He means to say that a flower as seen by the ordinary people under normal conditions is an object standing before the perceiving subject . . . the flower is represented as something different from the man who is looking at it. The flower in its true reality, however, is, according to Nan Ch'uan, a flower which is not distinguishable from the man who sees it, the subject. What is at issue here is a state which is neither subjective nor objective, but which is, at the same time both subjective and objective—a state in which the subject and object, the man and the flower, become fused in an indescribably subtle way into an absolute unity" (p. 9).

I believe that this way of putting the matter is distinctly unhelpful. Indeed, it is misguided, and there are many mystics whose articulations of the nature of mystical experience fall prey to the confusions inherent in the notion that in ordinary experience the perceiving subject is distinct from the perceived object whereas in mystical experience, the perceiving subject is not distinct from the perceived object. The perceiving subject is a person. Any statement of the form "_____ saw the flower," should have the blank filled in by a phrase which refers to a person, as perception of an object involves a personal perceiver to do the perceiving, perception being one of the constitutive elements of personality. Whether there can be any perception without other elements of personality such as planning, desiring, willing, and moving bodily parts in accord with immediate plans is a complex topic which we need not discuss at this point. The mystic, whatever else, is a person, and many mystics, as is clear from the Izutsu exposition, and many similar to it, claim to experience the world mystically even when continuing to function as persons. But now consider the consequences of holding that the mystic is one for whom the perceiving subject has become the perceived object. This would mean, in the case of the mystic looking at a flower, that the mystic has become the flower. The logician surely has reason to balk at this description. (Does the mystic have petals and stamens? Does the mystic exude a delicate floral fragrance—without daubing perfume in the morning?) There won't be maneuvering room for discussion if "the mystic has become the flower" exemplifies the type of description required for there to be mystical experience.

But surely, it will be demurred, the relation of subject and object which obtains in non-mystical experience is different from that which obtains in mystical experience, and it is this difference which makes for the difference between non-mystical and mystical experience. Then what is that difference? It is the task of this chapter to examine the concepts of subject and object, to sketch their relations in such a way that we can see what the difference is between mystical and non-mystical experience, and to do so in a way that does not offend basic tools of reason and logic. To prefigure the analysis, it will be shown that mystical experience must be understood with reference to particular conceptions of the object world. Once a particular conception of the object world is given—for example, "there are many objects," or "no objects exist," or "there is only one object in existence, an absolutely simple entity," then the subject may be placed within, or in relation to the world of objects as thus conceived. In each of these conceptions of the world of objects, including the first, the subject may be so placed that mystical experience results. In other words, it is at least the way in which the subject is placed in, or in relation to, the object world which makes for the difference between mystical and nonmystical experience. The difference between mystical and non-mystical experience is perhaps best explained at this preliminary stage with reference to a particular example of mystical experience.

In all non-mystical experience, the world of objects is conceived as a plurality. That is, the view "there are many objects" is affirmed. Further, in all non-mystical experience, the subject is placed as, or identified with, one of the elements of the world of objects, namely, the first person. The metaphysical picture results, "There are many objects, and I am one of them, namely, this very person."

If either of two things occurs, mystical experience results. First, if one replaces the conception of the world of objects by a non-pluralist conception, mystical experience results. Alternatively, if one retains the conception of the object world as a plurality of objects, but alters the placement or identification of the subject, then mystical experience results. The particular example of an altered identification of subject within the object world which may be most conveniently used to illustrate at this stage is mystical experience which results when, preserving the image of the object world as a plurality of objects, one identifies the subject as the object world itself, thus resulting in the judgments: "I am the cosmos. The first person is a mere part of me. The first person is looking at the flower. I am not the first person. I include five billion people on the planet earth." Perhaps this illustration provides enough by way of hint as to the sort of analysis to be presented here.

In general, then, a proper understanding of mystical experience requires understanding the relationship between *(a)* the subject, I, or self, *(b)* the object or object world, and *(c)* the experiencing person. It is the purpose of the following meditations to clarify this relationship.

Ego-consciousness

"I am this person. I am not anything else. I am not that tree, I am not that flower. I am not that desk. I am exclusively this person."

Comments

Ego-consciousness is the consciousness with which one begins mature reflections, or with which one begins philosophizing. It may be characterized as the exclusive identification of the self with a particular element of a world with many objects, namely, the first person. The subject story of this standpoint is the story of the first person beginning with earliest memories, skipping all events that are not remembered, but including events that are remembered if only in summary form ("I had a good time in grade one"). Other events enter the subject story at the points in which the subject of the subject story is presented with the data concerning them. ("It was only in my thirties that I realized how hard my parents had worked before I was born.")

The object story of this standpoint is supposed to be the same object story as anyone else's object story no matter who is telling it, but in fact many object stories are told: "First God created the heavens and the earth, and then . . .", or, "The Big Bang happened 15 billion years ago. After the first ten minutes, the temperature was about. . . ." Of course all the events of the subject story appear within the object story in appropriate chronology. ("Then there was this person named 'Leonard.' He was fond of certain special toys as a child. . . .")

From one angle, the subject story has primacy ("It's my story. It's the story of actual experiences only; the object story is a constructed story, and appears within my story as a constructed story.") But from another angle, the object story has primacy. ("It's a unified and general story in which everything can be seen in proper chronology, and includes everything in the subject story anyway. . . .")

Ego-consciousness is characterized by a constant seesawing between these two angles. It's also characterized by a feeling of delight ("Of all the objects in the world, this one, this person is so special—it's me. How delightful!") and by a feeling of isolation ("This person is me, and nothing else is me. How isolated it is to be me.")

There is also a considerable variation in the tone of the subject-object relation within ego consciousness not only in that having an ego, being a particular person, is sometimes delightful, sometimes lonely, but also in that the gap between self and other comes in a seemingly endless variety of flavors. The relationship one has with one's spouse has a mixture of distance and intimacy that constitutes a particular flavor within ego consciousness quite different from that of the relationship between an artist and the artist's materials, which is again different from that of the relationship between a hiker and the forest, and so on.

The seesawing that characterizes the ego-conscious standpoint issues forth in a series of philosophical problems ("How do I know other people are not contentless objects, but actually experience as subjects?" "Can I consider my doings as praiseworthy or blameworthy and also regard them, objectively, as the outcomes of causal sequences?" "Say I enter an atom sorting machine which takes half my atoms and puts them in location A, filling in the rest of the body with fresh atoms from an independent stock, and it puts the other half in location B, again filling in the rest of my body with fresh atoms. Say this procedure works and both Leonards go off their individual merry ways. What happens to me? Have I disappeared? Can I be in both bodies? Can I be in one body and not in the other?" And so on.)

Subjective and objective angles

These problems share an apparent insolubility factor: one attempts to solve the problem by looking at it from an objective standpoint only to find that subjectivity has not been accommodated. And yet subjectivity is a datum that must be accommodated.

So one is tempted to conclude something like this: there are two ways of looking at the world. There is the subjective perspective in which one takes account of the fact that "this very person is me"; and there is the objective perspective in which one leaves out of account that very phenomenon, taking it that "this very person is just one of many people without any specialness or centrality." And yet, each standpoint is incomplete in a fundamental way. The result of this is that any general statement of the way the subjective relates to the objective will remain forever elusive. This is how Thomas Nagel puts the matter, in a closely related discussion: "A general conception of reality would require a general conception of experience which admitted our own subjective viewpoint as a special case. This is completely beyond us and will probably remain so for as long as human beings continue to exist" (1979, p. 213). He might have added that not only does a general conception of reality require a general conception of experience, but it also requires a general conception of what is objectively present, the object world, into which each experiencing being experiences itself as a subject. Indeed, since Berkeley's celebrated criticism of the notion of material substance (if a date must be given for the inauguration of this mood), philosophers of the Anglo-American tradition have been loathe to attempt to characterize "reality in general" in such a way that our own subjective viewpoint—ego consciousness—appears as a special case. Thus, the situation stands even today. But need it?

Prospects

I will begin my analysis with a brief diagnosis of the problem. Consider the contrast between our attitudes towards being a person looked at objectively and considered subjectively. Let us express the objective reflexive perspective, that is, the objective perspective on the first person by the expression "This is a person," and the subjective reflexive perspective, the subjective perspective on the self by "I am this entity." These two statements combine together to form the statement expressive of ego consciousness, "I am this person." Ego consciousness, then, fuses an objective reflexive stance with a subjective reflexive stance so as to issue in what is perceived as a single indissoluble image of the self, namely, "I am this person."

Now we know how to look at "this person" as being an impersonal composite. We know how to see this entity not as a person, but as a "bunch of atoms strung together in a structure which behaves a certain way, is as subject to causal laws as anything else, so far as we know, and so on." That is, when we look at the world, including its persons, objectively, we know how to desubjectivize and depersonalize. This does not mean, of course, that as soon as we look at the world objectively we depersonalize its parts. Rather, we have a choice within the objective perspective. We can, if we wish, consider this (rational agent) as a person. That we can do so is made evident by the fact that in our everyday dealings with other persons we are characteristically dealing with them as persons, as do-ers, and not as embodied brains whose neurons' firings are explicable with reference to causal laws. On the other hand, we can choose to see the person as a physical system the behavior of which is explicable by causal laws (so many of which we are as yet so ignorant of, but never mind). Some circumstances make it natural to adopt this as our dominant image of the entity (e.g., the circumstance of being a brain surgeon at work on a patient's grey matter).

On the other hand, there is no corresponding flexibility within the subjective perspective as normally conceived. We don't know how to adopt the subjective reflexive stance, and yet still depersonalize. If we could we would end up saying something like, "I am this entity. I am myself, but do not see myself as a person." However, we have no idea what it would mean to have such a perspective. "I am a person" registers with a fixity that does not register with the objective stance "This entity is a person." Since we can take another person and analytically depersonalize the conglomerate that constitutes the person, we can conceive of doing the same to ourselves. But as soon as the subjective intuition is raised reflexively or towards another, the intuition that the subject is a person seems inescapable. "The subject of consciousness is a person, this person" seems to be a condition of intelligibility of experience. It is this lopsidedness, this asymmetry between objective and subjective attitudes which makes incompatible the two perspectives. On the one hand, this can be conceived as an impersonal composite, even when 'this' refers to the first person. But "I am this first person" does not seem to allow an interpretation, or an experience, expressed by "I am an impersonal entity." The only interpretation we can give of this is by way of taking 'I' in its other sense, as the logically or objectively reflexive self, to refer to this person, and through an objective view of this person, depersonalizing and seeing the first person as a composite of impersonal parts. In effect, the only way to interpret "I am an impersonal entity," or "I see myself as an impersonal entity" is to adopt the objective attitude.

If one were to discover a flexibility with regard to "I am a person" corresponding to the flexibility to see *this* as a person, and *this* as a composite of impersonal entities, the strain would vanish.

Such a discovery, I am going to suggest, is possible. The keys to deconstructing the exclusive identification of the subject of consciousness with a person are in the subliminal mechanisms of everyday consciousness. One needs only to bring them into the foreground of consciousness and discover that if what is left after attitudinally depersonalizing *this* is matter, atoms, and molecules, then what is left after experientially depersonalizing *me* is the world as the all embracing, impersonal, me. Attitudinally depersonalizing self, however, does not result in what clinical psychologists sometimes refer to as the abnormal condition of depersonalization of the first person.

It may be worth mentioning at this point that a somewhat different route towards establishing the distinction between the concept of the self and the concept of the first person is provided by Derek Parfit in section #80 of *Reasons and Persons*.

THE MEDITATIONS

First Meditation: On the Silence of the Subject

To produce this meditation, exclusively refer to the first person by proper name or other purely objective form of reference (e.g., 'the speaker,' 'this person'). One does this both in one's thoughts and in conversation. In the first meditation, the vocabulary of the subject,— 'I,' 'me,' 'self,' 'myself,' and so on—entirely drops away.

"This person, Leonard, is one person among many people and many things. Here is a person, here is another person, there is a third person. Leonard is but one amongst many. There are all kinds of things, and some of them are persons, and this is merely one of them . . . Leonard will now move his arm . . . He just moved his arm. Someone over there is looking (up) (down) (sideways). Someone over there is looking in the direction of the speaker who is Leonard. This person is the speaker. . . ."

Comments

In the first meditation, there is only one story to be told. Of course, it can be told in various orders. For example, the speaker can tell the story beginning with the speaker's first memories ("The speaker's first memories are of a large furry toy. He used to play with it in the crib. . . .") Or, he can tell the story in the most complete chronology he knows ("First there was the Big Bang. Fifteen billion years later, in a planet of a solar system of the Milky Way galaxy, people evolved. Which planet? this planet. . . . Human recorded history begins in the Middle East. . . . The speaker's first memories concern a large furry toy. . . .") But regardless of ordering, the story forms a single narrative, every element of which is presented from the same perspective.

The experience of ego consciousness, of course, is inexpressible with this meditation, as it requires the language of the subject for its expression. It is this aspect of the meditation which enables the empirical structure of ego consciousness to become clarified.

Needless to say, the meditation does not accomplish anything as it were by magic, and one can continue to experience ego consciousness while just temporarily suppressing the expression of it within the meditation. But one can use the vehicle of pure objectivity of thinking as a means of discovering the possibility of abandoning the intuition of the subject while retaining the concept of the first person. If one does so, then a new reflexive image takes the place of the reflexive image of ego-consciousness. The reflexive image of ego consciousness is "I am the first person". The reflexive image of purely objective consciousness is "The first person inhabits a world of objects. (There is no subject)."

One test for whether this meditation is accomplished is whether or not there is a seesaw of primacy or inclusiveness between the various orders of stories, particularly, the one beginning "The speaker's first memories are of . . ." and "First there was the Big Bang. . . ." When the meditation is accomplished, there is no seesaw of primacy or inclusiveness: one is capable of considering that there is a first person point of view without slipping into thinking, "the first person is me." For there is nothing in the concept of the point of view of a person, or perspectival awareness, which already contains the notion of subjectivity as given in ego consciousness. After all, 'person' has a purely objective connotation here, and even within ego consciousness one can ask whether other persons are subjects while recognizing that in some purely objective sense each person's cognition must represent the world in perspectivized format. Objective stories told by different people, will, of course, be missing different bits of information.

It may be objected that there doesn't appear to be much mysticism in this perspective. Interestingly enough, however, the perspective, if thoroughly digested, produces very powerful results. This is an empirical thesis, and it is not easy to suggest the mysticism of pure objectivity. Certainly, trying the perspective on for size for a few seconds is not likely to have profound psychological effect. On the other hand, judging from the results of informal tests conducted by students in various classes over the years, thorough use of this perspective for a mere day, including social interactions, will often serve to exhibit some of the power of the meditation. (One has to prepare those with whom one will conduct the experiment!)

When the subject stance disappears, not only for brief moments, but on a sustained basis, then a great deal of psychological energy which is stored in the effort to maintain the association of self-experience and first-person experience is released. It is in part the release of this psychic energy which results in the characteristic blissful equanimity of the subject-dissolved, ego-released person. One might describe the perspective by saying that when one occupies the purely objective stance, all events have the spontaneity that for the ego-identified person is associated with events outside one's personal body. For the ego-identified person, a leaf falling from a tree in autumn is a spontaneous occurrence. Of course it is understood to be caused, but the event is experienced as just spontaneously happening. It is not "my doing." On the other hand, when the ego-identified person raises her hand, she experiences the event as "my doing." "I made my hand go up." Thus, the ego-identified experience of first personal actions are not experienced as magic, or spontaneous occurrences. However, when one fully gives up the ego perspective, there is no experience corresponding to "I made it happen." Rather, the experience, "this very person, the first person, made it happen" is on a par with "that tree dropped its leaf," or "that person over there made it happen." Just as the ego-identified Leonard doesn't experience any effortfulness while recognizing that Pat is raising her arm, so, too, the purely objectively identified Leonard doesn't experience any effortfulness while recognizing that Leonard is raising his arm.

The first meditation, then, is to speak, at the deepest level of inner speaking, only of elements of the world of objects.

Second Meditation: Expanding the Subject

In the first meditation, we abandon the experience of subjectivity. In the second meditation, we expand the experience of the subject.

There are two ways we can accomplish this expansion of the subject: first, by expanding the extension of the first person, and, second, by retaining the limited extension of the first person, while expanding the extension of the subject which then is not exclusively identified with the first person.

(A) Expanding the first person: The avatar perspective

Let us return to the ego-perspective. "The world is comprised of many things, and I am one of them, namely, this very person." What is it to be a person? To be a person is to be a conscious rational agent. More elaborately, to be a person is to be an experiencer of qualia, to form beliefs about the world, to have desires, to form plans as to how these desires may be satisfied, to select from these plans a plan for immediate implementation, and to implement the plan selected as a final plan by initiating the bodily movement(s) by which that final plan is inaugurated. Since I identify myself as a being conscious of qualia, and as a rational agent, I identify myself as this conscious rational agent.

Further, in our experience of personhood we experience the coextensionality of three psychophysical systems: the experiential body, the volitional body, and the organic or causal body.

The experiential body is that particular physical system which I experience as present wherever I am whenever I am aware. As motion and change take place, there is one particular physical system the qualia proprioception of which or many parts of which remains more or less constant in my experience throughout the change; and that physical system is the experiential body. As change occurs in experience, there is a continuity of kinesthetic proprioception, for instance. I continue to experience kinesthetically these hands, these feet, the proprioceptive face and torso. Further there is a continuity of sorts in the visual field. There is a nose I look over or down, and the kinesthetic continuity of hands and arms, for instance, is reinforced by an interrupted visual continuity of arms and hands. Less obviously, but equally true, the kinesthetic and visual continuities are supplemented by aural continuities. It is the kinesthetic, and often seen, body I hear rustling against my clothes, however much the main focus of the aural experience is produced by changing, non-constant bodies. Further, there is a physical system which constitutes the perspectival locus of my sensory experience. Not only is there continuity in the object of proprioception and the object of the kinesthetic experience, but also there is continuity in the object from which I appear to see, from which I appear to hear, and from which I appear to experience scent. The visual orientation is to a certain physical body. Wherever that body goes, so goes the perspectival locus of visual experience. And so similarly for aural experience and the experience of smell. These facts are so basic and so deeply entrenched that it takes a moment to recognize that these are contingent facts of continuity. In general, then, the physical system which I am continually experiencing through proprioception or perspectival locus, wherever and whenever experience takes place, we may refer to as the experiential body.

Similarly, the volitional body is that part of the physical world which changes in direct response, as it were, to mental commands or volitions. The physical system which so responds is the musculature. I think (consciously, or subconsciously) "move left hand!" and lo and behold, this particular left hand moves. I think "tilt head forward!" and lo and behold, this particular head tilts forward. Another head does not so respond to my thoughts. Nor does the pen sitting on the desk rise no matter how hard I think, "Rise, pen!" It only rises if I first think, (consciously or subconsciously) "move hand, grasp pen, raise arm!"

The organic, or causal body is that physical system which is to an extraordinarily high degree causily efficacious in there being an experiential self, and a volitional self. So the brain, the heart, the sensory organs, the internal organs, in addition to the nervous system and the musculature are all parts of the causal body.

Now we notice that there is a high degree of empirical content to the organization of each of these bodies and their interrelation. That is, we can conceive of a world in which the extension of the experiential body does not coincide nearly as neatly with the the extension of the volitional body, nor with the causal body as these do in our world. A mind which has access to various limbs which are scattered about, this access being by degrees of proximity of the limbs to each other and the presence or absence of competing minds, say, and which has only a very limited experiential body, would still, conceivably, constitute an effective personal system in some world. But our world doesn't work that way. In our world, it is not the case that several minds share a single set of limbs which are scattered about. Nor is it the case that the brain sits in a protected vat and sends radio signals to some distant set of limbs. A science fiction story could be concocted out of such set-ups too. But our world doesn't work that way. The organs which support the volitional and experiential set-ups are packaged, so to speak, together with the volitional and experiential bodies. The coextensionality is by no means complete, but it is strong. For instance, the glands and the brain are parts of the causal body, obviously, but only indirectly parts of the experiential body and of the volitional body. The bones are obviously parts of the causal body and, in varying ways, of the experiential body, but only indirectly parts of the volitional body. However, the volitional body, which is the musculature, is physically tied, in rather tight ways, to the bones, the brain, the glands, and so on.

In any case, if I am a person, I am a being whose specific functional organization and makeup is contingent. To be this particular person is to be the person whose volitional, experiential, and causal bodies coincide to a very high degree in this one physical system, and for me to be this person is to be a psycho-physical system which happens to work a certain way, and which happens to be connected up a certain way.

But is it not possible to experience myself in a different way than I usually do, without the contingent set up being any different? Consider the causal body, for instance. The causal body is the physical system which happens to support the continued functioning of the succession of experiences and thoughts, and the efficacy of volitional states. It happens to coincide, more or less, with my experiential body and my volitional body. Indeed, it is understood by us why these bodies should coincide. I experience my causal body so that through pain-avoidance and pleasure-pursuit, the causal body is maintained. There are excellent evolutionary or teleological reasons for the coincidence of the experiential body and the causal body. Nonetheless, the causal body is defined only by degrees. The trees with their fruit, the soil with its nutrients, the air with its oxygen, these are all parts of my causal body by degrees.

Is it not possible, therefore, to think of the soil, the fruit trees, the atmosphere, and so on as parts of my causal body? I suggest that it is. The limitations on what one usually experiences as parts of the causal body arise from a complex series of conventions and habits of thought, habits, and conventions with deep empirical underpinnings no doubt, but which are metaphysically weak. There is no compelling metaphysical reason which leads one to say that fruit trees and the atmosphere are not to be regarded as parts of one's causal body, whereas the appendix, small toes, gall bladder, and hair are.

Then there is a meditation in which one strengthens the attitude of self in relation to the fruit trees, atmosphere, soil and so on. And from this meditation it is but a short further step to the meditation in which one strengthens the attitude of self in relation to the whole causally interactive universe, including other agents, as one's causal body. Assuming that one recognizes the whole universe as one's causal body, then one may take it that one's causal body is vastly larger than one's volitional body, and vastly larger than one's experiential body. One's causal body is not coextensive with one's volitional body, and not coextensive with one's experiential body.

> Q: "What am I then?"
> A: "I am a person. My causal body is the whole of the causally interactive universe. My experiential body is as per usually conceived. And my volitional body is as per usually conceived."

Let us explore the consequences of this shift in understanding or attitude one step further. Having come to regard the fruit trees, the soil, the atmosphere as parts of one's causal body, one also comes naturally to recognize that experiencing the fruit trees through sight or touch is the experiencing of parts of one's causal body. Moreover, it is readily understandable, once again, why one should have developed the capacity to see these things: it is evolutionarily advantageous to be able to experience such parts of one's causal body. Thus, having come to regard the fruit trees as parts of one's causal body, one also comes naturally to regard one's experiential body as encompassing the fruit trees. It is true that one doesn't necessarily continue to see fruit trees. One is in an orchard, say, and if one looks in the direction of the fruit trees, one sees parts of one's causal body. But as soon as one looks away, these parts of one's causal body are no longer experienced. So if the experiential body is that physical system which keeps being experienced, the fruit trees should not be regarded as parts of one's experiential body. But then, neither should one's feet. How often is one staring at one's feet? The experiential body given through the kinesthetic sense has good continuity and coextensionality with the conventional volitional and causal bodies. But the visually given experiential body has much less continuity and coextensionality with the conventional volitional and causal bodies. And this feature enables one to extend the visual-experiential body so that one comes to regard the fruit trees as parts of one's visual-experiential body. Constancy of visual experience is not a prerequisite for taking it that one's heels are parts of one's experiential body; and so we need not be constantly seeing fruit trees for them to be regarded as parts of our experiential bodies. Moreover kinesthetic discontinuities would not prevent our toes, say, from being perceived as parts of our experiential body. Assume I lose all kinesthetic sense of my foot. My foot would remain part of my experiential body in virtue of discontinuous touching of my foot by my hand, and of discontinuous seeing of my foot, and, indeed, in virtue of its connectedness to my causal body. By application, we may come to regard the fruit trees as parts of our experiential bodies when we see them because we know that these trees are parts of our causal bodies.

Moreover, for the sake of discussion, let us suppose one were to insist on a high degree of constancy in the experiential body. Then, if one regards, say, the Milky Way galaxy as one's causal body, one is always experiencing the Milky Way when one is experiencing anything. When one sees the fruit trees, one is seeing part of the Milky Way, just as when one sees one's hands, one is seeing some surface of one's hands, and this skin surface is part of one's hands. One sees a part of one's hands and takes it, or understands, that one sees one's hands. Similarly, although the scale is rather different, one sees a part of the Milky Way and one's intentionality can be directed towards the Milky Way, so that one takes it one is seeing the Milky Way when one sees a part of the Milky Way. Since more or less everything one looks at, touches, smells, hears, tastes, is part of the Milky Way, one is always experiencing part of one's causal body, more or less whatever one experiences. And one can strengthen one's intuition that in seeing part of one's causal body one is experiencing one's causal body. Stabilizing this contemplation produces the intuition that one's experiential body is the Milky Way. (See chapter 5 for a more thorough discussion of perceptual intentionality and the part/whole relation.)

What about our volitional bodies? Is there a similar flexibility? If I regard the causally interactive universe as constitutive of my causal body, will it be natural to come to regard the causally interactive universe as constitutive of my volitional body?

The answer here is, No, at least not so long as the volitional body is identified with the physical system that responds to conscious intentions and conscious volitional states or instructions. Consider, if you will, your stomach. Your stomach digests food. The fact that it can do so is not irrelevant to your survival. So your stomach is certainly an important part of your causal body. Yet your stomach is not part of your volitional body. There is nothing that you can consciously will to occur in your stomach, and be routinely successful insofar as its occurrence predictably following the volition is concerned. (Perhaps there are marginal exceptions: you can learn to relax and then feelings of anxiety associated with the stomach, if you have them, can be lessened. But the stomach does not move in direct response to the conscious volitional instructions the way the arms, legs, neck and so on, do.) However, your stomach is an important part of you, the person, and we say, quite properly, I think, you digest your food. You do not normally take it that you give it out somewhere else to be digested for you.

In this sense there is more to personhood than conscious volitional agency. It is the person who blinks even if the blinking is involuntary. It is the person who hears, even though there is no way for the person to shut off the hearing. The hearing is not in the voluntary or volitional control of the person, but it is the person who hears.

There are, then, verbal questions which need to be sorted out. In what immediately follows, I reserve the term *agency* for those aspects of the person which coalesce around conscious volitional acts. Over and above agency, but still parts or aspects of the person, are unconscious volitional acts, (such as automatic subroutines of complex actions, and some compulsive behavior at odds with conscious intentions) and, loosely speaking, doings of the person whether conscious or subconscious, such as the digesting of food, and involuntary blinking. I will call the body to which both conscious and subconscious doings are properly attributed, *the active body*.

Given the rich variety of types of doings, degrees of consciousness, voluntariness, and so on, the position, if anyone were to advance it, that there is a single, neatly defined agent, and that there is a single neatly defined active body, breaks down. If digestion is something that the person does, then why isn't the cooking of foods on a stove a sort of predigestion occurring in one's causal body? Can one not take it that when one is reading the newspaper while one's dinner is in a saucepan cooking on the stove, one is digesting the food in the saucepan on the stove in whatever sense, or a sense similar to the sense in which one is doing the digestion in one's stomach?

It is possible, then, for me to regard every process within my causal body as a subconscious doing of mine which I can bring into consciousness by perceiving it. And if my causal body is the causally interactive universe, then I see myself in the following way: "I am a person. My body is the universe. And at the tactile-experiential center of my body is a particular agent. I am a universal person at whose conscious center is a particular agent, Leonard, whose thoughts I am directly conscious of. The active bodies of other persons are parts of my causal body. However, I am not directly conscious of these other agents' thoughts."

I propose to call someone who identifies personally with the cosmos in this manner, an *avatar*. The avatar identifies with each process which occurs within the universe and regards it "as a subconscious doing of mine," to phrase it from within the perspective of the avatar. To the avatar, the first personal-agent is seen as "the locus of my conscious mind, or my conscious doings." Thus, for the avatar, there is the first person whose body is the active body, which is the whole universe. And there is the first person whose body is the conscious volitional body, which coincides with the first person as delimited in the usual way.

The avatar perspective has both a subject story and an object story. The subject story includes: "I produced the galaxies out of the big bang, I formed planetary systems, I shaped the planet earth, I developed life forms on planet earth, . . . I am doing all the things that are happening now. I am conscious of only one agent's mental events, this very person's."

The object story is the same as any object story, with the usual proviso, of course, that different tellers have different informational gaps.

Comments

An important point to observe is that the seesaw between objective and subjective viewpoints, which occurs in the ego-perspective, is paralleled in the avatar perspective. The reason is that the avatar regards the entire universe as the active body of the first person. The agent is the conscious center of the first person. Then what role is there for other agents, that is, other conscious subjects? The avatar must recognize such other conscious subjects as subconscious parts of the first person, whose consciousness, except as expressed in behavior, of course, is concealed from the conscious awareness, or agentive awareness, of the avatar. Thus, an important asymmetry of ego-consciousness is still present in the avatar perspective. The avatar still seesaws between the objective and subjective perspectives, however much the placement of subject in the object world is different from that of ego-consciousness. The avatar can still wonder, "What is it like to have the subjectivity of another agent, or the subjectivity of a bat?" The avatar can still feel the wonder of the contingency of having this particular agent as a conscious agent rather than another, even though, as the avatar puts it, "I am the entire universe." For the avatar to wonder about the subjectivity of another agent is for the avatar to wonder "What is it like to have the agentive awareness of an agent other than the one I am aware of? What is it like to have the agentive awareness of that agent, Pat, who is a subconscious part of me, but is conscious to herself?" Using 'first agent' to refer to the conscious agentive mind-body, and 'first person' to refer to the conscious and subconscious mind-body, these questions are phrased, "What is it like to have the agentive awareness of an agent other than the first agent? What is it like to have the agentive awareness of that agent, Pat, who is a subconscious part of me, the first person, but is conscious to herself?"

(B) The universal impersonal subject

The second way to expand the subject is to identify the subject as the whole, adopt a realistic perspective concerning the plurality of objects, realize that the whole is not itself a person as far as one is able to tell, and conclude that "Although I am the whole, I am not a person. I include persons." But how does one identify the subject as the whole? We return now to the first meditation on objectivity.

Having discovered the entirely objective perspective, one is in a position to articulate the perspective of the impersonal subject. One way to produce this meditation is the concentration on the consciousness of qualia while maintaining a rigorously objective language. (The quale of a sensation is the qualitative aspect of the experience which is impossible to put into words. The quale of a particular sensation of green is the way that green looks.) The first stage of the meditation, then, involves the recognition, "Leonard is listening to the bird and looking at the trees. There are qualia of sweet warbling sounds. There are qualia of green leaves, shimmering light." Now one asks oneself, whose qualia are these qualia? Normally one answers, "Mine. These qualia are mine." And the referent of 'mine' is understood, normally, as the first person. However, in this meditation one does not take the step of linking the first person with ownership of the qualia. Instead, one adopts a no-personal-ownership view of these qualia:

"These qualia belong to no person. They are out there. The sounds are unowned. The greenness of the leaves belongs to the world. But the greenness is mine. So if the qualia are out there in the world, and belong to the world, and the qualia are the world's, and also the qualia are mine, then I am the world. Qualia are mine, but do not belong to the first person. I define myself as the object to which these qualia attach. What object is that? Why, the universe is the object in question. The quale green belongs to the world. The quale sweet warbling sound belongs to the world. All these qualia belong to me, and the extension of me is the object to which the qualia belong.

I am the world." However, accounting for the perspectival facts surrounding the qualia (the sound is loud if its origin is near the first person, and dim if it is far away, and so on), is difficult under this path to the stance. One must maintain the view that the qualia are mine, not the first person's, as well as the awareness of the facts of perspectivization.

There is, however, another way to arrive at the universal impersonal self mystical stance. In this way one remains absolutely still and imagines that one is paralyzed and will no longer be able to move for the rest of one's life. Deprived of one's volitional body, one's experiential body only has the causal body by which to define itself. But the causal body is not sharply defined and, as we've seen in the course of development of the avatar viewpoint, the entire universe can be regarded as the causal body. Then the entire universe can be regarded as the experiential body. Yet one can also reflect, "I am the entire universe, but the first person is just little old Leonard, a small part of the universe." Once one achieves this point of view, even if the first person has the volitional function restored, the first person can be seen as a mere part of the self, and the self can be seen to be identical with the universe. This avenue, too, then, results in the impersonal universal self viewpoint.

It will, of course, be clear that in this meditation the speaker will also report, with full phenomenological conviction, "I am not a person. The world is not a person, and I am the world." Thus, one maintains the distinction between the subject and the first person that one has implicitly discovered in the first (objectivity) meditation. Only now instead of shrinking to nothing, the extension of the subject has expanded. The second version of the second meditation in final form, then, is expressed by thoughts such as these:

"What am I? I am all this. I am the cosmos. I am the green ball, the forest, the buildings, or at least, they are parts of me. Whatever object enters my consciousness is part of me. The first person is a part of me. All people, and all things are part of me. Every particular thing has the aspect of me. The tree is me. The flower is me. The desk is me. The first person is me. That person over there is me. The first person is no more me than the flower, or that person over there. The first person centers the first person's experience while all things are constitutive of me. All is me. But one person is not another person, one thing is not another thing. The world of objects is untouched. The relationship I have with the first person is not different from the relationship I have with any of the billions of persons on the planet, nor is it different from any extraterrestrial if one exists."

Comments

In the ego perspective there is an asymmetry between the subjective story and the objective story. In the fully objective perspective, there is an object story but no subject story. In the avatar perspective, there is a subject story as well as an object story, and there is an asymmetry, or seesaw between them. In the universal impersonal subject perspective, there is a subject story as well as an object story as well, but here, for the first time in a perspective which has both objective and subjective stories, there is no seesaw, but symmetry. The subject story and the object story are the same story told from two symmetrical points of view, two points of view which run in perfect parallel.

The subject story is the story of how I exploded in a Big Bang fifteen billion years or so ago; how I congealed into galaxies; how part of me became the solar system; (this was not an act of volition: I am not a person, nor do I know anything about myself at all, since only persons have beliefs or knowledge); how a part of me proved suitable for the evolution of life; how I include five billion people on planet earth, one of whom is the author whose first memories concern a certain large fuzzy toy; and so on.

The object story is the story of how there was a Big Bang fifteen billion years ago or so; how matter generated into galaxies; and so on. The object story may also be told as it was told the first way in the first meditation, namely, beginning the chronology from the earliest memories of the author. And the subject story may also be told using the speaker's chronology, but it is not the subject story of ego-consciousness, for it goes as follows: "About forty years ago various parts of me were in a room with a crib and a little boy playing with a large fuzzy toy."

As was the case with the first meditation, there is no feeling that one way of telling the story should have primacy over another. By contrast, in ego-consciousness the two stories seesaw in inclusiveness, and one thinks one ought to be able to find a way to settle the seesaw. In this meditation, as in the first, we can juggle various stories, and there is the first person point of view (which can be told in an object version and a subject version, each parallel to the other), but there is no feeling of pressure to stop juggling, or, for that matter, to start. Moreover, if Leonard wonders what it is like to be a bat, and so does Pat, neither of them have special status by being identified as me or the subject. I include both Leonard and Pat. The placement of the subject does not create imbalance.

It may be objected that it is a person who judges "I am not the first person," and such a judgment seems analytically false. But to object in this way is to rule out a priori the very phenomenological possibility at issue. A speculation for comparison sake may be of use. Suppose my bodily parts other than my brain are exchanged every hour. Then I might no longer regard any limbs as parts of me. I might take it that they were no more parts of me than my clothes are parts of me. Further, I might distinguish my volitional body from myself. My volitional body would be bigger than me, just as, for most people, "my family includes more than me" is true. A sort of inverse holds for the universal impersonal self mystic, namely, "I am more than the first person." Just as a person can judge "My family includes more than me," so a universal impersonal self mystic can begin with the no-self view of the first person, develop a particular impersonal self notion, identifying self as the universe, and judge that "I am more than the first person, hence I am not the first person." Clearly this requires that the concept of self be at least ambiguous, for 'self' is at least sometimes synonymous with 'the first person,' and 'self' sometimes is not restricted to 'the first person.' Linguistic evidence that it need not be true that 'self' exclusively means the first person is the presence of the 'self' concept in words such as 'itself.' Consider: "The chair was in the room all by itself." Obviously, the self of the chair is not anyone's first person. And that self is not phenomenologically identical to the first person is evidenced by the phenomenology of no-self experience. For in that perspective there is no subjectivity or self experience, but there is first person experience. In avatar phenomenology, the self is the first person, but the first person is identified with the universe, and the conscious agent is a mere part of the first person. In universal impersonal self phenomenology, for the first time, we assign extensional identity to the self, and extensional identity to the first person, but there is an extensional distinction between the self and the first person. The entity identified as the referent of the term 'self' is distinct from the entity identified as the referent of the term 'first person.' It is this extensional distinction which makes the universal impersonal self mysticism the most challenging and difficult of the three. In the first meditation, one forgets about self. In the second meditation, one ends up with a very large personal self. In the universal impersonal self meditation one ends up with a very large self which is not itself a person, though it includes all persons.

The discipline in this meditation is to experience the cosmos as self, and not merely conceptualize this. This meditation is to experience everything in the cosmos as having the aspect of me, the aspect of the subject while retaining the ordinary notion of the first person. This is not a matter of mere conceptualization, and may need to be supported by assiduous training.

Third Meditation: Attending to the Whole

So far we have left the conventional picture of the objective world unaffected by our meditations. We have, instead, been varying our view of the presence of the subject. We began holding the identification of the subject with the first person. For our first meditation, we let subjectivity be silent, and let our thoughts concern themselves only with objects. Then we articulated two paths towards identifying the self with the world: the expansion of the first person via the expansion of the understanding of the causal body, and so forth. And the experience of the world as me, as the subject that had been unexpressed in the first meditation of complete objectivity.

If we are to explore the flexibility of the object world in whatever way corresponds to the flexibility of the subject that we have now discovered, we should begin by coming back to the first meditation wherein the subject is unmentionable and we are explicitly dealing in our thoughts only with objects.

"This person is one person among many persons and many things," was the touchstone of this meditation. Having returned to the first meditation, we can now focus on the nature of our experience of objects. One moves forward to the next meditation by attending to the presence of the Whole: One attends to "this and this and this" and so on, and one supplies an object interpretation of "this and this and this" such that "this is this" statements are always true. What does this mean?

When I ask, "Is this this?" I understand that each 'this' has a referent, and I am inquiring into the identity or non-identity of the referent of the first 'this' and the referent of the second 'this.' The question is answered affirmatively when both uses of 'this' have the same referent; negatively when they do not. Naturally there are various conventions that we may use in helping communicate the referents involved. Suppose that we not only use 'this' but also point with a finger in a certain direction. Under the usual convention, the object intended is the smallest natural kind or conventionally defined object whose center is in the first visually given object in a direct line emanating away from the finger being pointed. But when one is asking the question oneself, one can be quite free with the usual conventions, as there is nothing to the context other than what one wants there to be. And as long as one is explicit about it, one can change conventions, and use new conventions of reference in situations in which one is communicating with another. Accordingly, one can ask whether a convention of reference might be adopted such that "Is this this?" questions will always be answered "Yes." A moment's reflection will convince one that such a convention is available, since the Whole is a referent that will make any such statements true. Then the new convention to be adopted is that 'this' refers to the largest possible object any part of which is in a direct line from the finger emanating away from the body. Under this convention, 'this' accompanied by any act of pointing always refers to the Whole. For those philosophers, for example, Peter Geach, who will insist that the Whole is not an object, or at least not identifiable, since it does not come under a sortal, there being no sortal "a whole," it will suffice to attend to this as our cosmos; our cosmos is everything since the Big Bang on. 'This' can now be interpreted to mean our cosmos, under which interpretation, "Is this this?" where each use of 'this' is accompanied by an act of pointing in whatever direction, will always be answered, "Yes." We now have the basis for the meditation we want. The cognitive instruction is to use only objective reference, and to do nothing but ask and answer, "Is this this?" questions under the novel convention.

Thus, one's meditation consists in the following sorts of reflections: "Is this, this? Yes. This is this. Is this this? Yes, this is this. And this is this, and this is this. And this is this, which is also this. This is the Whole. The Whole is here. Here is the entire cosmos. It is still here, and this is still it. Here it is, same thing. Yes, it's still here. What's this (pointing in one direction)? Why, it's this (pointing in another direction)."

Comments

Our meditation here turns one into a bit of an idiot, but it is a very pleasant meditation to dwell in. How much of the object story can be told within this meditation? Consider descriptions of the present properties of this. One would like to say something like, "The Whole is green here, and red there, and noisy from that direction," or perhaps, "The cosmos big-banged long ago, and is deskifying here and personifying here and here and here, and flowering here, and is likely to continue as it was," and so on. But even when one locates "here" as opposed to "there," and one has to do so if one is to understand "green here," one has, it would seem, attended to the Whole as a composite, for there is the part of the Whole which is here, and the other part which is there. And therefore one has attended, it would seem, however briefly, to the Whole as comprising parts. And therefore one has attended, however briefly, to individuals other than the individual which makes "this is this and this is this" true.

It is possible to respond to this criticism by insisting that so long as the mind of the mystic is focused completely on the content of the propositions asserted, no awareness of the Whole as having parts need arise. The mystic, then, is psychologically capable of articulating descriptions such as "This is green here, and blue there," without having to be aware of the Whole as being composite, just as one is psychologically capable of thinking of a child's red ball, which has a green stripe around an equatorial section, as a ball that is mostly red and striped green, without thinking of the ball as having three parts, two of which are red on the surface, and one of which is green on the surface.

If one does not accept that it is psychologically possible to maintain such pure focus on the Whole as the only object and still make attributions to the Whole, then at least we ought to acknowledge the logical intelligibility of the mystical expressions themselves. There is nothing logically infelicitous about a series of predications, each of which has the same (grammatical) subject. The degree to which the mystic is in fact capable of training herself in focused concentration on the referent of that (grammatical) subject is a purely empirical matter. A fortiori, there is nothing logically infelicitous about a series of expressions of object reidentifications each of which has the same (grammatical) subject. Also, the object reidentifications, "This is this. And it is this. And it is this," involve no qualitative predication. Consequently, there is no drift towards multiplicity through the construction of predicate polarities with their consequent various referents to bear the different predicates. Then the object reidentifications, "This is this. And it is this. And it is this," are psychologically easier to maintain without awareness of multiplicity creeping into one's consciousness. Further, there is the mathematical notion of the limit based upon which an account of the possibilities of the monist state of mind might be given. The limit of the practice of attending to only the single, entirely comprehensive object is the monist state of mind. Even if the monist state of mind is not entirely achievable, one can keep approaching that state of mind, much in the way an infinite convergent series approaches its limit.

And a fortiori again, one can be aware of a whole as comprising parts; one holds a complex image of the world all the time. In this case, one can tell far more of the object story. It goes "The cosmos exploded with tremendous force; then it cooled off; then it galaxified; then it alived here; then it personified; then it culturated," and so on.

There is, however, as we'll see again in the next chapter, a very real question as to whether any causal story can be told with only the cosmos as the grammatical subject of the sentence. And the difficulty becomes even more severe when one tries to describe interpersonal agency where the only object is the cosmos. However, to say that there is comparatively little language that is expressive of this meditation, or that language expressive of this meditation cannot describe agent activities, is not to say that one who adopts this meditation cannot speak. One can acquire a dominant object image other than that of multiplicity and still use language that is expressive of some other standpoint. (The time that it takes to be able to do this and not slip into ego consciousness or the multiplicity of the silent subject is indicative of the depth of one's habits of thought concerning the world of many objects).

Of course, our subject is still silent, or negated, and so there is no subject story to tell here. "This is this. And it is not me," are the twin foundational truths of this meditation. These foundational truths are elaborated by varying degrees of predication, depending on the specifics of the meditation, and the psychological capacity of the meditator to retain focus on the Whole while indulging in predication.

Finally, we want to observe that rendering intelligible mystical states in this way, while not entirely independent of one's metaphysical views, is not in and of itself a metaphysical enterprise. The explication whereby we rendered intelligible Parmenidean, Spinozistic, or more generally, monistic mysticism, does not strictly imply Pamenidean, Spinozistic, or, more generally, monistic metaphysics. The difference between a phenomenological and a metaphysical explication of a mystical pronouncement is fundamental. In order to show that mystical experience and descriptions of them do not violate logical constraints, it suffices to present a logically coherent phenomenological explication. To do so, however, is not to present a defense of the corresponding metaphysical schema.

This point was undoubtedly clear enough with the subject-altered mysticisms already treated, but since it is easily blurred with the object-altered mystical expressions, we explicitly treat the distinction here.

Suppose one accomplishes the meditation on objectivity. Then one's internal language of thought abandons references to the self. One says, "The first person would like the salt to be passed; the first person is hungry," and so on. Does this imply that there is no self? No, no more than forgetting about some unpleasant experience implies that the unpleasant experience never took place, or no more than forgetting about some unpleasant person implies that the unpleasant person does not exist.

Suppose one accomplishes the meditation on expanded subjectivity, either through expanding the first person and recognizing the universe as the active body, or by maintaining the limited first person and expanding the impersonal subject so that the impersonal subject is identified as the cosmos. Does this imply that there is an ultimate constituent of the cosmos, a substantial universal self? No, no more than identifying the experiences, beliefs, desires, plans, volitions, memories, actions, and bodily parts of the ordinarily constructed first person across time so as to have a conception of a single person across time implies that there is an ultimate constituent of the cosmos which is the substantial self. Rather, it may be that the reidentifications are arbitrary in some sense, or convenient merely, or conventional, and do not reflect fundamental metaphysical features of the universe .

So too, regardless of the degree to which a mystic is capable of abandoning thoughts of multiplicity, the mystic is not committed to a monistic metaphysic in order to render intelligible the mystical states of mind which are exclusively focused on the Whole. For it to be possible for the mystic to concentrate on the cosmos, or the Whole, it is necessary to render intelligible such notions as 'the cosmos' or the Whole. But the monistic metaphysics, which asserts that there is only one object, is not implied by the mystical phenomenology of awareness focused on the Whole. In the next chapter, we will further explicate this point.

Fourth Meditation: The Deconstructed Object

In the fourth meditation, one deconstructs any possible world of objects in the following way: one attends to "this and this and this" where 'this' is what is given in each occasion, as before, only now one attempts to supply an object interpretation of 'this and this and this' such that "this is this" statements would never be true. One adopts a convention of sentential referencing such that "this is this" is always false. The convention trades on the fact that in each question of the form, "Is this this?" or in each statement asserting "This is this" there are two uses of 'this,' each, as before, accompanied by an act of pointing. The convention adopted to launch the fourth meditation is to be governed by the rule that the reference of the first use of 'this' will always be the largest object in the line of pointing, if it refers at all; the reference of the second use of 'this' will always be the smallest object in the line of pointing, if it refers at all. Try to adopt this rule, and think of nothing but whether this is this or not under that convention. You will find that eventually, no use of 'this' succeeds in referring at all. Eventually, one has deconstructed the world of objects. The image of the world that one arrives at through such a meditation may be referred to, not too misleadingly one hopes, as the image of nothingness or zero object.

Thus: "This is not this; nor is it this; nor is this, this; nor is this, this."

Comments

There is precious little other language expressive of this standpoint than "this is not this." However, it needs to be stated that living within a standpoint does not require adoption of the only language that is expressive of the standpoint. If one is sufficiently habituated in one's consciousness to the deconstructed world, one can automatically, perhaps, interact in the world using the language of ego consciousness, but be consciously experiencing within the dominant framework of "no object." Second, we should also observe that the more nominalistically inclined will hold that it is possible to use predicates without adding ontological commitments. Then language which is grammatically subjectless and accomplishes predicate placing only may be consistent with objectless mysticism. ". . . green here; raining; blue there," may, then, be possible. In other words, pure particular-free feature-placement languages such as P. F. Strawson considered in *Individuals* (and rejected as inadequate for general purposes) might be constructed and would presumably be capable of expressing some facts about the world. As we shall see again in the next chapter, the degree of success one might have along these lines is not clear.

As with the third meditation, the fourth meditation is free of any subjective reference. "This is not this; and there is no me anywhere" are the two fundamental judgments of this form of mysticism.

Also, the phenomenology of objectlessness does not imply that there are no fundamental or ultimate substantial constituents of reality. What we have done is to have rendered intelligible a psychological practice in which consciousness is focused or maintained in such a way that nothing is ever sufficiently reidentified in order to allow for any conceptions of objects to survive. If the mystic is right, it is possible to train oneself in this form of awareness to a remarkable extent, and there is a great bliss which accompanies such training. But, once again, to be psychologically capable of training oneself to forget all about objects does not imply that there are no objects, any more than being capable of forgetting about an unpleasant individual implies that that individual never existed.

The purpose of these meditations

These four meditations help to clarify the structure of the phenomenology (but not the metaphysics) of the subject-object relation. The first meditation was on the objective world. When one meditates on the objective world what is clarified is the non-necessity, indeed, the ludicrousness, as it appears from the achieved meditation, of identifying the subject with the first person. The objectivity meditation drops away the subjective order in favor of the objective order. "I am a person" is replaced by "This is a person." The subject entirely disappears. So the first meditation clarifies the possibility of universal negation of subject identification with any object.

The second meditation in its first form shows us how to expand our extensional identification of the first person. The second meditation in its second form shows us how to experience and articulate qualia as self or the universe as self, and use such reflections together with the first meditation's objectivity in regard to the first person to result in an articulation of the impersonal universal self. Just as we can universally negate the identity of the subject with any object, we can universally affirm the identity of the subject with the world.

Following our meditations on objectivity and the two main paths to expanded subjectivity, each of which altered subject placement, we adopted the meditation on the expanded object, and, finally, on the contracted object. We found that within these latter two meditations, there are only limited linguistic expressions of the dominant images.

The Seven Primary Images Of The World

We are now in a position to grasp the general structure of the relationship of subject and object, and the seven phenomenological images of the world vis à vis subject-object placement, which a person can bring to the foreground of consciousness. I should perhaps mention that this section is rather technical and of special interest to those seeking a thorough and precise classification of the phenomenology of the subject-object relations. Understanding the classification procedure, and indeed, the classification system as a whole, is not essential for what follows afterwards.

Our meditations have been based on the following facts: The subject may be (1) universalized, that is, identified with whatever is, as in the expanded subject meditations; (2) seen as having an extension, but not a universal extension, in which case the subject is extensionally identified with some, but not all, of what there is, as in ego-consciousness; (3) negated or denied or dissolved or cancelled, as in the meditation exclusively on the objective world. And the object world may be seen (1) as consisting of a single simple object, as in the meditation on the Whole or the cosmos; (2) as a whole comprised of a plurality of objects, as in ego consciousness, for instance, but also in the other two (or three, depending how you count them) forms of altered self-placement (cancelled subject meditating on the objective world, and expanded subject in both forms) so far considered; and (3) as nonexistent, as in the fourth meditation on the deconstructed object world. Thus:

Subject	*Object*
1a expanded subject	1b one simple object
2a partial subject	2b many objects
3a contracted subject	3b deconstructed object

Further, we can characterize the functioning of consciousness of subject and object in terms of judgments of subject and object identity. "I am" and "I am not" are subject identity judgments. "This is this" and "This is not this" are object identity judgments. Thus:

Type	*Affirmative*	*Negative*
Subject identity:	I am this	I am not this
	(The subject is this)	(The subject is not this)
Object identity:	This is this	This is not this

In the above extract, each judgment in parenthesis is synonymous with the judgment directly above it. Of course each such judgment requires a context or a convention of reference for an interpretation to be possible.

Further, there are three types of sequences of each type of judgment:

1. All affirmative judgments
2. Mixed affirmative and negative judgments
3. All negative judgments

Sequences are atemporal composites, each composite forming a possible fundamental image of experience. For example, a composite formed of mixed affirmative and negative identity judgments both of subject and object might yield an image of many objects of which one is me: "This person is me. This person is not this table. This cup is not this table . . . and so on."

Combining subject sequence type #1 (found implicit in 1a, above) with each of the three types of object sequence, then subject sequence type #2 with each of the three types of object sequence, and finally subject sequence type #3 with each of the three types of object sequence, we derive nine potential fundamental images of What Is. These are (in the order just described):

A1: I am everything; and there is only one object.

A2: I am everything; and there are many objects.

A3: I am everything; and there is no object.

B1: There is some me and there is some not me; and there is only one object.

B2: There is some me and there is some not me; and there are many objects.

B3: There is some me, and there is some not me; and there is no object.

C1: There is no me; and there is only one object.

C2: There is no me; and there are many objects.

C3: There is no me; and there is no object.

However, B1 and B3 are unintelligible, since the division of a world into that object which is the subject and that object which is not the subject presupposes object plurality. This leaves seven primary possible fundamental images of experience: A1, A2, A3, B2, C1, C2, C3.

Comments on the seven perspectives

There is no way both to carry on worldly functions and also use a linguistic vehicle expressive of A1, A3, C1, and C3 to refer to these functions, since language used for ordinary worldly purposes must be capable of referring to a multiplicity of objects. However, it does not follow from this that the states of mind of A1, A3, C1, and C3 are wholly unintelligible, or that there is any violation of the laws of logic involved in describing the intentionality of these states. Nor does one have to be a mystic to appreciate this. The precise description of the state of consciousness of one who has wholly focused consciousness within any of these four states is as subject to correction and analysis by the non-mystic metaphysician as is any state of mind. The logically possible still governs the descriptions involved. And the input of the metaphysician we will concern ourselves with in the next chapter. Here we want to remember that rendering these states generally intelligible depends on reflecting on how consciousness is always selective. One who is in the middle of performing *Swan Lake* before an audience of thousands, and in a good state of flowing concentration, has his or her consciousness filled with the steps of the ballet and their expressive content, and the sensory experience of the event. It is overwhelmingly difficult, if not impossible, for someone who is driving a car for the first time to be simultaneously learning how to solve quadratic equations. The conscious mind must always be filled with some matters, and blocking out or forgetting other matters. There is, then, an issue of logical coherence in the vocabulary of the reports of the experiences. Distinct from this issue is the metaphysical issue: Do these selective directions for experience give grounds to form various metaphysical judgments? The psychological question is the degree of one-pointedness one can achieve in respect to these meditations. The metaphysical issue is the question of the correct description of the mental contents of them in terms which accurately reflect what fundamentally exists.

In the case of the subject, then, the three types of sequences of judgments (sequences in which the subject is always affirmed; sequences in which there are mixed affirmations and negations of subject in judgments; and sequences in which the subject in judgment is always negated) are practical instruments of meditation together with carrying on worldly functions and being capable of expressing the perspective at the same time in language. The sequences of universally affirmed object judgments; sequences with mixed affirmative and negative object judgments; and sequences with universally negated object judgments, are also practical instruments of meditation. But only in the cases in which there are mixed affirmative and negative object judgments (A2 and C2) can one simultaneously carry on worldly business, and express one's worldly business, and, simultaneously, how things appear from the mystical perspective, in language.

Another way to put it is to note that A2 and C2 are two forms of extrovertive mystical experience, and A1, A3, C1, C3, are four forms of introvertive mystical experience. There are still some important metaphysico-logical questions which we'll be looking at with regard to A1, A3, C1, and C3, in the next chapter. But it is strikingly clear that at least two powerfully mystical states, A2 and C2, ("I am the cosmos," and "There is no me") have been explicated in such a way as to do no violence to the laws of logic. Wainwright's anticipation that "I cease to exist and yet continue to exist" will be explained as stating that the empirical ego ceases to exist, and yet the pure or true self, or Atman, *nous, purusa*, exists, has been, in a sense, fulfilled. However the Atman, *nous, purusa* or True Self is usually regarded as Transcendental in some strong sense, and is so regarded by Wainwright, and thus in need of a good bit of metaphysical explication. Whereas what I am in A2 is simply the cosmos or, if one wants to go a little further, the meriated Whole.

B2, of course, is ego-consciousness. But we should note that it would be more accurate to say B2 includes ego-consciousness, as the formulation of B2 allows for John to experience self to be Mary, while recognizing that the first person is John, and judge that John is not me. This might be John's dominant image. (A weird one no doubt, even in the context of the expected weirdness of mysticism, but Tantric practices in which the disciple imitates the mouth movements and gestures of the teacher for hours and hours on end could produce this state: the disciple still feeds the disciple at mealtime during periods which the disciple is, in other respects, imitating the teacher.)

It does follow, then, that we can characterize the nature of subjectivity and objectivity in general terms in such a way as to admit the usual ego-based subjectivity as a special case. The structure of subject-object judgments provides for seven fundamental types of states of consciousness. The psychological aspect of the discipline of meditation is training in the ability to bring to the foreground each of the six primary non-ego conscious, or non-ego based, states of consciousness.

It should also be noted that the psychophysical aspect is distinct from the practical wisdom aspect, the latter of which is the training in the appropriate use of the six primary non ego-conscious states, and the appropriate use of expressive means (language and so on) of all seven states of consciousness in everyday circumstances.

This is by no means, then, a preferential account in which one of the seven states is to be singled out as being "best" or "closest to enlightenment" or most descriptive of "ultimate reality." The point is, rather, that the philosopher would do well to become familiar with these seven ways of calling into the foreground the relation of subject identity and object identity. Without such familiarity, one is stuck on a single version, ego-consciousness, and one does not experience the structure and functioning of subjectivity and objectivity vis à vis consciousness in a clear way. At the same time, there may be some purposes for which some of the seven states or images are preferable to others. For example, as mentioned, there are two main mystical, or non-ego perspectives in which the object world is conceived as a plurality. These perspectives consequently can be fully expressed in a language suitable for carrying on worldly business. One could carry on a court case and express everything mystically without violating the laws of logic. On the other hand, there are four non-ego perspectives which may not be amenable to full linguistic expression of worldly activities in the light of the mystical state. These four are, however, appropriate vehicles for meditation in stillness. When you are driving your car, it helps to bring to the foreground of consciousness an image of the object world in which there is a plurality of objects!

Are the six mystical states mutually consistent?

When raising the question of the intelligibility and logical possibility of mystical experience, we must distinguish between the following four distinct questions:

1. Does the description of the mystical state involve a logical or metaphysical contradiction, incoherency, or infelicity?

2. Is the one who describes the mystical state also making a metaphysical claim?

3. Given that mystics sometimes take themselves to be making a metaphysical claim while providing a description of the experience, are the various mystical descriptions consistent with each other?

4. Does mystical experience provide prima facie evidence for the truth of mystical metaphysical claim?

In this chapter, I have been concerned almost entirely with question 1. In the next chapter, I will be concerned with 2, 3, and 4. Here I have been concerned to provide the basis for a typology of mystical phenomenology in which each of the various mystical states can be rendered internally consistent. Thus, the mystic says, "I am the cosmos" and is thereby endorsing a certain form of extensional self-identification. The mystic's self-identification fails to satisfy the most minimal conditions of intelligibility if the very phenomenology is incoherent. The description of incoherent mystical experience would be analogous to the following description of an experience: "Suddenly I saw a tetrahedronal sphere floating in front of me." If someone says, "I saw a snake on the ground before me," we understand what is being said. We find it intelligible. The report of a floating spherical tetrahedron we do not find intelligible. The very phenomenology is uninterpretable. In this chapter, I hope to have shown that some difficult descriptions can be rendered intelligible in the phenomenological sense. But for "I am the cosmos," "There is no me," "There is only the One," and "There is nothing" to be rendered intelligible in this phenomenological sense does not imply that the mystic in asserting one of these statements is indeed making a metaphysical claim.

Summary

I have had three principal goals in this chapter. First, I have tried to make intelligible the claims of the mystical enlightenment project that appear to violate the principle of non-contradiction.

Second, I have tried to provide instructions for cognitive practice which are clear and followable. (Even if the contradictions can be theoretically removed, it won't help if the only instruction one has from the mystic is to "dissolve into emptiness.") I take it that, of the key cognitive meditation practices I have described, those which allow for a multiplicitous object picture are perspicuously clear and easily followable. The intelligibility of the others may depend on some degree of familiarity with the first sort.

Third, I have tried to hint at the import of mysticism and meditation for the practitioner of philosophy of mind. The mystic may be claiming that, by engaging in these meditations, the basis whereby one experiences or tends to experience the subject as the first person clarifies. One comes to see how the ego construct is the result of a particular conception of the object world into which a particular conception of the extension of the subject has been fitted or placed. However, the subject can be identified as the universe, as a stone, or a flower as easily as it can be identified as the first person.

If one has trouble understanding how the self can be identified with an object other than the first person, it is because one is unfamiliar with a range of standpoints. The ego-standpoint is the natural result of the habituation that occurs through the formation of ego consciousness from birth to the age of three or so. But it is not necessary to be stuck on that standpoint. To unpack the structure of ego, one needs to de-habituate the image which preserves it, and this one does through such practices as attending to the Whole, deconstructing any possible object world, attending to objects as objects, expanding the extension of the first person, and articulating the subject as qualia.

Taking these three points into consideration, then, the overall structure of mysticism and meditation practice should be clear. "I am the cosmos" is not a logical contradiction, nor does it imply one, because the subject need not be identified with the first person. Indeed this is the very content of the assertion: "I am not the first person! I am the cosmos." But the experience corresponding to this new form of identification eludes people until they understand the flexibility of subject extensional identification. And people tend not to understand this flexibility through philosophical analysis alone, but through acquiring it in their experience.

Five

Mysticism, Metaphysics,
and the Philosophy of Mind

I've been concerned, thus far, to show that:

1. Genial mysticism, which advocates the cultivation of blissful awareness of Ultimacy in everyday living, plays a fundamental role in value theory, since the realization such cultivation produces is the greatest monadic good.

2. Esoteric expressions of mysticism can be rendered phenomenologically intelligible within the most rigorous standards of logical and linguistic analysis.

At the outset of the project, however, I announced as a goal the task of showing not only the importance of mysticism for ethics, but also the importance of mysticism for our understanding of the cosmos. In chapter four, I tried both to eliminate the objection that the puzzling mystical expressions are unintelligible, and also to make accessible the practices which the mystic links with the achievement of the mystical goal. If I have succeeded, I have hinted at the value of doctrinal mysticism for the metaphysician. In this chapter, I wish to draw out these hints more fully, show the importance of mysticism and meditation practice to the achievement of the aims of the philosopher, not only qua monadic individual, but also qua metaphysician and qua philosopher of mind. Simultaneously, I will be concerned to show the limits of the relevance of mystical experience to metaphysical inquiry. According to the view to be sketched here, although mystical experience of the rather esoteric sorts can be rendered intelligible without doing violence to the laws of logic, the value of mystical experience as *empirical evidence* for particular mystical metaphysical views is extremely limited indeed.

I.

We begin by sketching in general terms the relationship between mystical experience and mystical metaphysics. Each of the six mystical approaches to the world which was delineated in chapter four can be understood in a corresponding metaphysical manner. That is, given each of the six mystical approaches to the world, there is a metaphysical view which corresponds to it. The six mystical approaches to the world are captured in these summary images:

A1: I am everything; and there is only one object.
A2: I am everything; and there are many objects.
A3: I am everything; and there is no object.
C1: There is no me; and there is only one object.
C2: There is no me; and there are many objects.
C3: There is no me; and there is no object.

The corresponding metaphysical views are:

A1': There is only one object, ultimately, and there is an ultimate, or substantial self.
A2': Every object is a part of the unique substantial self, and there are, ultimately, many objects.
A3': There is a unique substantial self, but no object ultimately exists.
C1': There is no substantial self, and ultimately, there is only one object.
C2': There is no substantial self, and, ultimately, there are many objects.
C3': There is no substantial self, and, ultimately, there are no objects.

The difference between the summary image and the metaphysical assertion is that whereas the report of how the world looks from the mystical standpoint expresses the state of mind of the mystic, or shows how the mind of the mystic is filled with an image or a picture of what is, the metaphysical assertion holds that a particular image corresponds to what is ultimately or finally true about the fundamental constituents of reality. Another way to express the difference is to note that the summary images can be held one after another without implying any logical inconsistency, whereas if one of the mystical metaphysical assertions is correct, then the others are incorrect. The phenomenalistic expression presents appearances as appearances. The metaphysical expression makes assertions about the ultimate constituents of the world.

"What, ultimately, is there?" asks the metaphysician. Some answer, "Matter in motion only." Others answer, "Material and immaterial substances." Still others say, "Many things of many sorts: impersonal material objects, persons, thoughts, actions, relations, properties, truths, numbers, other conceptual entities, and so on." Still others say, "There is only one thing, which manifests both as material and as mental." Still others (the solipsists) say, "There is only one thing, me." Others again say, "There is only one thing, the One." And, finally, according to the most rarefied metaphysicians, "Nothing whatever exists."

Now from the fact that I forgot my wallet, you are not entitled to conclude that my wallet does not exist. If the no-self mystic forgets about the self, we are not entitled to conclude that the mystic has no self. Nor, therefore, is the phenomenological no-self mystic committed to the metaphysical view that there is no substantial self.

The matter is clear with regard to that case, it might be responded, but how can it be, it might be further asked, that when the mystic says, "There is *only* the One," she is not making a claim, a claim, moreover, subject to refutation by noting, "There must be more than the One, because there are flowers and stones, and a flower is not a stone, and so there are several things?"

The answer can be given by analogy. Suppose I am focusing my consciousness on the view from the mountaintop on which I'm standing. The colors of the sunset and the fields below fill my consciousness. Mightn't I say, "There are *only* the colors of the sunset and shapes of the furrowed fields below?" By this I mean that my consciousness is filled with this and nothing else. Of course subconsciously I am able to operate with many more concepts, and am operating with many more concepts. Similarly, the mystic's consciousness may be filled with the One, and the mystic is aware only of the One, and in this sense, it may be true for the mystic to say, "There is *only* the One." This assertion is expressive of a one-pointed state of consciousness in which all else but the comprehensive object, or the cosmos, or the Whole, is placed into subconsciousness. But sweeping multiplicity under the mental carpet does not obliterate the many, if many things ultimately exist. The analysis of chapter four leaves untouched the gulf between mystical phenomenology and mystical metaphysics. The mystical phenomenologies of chapter four do not commit the mystics to the corresponding mystical metaphysics.

This does not, however, imply that the practices of no-self mysticism, and other forms of mystical meditation, have no value for metaphysics and the philosophy of mind. No-self mysticism, understood phenomenalistically, can be valuable for the philosopher puzzled about personal identity, self-placement and the ego stance. Similarly, the availability of the universal-self mystical standpoint, the mystical standpoint directed toward the One, and the standpoint released from object conception, encourages the metaphysician in practices which are useful. The metaphysician and philosopher of mind ought to have a vigorous interest in the purported phenomenologies for obvious reasons. These are precisely the sort of phenomenology which informs one's theory of personal identity, for example, whether there is a substantial self or not, one's theory of the relation between subjective and objective perspectives, their implications for moral rationality and so on. To cite one of many possible examples, many of Derek Parfit's arguments in *Reasons And Persons* depend upon the availability of the entirely objective, no-self perspective. In the first instance, it is the phenomenology of the perspective which makes possible the inquiries into moral rationality and what matters about personhood which animate the book. It would also be worth investigating the ways in which moral concepts might be challenged not only by the seesaw between the phenomena of ego-based subjectivity and complete objectivity, but also by the seesaw between, say, the phenomena of complete objectivity and avatar-based subjectivity. Metaphysical commitments are not immediately generated, but moral and metaphysical questions are immediately raised.

Further, when no-self mysticism is complemented by universal-self mysticism, of either avatar, or impersonal type, not only is the bliss strengthened, according to the mystic, (in accordance with the Law of Mystical Bliss: mystical bliss is directly proportional to the difficulty of acquiring the perspective), but also the understanding of the self concept is deepened. To the extent that one comes to recognize the indefinite extension of the indexical term 'self,' one will not be tempted by a simplistic acceptance of the concept of the substantial self.

Plainly, making the discoveries, if these discoveries are there for the making, that I can take myself, personally, to be the cosmos, and all the events as my conscious or subconscious doings, and that I can take myself to be the impersonal cosmos which contains as proper parts the first person and multitudinous persons besides, is of signal importance in the philosophy of personal identity. If it is indeed a confusion to take the judgment "I am this very person, a part, and not the whole," as a metaphysical or analytic necessity, when it is a psychologically supported judgment which is in any case only sometimes true, we can see that the practice of universal-self mysticism is of fundamental interest for those, like Parfit and Nagel, who wish to understand fully the nature of subject-object placement, and the practical empirical bounds of possible extensional identifications.

Are mystics metaphysicians?

Since James' analysis, it has been standard to emphasize the alleged noetic content of mystical experience, and hence to hold that mystics in their descriptions of mystical experience are simultaneously being metaphysicians. I hope that one of the principal benefits of the analysis of chapter four is the way it facilitates separation out of mystical experience and expression of this experience, on the one hand, from mystical metaphysics on the other hand. The analysis presented here may be contrasted in important respects with that of Steven Katz and Wayne Proudfoot. Katz and Proudfoot, in somewhat different ways, emphasize that mystical experience comes conceptualized as it were, and the conceptualizations are supplied by the traditional context of the mystic. However, they both regard the mystic as taking it that the conceptualizations are to be understood as implying metaphysical realities (Katz, pp. 49, 50; Proudfoot pp. 136-148). They don't realize that the conceptualized descriptions may be presented phenomenologically, and not metaphysically, by the mystics themselves. Once we can see clearly how to construct a typology of mystical phenomenology which is free to a very large degree, if not entirely free, of the corresponding metaphysical commitments, we can both justify mystical practice for its central role in value theory, and also inquire properly into the relation between mystical phenomenology and mystical metaphysics.

For instance, it might be assumed that some one of the avatar stance, the no-self stance, and the impersonal-self stance, or any of the other mystical stances, is in some sense to be preferred on metaphysical grounds to the ego-based conscious stance. Certainly, there are many Buddhist systems, for instance, in which the release from the ego is suggested to be a release from ignorance and delusion. However, there are two ways to take such suggestions. One is to hold that the metaphysical perspectives of ego-released stances are preferable, more accurate, or in some sense truer than that of the ego-stance. The second is to hold that the release from delusion is only a release from the delusion of thinking that the ego-stance is fixed as the only possible stance. The analysis presented thus far requires only the latter view. Indeed, the very fact that there are universal-self and no-self paths to release from the ego stance tends to support the view that it is the flexibility which is to be desired, and not that the perspective revealed under one or the other ego-released stance is the *true picture*. Once again, it should be emphasized that so far we are only entitled to support the mystic's preference for the ego-released stances, comparing any one of them with the ego-stance, on account of an alleged empirical connection between release from the ego-stance and the heightening of the individual's capacity to sustain the experience of joy in Being, and on account of the greater understanding of philosophical psychology produced by the direct experience of the range of modes of identification. The mystic prefers to adopt the ego-released stances because the ego-released stances reveal the monadic summum bonum, immerse the practitioner of those stances in it, and confer greater understanding. The superiority of the mystic's view lies in the freedom of the mystic to see things from the ego perspective, *and* from the non-ego perspectives at will. The non-mystic looks at the world from an unnecessarily fixed point of view. And the mystic finds that this flexibility is strongly connected with strengthening the experience of bliss in Being.

To what degree mystics have regarded themselves as reporting mystical phenomenology as opposed to propounding mystical metaphysics is a historical and interpretive project we will not take far in this context. Undoubtedly many mystics have not been clear on the distinction, and that has confused things. Undoubtedly, too, philosophers studying mysticism have been confused by the mystics' confusion on this point. For instance, one of the most vexatious questions in the philosophical literature concerning the nature of mysticism is the issue whether there is a common core to mystical experience. The analysis of chapter four, because it is phenomenological, enables us to propose an elegant solution to the problem: What mystics have in common is the claim to experience blissful release from ego-identification, for which state of identification we have provided a precise analysis: ego-identification is the experience of the self as the first agent (the first person as normally conceived). But then there are six main ways to accomplish such release, and two ways to interpret what has happened when any such release occurs, one phenomenological, and one metaphysical.

It may well be that, for many mystics at least, the important feature of mystical experience is blissful ego-release. And the claim to blissful ego-release is shared by mystics, and so for some mystics what really counts about mysticism is shared by mystics. For others, however, blissful ego-release is not enough. If the metaphysics isn't right, by their lights, then something important is missing. For such mystics, the differences between mysticisms can be more important than the commonalities. The vexatiousness of the problem of the common core arises because the full analysis of ego-identification itself can only be undertaken when the various possibilities for its dissolution are grasped. Few mystics practice all six directions of ego-release, and as a result it is easy for mystics to fall into the metaphysical interpretation of one direction or other. It should not be surprising, then, that the distinction between making a phenomenological claim and making a metaphysical claim has not always been clear to mystics themselves. The elegant solution to the common core question depends on understanding that the distinction is fundamental and does not itself prejudge the issue of whether mystical experience provides grounds for mystical metaphysics.

We should also note that the availability of the distinction may be of use in exegetical and critical contexts. For instance, suppose we interpret Nagarjuna's views as primarily directed at getting us away from attempting any final analysis of the metaphysical truth, somewhat along the lines of Kalupahana (1986, and 1992). Under this interpretation Nagarjuna is not emphasizing the unreality of individual phenomena, as T. R. V. Murti (1960), and A. L. Basham (1972) would interpret him, but rather is asserting, among other things, a form of pragmatic skepticism about any final or absolutist metaphysics. But to interpret his Madhyamika philosophy this way is not yet to say anything about the range of phenomenalistic experience held to be possible. That is, there may be a Hindu monist metaphysical view expressed in the mahavakya (key doctrine) "Atman is Brahman," or "That art Thou," which is being criticized or rejected by Nagarjuna. One who interprets him as ontologizing emptiness or presenting a metaphysical view will have an account of why he prefers anatman phenomenology over "Atman is Brahman" phenomenological experience, if such were conceded: the former is in tune with Reality, the latter is not. But without the distinction between phenomenalistic and metaphysical mystical claims, we are unable to clarify a certain exegetical question, nor to present an important criticism of Buddhism on phenomenological grounds which arises on the other interpretation. The exegetical question is whether Nagarjuna, or, for that matter, the Buddha, means to deny the avatar phenomenology. Indeed, whatever one's interpretation of the Buddha's teaching, the question should be raised whether the avatar phenomenology is possible. If the account of chapter four is correct, an account which does not allow for this possibility is too limited. So many forms of Buddhism, Madhyamika Buddhism under certain interpretations included, might be criticized for having too restricted a mystical phenomenology, whatever one's views on the ultimate reality, whether it can be known, and how phenomena are to be regarded in relation to it. Further, under Kalupahana's interpretation of Buddhism, one must wonder why anatman phenomenology is to be preferred over atman phenomenology.

Similarly, Kantian skepticism concerning our knowledge of noumena might be accepted, while one rejects the Kantian restrictions on the form of phenomenalistic experience, which effectively exclude the mystical phenomenologies. In this case, the exegetical issue is clear, for Kant was clear on what he took to be the bounds of possible experience, but the critical question remains: perhaps one *can* phenomenalistically experience subjective identity with the whole realm of phenomena. In this way, critiques of the phenomenological range of mystical schools and of various philosophical positions are made possible by an account of the variety of states of release from ego-based experience conjoined with a distinction between phenomenological and metaphysical construals of these experiences.

The distinction may also provide a tool in exegesis in this way: the more one wants to apply the principle of hermeneutic charity to a mystical position which appears to contain logical contradictions, the more seriously one ought to take the strictly phenomenological interpretation as an exegetical possibility. For instance, in *Sankara's Philosophy of Appearances*, Kazi Nurul Islam calls attention to the way Shankara argues both for the proposition "The world (of multiplicity) is not real," and for the proposition "The world (of multiplicity) is not unreal" (pp. 190-191). The more one recognizes such arguments, the more pressure there will be on one to adopt a phenomenological construal of the mystical states. S. S. Roy in *The Heritage of Sankara* adopts an unequivocally metaphysical interpretation, and in order to make good this interpretation, the production of parallel propositions, which if interpreted metaphysically are inconsistent, will have to be ignored, somehow downplayed, or supported by a fully intelligible two-levelled theory of truth, which latter is rather hard to come by. In principle, then, having available a variety of phenomenological mystical states can be an aid in interpreting a mystic who might otherwise be accused of internal incoherency. Concomitantly, the phenomenological possibility places a constraint on anyone who wants merely to assume the metaphysical interpretation of a mystic: grounds ought to be found to justify the assumption.

To return now to our main theme, our primary question is the relation between the capacity for mystical experience and the forming of mystical metaphysical conclusions. Since James, the relation has been understood as supposedly evidential. The resulting question for the philosopher is: Does mystical experience provide experiential evidence for mystical metaphysics? And we should also remember that we ought to inquire into whether there are grounds, independent of the evidence provided by mystical experience, to defend or refute mystical metaphysics.

Definitions

For the discussion that follows, we define *ontological monism* as the view that there is only one object. In other words, ontological monism is a token or numerical monism, whereas, for instance, materialism as usually defined, is a type monism, for it asserts that if something exists it is material. Under type monism, there may, of course, be many distinct material things. But under ontological monism, any two successful individuating terms pick out one and the same individual, since there is, numerically, only a single individual. *Ontological pluralism* is the view that there are many objects. *Ontological nihilism* is the view that no object exists.

Do mystical experiences provide warrant for mystical metaphysics?

If the phenomenological analysis of chapter four is along the right lines, then it is extremely unlikely that much evidential value can be placed on mystical experience for the truth of mystical metaphysical doctrine. The varieties of mystical experience arise from the unbounded indexicality of the self concept on the one hand, and elementary features concerning judgments of reidentification and non-reidentification, on the other hand. There seems to be no reason to think from the outset that the symmetries of the phenomenological dynamics can ever be overcome by one or another mystical experience. That is, if mystical experience is to provide empirical evidential grounds for some mystical metaphysics, it will never be against its corresponding type. Mystical experience of type A1 will never provide evidence for mystical doctrine A2', A3', C1', C2', or C3'. A1 experience will only provide evidence, if it does, for metaphysical doctrine A1. And so on. Further, the metaphysical doctrines A1' through C3' are pairwise inconsistent, even though their phenomenological expressions are insufficiently metaphysical to be inconsistent at all. And finally, if one type of mystical experience provides evidence for its type of mystical metaphysics, then so do the other types of mystical experience provide evidence for their respective types of mystical metaphysics. But then the evidence for any one type of mystical metaphysics provided by its type of mystical experience must be cancelled out by the evidence provided for other types of mystical metaphysics by the other types of mystical experience.

William Wainwright, who holds that mystical experience provides prima facie evidence for mystical metaphysics, deals with a similar problem, but misses the force of the objection. He says, "It is true that nature mysticism, monistic mysticism, theistic mysticism, and numinous experience (immediately?) support *different* claims—that nature is one and sacred, that there is an undifferentiated unity transcending space and time, that an overwhelming loving consciousness exists, that there is a holy Other. But it is not clear that these claims *conflict*. (Monistic and theistic experiences might be experiences of different objects, for example.) . . . I therefore conclude that the objection from conflicting religious experiences or intuitions is inconclusive" (p. 110).

Once again, Wainwright has failed to consider the plain meaning of monistic mysticism. Certainly there are, or seem to be, numerical monists, and numerical or ontological monism constitutes a form of mystical metaphysics. Parmenides is usually interpreted as asserting numerical or ontological monism, even though it has become suddenly fashionable to interpret Parmenides' position as being consistent with ontological pluralism. (Milton Munitz, 1986, p. 39, goes so far as to state that the standard antipluralist interpretation is "outrageous." See also Barnes, 1979; Mourelatos, 1979; Hatab 1990; and Curd 1991 for the various interpretations other than ontological monism.) In any case, Spinoza seems to advocate a numerical or ontological monism. Among the Eastern mystics, Shankara and other Advaitins apparently advocate numerical monism. Moreover Shankara's monism is the paradigm case of monistic mysticism for Wainwright, and he glosses Shankara's monism in the standard way: "According to Advaita Vedanta, the 'object' of mystical experience is the Atman-Brahman. The Atman-Brahman is the *unique* ground of both world and self. In the last analysis, it alone is real" (p. 32, emphasis in the original). The assurance that mystical monism and mystical theism assert different doctrines but doctrines which might be consistent on the grounds that God and the One might be two distinct items in the ontological inventory comes about as close to self-refutation as one can get. For if ontological monism is true, nothing exists but the One. So if monistic mystical experience is prima facie evidence for the existence of the One, then theistic mystical experience provides prima facie evidence for something other than the One, thus cancelling out the evidential value of the monistic mystical experience! Anyhow, if the monist's One exists, nothing else exists, and to forget this simple fact is to forget the very heart of the problem.

Wainwright's treatment of what he takes to be the relation between Buddhist doctrine and the experience of Buddhist practitioners is similarly flawed. His position, using our terminology, is that *(a)* ontological nihilism or metaphysical skepticism is at the heart of orthodox Buddhist doctrine; and that *(b)* Buddhists probably experience the Transcendent One, but are reluctant to report their experiences in such terms because they are steeped in a tradition which repudiates the existence of atman. It would be impossible in this context to do justice to the complexity of the exegetical issues involved here. For our purposes it is sufficient perhaps to point out the peculiarity of Wainwright's interpretation: He disallows any straightforward phenomenological *or* metaphysical interpretation of Buddhist experience. If, for instance, the Buddha claimed that metaphysical nihilism is experientially confirmable, then why wouldn't such claims be evidence against ontological monism? Indeed, according to much Buddhism, it seems, as one's mental discipline and clarity increases, one comes to understand how all phenomena are empty of final or ultimate identity. Each object at the relative or phenomenal level is causally dependent, no object is simple, and the terms we use are mere designations. It is one's experience in meditation, combined with analysis, which enables one to see this. This sounds very much like an assertion that experience, in the broad sense, confirms either some form of what we're calling "ontological nihilism," or that we must be pragmatically skeptical on metaphysical matters. If monistic mystical experience is, according to Wainwright, prima facie evidence for the existence of the One, why isn't the attainment of nirvana prima facie evidence for the truth of the doctrine of anatman, interpreted either pragma-skeptically or ontologically?

Wainwright opines that many Buddhists experience a Transcendental object but tend nonetheless to repudiate the cognitive implications of this experience. Why do they repudiate it? "Most important . . ." he says by way of explanation, "is the anatman doctrine. The repudiation of any kind of permanent self or substance is at the very heart of Buddhism. Belief in self *(atman)* is both a cause and effect of self-assertion and the will to live. It is thus inextricably bound up with the attachment to self which binds us to this world. Since monistic experiences almost invariably lead to talk of a 'true self' or 'real I' (an Atman or *purusa*, etc.) it is not surprising that Buddhists are suspicious of them. There therefore seems to be no reason to suppose that Buddhists have noticed something which has escaped other observers, viz., that mystical experiences are not really noetic. Furthermore, the Buddhist's rejection of the ontological claims that appear to be built into these experiences is inextricably bound up with the anatman doctrine, the attack on 'views' and other teachings peculiar to Buddhism. No reason for repudiating the cognitive implications of mystical experiences has been provided which is independent of the idiosyncrasies of Buddhist doctrine" (p. 124). Suddenly "the very heart of Buddhism," namely, the anatman doctrine, which entails ontological nihilism or metaphysical skepticism, is demoted to "an idiosyncracy." Wainwright refuses to allow either a "phenomenology only" interpretation of Buddhism, or the metaphysical interpretation. In other words, Wainwright arbitrarily and question beggingly ignores the two standard interpretations of the Buddhist teachings at issue. Wainwright doesn't support his assertions with anything like a proper exegetical account.

Second, if there are practical reasons why Buddhists experience the Transcendent One or the Transcendent Reality but are reluctant to ontologize it, then we must also consider the possibility that those monists, for instance, who regard their experiences in the metaphysical light, and as providing evidence for the truth of monist metaphysics, may be doing so more for practical reasons than for metaphysically grounded reasons. Perhaps Shankara wants us to concentrate so hard that he says the Self is the only Reality. That would encourage us to concentrate in the requisite manner, wouldn't it? If such practical interpretations prevent us from taking some apparent Buddhist ontology (either skeptical, or nihilist) at face value, why shouldn't such interpretations undercut the evidential value of monist mystical experience for monist mystical metaphysics? Considering remarks such as Sengaku Mayeda's that "Philosophy is not [Shankara's] aim but is rather a vital weapon with which to fulfill his aim, which is to rescue people from transmigratory existence" (1979, pp. 11, 12), this is not an entirely idle issue. How can one ever factor out the practical and expressive functions of mystical teachings so as to conclude that a mystic is committed to a metaphysical view rather than expressing a phenomenalistic experience in emphatic and exaggeratedly metaphysical terms for various practical reasons?

All in all, then, the many exegetical difficulties involved in establishing whether a given mystical expression or claim is meant phenomenologically or metaphysically complicate matters when one tries to use mystical reports as evidence for mystical metaphysical claims. The evidentialist would first need to establish that the descriptions are meant metaphysically, and in some cases, this would be difficult. But even if one ignores such problems, and assumes the accuracy of the metaphysical interpretations, the symmetries in the relations between the diverse mystical experiences and their corresponding metaphysical construals make it very difficult for the evidentialist to assert that mystical experience provides prima facie grounds for the acceptance of any form of mystical metaphysics. Indeed, the symmetries, if anything, provide evidence for skepticism on metaphysical issues because they emphasize the gap between the realm of phenomena and of noumena.

Aside from the evidential value of mystical experience, however, there is the question of a priori analysis of mystical metaphysical views.

A priori consideration of mystical metaphysics

Can ontological monism be defended? Alternatively, can we rule out ontological monism by some elementary consideration? True enough, all language seems to presuppose multiplicity. And multiplicity seems to be multiplicity of objects. But Spinoza pointed the way to a metaphysical middle ground, and it seems that Parmenides and some Eastern monists held, or were reaching for, the Spinozistic view. Let 'the One' be the only noun phrase in our language. Then all the multiplicity gets forced into being expressed via sentential predication: Instead of "The dog is barking here, and the cat is meowing there," we say "The One is barking here, and the One is meowing there." Multiplicity is expressed but there is no plurality of objects. It is false to say "There is a dog," because only the One exists, and the One is not a dog. Nor is it even correct to say that the One includes a dog as one of its proper parts. The One does not include a dog as one of its proper parts, for if it has proper parts, then more than one thing exists, namely, one of its proper parts, and another of its proper parts. Thus, so long as the only nominal expression occurring in our every sentence is 'The One,' or refers to the One, we will not be presupposing ontological pluralism. (The language of this discussion, however, as the reader has surely noted, presupposes ontological pluralism!)

Let us call a set of sentences in which the condition obtains that each nominative phrase refers to no object except the One "monist sentences," and the language which consists of nothing but monist sentences, "monist language." How much can we express in monist language?

There are serious shortcomings of monist language if it is intended to be capable of expressing worldly concerns. Only persons can act. But can the One be a person? No, it will be argued, because a person has proper parts. It is not adequate to say, "The One thinks, the One plans, the One moves here, the One moves there." Rather the concept of a person is the concept of one who has beliefs, desires, intentions, and so on. And a belief is not the One. Moreover, even if one were to get around this by suggesting that the desire need not be individuated, still there will be the problem of interaction. What happens when two people communicate? "The One says. . . ." What does the one say? And to whom? To Itself? Perhaps there are convoluted solutions: "The One here spoke to the One there, saying," and so on. But for many at least, the convolutions will seem to be maskings of ontological multiplicity rather than genuine elimination of it. I must confess that I share such suspicions. Further, for those brave and radical souls who will accept that the elimination of multiplicity is genuine, there is the problem of scientific thought, which, on the face of it seems to require multiplicity. When one makes an experiment, sets up a control, and so on, it seems that one presupposes multiplicity. After all, one is checking for causes and correlations, and it is hard to see how the multiplicitous concepts can be eliminated. Once again, it is dubious whether one can successfully eliminate the multiplicitous thinking and carry on scientific enterprises, make sophisticated predictions, and so on.

An argument might be raised as to the possibility for conscious monism, subconscious pluralism. The idea rests on the empirical claim that a person can maintain the monist perspective consciously, while subconsciously processing information in ways similar to the ontological pluralist. In principle, this is not as implausible a salvation of monism as might at first be thought. If the elements of the many are regarded in the same manner as one regards the square root of minus one, then the burden of the question is thrown onto the empirical foundation of the position. To what degree can one regard the linguistic forms associated with multiplicitous metaphysics as mere algorithms, thus enabling one to remain conscious only of the One and its modes? However, whatever the merits of the empirical foundation, the moral objections once again surface. For it may be that one needs to bring moral deliberation into consciousness. The question must be raised: Can a mystic carry on fresh moral deliberation subconsciously, while consciously maintaining the monistic language of thought? This seems rather unlikely. Rather, the moral life, it would seem, requires the mystic to shift from monistic mysticism to ontologically pluralistic altered-self mysticism as circumstances dictate. It would seem to be forbiddingly hard to relegate to one's subconscious processes the task of figuring out whether such and such an expense is a genuine business deduction, while the conscious mind is thinking "The One, nothing but the One!"

This also opens up a rather arcane discipline: ethics of metaphysics. A typical question of this discipline is: Is it ethically permissible for one to train oneself to think monistically in one's conscious life while processing information subconsciously along lines similar to the ontological pluralist? This is similar to the question as to whether it's permissible to be a hermit, only it's harder, since the external action of the conscious-monist subconscious-pluralist individual might be saintly and altruistic, despite the fact that the conscious life of the agent is always focused in the monist language of thought which effectively eliminates any interagency modality!

The same points can be made for ontological nihilism as for ontological monism, although the points of suspicion become stretched a bit further. For whereas 'The One' is a suitable expression to serve as grammatical subject of a sentence, the language of thought of ontological nihilism has no nominal terms at all. Rather, predicates are concatenated. "Barking, clouding, raining." The restrictions on expressive scope are even stronger than with ontological monism, it would seem. However, the paucity of a language of thought, or an idio-language of thought (adapted from 'idiolect,' not 'idiot,' though one is excused for wondering) is a defect in it if it is meant to replace altogether the usual language of thought. It is not a defect if it is meant to expand one's perspective by refreshing a dimension of experience. Just as the tennis player's game is enhanced by arbitrarily adopting a restriction on the rules in practice sessions (e.g., "Always hit backhand, even though the rules permit forehand") so, too, one's philosophical acumen and insight can be enhanced by adopting, for a period of time, a restricted language of thought, so one becomes fully familiar with the perspective restricted to that language of thought.

The relevance of the dynamic of restriction to mystical metaphysics is this. The possibility, at some level of epistemic possibility, exists that either monist or nihilist ontology is correct, and that pluralist ontology is delusional. If that were to be true we would want to understand as best we could how things stand with the world. Even though we cannot take it that our practical experience in maintaining nihilist or monist ontological consciousness provides evidence for the truth of the metaphysics, nonetheless it would be of supreme value for the philosopher to practice these states of mind as much as possible in order to align cognition with what, possibly, is real. Training the mind in mystical cognition would then count as supremely important metaphysical lab work.

Despite the weakness of the view that mystical experience is prima facie evidence for mystical metaphysics, and despite the inconclusiveness of a priori treatments of mystical metaphysical positions of any of the six sorts, mystical metaphysical positions are deserving of serious consideration. They are not mutually consistent, but none of them can be ruled out by immediately obvious a priori means.

The implications of this for the practice of philosophy are, I think, striking. The practice of analysis and logic, especially in an information-overload society, has led to a discipline of philosophy whose practitioners' familiarity with phenomenology is wonderful in some areas, but astoundingly weak in others. Consider how fine grained is the phenomenology of emotional life reflected in two such different works as *The Passions* by Robert Solomon, and Ronald de Sousa's *Rationality of Emotion*. Why shouldn't the range of possible self-identifications be as well grasped by philosophers of personal identity as the range of emotional life is grasped by philosophers of the emotions? Even those philosophers of personal identity who are concerned with living life in some image other than ego-placement are working with an unnecessarily restricted palette.

Consider, again, Derek Parfit's analysis resulting in something similar to what we're calling an "exclusively objective view" of the first person. He says that when he realized the truth of the Reductionist View he felt liberated. "When I changed my view, the walls of my glass tunnel disappeared. I now live in the open air . . . I am less concerned about the rest of my own life and more concerned about the lives of others./ When I believed the Non-Reductionist View, I also cared more about my inevitable death. After my death there will be no one living who will be me. I can now redescribe this fact. . . . My death will break the more direct relations between my present experiences and future experiences, but it will not break various other relations. This is all there is to the fact that there will be no one living who will be me. Now that I have seen this, my death seems to me less bad" (p. 281). Given the phenomenology of the avatar, and of the universal impersonal self mystic, though, one must wonder whether Parfit is still holding to too limited a view of the possibilities. Perhaps what matters, or can matter, is my self, after all, or I can matter as much as psychological continuity matters. If so, the impersonal universal self mystic experiences more of what matters than someone familiar only with what Parfit calls the impersonal stance, and will not take it that the self disappears with the death of the first person. Also the avatar and impersonal universal self mystics have rather surprising answers to some of the dividing self conundrums, and these answers, one would expect, could lead to fresh analyses overall.

In summary, then, the ego-released perspectives, and particularly, the no-self, avatar, and universal impersonal self perspectives should be of great interest to the metaphysician and philosophical psychologist. They arise from a view of selfhood and personhood that holds that there is a wide empirical range and flexibility in the phenomenology of extensional self-identification. The a priori availability of the perspectives together with the mystics' claims of the empirical availability of sustained maintenance of the non-ego perspectives ought to be considered grounds by all serious philosophers interested in personal identity and ontology to devote several years of assiduous work towards the mastery of the mystics' claims concerning the modalities of extensional self identification and concerning the various metaphysical interpretations of the mystical experiences.

II.

So far we have seen how mystical experience can provide insight into the philosophy of mind and personal identity. There is another way in which mysticism can contribute to metaphysics. This second way revolves around the controversy concerning the existence of an Ultimate Reality underlying the worldly multiplicity, or a Transcendent Being.

As we've seen, according to the standard view of mysticism as noetic, mystics claim there is a mysterious object or entity, Transcendent Being, or The One, or Emptiness, or Transcendent God, or Godhead, whose reality the mystics claim to directly perceive or experience. The question as it has been raised in the writings of Broad, James, Russell, Stace, Gale, Ninian Smart, Scharfstein, Wainwright, Katz, Proudfoot, and others is whether or not the mystical experience can provide warrant for the truth of the metaphysical claims, and whether mystical experience can be interpreted as being a type of perception or akin to perception. It is not difficult to see how such a view of the relationship between mystical experience and metaphysics arose. The view that there is a Personal God could, in principle, be supported by experiencing communications which must be at least from a great and powerful supernatural source, for example, experiencing apparent communications in the form of galaxies spelling out messages. The analogy with mystical experience is a natural one to make.

However, it may be that this way of construing the problem is not only unsatisfactory for reasons previously discussed, but also distorts the relationship between mystical experience and metaphysics in the way it sets up the problem. In what follows I would like to present an alternative way of construing the relationship between mystical experience and mystical metaphysics. It's not that the existence of the Transcendent Being is established by having a special kind of experience. Rather, if there is a Transcendent Reality, or a Transcendent Object, it is something the existence of which is guaranteed by the existence of any kind of object at all. Whether or not there is a Transcendent Reality we discover by philosophical contemplation aided by philosophical analysis. This philosophical contemplation is a genuine form of meditation, but the philosophical component is decisive. Once we have come to the conclusion that the Transcendent Object exists, then we come to understand that the Transcendent Object is being experienced whenever any object is being experienced much the way a table is being experienced (directly or indirectly) whenever someone with normal vision with unobstructed view looks in the direction of the table from a few feet away.

What, then, is the relationship between mystical experience and the Transcendent Object? Just this: mystical experience construes its object as the object that is always experienced whenever any object is being experienced. Mystical experience is heightened attentiveness to the Transcendent Object, that is to say, that which is always experienced whenever an experience occurs.

Parts and wholes

We will begin with an examination of the part-whole relationship. The purpose at this stage of the inquiry is to establish the truth of the proposition that if one perceives any part of an object, then the object of one's perception can be construed as the whole as much as the part. 'Perceives' is being used veridically here. That is, to say that someone perceives a snake presupposes the truth of the proposition that the snake exists. If someone thinks he perceives a snake, but it is not a snake, but rather a rope, then we will say he thinks he perceives a snake, but actually is perceiving a rope.

Suppose I am sitting facing a computer at the moment. What do I see? I see various surfaces of the computer, or surfaces of some parts of the computer. When I see a cat, I don't see the cat's liver. I see the fur, or the surface of the fur, the nose, or some surfaces of the nose, and so on. Yet, still, what I see is what caused me to see what I'm seeing. If the cat is there, and I am looking there, I see the cat. If the computer is there, and I am looking there, I see the computer. I see what I'm looking at, even though there is a sense in which all that I see is the surface, or some part of the surface.

It may be useful to prevent a confusion from arising concerning what's been said so far. The account given so far is neutral with regard to direct versus indirect realism. (The terminology follows Dancy 1985, pp. 147-155.) Whether I see the object indirectly in virtue of directly seeing a percept (an internal object of perception) of some sort, or I see the object directly, still, I see the object. So the observations concerning our ability to see things despite seeing only the surfaces of the things requires only the semantics of perceptual realism, that is, the possibility that there are objects out there to be perceived. We are not asserting the truth of the realistic interpretation of the bulk of our ordinary perceptual beliefs, but rather that the propositions asserting perceptual facts of the usual kind are to be understood as being either true or false according to whether or not there are objects there corresponding to what we think we see. If I say "I see a cat on a mat," and I'm a brain in a vat, then I'm deluded. If I seem to see a cat on a mat, and I'm not a brain in a vat, then I see a cat on a mat.

We may distinguish, further, between the construed objects of perceptions and the objects of perceptions. I look at a rope but construe my perception as being of a snake. In this case, the construed object is not the object of my perception.

The question we want to raise now is whether or not there is an object whose description is such that there can be no distinction between the construal and the reality. The essential idea of monist mysticism, on this interpretation, is that there is such an object. We can orient towards that object in two ways. The first is the orientation away from parts and towards the whole; the second is the orientation away from the phenomenon (the appearance) and toward the noumenon (the reality).

The orientation from parts to the whole works this way: I see myself as a finite being, a part of a larger plurality of entities. I perceive myself, I perceive other things. This is the ego-perspective. For most of my tasks in life, I must focus at a rather small scale. I think about whether the fridge is full of food or not, whether I have the books with me that I will need, and so on. But if I like, I can keep in mind objects of a much larger scale. I can think of the Milky Way, which is a very big object. I can think of the billions of galaxies that surround it, which together constitute a much bigger object still. And I can think of the whole universe, the entire physical cosmos from the Big Bang and on, assuming there was a Big Bang. Then I can think of the possibility that the physical universe from the Big Bang and on could be part of an enormous assembly of universes. Perhaps some of these universes are causally interrelated. But perhaps there is an infinity of parallel universes which are causally uncoupled. The largest entity that can be conceived would seem to be the entity which would exist if every logically possible state of affairs actually obtained in some particular one of the infinities upon superinfinities of parallel universes. Now when I think of the entirety of what exists, I am thinking of the Whole. I take every thing which exists, and include it.

Is it not correct to say that whatever I am experiencing, I am experiencing the Whole? Obviously, I am not experiencing all the details. But then when I experience any material object I am not experiencing all the details. But there is no significance to such features of scale for the philosophy of perception. Therefore when I look at a tabletop, I can take it that I see the table, and I can take it that I see the planet earth, and I can take it that I see the Milky Way, and I can take it that I see the Whole. Furthermore, when I look at the tabletop, and take it that what I am seeing is the tabletop, nonetheless I am experiencing the table. It follows that I am always experiencing the Whole, regardless of how I construe my experience. Finally, if I am looking at a rope, and take it that I see a snake, I am experiencing the rope and misconstruing my experience as being an experience of a snake.

There are, then, two ways to experience the Whole. We can experience the Whole as the Whole. That is, we can experience the Whole and construe it as the Whole. Or, we can experience the Whole, and construe the experience as an experience of one of its parts. If I look at a rope, and construe the object of my perception as a snake, then I am experiencing the Whole, and construing the object of my perception under the mistakenly construed aspect (snake) of one of the Whole's parts (rope). If I look at a rope and construe the object of my perception as a rope, then I am experiencing the Whole, and construing the object of my perception in terms of one of its parts, the rope. If I look at a rope and construe the object of my perception as the Whole, then I am experiencing the Whole, and construing it as the Whole.

It is important not to be misled by these examples. If one looks at a rope and construes the object of one's perception as the Whole, it is *not* the case that one is construing the rope as the Whole. Such a construal would be at least as mistaken as a construal of the rope as a snake. One is looking at the rope, yes, but one is construing the object of one's perception as the Whole, and indeed, it is the Whole which is the object of one's perception. Just as one can look at a tabletop and see a table, so one can look at a table and see the Whole. What one is perceiving is an intentional matter, so long as one's intention is not fictitious, and the object so intended is causally involved in the perception in the appropriate manner.

Once again: I look at the top of the table, and construe the object of my perception as the table. If I look at the top of the table, and construe the top of the table as the table, then I am surely mistaken. But if I look at the top of the table and construe the object of my perception as the table, then no mistake is being made. (The table exists, since by hypothesis, I am looking at the top of the table.)

Thus, the philosopher contemplates the Whole, and at any point can construe the object of her perception as the Whole, wherever she is looking, whatever she is listening to, and even whatever she is tasting.

The Whole as given through the resolution of skeptical doubt

Ever since the Greek skeptics we have trained ourselves in the systematic doubting of, or inquiry into, the relationship between the construed object and the object of perception. Accordingly, although we may understand that if one is looking at a tabletop one may construe the object of one's perception as the table, nevertheless, we may have profound doubts as to what it is that we are looking at, or if anything at all exists to be looked at in the way we naively think we are looking at things.

There are several avenues we might pursue to resolve these doubts. The first avenue, the standard one these days, and the one suggested at least as far back as John Locke, is to look for the best explanation of our experience of apparent objects. Since the simpler explanation is the better one, other things being equal, and it is simpler to suppose our experiences as veridical than as illusions generated by a higher order of reality, we are justified in accepting the apparent world as the real world. A second method is to ask ourselves what we need in the way of a reality. And when we sincerely look at what it is we need in the way of a reality, according to this view, we will tend to find that we have what we need. The details whereby we come to discover this are variable. Perhaps we will adopt J. L. Austin's line in *Sense and Sensibilia*: something can only be unreal by diverging from the standard in some particular way, by being fake or ersatz, or a fictional character as opposed to a historical figure. But this presupposes that we don't question the standard as to whether it is itself real. Or perhaps, finally, we will adopt a moral line of thought. If we are really prepared to adopt an evil demon hypothesis, or a brain in the vat hypothesis, then there is no reason to think that those other apparent persons out there are persons at all. And if not, the only interests we need take ultimate account of, or account of as ends in themselves, are our own phenomenal or experiential interests. Phenomenalistic egoism is a perfectly viable moral philosophy for the skeptic who adopts the systematic error hypothesis. But most people are not prepared to adopt phenomenalistic egoism as their ultimate moral principle. When one realizes one is not prepared to give up the idea that there are other minds out there that one is communicating with, and so on, then one realizes that one's moral stance cancels out one's skepticism. Thus, there are these three standard avenues for resolving skeptical doubts about an objective reality.

There is also, however, the mystical avenue for resolving at least some skeptical doubts. The mystical avenue is orientation toward the Whole. To see how this works, let us adopt the standpoint of the systematic skeptic. Every judgment that is subject to doubt I will doubt. I pick up a book by Descartes, and immediately subject to doubt that there ever was a Descartes, even that there is a person who has just picked up a book. But I read, or seem to read, anyway. I read that nothing "can cause me to be nothing so long as I think that I am something. So that after having reflected well and carefully examined all things, we must come to the definite conclusion that this proposition: I am, I exist, is necessarily true each time that I pronounce it, or that I mentally conceive it" (Meditations, No. 2).

This seems clear enough, then, that I am, at the moment I question whether I am. I am, at the moment I conceive of myself in any form or fashion. Of course Descartes immediately goes on to limit what it is that has been discovered: "But I do not yet know clearly enough what I am, I who am certain that I am; and hence I must be careful to see that I do not imprudently take some other object in place of myself, and thus that I do not go astray in respect of this knowledge that I hold to be the most certain and most evident of all that I have formerly learned" (ibid.).

This cautions me against jumping to the conclusion that I am a particular person, one small element in a vast plurality of objects, let alone that I am Leonard Angel.

Having realized that I am, however, I might also realize that This is. In other words, it is not the case that nothing exists. Since I exist, then it is not the case that nothing whatever exists. And if something exists, then that thing is either the Whole, or a proper part of the Whole. And if it is the former, then This, the Whole exists; and if it is the latter, then This, the Whole, exists and comprises both the first proper part, and whatever else there is. Thus, since there is thinking, or there is consciousness, or there is phenomenological content, therefore This, the Whole, actually is.

From this it should be clear that I needn't originally have thought of what appears to be as myself. I might have thought merely of the appearance of something. In other words, I might have adopted a purely objective perspective, a perspective which makes no reference to selfhood. I might have affirmed that so long as something appears to exist, then something exists, even if it is nothing but the appearance of something. This, too, would lead directly to the proposition, This, the Whole, is.

In this case, too, one would need to immediately add a cautionary note: "But there is as yet no clear enough knowledge what This, the Whole, consists in, despite the knowledge that This, the Whole, is, so care must be taken, lest the Whole be construed in ways other than it is, and the knowledge that is most certain and evident be betrayed by these false construals."

The reader may note that the above reasoning shares important features of what is usually called in natural theology, "the ontological argument" for the existence of God. It is worth our while to reconstruct it somewhat more formally in that light. The version of the ontological argument which we will be constructing and examining I shall call "the existential ontological argument."

The existential ontological argument for the existence of God

An argument is a sound ontological argument for the existence of God if and only if it (1) begins with a true premise asserting that there is a conception of something; (2) validly draws out from that conception, the real existence of the thing which the conception is a conception of; and (3) concludes without violence to language or the history of thought that the thing whose real existence has been demonstrated, is God, or has been plausibly regarded as God in some (important) religious or philosophical tradition(s).

The usual criticism of the ontological argument is that it commits the existential fallacy. It attempts to derive from the mere logical possibility of something the real existence, even the necessary existence, of the thing. For the sake of discussion we may grant that the ontological arguments as usually conceived do commit some form of existential fallacy, or beg some modal or existential question. However, it is not clear that every argument which satisfies the three criteria will commit the existential fallacy. In order to show how one can satisfy the three criteria while begging no question, nor even attempting to derive existence from mere logical possibility, we note that there are two quite distinct ways in which one can assert the existence of a conception.

There is the purely possibilistic assertion of the existence of a conception, according to which to say that there is a conception of God is to say that the existence of God is logically coherent, or logically possible. Then there is what I will call the "occasionalistic assertion of a conception." Under the occasionalistic assertion of a conception, to say that there is a conception of God is to say that there is an occasion of experience whose intentional object is the existence of God.

It is interesting to note that Anselm's ontological argument makes frequent use of the occasionalistic notion of conception. For example, Anselm says, ". . . it is one thing for an object to be in the understanding, and another to understand that the object exists. When a painter first conceives of what he will afterwards perform, he has it in his understanding, but he does not yet understand it to be because he has not yet performed it. But after he has made the painting, he both has it in his understanding, and he understands that it exists, because he has made it" (*Proslogion* II). Here the clearly temporal language shows that Anselm's notion of having a concept in the understanding is occasionalistic.

In what follows, the assertion of the existence of a conception, or the occurrence of a conception is meant in the occasionalistic sense. To say "there is a conception of the Whole" is to say that there is an occasion of experience whose intentional object is the Whole. That is, there is a state of consciousness directed towards the Whole. Note that to assert an occasionalistic conception is to make an existential assertion to begin with. It should not be too surprising, then, to find that adopting the occasionalistic interpretation of asserting that there is some conception or other will allow us to satisfy our three criteria for an ontological argument without running afoul of the existential fallacy.

Adapting our previous reflections on parts and the Whole, we begin with the mere (occasionalistic) conception of the Whole. That is, we allow the mind to direct itself toward the Whole, and thus bring into being an occasion of experience whose intentional object is the Whole. In this way, we satisfy criterion (1) of the ontological argument. We bring into being the conditions under which it becomes true to say, "There is a conception of the Whole." Next, we reason that if there is a conception of the Whole, then either the occasion of conception of the Whole is all there is, or there is more, in which case there is a Whole consisting of the occasion of conception of the Whole, and, in addition, whatever else. Thus, we have found something such that the mere existence of a conception of it guarantees the real existence of that thing. In other words, it is true to assert, "If there is an occasion of conception of the Whole, then the Whole exists." Thus, we have satisfied criterion (2). From the two assertions whose truth we have now found, we are entitled to conclude the truth of the assertion, "There is the Whole," or "The Whole exists." Finally we note that it is plausible to define 'God' as the greatest actual being, rather than as the greatest possible being. The history of the concept of 'God' shows that for centuries God was conceived of as the greatest reality, rather than the greatest possible reality. Seneca seems to have introduced the notion that God is the greatest conceivable being, saying that God is "everything that you see and everything that you do not see. His greatness, than which nothing greater can be conceived, is only attributed to him if he alone is everything" (*Naturales Quaestiones* I, 13). Even here, that God is the greatest conceivable being is assumed as a premise for a pantheist conclusion. Anselm appears to have picked the notion that God is the greatest conceivable being from this passage in Seneca. Given the lateness of this development, and, as well, that in any pantheistic conception ancient or modern, God is conceived as the Whole, or the greatest actual being, our third criterion for a successful ontological argument for the existence of God is satisfied. There is, then, a sound ontological argument for the existence of God!

It will be noted, of course, that the argument has as much logical force when 'cat' is substituted for 'the Whole' in the first premise, but not everywhere in subsequent steps. That is, the argument can be restated as follows: There is a conception of a cat, therefore there is a Whole which is either nothing but the conception of the cat, or the conception of the cat plus whatever else. In either case, we derive the existence of the Whole. From an occasional conception of a cat we derive the existence of an actual Whole. The argument works because we have actual existence wherever we have any occasionalistic conception occurring at all. (We do not, then, commit the existential fallacy.) But when we substitute 'the cat' in the first premise, the argument no longer embodies the defining characteristic (2) of the ontological argument, namely, that from a conception of God we validly derive the existence of God. That we can present the argument in the way we originally did, deriving from the conception of the Whole, the existence of the Whole, stems, from the logical point of view, from an accidental feature of the argument, namely, that anything at all could be the object of the conception. It is, from the logical point of view, an ontological argument for the existence of (the pantheist) God, only accidentally, as it were. But from the experiential viewpoint, there is real beauty and power in the contemplation indicated not only in the inference from the conception of a cat to the existence of an actual Whole, but also, and all the more so, in the inference from the conception of an actual Whole to the existence of an actual Whole.

Also we may note that a Cartesian-Vedantic version of the existential ontological argument is available. For if we substitute, 'I' or 'me' or 'the self' or 'Atman' in place of 'the Whole' in the version of the existential ontological argument given, we still have a highly plausible version of the existential ontological argument, viz:

(a) There is an occasion of conception of myself. (This is, or becomes true, as soon as I direct my consciousness toward myself, which I do as soon as I try to assess the truth of the premise!) *(b)* If there is an occasion of conception of myself then there is the subject whose conception the conception is of. (This is more controversial then the second premise in the first argument form. But some metaphysicians will allow that if there is thought about myself, I must exist.) *(c)* Therefore I, the subject, exist. (Valid inference) *(d)* And the subject that I *must be* for any thought to occur is the pure subject or Atman, which is Brahman, or God in Advaita metaphysics. (This step, again, is controversial, since some would say that I need not be the pure subject; however, others would hold as a basic metaphysical intuition that built into the notion of selfhood is the pure subject or self. Because of the controversial status of this intuition, the Advaitin version of the existential ontological argument is weaker than the original, pantheist version.)

Descartes might have regarded the ultimate conclusion as somewhat blasphemous. In the *Meditations*, while speculating about himself in the phase in Meditation II in which he does not yet know what he is, he assiduously avoids any speculation that he is either infinite or Divine, and in Meditation III it seems to him that the finitude of the conceiving subject is self-evident. So perhaps it is fairer to Descartes, in view of step *(d)*, to remove his name from this argument, and conceive of it simply as the Advaitin existential ontological argument for the existence of God.

Thus, we can resolve systematic skeptical doubt about objective existence with the propositions: I am; and This is, or the Whole is. Whether one can go any further in establishing descriptions or construals of the Whole without making use of at least one of the three standard avenues for resolution of skeptical doubt, namely, inference to the best explanation, the Austinian avenue, and the moral avenue, is another matter, a matter not strictly germane to our purposes. For our purposes we need only consider that the effort to resolve global skeptical doubt also gives rise to the orientation or intentionality directed perhaps toward the Self, and, in any case, toward the Whole.

Mystical and non-mystical metaphysics

Non-mystical metaphysics, we can see now, is metaphysics that denies that there is any object which can be identified without a particular sortal. Mystical metaphysics, in one form at any rate, holds that there is something which can be identified without a sortal, namely, This, the Whole, that object of perception which is always being perceived regardless of what is being perceived, and regardless of how misconstrued the perception is. It is in this sense that the Whole may be regarded as the Transcendent Object. No matter how deceived I am, no matter what errors I make in identifications, whether I wake up and discover I apparently had been a brain in a vat stimulated by mad scientists, or whatever, my intentionality toward the Transcendent Object, the Whole, guarantees transparency, or success in my construal. Mystical experience, or a paradigmatic type of mystical experience, is experience of This, the Whole, as This, the Whole. The mystic, or a certain sort of mystic, sustains in her consciousness the construal of This, the Whole, as This, the Whole. And the mystical practice of orienting toward This, the Whole is not only a wonderful vehicle of blissfulness, but also, a practice through which one comes to understand the metaphysics of Transcendence.

We don't transcend the world when we discover the Transcendent, for the Transcendent is the world. Then what is transcended when we discover the Transcendent? What is transcended is the possibility of error.

III.

The skeptic may have two retorts to the monist mystical metaphysics of the sort just presented. The first, more modest point, is that the possibility of error which the mystic has or claims to have transcended is a very limited possibility of error. For although the skeptic, who denies that any form of knowledge is possible, has been shown an avenue or two to knowledge (perhaps I realize that I exist, or, in any case, I realize that the Whole exists), nonetheless there is no connection between such transcendental realizations and the sort of specific knowledge concerning construals of the Whole which people rely on for their activities. What good does it do me to know that I exist if I'm not entitled to the conclusion "I'm not a brain in a vat being stimulated by an array of scientists in some super-reality; rather I'm a human being on planet earth?"

More generally, and this is the ambitious second point, how does the monistic mystic guarantee the actual existence of the Whole from intentionality directed toward the Whole? What guarantee, that is, does the mystic have that the first premise of the existential ontological argument, "There is a conception of the Whole" has been expressed in terms which reflect what ultimately is? The first premise of the existential ontological argument asserts that there is an occasion of conception of the Whole. This premise is held to be true every time I direct my mind toward the Whole. But a strictly substanceless Platonic Formalism needs to be contrasted with a substantialist metaphysical picture prior to an assessment of this premise.

A strictly substanceless Platonic Formalism holds that no substantial individual exists, and that every expression concerning a spatiotemporal object of the form "X is y" receives its metaphysically perspicuous expression in a statement of the form, "Y-ness is here." According to the strict Platonic Formalist, there are no tables or chairs ultimately; there only are the Forms being instantiated spatiotemporally in various patterns of continuity. On the other hand, according to the substantialist, *something is always there* which holds the properties ascribed. According to the substantialist, properties are not genuine things. Rather, something is there which takes on the form of a chair, or which has the property of being chair-like. The substantialist, then can be either an ontological pluralist, as most substantialists from Aristotle and on have been, or a numerical monist, as Spinoza and Shankara, and Parmenides were, or seem to have been, according to standard interpretations of their works.

Next, let us ask ourselves whether or not the strict Platonist is advancing a form of ontological nihilism. As defined, ontological nihilism holds that no object exists. Clearly, strict Platonism is a form of ontological nihilism if by 'object' is meant 'substantial object' or 'object of the sort which bears spatiotemporal properties and can stay the same through change in location or across time.' To some it would appear to be a form of skeptical overkill to argue that no object exists whatsoever, not even forms. However, it is worth considering a position which holds both *(a)* that reification of predicates is incorrect when considered from the ultimate viewpoint, as Gilbert Ryle, for instance, does in "Systematically Misleading Expressions"; and also *(b)* that the substanceless view of identity over time of spatiotemporal objects is correct. In other words, the anti-Platonism of the substantialist is correct; but the antisubstantialism of the analysis of material object identity over time is also correct. What is left is a metaphysical view according to which the expressions which are most metaphysically perspicuous of what ultimately obtains are pure feature-placing expressions such as ". . . raining here; green there; brown there. . . ."

The issues surrounding the two points, *(a)*, and *(b)*, can be argued entirely independently of each other, so that the conjunction of *(a)* and *(b)* would appear to have no prima facie or obvious internal inconsistency. Here's what the two points amount to in summary form:

(a) When we nominalize predicates, and talk about greenness or justice we are using grammatical forms which have great convenience, but which suggest misleading comparisons due to the new grammatical roles they take on. We tend to think of noun phrases along lines suggested by those which refer to spatiotemporal entities. So once 'green' becomes nominalized as 'greenness,' we start to think of greenness as something that occupies a spot in the ontological inventory. To think this way, however, is to be misled by its grammatical role. We're best off recalling that the nominalizations were undertaken for linguistic convenience in the first place, and we're best off ceasing to accord such nominalizations ontological status. People and their actions can be just or unjust. It is convenient to refer to that which they are when we say that they are just. But this doesn't imply that there is a justice in the order of things which has being, or which exists. We can deny the existence of justice, and still affirm whatever it is that needs affirmation.

(b) Consider the question of what it is that stays the same when an object moves about in space and endures in time. Consider, for instance, a ship. There are two views of the identity over time of such an object. According to one view, there is something which stays the same when the object endures. Even to say "the object endures" seems to presuppose that something is staying the same. According to the other view, there is no ultimate bearer of properties which stays the same over time. There is no substance which stays the same whose properties change. Proponents of the first, substantialist

view, hold that we cannot have a viable conceptual scheme unless we can use the concept of endurance over time, and, as mentioned, this concept, according to this viewpoint, requires the notion of identity over time, which itself presupposes that something is the same while the properties change. Proponents of the second, insubstantialist view, hold that the concept of a substance staying the same over time breaks down under careful analysis.

The first weak spot is the relation between our way of identifying something as being the same and the substantialist's belief that the identification has been correct. According to the insubstantialist view, the only epistemic criterion of an object's identity over time available is the continuity of some set of properties. For instance, I identify a pen as enduring over time by noticing the continuity of shape. If it is said that I identify a pen as enduring over time by noticing the continuity of its parts, then I must be able to judge concerning the continuity of its parts. And these in turn would only be the same parts if *their* parts were the same. Since I do not move down through the part layers infinitely many times, the actual epistemic criterion of an object's endurance through time terminates in continuity of features. Now if our judgments of identity over time were for the purpose of identifying anything other than continuity of features, we ought to be concerned, and would be concerned, about the potential gap between our epistemic criterion and the metaphysical truth of the matter. But for none of our purposes are we so concerned. We don't care a whit whether metaphysical substances are popping in and out of existence at the rate of one an hour so that my pen is really a hundred different ontological items every hundred hours, each of which resembles the other and comes into existence just as the other goes out of existence. Thus, operationalists, pragmatists, verificationists of even mild stamps, and many more, will hold that all that matters is continuity of formal features, which is a variegated business, and one that obtains by degree. There is no need for the concept of substance, and no function that it performs. Against this it might be argued that our conceptual scheme requires the concept of substance, even if our epistemic criteria for object reidentifications are always in principle removed from the metaphysical facts and possibilities. This rejoinder requires, however, that the conception of substance be at least coherent, and the coherence of the notion of substance is what is attacked in the second insubstantialist argument.

Second, according to some insubstantialists, the notion of substance extended in space and time is incoherent. For assume that there were a substance extended in space, say a spherical lump of gold. Then the gold would be conceptually divisible. Then there would be a possible world in which the substance were in fact divided into two lumps of gold. And there is a possible world in which the two parts were moved away from each other. And there is a possible world in which during successively smaller intervals in time, each part resulting from a previous division is divided into two parts. Within a finite period of time, then, infinitely many such successively quicker divisions can have taken place in some possible world. At the end of such a period of time, in a world in which all of the divisions had taken place, there would be no location in all of space which held any part of the gold, yet all that happened was the rearrangement of the parts of the gold. At the end of a dense division of the gold, then, no material particle would be left. But each operation was a mere rearrangement of parts, and a series of operations each of which is a mere rearrangements of parts in space, which series is concluded in a finite period of time, cannot effect the removal of a substance from existence. Therefore there couldn't have been any substance there in the first place.

Such considerations, then, lead to the conclusion, according to the insubstantialist, that the feature-placing language is more expressive of the ultimate truth of things than the substantialist language. Moreover, there is no inconsistency between denying the Platonic reification of features or properties, and denying the real existence of substances. What is left, then, if one affirms both *(a)* and *(b)* is a pure feature-placing conception of the world.

There are, then, two forms of ontological nihilism to consider: strict Platonic Formalism, according to which no substantial entity exists, but according to which Forms exist, and may even have predicates ascribed to them. Then there is the stronger form of ontological nihilism according to which no expression of the form "X is y," even where 'X' refers to a Form, is metaphysically or ontologically perspicuous.

The skeptic's question, then, addressed to the monistic mystic of part II, is whether or not the monistic mystic's existential ontological argument itself is a genuinely metaphysical argument, or, rather, merely points out the possibility of a form of experience which may or may not correspond to what ultimately exists.

It is through consideration of this question that a further value of mystical experience for metaphysics emerges. According to Strawson's program for the resuscitation of metaphysics in the 1960s, as found in *Individuals*, we distinguish between descriptive and revisionist metaphysics. The revisionist metaphysics was concerned with what is ultimately real. Descriptive metaphysics concerns itself with the presuppositions of the conceptual scheme which we require in order to carry on speaker-hearer discourse.

For two reasons, mystical experiential phenomenology of the sort exposed in chapter 4 shows the limitations inherent in the restriction of metaphysics to descriptive metaphysics. First, the mystic is interested in representations of the world whose viability ultimately pertains to monadic experience outside the contexts of speaker-hearer discourse. For this reason, accounts which prefer one or another such representation will not operate on criteria discovered through the exploration of presuppositions of speaker-hearer discourse. Second, we have already noted the possibility for what we called "conscious monism, subconscious pluralism." That is, it is conceivable that the mystic can train herself to remain consciously aware of the world in the manner of the ontological monist, while still subconsciously processing information in the language of thought of ontological pluralism. But since the processing is subconscious, it is as appropriate to hold that there is no pluralist metaphysics genuinely being used by such a mystic. What appear to the nonmystic to be the pluralistic pronouncements of the mystic, or pronouncements of the mystic presupposing pluralism, are the result of subconscious algorithms or processing methods. Thus, it is no longer clear whether ontological pluralism is a genuine presupposition of speaker-hearer discourse, even if it is embodied in the concept of a speaker distinct from a hearer.

To resolve the metaphysical questions posed by mystical experience, we need to abandon the assumption that contexts such as speaker-hearer discourse are definitive for all proper metaphysical work. Rather, mystical experience revives our sense of the metaphysical controversies between ontological monists, pluralists, and nihilists. And to adjudicate between ontological monism, pluralism, and nihilism, it will be necessary to resuscitate old style pre-Kantian revisionist, or speculative, metaphysics rather than rest content with the pluralistically biased description of the presuppositions of speaker-hearer discourse. If there is no way to do so, because we lack the epistemic tools to get at the noumenal realm, then no amount of mystical experience will come to our rescue. Although some of the mystics have or might have transcendent knowledge, depending on the degree of externalism allowed one in one's theory of knowledge, there is still tremendous difficulty, for the widely experienced mystic no less than the nonmystic, in figuring out which one. The variety in forms of mystical experience makes for the severity of the problem.

Thus, understanding mystical experience and paying it its due in metaphysics both reawakens our need for what Kant called "speculative metaphysics" and, at the same time, compounds our efforts to accomplish the tasks inherent in speculative metaphysics. This is not the happiest of outcomes, but it is better to face the problem squarely than to ignore it.

Six

Enlightenment Sacred and Secular

Knowledge is a monadic good, and so, in a sense, the inquiry of our last two chapters was in pursuit of a monadic good. Now, practically speaking, monadic fulfillment exhausts ethical pursuit for the hermit. But for everyone else, monadic fulfillment is a mere part of ethics. And so mystical realization for all but the hermit can be only a partial fulfillment. One must also consider interrelational, or non-monadic fulfillment. Moreover, the hermit's life-style itself presupposes an evaluation of interrelational obligations under which hermitude, at least sometimes, is acceptable. Thus, one is inescapably led into the complexities of interrelational ethics.

If we return now to the terms under which the irreconcilability of Enlightenment East and Enlightenment West traditions appeared, and apply our relational ethical framework to them, we find that these problems are role prioritization problems. For to grant that the monadic life finds its fulfillment in *samadhi*, is not to grant that the pursuit of one's own monadic bliss takes so much priority over the interrelational life, or over helping others pursue their monadic bliss, that all interrelational activities may as well be abandoned. And from the other side, even granting that everyone has some minimal citizenship relation with everyone else, we do not yet know what sort of claims the citizen relation places upon people in practical terms. Only when we answer such questions can we say whether systems which idealize *sanyasin* renunciation, to take the most extreme case, are morally deficient.

We have also seen in what direction we may look to find a way to harmonize the results of such an investigation with the maintenance of a mystical theory of value. So long as there is no insuperable practical obstacle to developing mystical value within a healthy interrelational life, mystical value and vigorously interrelational living can be combined. So long as it is not an absolute requirement that one live as a hermit in order to cultivate *samadhi*, it will be possible to adjust the balance between pursuit of mystical monadic value in quasi-hermitude or periods of retreat, and pursuit of social and interrelational value during periods of social interaction. We have seen how mystical values are, fundamentally, monadic values, and so a critique is always possible of any particular cultural and social implementation of an overall ethical schema which includes mystical value as the central monadic value. To say everyone would be happier, more blissful, if he or she strengthened and sustained the experience of ultimacy in every day living is not to say that one needs to be a hermit to do this.

Our task, then, is threefold: *(a)* to determine whether mystical practice requires hermitude or near hermitude, and if so for what sorts of periods of time; *(b)* to locate a point of proper balance between the self relation and the other relations; and *(c)* to see whether the main exponents of Enlightenment East have in fact been deficient in the way they have located the point of balance between self fulfillment and interrelational fulfillment. The first question is easy to resolve: given the many gradations of mystical monasticism, and given vigorously mystical householder paths within Buddhism, the Sant Mat tradition, Taoism, esoteric Judaism, Sufism, and others, we can be sure that neither extended hermitude nor celibacy is a necessary condition of mysticism. The second and third questions, however, are more difficult. In this chapter, our inquiry into the second issue will lead us to consider religious and secular values in the context of the Enlightenment East and West controversy. In the next chapter, we will see whether the critique of Enlightenment East as originally presented in chapter 1 is either accurate or justified, and if justified whether the Enlightenment East vision can be rectified.

I.

Two Types of Value Theory: Monadic and
Interrelational; or, the Life of Experience
Versus the Life of Dialogue

Underlying the Enlightenment West critique of mysticism lurks an assumption that has not been fully articulated and that perhaps may best be articulated in terms of a contrast between two types of ethics. The first type revolves around monadic value, and hence may be called a "monadic theory of value"; and the second type revolves around interrelational value, and hence may be called an "interrelational theory of value." By 'interrelational value,' we mean an intrinsic value that only arises in a context in which two or more distinct persons are in relation to each other. The monadic theory of value revolves around monadic value in these ways: it depicts all intrinsic value as monadic value; or it emphasizes monadic value over interrelational value in that it prioritizes monadic value over interrelational value. The interrelational theory of value revolves around interrelational value in that it prioritizes some interrelational value over any monadic value.

Let us examine how this contrast works in practice. No ethical theorist can altogether ignore monadic value. Everyone, that is, should be willing to acknowledge that some intrinsic goods are monadic. Yet there are some people who hold that the hermit's existence is fundamentally barren. No matter how deeply one realizes the ultimacy of the present moment, unless there is another person to somehow share that realization, the realization is fruitless, or barren, according to this viewpoint. It follows from such a point of view that there is something missing in any life which revolves around the exclusive pursuit of monadic value.

In representing interrelational values, we must take care to note exactly what the position states. The view not only holds that something is missing in a life in which one pursues one's own monadic value exclusively, but also that something is missing in a life in which one's actions on behalf of others are pursued with the sole ultimate aim of increasing the others' monadic value and one's own monadic value! In other words, something is missing in any life in which the interrelational activities are seen as purely instrumental to the fulfillment of the parties' respective monadic interests or goods. What is missing is the experience of full mutuality, or love, the experience of the relationship itself as being of intrinsic value.

There are some simple ways in which the reader can test for the monadic versus interrelational ethical viewpoint. Consider the question, "Can you conceive of being fulfilled if you were the only person left alive in the world, or if you were abandoned alone on a distant planet with no hope of ever being picked up and brought back to planet earth?" If a life of complete and uninterrupted solitude seems to you to be pretty much not worth living, then you most likely have an interrelational ethical intuition. On the other hand, if you can conceive of fulfillment under such conditions, or, more generally, if you see interrelational life as instrumental toward everyone's monadic fulfillment, then you have a distinctly monadic intuition.

To state this another way, if you think it is the character of a relationship itself which has ultimate, intrinsic value; if you think the unit of fulfillment in a marriage is the marital partnership; if you think the unit of fulfillment in a society is the community; if you think the unit of fulfillment in the relation of parents to children is the family unit itself; and, if you think these interrelational fulfillments are deeper than any monadic satisfaction or pleasure, then you have the intuition of interrelational ethics.

If we were to apply this distinction to Enlightenment East and Enlightenment West visions, we would expect that Enlightenment East ethics is monadic, whereas Enlightenment West vision is interrelational. However, the contrast between monadic and interrelational thinking does not apply so neatly across Enlightenment East and West visions. For instance, the Enlightenment West vision of eudaimonian individualism from Thomas Hobbes right on through John Stuart Mill and Bertrand Russell, conceives of individuals in overwhelmingly monadic terms. Relational life under utilitarian philosophies as standardly given in the classic literature is, typically, conceived of as instrumental toward the fulfillment of each and everyone's monadic interests. And Advaita Vedanta, which is mystical monism, is sometimes encased in an overall moral and social vision, as expressed, for instance, in the *Bhagavad Gita*, which centers on the injunction to fulfill your relational *dharma*, abandoning the fruit of the relation for the purity of the action itself, and this seems to be interrelational rather than monadic. The fruit of the relation would be monadic value, for you, or the recipient of your action. The *dharmic* purity of role fulfillment is an expression of interrelational value.

It may also be that the controversy over the relationship between deontological ethics and rule utilitarianism is best expressed in terms of this contrast between monadic and interrelational ethical thinking. Rule utilitarianism holds that the proper way to calculate utilities is to do so over practices or rules, not over individual actions. For example, instead of asking oneself whether telling some particular lie is likely to maximize happiness, one asks oneself whether following the practice of telling lies is likely to maximize happiness. Some analysts have held that rule utilitarianism is indistinguishable from deontological ethics. Yet there is some stubborn feature of deontological thinking which does not seem to be adequately captured within rule utilitarianism. Perhaps this feature is an assessment of interrelational life, that is, polyadic relations, as being more important than the monadic relation, that is, the self relation. Technically speaking, then, it is possible to have two versions of a utilitarian scheme: a utilitarian scheme that regards interrelational life as instrumental toward monadic fulfillment, and, on the other hand, a utilitarian scheme that regards interrelational life as intrinsically good, and, perhaps, as ranking higher in priority than monadic fulfillment. But perhaps it is not similarly possible to have two versions of a deontological scheme. The deontological scheme regards interrelational value as paramount. However, neither utilitarian nor deontological expressions have been given in explicitly relational terms. Relational ethics helps to clarify the point.

Further, although utilitarian ethics can be either monadic or interrelational in theory, one will search in vain for explicit exponents of utilitarian ethics to express themselves in decisively interrelational ways. Consider Kai Nielsen as a representative contemporary eudaimonian theorist. He writes, "A man could be said to have lived a happy life if he had found lasting sources of satisfaction in his life and if he had been able to find certain goals worth while and to achieve at least some of them. He could indeed have suffered some pain and anxiety, but his life, for the most part, must have been free from pain, estrangement and despair and must, on balance have been a life which he has liked and found worth while. Surely we have no good grounds for saying that no one achieves such a balance. . . . We all have some idea of what would make us happy and of what would make us unhappy. . . . What are these relatively permanent sources of human happiness that we all want or need? What is it which, if we have it, will give us the basis for a life that could properly be said to be happy? We all desire to be free from pain and want. . . . We all want a life in which sometimes we can enjoy ourselves and in which we can attain our fair share of some of the simple pleasures that we all desire. . . . We also need security and emotional peace. We need and want a life in which we will not be constantly threatened with physical or emotional harassment. . . . Human love and companionship are also central to a happy life. . . . Furthermore, we all need some sort of creative employment or meaningful work to give our lives point, to save them from boredom, drudgery and futility. . . . We want and need art, music, and the dance. We find pleasure in travel and conversation and in a rich variety of experiences. The sources of human enjoyment are obviously too numerous to detail. . . . Only a Steppenwolfish personality, beguiled by impossible expectations and warped by irrational guilts and fears, can fail to find happiness in the realization of such ends. But to be free of impossible expectations people must clearly recognize that there is no 'one big thing' (or, for that matter, 'one small thing') which would make them permanently happy; almost anything permanently and exclusively pursued will lead to that nausea that Sartre has so forcefully brought to our attention. But we can, if we are not too sick and if our situation is not too precarious, find lasting sources of human happiness in a purely secular world" (*Ethics Without God*, pp. 51, 52).

Aside from the references to love, companionship, and the pleasures of conversation, all other sources of happiness listed are clearly monadic. And even the experience of love, companionship, and the pleasure of conversation might be interpreted by degrees in monadic and interrelational ways. Sexual happiness is a good model to see how a relationship can be experienced primarily monadically or primarily interrelationally. Orgasm is itself a monadic pleasure. For some people, the loving sexual relation is primarily instrumental toward the monadic pleasure of each partner. For others, the monadic pleasure is an expressive by-product of what is central, namely, the relational experience of loving mutuality.

Where, then, do we look to find an explicitly polyadic ethical vision within Enlightenment West? I suggest that even more clearly than in Kantian deontological ethics we find it in Martin Buber's *I-Thou*. For Buber, the life of dialogue, of living interrelation is paramount, and no monadic, even mystical, experience can compare in value. Buber begins his exposition, "The world is twofold for humanity in accordance with humanity's twofold attitude. The attitude of humanity is twofold in accordance with the two basic words a person can speak. The basic words are not single words, but word pairs. One basic word is the word pair I-You. The other basic word is the word pair I-It; but this basic word is not changed when he or she takes the place of It. Thus the I of a person is also twofold. For the I of the basic word I-You is different from that in the basic word I-It. Basic words do not state something that might exist outside them; by being spoken they establish a mode of existence. Basic words are spoken with one's being. When one says You, the I of the word pair I-You is said, too. When one says It, the I of the word pair I-It is said, too. *The basic word I-You can only be spoken with one's whole being. The basic word I-It can never be spoken with one's whole being*" (*I and Thou*, 1970; emphasis added). [Translation altered to update gender references. Also, in the original each of these sentences begins a paragraph.] The roots of this vision are to be found in the thought of William James, for whom the essence of the religious vision is described this way: "The universe is no longer a mere *It* to us, but a *Thou*, if we are religious" (*The Will To Believe*, chap. 10). They are also to be found in the thought of C. S. Pierce, whose first metaphysical system was based on the relations between I, Thou, and It; and all the way back to Augustine's agapistic solution to ethics, namely, the effort to "love and do Thy will."

Both in Augustine and Buber, the paradigmatic exponents of the interrelational ethical vision, the life of dialogue is the religious life par excellence, and the paradigmatic dialogue is the dialogue with the Divine Being. Indeed, for Buber, the life of dialogue is always dialogue with the Divine, for it is in the life of interpersonality, of interrelationship, of dialogue, that the Divine is revealed.

Paradoxically, the interpersonal polyadic ethics, which should have been the ethics of Enlightenment West, is articulated as a religious vision in western sources. The ethics of utilitarianism, eudaimonian ethics, which is paradigmatic for the ethics of Enlightenment West, is not only secular, as is to be expected, but also monadic, as is not to be expected. What do we make of this crossover? Enlightenment East traditions tend to be deeply religious in feeling and in institutional expression. Enlightenment West is explicitly secularist in its thrust, and, as well, finds its center in its valuation of individual autonomy, and its antitraditionalism in its assessment of patterns of social authority. But the ethics of interpersonality and dialogue, in the west is a religious vision, and the ethics of fulfillment in Enlightenment West is secularist. In Enlightenment West the ethical theory tends to be monadic, and in Enlightenment East the ethical theory is in the first instance problematic in relation to the metaphysics. In any case, the encasing ethical and social vision of an Enlightenment East tradition is likely to be interrelational.

I suggest that to find a method of establishing a proper balance between monadic and interrelational values, we need to make sense of this tangled skein of conceptual relations. And to make sense of this tangled skein of conceptual relations we need to look afresh at the relationship between religion and ethics.

II.

Religion and Ethics: The Standard Picture

The usual view of the relationship between religious ethics and Enlightenment West secular ethics turns on the Enlightenment West rejection of Divine Voluntarism, the latter being the view that the Divine Will for humans, what God wants us to do, is the ultimate foundation of ethics. Ethicists in general, according to the standard picture, come in two varieties: *(a)* Divine Voluntarists, for whom there is a strong connection between ethical practice and theistic religious belief, and *(b)* those who reject Divine Voluntarism, which includes both *(b*.i) believers in a Personal God who reject the notion that the Divine Will is the ultimate criterion of the good, and (*b*.2) secular humanists who do not believe in a Personal God but maintain that there is intrinsic value as described in theories eudaimonian, deontological, or some complex combination of these. Once one rejects Divine Voluntarism, it is thought, whether one believes in a Personal God or not, the ultimate foundation of ethical action lies in what is intrinsic to sentient beings as sentient beings, for example, in the fulfillment or realization of the potential which sentient beings, such as human beings, have for happiness.

Despite its currency at the popular level, the Divine Command or Divine Voluntarist view (we'll use the two titles interchangeably) has been very largely discredited. It has been widely held to be true by recent philosophers of the west, influenced by Plato's *Euthyphro* as the ancient model, and Cudworth's *Eternal and Immutable Morality* as the modern (i.e., post-Medieval) statement, that if God exists, what God plans for human beings God plans for the good, and correlatively, what is good is not good merely in virtue of God's holding those plans or commands.

Enlightenment West, indeed, can be seen precisely as the vision which posits an enlightenment which is an unburdening, a liberation, from the weighty oppressiveness of theocratic authority patterns, and an enlightenment which brings the light of reason and understanding to the darkness of a society founded on ignorant, uncomprehending obedience to prophetically delivered commands and prophetically sanctioned monarchic rulership.

Enlightenment East also sees itself as an enlightenment which is an unburdening, and an enlightenment which illuminates a darkness, but the burden is that of the cycle of existence, and the illumination is a monadic, inner illumination. At least so the matter is presented for both Enlightenment West and East in stereotypic expositions of them. How odd, then, that interrelational ethics, which should be an Enlightenment West ethics, is expressed as a religious ethic. And yet this religious ethic is not a religious ethic in virtue of the point of connection between ethics and religion as that point is standardly identified. Something must be wrong with the standard picture of the connection between religiosity and ethics!

There are two elements in the standard picture of this connection. The first is the view concerning the central point of potential contact between morality and religion, namely, Divine Voluntarism or Divine Command theory. The second is the negative assessment of the Divine Voluntarist position. In what follows I will try to show that the standard picture misses the mark, at least partly, on both scores. Divine

Voluntarism is not quite the incoherent hash it has been taken for. Divine Voluntarism could be of practical importance in establishing balances between interrelational and monadic value. The theory, however, is not matched by the facts it requires to engage, and so the justification of the modified Divine Voluntarist theory will not ultimately result in a practical difference for us. Second, and this point is ultimately germane for us, the Divine Voluntarist position is only one of two main points of possible contact between morality and religion; and whatever one's views of the Divine Voluntarist issue, the second point of possible contact between religion and ethics must not be ignored. It is this other point of contact, to be developed in section IV of the chapter, which will enable us, finally, to see our way through the tangled relations of religiosity, secularism, monadic and interelational value, mysticism and nonmysticism, that we have uncovered.

III.

Divine Voluntarism

Can we look to Divinely revealed answers to our questions concerning the proper point of balance between monadic and interrelational values? The standard response to Divine Voluntarism holds that even if the Supreme Personal Being, (God, unless otherwise noted) exists, and God commands us to do x, God's command issues from God's recognition, so to speak, or God's knowledge that x is good. It is not the case that x is good because God commands it. Therefore, the argument goes, it is ultimately irrelevant for us to know that God commands x, since our knowledge that God commands x is derivative of our knowledge that x is good. If we didn't know that x is good, we would never be in a position to properly confirm x as being a Divine command rather than the command of a malevolent devil or spirit masquerading as God. This is putting the criticism from our epistemic viewpoint. The criticism can also be put from God's viewpoint as well. If the ultimate criterion of the good were the Divine Will, then it would have to be God's criterion as well. But if it were, God would have no way to apply this criterion so as to distinguish an action God would command from an action God would prohibit. Then if the ultimate criterion of the good were the Divine Command, nothing would ever get to be commanded by God!

There have been several attempts to rethink the standard critique of Divine Voluntarism in recent decades, as, for example, in Baruch

Brody's "Morality and Religion Reconsidered"; Peter Geach's *God and The Soul* (pp. 117-129); and in Robert Adams's "A Modified Divine Command Theory of Ethical Wrongness." The basic idea underlying these modifications of the original Divine Command Theory is this. The original Divine Command Theory asserts that there is an important relevance of theistic belief to moral consciousness because the ultimate criterion of the good is the Will of God. The implication is that if we don't know the Will of God we won't know what is good. The standard criticisms of the original Divine Command Theory can be seen as consisting of two elements: *(a)* the refutation of the view that the ultimate criterion of the good is the Will of God; and *(b)* the conclusion or implication that because the Will of God cannot be the ultimate criterion of the good, there is no relevance, or no reason to think there is any relevance, of theistic belief to the practice of ethics. The modified Divine Command theories attempt to show that even if the refutation referred to in *(a)* is accomplished, it does not follow that *(b)* there is no relevance of theistic belief to the practice of ethics. It may still be, for example, that only from belief in God can one properly derive deontology; or it may be that when one factors in the duties of obedience humans would owe their Divine Creator, and the rights of a Creator to design the creation according to his own wishes and specifications, permissions could be given by God for actions that would on purely rational grounds be prohibited, for example, the killing of the higher animals for food on the part of people aware of how to thrive on vegetarian food, and prohibitions may be given by God for actions that might on purely rational grounds be permitted, for example, consensual adultery, or bowing before statues representing God; or it may be that Divine Command is identifiable with the good because of the character of God.

In what follows I'll focus on the most practical concern of all, the potential relevance of belief in Divine Command to an ethical system. In line with the modified Divine Command theories, I'll suggest that it would be plausible under some circumstances to maintain that Divine Command is the best working criterion of the good we have, just as the instructions of a parent may be the best working criterion of the good a child at a certain stage of moral development may have. Thus, it is still relevant to try to determine if there is a Personal God and if the Personal God has left identifiable commands for us. I'll then assess in detailed terms whether such a modified Divine Command theory is not only a theoretical possibility but plausible in substance. The conclusion will, in the end, be negative. However, our excursion will not be in vain: some considerations arising in connection with fideistic, or faith-based belief in Divine Voluntarism, will prove fruitful in an important area of the theory of knowledge, enabling a fuller response to relativist and antifoundationalist criticisms of Enlightenment West epistemology than was given in chapter 1. (The reader who is not tempted by modified Divine Voluntarism to begin with can skip directly to the section entitled, "Imaginaction and the theory of knowledge," p. 205, reviewing the section called "Some cases," p. 193, and the discussion surrounding it as required to make sense of the imaginaction and the theory of knowledge discussion.)

To see the alternative route to modified Divine Voluntarism, consider the following thought experiment: imagine that your blood cells were self-conscious creatures, autonomous and rational. Suppose further that your blood cells wanted to hang around your pancreas all day, because that, to them, was the equivalent of your sunbathing in Hawaii. They enjoy hanging around your pancreas. But your welfare depends on their doing their appointed job of circulating through the body and attacking the various microbes or noxious invaders. You might therefore issue a command to them to do what you want rather than hang around the pancreas. They may not be able to fully comprehend the scale on which your benefits and consciousness occur, but in some sense they should take it on faith that their proper role is something other than hanging around the pancreas, and sunbathing as it were.

To be sure, they are capable of understanding that the command issues from a being whose life is lived on a vast scale compared to theirs, and that this being has a welfare which is dependent on their doing what are to them onerous chores. So it is not as though you cannot explain to them at all why they must do these chores. Rather, they can be expected to understand that were it not for the command, rationally intelligible to them, that they should do these chores, they would do quite different things, such as hang around the pancreas all day.

Now consider the analogous situation. Suppose a supermind has created our cosmos for various purposes of its own. We are tiny, miniscule creatures, and we have some sort of function to play in God's vast scheme of things. Is it not reasonable to hold that what we really ought to do, above all other things, is figure out what the supermind wants of us, and do that, even if it involves sacrifice of many of our own interests? Moreover is there not a consistency at the metaphysics of morals level in holding *both* that a principle such as the principle of utility supplies the *ultimate* criterion of the good, and also that the ultimate *working* criterion of the good is what is in God's interests? If a personal God exists, then there is an interrelational fulfillment, a fundamental or basic relational category, and this relationship must be looked at with regard to role fulfillment, role prioritization, and defeasible or nondefeasible status. Further, the relation with God is non-defeasible the way that the citizen relation is non-defeasible, and in prioritization questions, God wins, hands down.

If God exists, then God's good must be taken into account in the moral calculus on any naturalistic or utilitarian ethic. What makes something good is not so much that it is commanded by God, but that it is desired by, or constitutive of the good of, some sentient being. But then it is surely relevant to find out whether God exists or not: God's good must count for so much. Alternatively, if a Personal God exists and has omnipotence over every bit of matter in our cosmos, then we are proper parts of God. Since, assuming God exists, we are proper parts of God, it can be argued, it becomes impossible to fully distinguish our interests from God's interests.

Thus, the critic of Divine voluntarism will win the meta-ethical battle, but lose the hypothetical-practical ethical war. Interestingly, the relationship between utilitarianism, theism, and Divine Voluntarism is thus revealed to be similar to the relationship between utilitarianism, solipsism, and egoism. If the utilitarian is a solipsist, then her pragmatic criterion for action is egoism, such egoism emerging on broadly factual grounds. If the utilitarian is a theist of a certain sort, Divine Voluntarism can result as the pragmatic criterion of action. Utilitarianism provides the ultimate moral criterion, but a factual picture has to be filled in in order to know what sentient beings populate the moral community.

The main pragmatic thrust of anti-Divine voluntarism is to reassure the moral practitioner that the existence of God need not be taken account of in the moral calculus. And this is precisely where anti-Divine voluntarism fails. We can do *metaethics* without concerning ourselves whether a personal God exists, but we cannot do *ethics proper, practical ethics*, in the first instance, without concerning ourselves over such a God's existence. If we are to fulfill our relational ethical lives we must raise the question: Does a God exist who issues commands which are not independently deducible by us?

It is important to call attention to the relative clause. We are not at this point interested in the existence of God per se. The mere question of God's existence we are interested in as a matter of deep curiosity, or deep intellectual moment. However, as far as the relation between ethics and religion is concerned, if a Personal God exists, but there is no explicit communication required from such a Being to us in order for us to deduce our ethical practices, then the question of a Personal God's existence is not a matter of practical ethical import to us, with only two qualifications.

The first is that any important piece of knowledge contributes to intellectual fulfillment, and so learning whether a Personal God exists contributes to monadic fulfillment. The second, and more important qualification with regard to our concerns, is that if a Personal God exists, there will be an interrelational good which is to enter into some kind of dialogue with the Personal God. This dialogue need not begin by an announcement or instruction on the part of the Personal God. It is the human who can initiate the dialogue by calling, praying, listening for the Divine Voice, and so on. But if the Divine Person responds by coming close as it were, by manifesting as a great Wise, Loving, Enveloping Presence, then the specific forms of activity issuing from such experiences of Divine exchange are not obligatory, mandated, or in any way heteronomously derived.

We must distinguish carefully, then, between the following conceptions of God: *(a)* The Specific Revelatory Personal God, that is, the God who reveals specific intentions or wishes or commands to people, such intentions, wishes, or commands not being independently rationally deducible by us; *(b)* The Non-Revelatory Personal God, that is, the God who is Personal, (has knowledge, purposes, plans, volitional states), but who does not explicitly communicate plans to people which they are not able to deduce independently, and so either does not communicate explicitly with people at all, or else communicates intentions, which are rationally deducible by people even if they hadn't been communicated, or enters into communication with people by manifesting as the Divinely Wise Loving Enveloping Presence; and *(c)* the Impersonal God, that is, the God who is, say, First Cause, or Infinite Being, but whose nature is such as to preclude the literal attribution of Personal characteristics such as knowledge, goals, plans, and volitional states.

The first argument we should consider is a general one to the effect that God cannot be Personal. The argument goes as follows: Suppose God were personal. Then the Ultimate Being would have various states which we can imagine to have been otherwise. Then, further, the Ultimate Being would have contingent states. But that which is Ultimate has no contingent states. Therefore God cannot be Personal.

This simple argument has not been given nearly the amount of philosophical airplay that it deserves, in my opinion. However, although it is a compelling argument, the question we are considering could still be raised in another way even if it were conceded that no super-person were God or fully God. For in order to consider our ethical obligations we must consider whether there is any super-person, regardless of whether it is deserving of the title 'God.' If there is a super-person, who created our cosmos and has total control over it, and has omniscience concerning it, and is benevolent with respect to all sentient beings in it, and so on, then the argument we were considering above still applies to such a super-person even if it is not proper to regard such a super-person as Ultimate, and therefore it is not proper to regard such a super-person as God or as fully God. There might well be other super-persons controlling other universes out of causal relation with ours, or responsible for the existence of the super-person who created our cosmos, none of whom is deserving of the title 'God' either. Still, we might have obligations to the super-person who created our universe.

If such a super-person exists, its desires always correspond to its interests, since it is omniscient (over its own states and our cosmos), and so its commands take proper account of its interests, and its interests are relevant in our moral calculations. So we need to know about its existence, and its nondeducible will, if it has any, if we are to do our best.

In the relational vocabulary, assuming a Personal God exists, then belief in the second, or *(b)*, type of God can result in a new relationship, a worshipping or loving relationship between a Wise Loving Super-person and the worshipper-communer. Belief in the first, or *(a)*, type of God can result both in new interrelational value and new specific practices conducive either to independently undeducible human fulfillments or the fulfillment of Divine interests, the fulfillment of the Divine Self.

We are now ready to address our question directly: Does a specifically communicating cosmic super-person exist, a cosmic super-person who issues instructions we could not have deduced on our own? To do the question justice, we want to consider both fideistic and fully rationalistic approaches.

Fideistic approaches to modified Divine Command

The fideistic approach to religious life has been most forcefully argued by James in *The Will To Believe*. According to James, belief in a Personal God is a genuine option. By 'genuine option' he means *(i)* a live option, not something either established by, or ruled out by our previously held beliefs; *(ii)* a forced option in that indifference amounts to disbelief; and *(iii)* a momentous option, an option which carries with it supremely important consequences for us. James holds that in any situation in which belief in *x* is a genuine option, we may choose to believe in *x* with full philosophical legitimacy or justification. His argument is that since the choice is forced, the view that in the absence of sufficient evidence one ought not to believe is unjustifiably biased in favor of agnosticism or atheism.

Our first criticism of James's view is that James does not adequately distinguish between imagining that *x* is the case, acting under the image that *x* is the case, and believing that *x* is the case. Specifically, so long as the existence of *x* is logically possible, I can conceive of how things would be if *x* existed. In this case, I am imagining *x* to exist, or conceiving of *x* as existing. It seems clear that to imagine that *x* exists does not normally produce in me the belief that *x* exists. For example, I can imagine that there is extraterrestrial life on a planet orbiting a star that I notice in the night sky. But this doesn't in and of itself produce the belief in me that there are such extraterrestrials. Further, if I am sufficiently motivated, it is possible for me to continue to imagine the world as though *x* exists, and to act as I would if *x* existed. However, such decisions to imagine the world a certain way, and to act as though the world were that way do not normally produce, nor constitute, belief that the world *is* that way. Only people who have no notion of being part of an objective reality can regard such acts of imagination and concomitant activities as constituting belief. This emerges clearly when one takes into consideration the sorts of motives which might lead one to decisions to imagine and act as though the world were a certain way in the absence of initial belief that the world is that way.

Some cases

Consider, for example, scientists for whom the belief in Extraterrestrials (ET's) is a live option, that is, the evidence neither establishes their existence nor rules out their existence. Some scientists in such a situation will actively send out messages into outer space in the hope that if there are ET's, they may answer, and future generations will receive the message. Does this imply that those scientists who send out such messages believe in ET's? Of course not. It is entirely consistent for someone to believe that the existence of ET's is unlikely, and yet imagine the world as though there were ET's and act as one would if there were, by sending out coded mathematical theorems as messages to them. Such hopes, acts of imagination, and activities, do not yield the belief in such scientists that there are ET's.

Or take the case of someone hoping against hope that the victim of a plane crash in a remote forest in winter is still alive after ten days of fruitless search. A decision to imagine the person still alive and a decision to act as if he were still alive by continuing the search is a fully rational activity even if one believes that there is only a one in a thousand chance that the person is still alive. Such hopes, imaginings, and activities are fully compatible with the maintenance of the original assessment of probabilities, and do not yield belief that the person is still alive, nor even that the person is probably still alive. To be sure, there are some people who are sufficiently subjectivistic as to find it difficult to maintain the fundamental distinction between imagining that someone is still alive, and acting under that image, on the one hand, and, on the other hand, believing that the person is indeed still alive. But to one who has a healthy sense of an objective world, which is unaffected by our beliefs and imaginings, and of the evidence being unchanged by one's acts of imagination and correlative activities, it is apparent that beliefs are not substantially altered by such decisions to imagine and to act-as-one-would-if. Nor is it by any means necessarily irrational to imagine the world in an unlikely way and to act as one would if the world were in what one takes to be an unlikely state. There is *rational imaginaction*, to coin a term, without belief. The unlikely rescue effort scenario is a conclusive example of this, for this is a case in which it can be not only rational to act under a hypothesis that is unlikely to be true, but also morally obligatory to act under a hypothesis that is unlikely to be true. There is, then, not merely weak rational imaginaction, but also strong rational imaginaction.

It is also worth noticing that rational imaginaction can include imaginaction under the image that *p* when one firmly believes that *p* is false. For instance, suppose A has embarrassed herself before B. A has said the wrong thing, and is of the belief that B must think horrible things of her. A decides, in the interests of restoring her own confidence, to imagine that the embarrassing incident never occurred and that that (disastrous) meeting between A and B went smoothly. A goes about imagining that A's last meeting with B went smoothly, and acting under that image, despite the fact that A firmly believes that the last meeting with B went poorly. The image of the meeting is suppressed in A's consciousness, and another image takes its place. But the belief is not being suppressed. A need not delude herself in order to restore her confidence.

The problem with James's analysis, then, is that he has not distinguished between what I'm calling "rational imaginaction" and belief. If fideism contains an important grain of truth, then, what is justified is only a decision to imagine the world a certain way, and a decision to act as one would if one believed the world were that way. What is forced is imaginaction in one direction or imaginaction in the other direction, and so one is never forced to choose to believe. Without the notion of the forced choice to believe one way or the other, however, James's legitimation of deciding to believe in God collapses.

Interestingly, the philosophical literature has been slow to distinguish clearly between rational imagination, both weak and strong, on the one hand, and belief, on the other. William Clifford catalyzed the ethics of voluntary belief debate in the last century without paying much attention to the psychology of voluntary belief (1879). He recognized no distinction between *philosophical fideism* and *psychological fideism*. Psychological fideism is the view that people can in fact come to hold beliefs—for example, in the existence of a super-person—by an act of will, independent of an assessment of evidence, so long as one has not positively rejected the belief. Philosophical fideism holds that psychological fideism is at least true to a degree, and second, that the process referred to in psychological fideism is justified in at least some circumstances. (For a recent account, which both examines the history of these distinctions and also contributes to the topic, by emphasizing the role that hope without full belief can play in religious consciousness, see Louis Pojman's *Religious Belief and the Will*. See also Bernard Williams, 1973, "Deciding To Believe.")

This brings us to the second criticism of James. James writes, "[R]eligion says essentially two things. First she says that the best things are the more eternal things, the overlapping things, the things in the universe that throw the last stone, so to speak, and say the final word. 'Perfection is eternal'—this phrase of Charles Secretan seems a good way of putting this first affirmation of religion. . . . The second affirmation of religion is that we are better off even now if we believe her first affirmation to be true." The problem here is that the first affirmation is too ambiguously and vaguely sketched to be capable of giving rise to a forced option of any kind; and the second affirmation is entirely psychologistic and can be established in the ordinary way without recourse to volitional belief. It will not give rise to a forced option because it will not meet the condition of being indeterminate on the evidence. It shows every sign of being determinate on the evidence. James claims to be defending an option to believe when all he is entitled to defend is either theistic imaginaction, or else the superiority of adopting a certain generalized pietistic, or contemplative, attitude toward the world, the superiority of which ought to emerge, and I think, does emerge, on a strictly naturalistic psychological account.

The only question remaining, then, is whether volitionalistic imaginaction (that is, imaginaction without belief) under a tradition of not independently deducible Divine Command can be legitimized as the exercise of a genuine option. In other words, suppose James were to concede that we're not entitled to volitionalistic *belief*. Couldn't he still say we're entitled to volitionalistic *imaginaction*?

In order to answer this question, we note that there are two possibilities: *(a)* the imaginaction does not conflict with any of our factual or ethical beliefs; *(b)* the imaginaction does conflict. For instance: suppose I take it that eating meat is cruel to animals whenever vegetarian know-how is available, and that vegetarian know-how is currently available. Then my reason leads me to the view that vegetarianism is currently preferable to carnivorism. Suppose I consider adopting Jewish, Christian, or Islamic Divine Voluntarist imaginaction. That is, I consider imagining the world as though God permitted Noah and Noah's descendants to eat meat, (*Gen*: 9: 3), even though this permission would not be rationally deducible, and I consider acting under this image. But then I must, in the process of considering this imaginaction, determine that such imaginaction is not currently permissible, because it does conflict with my moral and factual beliefs about the existence of sentient animals who are part of the moral community and whose welfare will needlessly suffer under this imaginaction. So I will only be permitted Divine Voluntarist imaginaction in the other cases, the cases in which the imaginaction would be consistent with my already established moral and factual beliefs. For instance, I would be permitted Divine Volitionalist action under the image that God is pleased when I worship a certain way, utter certain words, bow before certain statues, or refrain from bowing before any statues. In these cases there is, or may well be, no conflict with already established moral or factual beliefs, and so the imaginaction is permitted. But if the only imaginactions permitted are of the *(a)* variety in which there are no conflicts with independent moral or factual beliefs, opting for imaginaction under a Divine Volitional scheme will only have the very weakest effect on my interrelational moral life, if any, for it will be essentially an aesthetico-religious decision. One may become so happy, loving, and blessed through one's discovery of an inspiring myth under which to live that one's relational life is enhanced. But this is not a contact which yields specific conceptions of interrelational obligation and so on. There will be no effective impact of Divine Voluntarism on one's ethical obligations coming from a fideistic base.

Evidential belief in modified Divine Voluntarism

Is there proper grounding for Divine Voluntarism based upon evidential sources? Once again, justifying such belief requires not only justification of belief in a super-person, but also justification of belief in the identifiability of otherwise not deducible specific instructions as instructions issued by the super-person.

Justification for such belief cannot come through the various forms of the cosmological argument, nor through the ontological argument. The direct cosmological argument holds that everything which exists has a cause of its existence, and therefore the universe, being something that exists, has a cause of its existence, which cause we call "God." The finitistic cosmological argument holds that everything has a cause, and as there cannot be an infinite regress of (spatio-temporal, or, alternatively, formal) causes, therefore there must be a first cause of the universe, which we call "God." The infinitary cosmological argument holds that every series of causes either has every element contingent, or else some non-contingent element. But if every element were contingent, then, the infinity of causes would never suffice to explain its own contingent character. Then there must be some noncontingent cause, which we call "God." The (traditional) ontological argument holds that by definition God is a being who or which contains every attribute which is a perfection; but since existence is an attribute which is a perfection, therefore, by definition God is a being who or which has the attribute of existence. Therefore, we cannot conceive of such a being as nonexistent. And whenever we conceive of God, we must conceive of God as existent.

However interesting the issues raised by these arguments, none of them lays the ground for belief in a Divine Super-person. This is especially clear in the case of the cosmological arguments, none of which makes any direct or indirect reference to personal attributes or capabilities. Since not all causes are personal, the cosmological arguments need augmentation in order to yield a personal cause of the universe. Such augmentation comes through the considerations which give rise to the various forms of the design argument, and to the arguments from moral and prophetic experience. As for the ontological argument, it might be claimed that benevolent personality is a perfection, so that God is not only existent, but personal and benevolent.

However, all personality is complex rather than simple, and complexity, multiplicity, and plurality, are traditionally (and justifiably) seen as a lack of the perfection of simplicity. So this approach to the ontological argument runs into trouble. If the cosmological and ontological arguments are to be augmented so as to yield Divine intelligence or personality, it is likely to be through the design argument or through the argument based on religious experience or prophetic transmission.

There are four principal forms of the design argument. The direct design argument holds that wherever there is design, that design was caused by a designer. The universe exhibits design, and its design must therefore have been caused by a designer, to whom we give the name 'God'. The analogical design argument holds that the principle of analogy, (which states that if A is like B then for any x which has relation R to A there is a corresponding y which has relation R to B), yields the premise that like effects were caused by like causes. The effect, namely, the universe, including design-exhibiting beings, namely, persons, it follows that the cause must be personal or must at least include persons. The third argument proceeds from a similar principle as the second, but purports to derive it in a less general way, and purports to be free from the weakness arising from the vague generalism of the second argument. This argument accepts as a fundamental proposition or axiom of metaphysics that any cause must have at least as much reality as its effect. Since the effect includes persons, then the cause must have as much reality as the persons in the universe, and so the cause of the universe must in some way be personal. The fourth design argument suggests that the early stages of our universe are fine tuned for the evolution of life; and the only adequate account of such fine tuning is that the evolution of the cosmos was designed so as to be capable of producing life.

These are rich arguments and the philosophical issues embodied in them are as tangled and difficult as they are rewarding. However I do not propose to analyze the issues they raise until it can be shown that the second part of the belief required to connect theism with ethics, the identifiability of instructions not deducible by us, can have a plausible defense. Let us concede for the sake of discussion that there is reason to believe in the existence of a cosmic super-person. Is there any plausible defense of the notion that we can identify as issuing from such a super-person specific instructions for practice which could not have been independently deduced by us?

Let us look at the case in its most exaggerated possible form, namely, universal direct experiential basis of belief in such communications. Say the galaxies started spelling out messages, and this happened repeatedly and was confirmed with complete regularity and unanimity by all magicians, scientists, philosophers, skeptics, and so forth. Say that the messages purported to be from an omnibenevolent Supreme Being, and that the messages gave us humans specific instructions of all sorts, some of them apparently good, some apparently harmful or evil, some of them just weird (but for all we are able to tell, morally neutral). Surely some people would say that the instructions might just as well be from a Devil let loose on the world as from God, an omnibenevolent being. Others would be persuaded that the instructions are for the ultimate good, even the ones we can't see as good, both the apparently evil ones and the merely weird ones. How might such differing responses be rationally assessed?

Interestingly enough, there is no readily apparent rational procedure for the assessment of rival responses to the instructions of a cosmic super-person. According to some, the uniqueness of such a situation would parallel the uniqueness of each individual's birth into a particular family whose language and culture, and first sets of instructions the toddler of necessity trusts as embodying appropriateness. According to others, however, the uniqueness of the situation would be without parallel, since the super-person would be dealing with adults who had presumably acquired the ability to think and reason autonomously. Finally there would be those who would hold that the situation would have its proper parallel in the instructions issued from a position of authority by such individuals as government officials claiming that x ought to be done, the reasons wherefore having to be held confidential so as not to jeopardize national security or the like.

In order to sort out this question, we need to look at the nature of instructions given by parents and teachers to children and students, and the degree of intelligibility we may expect such instructions to have. As a psychological point, I offer the following empirical theses: Proponents of the first response have probably been asked to follow a lot of arbitrary authority in their youth. They have probably been told by parents or teachers that x or y or z is in their best interests though they (the parents and teachers, that is) couldn't possibly be expected to explain how that is so. Proponents of the latter two responses, on the other hand, have been taught in such a way as to place a premium on understanding, development of autonomous capacity to make decisions, and have been given only a minimum of "trust me and my reasons" instructions in their early years.

Psychological guesses aside, though, the first issue here is whether children need a good deal of "just do it" instructions, or whether, rather, wherever instructions are appropriately given to children it is also appropriate for the children or students to understand and identify positively with the ultimate task to be accomplished by them or ultimate benefit to be acquired by them as well as the immediate task which is the direct focus of the instructions.

On this score, the earliest educational situations are useful tests. The child who has never seen a car may not understand why she must stay off the road. An instruction to stay off the road may not be intelligible to her, even if a description of a very fast moving object that might harm her is abstractly understood by her. The problem is that she might not believe it, or might be distracted by the task of chasing after a ball. In such a case, the parent must ensure that adequate fencing, or adequate adult supervision is available. But as soon as is possible, the adult wants to explain to the child in such a way that the child can understand, and act on the understanding. Every child, soon enough, has the experience of physical harm, and so even if the child doesn't adequately assess the danger of playing alone in a swimming pool, say, the child at least identifies with the ultimate purpose of the rule that she mustn't play around the swimming pool unsupervised.

In general, it seems to me that there is no stage of life at which a rule can be verbally given whose general aim or rationale cannot be given. If a child or student is at too early a stage to be given even a vague idea of the ultimate purpose or purposes (since there is no rule-governed learning practice which is not educationally multidimensional) then the practice must be induced non-verbally (by building the fence, supervising the child, etc.) But once the rule can be grasped, so can the general purpose or purposes of the rule. (And naturally, there are transitional phases in which the purpose is given verbally, but the child is not yet competent to be without supervision or the fence.) Children old enough to learn the rules of volleyball are old enough to identify with the values of health, teamwork, physical coordination, stamina, and so on.

If this is so, then a God who has so created human beings that adult human beings must learn from Her in a way discontinuous with the way in which children best learn from their parents, and in a way which cannot be made rationally intelligible to them, is a God who lacks, or seems to lack, in the perfection of creative or pedagogic excellence. The third response, then, makes most prima facie sense: if the galaxies spelled out messages instructing us to do strange things, some of them apparently evil, and purported to be all for the good, we would rightly deal with these instructions in the light of the overall circumstances, just as we would if people in a position of power and authority issued commands without fully adequate explanation. How well, then, do the cases that are actually made out on experiential and prophetic bases work?

Alas, for every prophet transmitting, or claiming to transmit Divine not-rationally deducible instruction there are two or three counterprophets or countertraditions with comparable provenances transmitting contrary instructions.

For instance, the Jewish prophets transmitted the instruction that worship of God through statues of God, angel, man or beast, is an abomination to God, and brings dire consequences. Hindu avatars proclaim that God is pleased by worship through images, and the various aspects of Deity have associated images. Some Hindu traditions insist that the Deity is present in and through the physical statue, which must therefore be bathed, dressed, and fed accordingly. Mohammed's revelation sided with Moses' on this score, and Mohammed claimed that he had Divine authority in doing so. But the theistic or quasi-theistic Mahayana Buddhists proliferate Buddha images in their temples, and contemplation is frequently through the various Buddha forms. In some later Buddhist systems, salvation, or at least the gaining of merit, is held to be connected to appropriate use of images, specific sutras, ceremonies, and scrolls. Christians, meantime, refer approvingly to the Ten Commandments that state first and foremost the prohibition against the imaging of God. However, some Christians believe that God literally incarnated as Jesus, and place statues of Jesus prominently in churches for the faithful to bow before, in apparent direct contravention of one of the Ten Commandments, and, in any case in opposition to Divine Command as interpreted by literalist Jews and Muslims.

What rational response can be made to these sorts of conflicts of claim about what the Supreme Person wants of people? Some will try to defend an identification of the will of God on grounds of prophetic authority backed by miraculous accounts as experiential support transmitted through the generations to support the bona fides of the source. Others, religious pluralists, will defend the rationality of the various traditions, seeing in each such tradition, a discipline of holiness with its own benefits and, possibly, potential traps, for the spiritual aspirant. Others still will regard the apparent prophetic contradictions as disconfirmations of them all, and as warrant for the conclusion that none of them is likely to be in possession of the truth.

Only a defense of the first response will do for our purposes, the latter two being equivalent, as far as evidentially yielding the Commanding God is concerned. Obviously it would be an enormous task to take all the prophetic instructions and subject them to detailed inspection as to their plausible origins. Rather, it suffices to show that each main religious tradition is subject to enormous difficulties if its scriptural materials are interpreted literally.

The book of Genesis presents two inconsistent, and in any case scientifically unacceptable accounts of the stages of evolution of the cosmos, accounts, further, which are of a piece with other documents of similar antiquity. There is a good deal of literature current about the amazing prescience of the book of Genesis. Such accounts invariably leave out the most obvious, overwhelmingly damaging objections to the view that the Genesis account parallels that of the Big Bang, for example, the objection that in the Genesis account water preexists the creation of the first light. Moreover, the Genesis lineages are incoherent if interpreted literally. For instance, Javal is supposed to be the ancestor of tent dwellers, (Gen. 4:20) but his line, which is determined by male descent, disappeared in the flood, since Noah was not his descendant (Gen. 5). As far as Christian lineages are concerned, the Gospel of Luke presents an ancestry of Jesus which goes back to Adam, whose direct ancestor was God, thus committing the Christian literalist to acceptance of the Genesis lineage from God through Adam to Seth and so on as endorsed by Luke. (For a treatment of the discrepancies between the Luke and Matthew lineages of Jesus see Howard Marshall, 1979.) The acceptance of Islamic dietary commands as Divine Will could not have been expected of us by independent reason, but certainly could have been developed as a discipline of holiness by a people. Similarly, Islamic insistence that religious worship through images is abominable to God cannot be made rationally plausible. This is not to say that practicing aniconic worship of God cannot be rendered rationally intelligible, for it certainly can. The point is, rather, that the hostility of one style for another justified on the grounds of undeducible Divine Command is not rationally defensible without at least support from indicators of authenticity such as miracles. But the Islamic guarantees of the Jewish and Christian miracles such as the virgin birth of Jesus and the healings are obviously as weak as the Jewish and Christian sources themselves. Further, the Qu'uranic revelations are plainly ethnocentric, making only references to historical elements, religious traditions, and social concerns which Mohammed himself had access to. How plausible is it that Divine revelation meant to seal all prophecy would clothe itself so ethnocentrically? The Hindu caste system is easy to see as a social invention, hard to see as a literal instruction of an omnibenevolent supreme being, or literal management system of an omnibenevolent or just karmic process, and so on. On the other hand, all these literalist beliefs, practices, exclusivisms, ethnocentrisms, and so on are extremely easy to account for on naturalistic lines.

But once we reject the notion that there are specific instructions left by a Personal God for us, which instructions we must follow faithfully because we lack the capacity to independently deduce them or even confirm their morality, there is precious little point of potential connection between the development of ethics and religion through the route of Divine Command.

To put all this simply, if each major religion is an appropriate discipline of holiness, then none of them is literally correct in any exclusivist claim, and the scriptural materials including the instructions for specific modes of worship and ritual practice are to be regarded as the evolving disciplines of holiness of their creating peoples and groups.

Earlier I tried to show that the critic of Divine Command wins the battle but loses the hypothetical-practical war. Now we see that the success of the Divine Command proponent in showing the possibility of a connection between religion and ethics through Divine Command does not in fact translate into fruition for ethics. Both theists and atheists need to think practical ethics through.

What of one who believes in a God of the second category, who issues no specific non-deducible instructions? It would seem that such a person rationally enters into what might well be construed as an intrinsically fulfilling relation with that God. The question then arises, do we need to judge the truth of the proposition that such a God exists, in order to assess the relation between ethics and religiosity? I think not. If such a relation is genuine because there are two distinct parties in it, rather than a worshipper and the worshipper's fictionally interpreted experience of a subconscious projection of a Wise Loving Enveloping Presence, then the relation is fulfilled. If it is not fulfilled, then there is monadic value which is being improperly construed. The cognitive debate must be carried on according to its merits. Either way, a relational ethic will accommodate these values, and role prioritization issues can be, at least, largely considered without resolution of the question whether the object of belief exists.

There is only one further argument potentially relevant to the connection between theistic belief of the second kind and the practice of ethics, which I am aware of. That is Peter Geach's view that deontology, and specifically, the view that evil can never be practiced to bring about good, is only properly derivable from theism. However, a close examination of Geach's tangled exposition, shows that he leaves unargued the crucial premise that the deontologist, who derives deontology from intrinsicalist considerations alone, is mistaken. The reasoning is empty at the crucial spot. Geach says, "So *unless* the rational knowledge that these practices are generally undesirable is itself a promulgation of the Divine law absolutely forbidding such practices, God has left most men without any promulgation of commands to them on these matters at all; which, on the theological premises I am assuming is absurd"(1969; emphasis added, p. 124). However, this Providentialism does not show what it claims to, that is, not only that theism of this kind yields deontology, but also that deontology presupposes theism. The only way to show that deontology presupposes theism is to show where pure deontological intuitions or arguments which have no Providential theistic ingredient go awry. Such deontological positions abound. The characteristic rejection of pure utilitarianism on grounds that it cannot accommodate intuitions of justice is of that kind. Yet Geach does not even attempt to show the groundlessness of the deontological intuition when presented as a pure intrinsicalism. Further, our relational framework, if anything, helps clarify how it is that a pure deontology, with no theistic ingredient, can be derived.

Within a relational framework, each relationship has its own intrinsic character and task. So long as one has an intuition of pure interrelational value, in addition to monadic value, one can understand how deontology is derivable without theistic Providentialism. Each actual concrete relationship gives rise to concrete interrelational value. Promise keeping, truth telling, and the like, to cite examples from Geach's range, arise from within the citizen to citizen relation. Just as monadic value arises directly from the nature of an individual qua rational agent in nature, so, too, citizenship values arise directly from the relation between two individuals qua agents sharing agency in nature. The fulfillment appropriate to this relationship entails the practices of promise keeping, truth telling, and the like. Theistic Providentialism need not be invoked at all.

We have made a long study of Divine Voluntarism. Our conclusion is that the existence of God is of no practical significance in determining our interrelational obligations. This is a negative conclusion, and so we should now try to see what fruit the inquiry may have yielded along the way.

Imaginaction and the theory of knowledge

The cases discussed during our exploration of fideism indicate an important pathway through the theory of knowledge, and in particular, one which enables us to respond to skeptical and antifoundationalist charges that Enlightenment West aspiration for cognitive rationality can never be fulfilled.

The first point that we want to note is that ethical activities of the usual sort are only intelligible in more or less realistic metaphysics and semantics. That is, if you don't think the term "the sentient beings on planet earth" refers to a plurality of objectively existing sentient beings, interrelational morality becomes unintelligible. If you can't justify belief in objectively existing others, how can you render moral restraints intelligible? Thus, the intelligibility of our moral practices seems to require a justification for the belief in the objective existence of others.

The second point is the extreme difficulty of coming by such a justification. In particular, each of the seven main possible sources of belief seems inadequate as the basis on which to acquire knowledge or justified belief that there is a plurality of sentient beings, and that one is not, say, a brain in a vat: *(a)* Sense experience is phenomenalistic, and would not be different if one were a brain in a vat; *(b)* Memory is likewise phenomenalistic; *(c)* Scientific inference, which relies on the principles of simplicity, predictive power, scope, and depth of data explained, internal consistency, consistency with other beliefs, and capacity to render the data intelligible, is not self-justifying. How do we know, for instance, that the simplest theory (our experiences are caused by objects in an external world) is the most likely to be true? Why can't the facts be arbitrarily complex at certain junctures? For this reason, one turns to *(d)* A priori reasoning, in search of a justification of scientific inference or some other justification of knowledge claims concerning other minds and the objects of the external world. Mathematical, semantic, and logical reasoning won't appropriately engage this issue, and epistemic reasoning is what we're doing throughout here. So one focuses on metaphysical reasoning. Now one might suggest that there is a cogent argument whose conclusions are the principles of scientific reasoning, relying on the principle at the border of scientific and metaphysical reasoning, as follows: *(i)* The more intelligible an account, the better the account; *(ii)* The simpler the account, other things being equal, the more intelligible; *(iii)* Therefore, the simpler the account, the better the account, other things being equal. In other words, intelligibility is used to justify the other principles of scientific reasoning. These arguments appear promising, but the promise vanishes in the face of further considerations.

The second phase of the critique of the seven possible sources of justified belief uses scientific reasoning to ultimately undermine itself. If we accept *(i)*, then we must also accept the following: *(iv)* Given two explanatory accounts of data D, the account with less arbitrariness is better. But this principle of minimizing arbitrariness leads one to accept modal realism, the view that every possible world is objectively real. (See Peter Unger, 1984a, for what I believe is the first exposition of this implication.) The basic idea is that so long as there are unfulfilled, or unreal, or unembodied possibles, then there is an account with less arbitrariness that can be conceived, namely, an account in which all possibles are real. If all possibles are real, there is no arbitrariness at all. And so long as there is an asymmetry between real possibles and the possibles that never made it to being real, so to speak, there is an ultimate arbitrariness. Thus, *(i)* implies modal realism.

But if modal realism is true, there are infinitely many uncoupled universes. And as many of them feature experience just like mine, but with the experiencer being a brain in a vat, as feature experience just like mine, but with the other sentient beings having objectively real existence. Therefore, the probability that in this world I am a brain in a vat is incalculable, or 50 percent, and I am not justified to believe that I am not a brain in a vat. In other words, the more we rely on minimizing arbitrariness, the less we are able to justify any belief concerning what Lewis (1986) calls the "actual universe," (this world) whose modality is not that of necessary truth. For there are as many universes in which the evidence is just like ours and the fact does not correspond to the apparent probabilistic calculation as universes in which the probability calculation works. Looked at another way, the infinite order of universes undermines all probabilistic calculations concerning this universe. Even the most absurd story told by what we'd normally regard as an obvious liar to the judge, so long as it is logically possible, is true in as many universes in which the evidence looks as bad as it does here, as universes in which it isn't true. Further, for every universe like this one in which I'm not a brain in a vat, and am doing the good it seems I'm doing by giving food to the needy and so on, there is a universe in which the experiencer is a brain in a vat, and every time the experiencer tries to do something good in the phenomenalistic realm, the mad, and evil, scientists, experimenting on the brain in the vat, cause immense harm to various real people in the superworld. Recognition of this undercuts an expected utility justification of one's choices.

Thus, none of the phenomenalistic, scientific, or metaphysical potential sources of justified belief concerning other minds and the external world has been fruitful. We continue further, then, with our critique of the seven possible sources of justified belief in other minds and the external world: *(e)* Fideistic belief has been shown to be either self-deceptive, or, worse, incoherent; *(f)* Evaluative reasoning cannot lead us to a conclusion on the existence of other sentient beings. It would appear that only what we might call *(g)* "prophetic intuition" remains. A person P prophetically intuits the truth of proposition *p* just in those cases in which, first, the proper source of a justified belief in *p* includes phenomenalistic experience, or scientific reasoning, or a general metaphysical principle or other a priori principle, and yet, second, without the involvement of, or reliance upon, such a source, P has the unshakable belief that *p*. Prophetic intuition doesn't seem to hold much promise at all. Indeed, it holds no promise to give a foundation either for knowledge of the external world or justified belief in the external world. Knowledge implies justified belief, and by definition, justified belief through prophetic intuition will not be present since the source is not adequate to it.

However, our critique of fideism has yielded some crucially important cases. In particular we have discovered that there is a difference between imaginaction and belief, and that there is a study of the rationality of imaginaction distinct from the study of the justification of belief. In the case of the embarrassed friend, imaginaction under hypothesis not-*p*, (the incident never took place) when one justifiably believes that *p*, is weakly rational; and in the case of the searcher, imaginaction under the hypothesis *p* (the hiker is still alive) when *p* is rather unlikely to be true is strongly rational. Similarly, it may well be that imaginaction under the hypothesis that there are other sentient beings is strongly rational even if the belief in other sentient beings is not justified. And this would be enough for all practical purposes.

Consider, now, the position of someone suffering from delusions. Suppose she thinks that unless she washes her hands immediately, a child across the way is in grave danger of being brainwashed into joining an evil gang by radio waves coming in from Mars. Now assume that she has no phenomenalistic experience which, interpreted by the lights of scientific reasoning, and so forth, would warrant such a conclusion. Yet she has an unshakable belief that it is so. So her belief is a prophetic intuition. Her belief is unjustified. But what does rationality require of her? Since she has the unshakable conviction that she must wash her hands or grave harm will befall the child across the way, she is in a position not entirely unlike that of the searcher whose belief is that the hiker has probably succumbed. Both are obliged under rationality to act under a hypothesis contrary to the objective determination of the probabilities. The searcher doesn't believe in the survival of the hiker, and believes rather that the hiker's death is more likely, but is obliged to act under the hypothesis of the hiker's survival for reasons having to do with expected utility. The victim of delusions believes, unjustifiably, in the danger and its prevention by hand-washing, and is obliged to act under the unjustifiable belief because it is a prophetic intuition, and carries with it a strong form of conviction. In other words, it's strongly rational to act under a belief, even if the belief happens to be unjustified, and even faced with the evidence that it's unjustified, so long as you are misappraising the evidence. It's not just that the victim of a delusion has gone beyond the pale of rationality. The victim of a delusion has lost rationality in appraisal of the evidence, but not in the rationality of which belief to act under given the misappraisal of the evidence. The commonsensical reasoning concerning the evidence is merely abstract, a shadow, a piece of intellectual puffery to one suffering from delusions, (just like skepticism to the non-philosopher, or idealism to Dr. Johnson). The prophetic intuition yields an unshakable representation of how things stand, or more modestly, the conclusion that the delusion is extremely probable. Rationality does not require that the victim of a delusion believe in the delusion, but it does requires imaginaction under the image of the delusion in preference to imaginaction under what is appraised as a shadowy piece of intellectual puffery.

And so, finally, consider the predicament that you and I are in. Accept the worst case for the sake of discussion: we have clear evidence that none of our beliefs concerning the external world is justified. Indeed, we have what seems to be clear evidence that there's as good a chance that every time we think we're doing good we're doing great harm as that we're doing the good we think. Yet we have a prophetic intuition that the external world exists and that the other minds are as we think they are, and that when we think we're doing good we are. We are not entitled to believe in the other minds, but we are obliged under rationality to act under the hypothesis that they are as we imagine they are.

This modifies Pyrrhonian skepticism and Humean skepticism on the one side, and foundationalism on the other side, in a fundamental way. It reconstructs a rational foundation for ethical and cognitive practice without giving in either to unjustified belief out of habit or convention, or to a pseudo-foundation for justified belief which does not stand up to rigorous inquiry. It also points to a direction of training for the mind: Our efforts should be to release from belief, in the Pyrrhonian manner, while maintaining the foundationalist's insistence on making intelligible the practical life under the canon of rationality. The life of rationally grounded imaginaction is a Middle Path between a skepticism which cannot justify its conventionality or practice of whatever sort, and a foundationalism which aims at justification in belief, rather than rationality of imaginaction, and so aims too high, and always fails.

Along the way we've also seen that religious imaginaction may be highly rational, so long as the religiosity is of the nonauthoritarian theist variety, or the Impersonal God, or sacralist variety. And this feeds directly into our next topic.

IV.

Sacralism

I now want to show that there is a stronger and more interesting connection between ethics and religious doctrine than that potentially provided by Divine Voluntarism. It is in terms of this more interesting connection that the relations between religiosity and secularism, monadic and polyadic ethics, mysticism and nonmysticism can be sorted out. I will suggest that religious ethics is distinct from secular ethics. However, religious ethics in this second sense is entirely consistent with humanist and secularist metaphysics with regard to divine or cosmic super-persons and prophetic authority. This view of religious ethics as sacralism will then be applied to Enlightenment East and Enlightenment West issues.

Having seen that the scriptural injunctions of any of the prophetic traditions of the world cannot be plausibly accepted as literal communications of otherwise nondeducible instructions from a cosmic super-person, we are left with the question of whether the instructions of the religious traditions themselves can be of any value to us. If a Jew no longer thinks of thrice daily prayer or the detailed Talmudic instructions for the ritual practice of the Sabbath as specific, literal communications from a Divine Super-person, then what value can such practices have? If the dressing and bathing of statues of Krishna are not literal expressions of obeisance to a Divine Super-person, who receives or responds to these expressions with some distinct form of favor, what value, if any, can such activities have?

I want to suggest that they can continue to have enormous value. More particularly, there are two main practical differences between religious ethics and secular ethics. The first has already been touched on in chapters 2 and 3: religious ethics posits as the central value, the blissful experience of Ultimacy and Mystery permeating everyday life. Secular ethics does not center values on metaphysical Mystery and the experience of Ultimacy. The second is the expression of this central religious value of the contemplation of Ultimacy in a system of ritual and symbolic expression which makes one's life a religious expression par excellence.

Religious ethics is indeed filled with traditionalist instructions: The Confucians said, practice the rituals! (An insightful interpretation of Confucianism, which emphasizes this aspect of the teachings, is found in Herbert Fingarette's *Confucius, The Secular As Sacred*, "Human Community As Holy Rite." Also Rodney Taylor's *The Confucian Way of Contemplation*, and *The Religious Dimensions of Confucianism* emphasize the religious side of the tradition in general. Roger Ames's and David Hall's *Thinking Through Confucius* emphasizes the aesthetic immanentalism in Confucius's thought and this, too, ties in with the sacralist theme. Robert C. Neville's *The Puritan Smile* shows how Confucian sense of responsibility can be integrated with liberalism. The reconstructive theme will emerge in what follows as well.) Observant Jews practice an elaborate set of rituals governing so many facets of everyday life. For instance, during the course of a typical weekday, an observant Jew recites approximately one hundred blessings. Anyone who has experienced the warmth and joy of the Jewish Sabbath knows the power of this twenty-four hour ritual. The Buddhist traditions are many and varied, but both the clerics and the lay practitioners are enjoined to practice ceremonies of great power and beauty, though the metaphysics underlying many of the ceremonies (if the myths are interpreted literally) has dubious standing. The Christian Eucharist is a deeply moving ceremony of mystic participation. The five daily prayer periods of the Islamic tradition provide a deeply stabilizing regular routine within which to orient towards Ultimacy, and so on.

However, the usual antiliteralist response to religious life is this: if the myths and instructions are not the literal instructions of a supreme personal being, or if they're not the literal ways of conforming to the occult karmic requirements for progress through the cycles of existence, then there is no point practicing the traditions of the religion. If ethics is the human response to the fact of moral community and moral agency, and no literalistic guidance is provided from some transcendent personal being, or occultly or prophetically delivered ritualistic recipes, then the traditional observances of religion are barren and without purpose. Indeed, having discarded literalism as naive and authoritarian, the non literalist will want to be careful to clarify and express this rejection, and will not want to engage in ritual that reminds the practitioner of the rejected literalist interpretation. Many do not want to engage in petitionary prayer ostensibly addressed to a personal God even when that petitionary prayer is interpreted along metaphorical lines as suggested by Paul van Buren in *The Edges of Language*, for instance. There is much substance in this rejection of ritual by those for whom literalism is rejected. After all, the social authority patterns associated with the literalist interpretation tend to coagulate and remain encrusted on the rituals themselves, and these authority patterns are held by the antiliteralists to have been frequently objectionable. Therefore there is a real question as to whether or not a religious ritual introduced in a literalist manner can ever be rehabilitated, so to speak, in the eyes of one who rejects the literalist metaphysics.

Of course, there are many traditions for which there is no equivalent question. For instance, religious systems whose myths remain pluralist and folkish, such as the aboriginal traditions, tend not to be subject to the tensions of literalism to begin with. It has always struck me as telling that supposedly primitive aboriginal shamans are sophisticated enough to react with amusement if anyone thinks that *they* think that there once literally was a raven who stole the sunlight, for instance, yet some supposedly sophisticated contemporary Westerners are not similarly sophisticated in relation to their own ancient materials.

It is commonly thought that the dominant clashing world views of our time are religious versus secularist world views. In some sense this is undoubtedly true. But if the contrast between religiosity and secularism is then identified with religious literalism versus secularism, a great distortion of the currently available world views is created. A minimally interesting classification of dominant world views at the present time requires distinction between the three religious world views mentioned in the first part of the chapter, and one nonreligious world view. In what follows, I will try to show the relevance to ethics of the religiosity of the second two of the three religious views. To recap, and to reframe somewhat to suit our context, these four world views are:

(a) Theist literal authoritarian revelationalism: God is a personal being who reveals specific not independently deducible instructions

to humans, and these instructions form the basis of social and political organizational authority.

(b) Theist non-literal revelationalism: God is a personal being whose intentions and glories are diffuse throughout all of nature. *In some metaphoric or attenuated sense*, God reveals personal attributes through the natural order, which, of course, includes the human social order, the creation of scriptures channeled through people and the like. But the critical point here is that scriptures are channeled through people just as mathematics and poetry are Divine cognitions channeled through people. It is metaphorically, not literally, that scriptures reveal Divine Nature. The Divine Nature is accessible through botany and sociology as well as through the study of Scripture. The Divine Nature may also be revealed in special experiences of being in the Presence of a Loving, Wise, Enveloping Mind, but such experiences transform the individual in global, not content-specific ways. Such experiences are more like watering a plant at its roots than like clipping and binding specific branches. Consequently, social authority cannot be derived through one or another scripture.

(c) God is the Ultimate Being, the Infinite, Boundless, Ineffable, Absolute Being. God is (perhaps) Ultimate Consciousness. But either the nature of this consciousness is inexpressible, or this consciousness is entirely unlike personal consciousness.

(d) None of the above. For, according to the proponents of this fourth view, there is convincing evidence against *(a)*. There is either no or insufficient evidence for *(b)* and in any case, no ethical relevance of *(b)*. Finally, there is no clear meaning to *(c)*, or insufficient evidence for *(c)* if it is meaningful; nor is there any ethical relevance of *(c)*.

What I would like to show here is that there is ethical relevance to *(b)* and *(c)*, so that nonliteralist religious practitioners can be seen to share an ethical practice, which is distinctly religious, and which indeed they may share with some proponents of *(a)*, some religious literalists, which religious ethics is entirely independent of the Divine Voluntarist ethics.

In a word, the religious ethics which is, or may be, common to literalist and nonliteralist religious proponents and practitioners, is the ethics that is centered on the *practice of the awareness of the sacred*.

Both of the main terms, 'practice,' and 'awareness to the sacred,' in the central phrase are important. For there is not only the recognition on the part of the religious ethicist of the centrality of the *experience* of the sacred, but also the recognition on the part of the religious ethicist of the centrality of the *practice* of the sacred.

Religious ethics, then, the general religious ethics over and above Divine Voluntarism, is founded in a tripartite religio-psychological thesis:

First, there is an experience of the sacredness of life, and the sacredness of nature, which is distinct from the experience of beauty, sympathy, or love, or the intuition of obligation, duty, and similar central elements in the secularist theory of moral value.

Second, the experience of the sacredness of human life and the natural world is somehow worth cultivating and promoting as involving a kind of happiness or fulfillment in people that is supreme, unique, or at least important.

Third, deep, fully founded stabilization of the experience of the sacredness of human life and the natural world is cultivated through disciplined, regular practice every bit as much as the stabilization of an understanding of modern physics, for instance, is cultivated through disciplined practice of the concepts involved.

The first and the third of these points are broadly empirical. The second is evaluative. We will examine these three pillars of *sacralist* religious ethics in turn.

(1) *The experience of the sacred.* In *The Idea Of The Holy*, Rudolf Otto states that the experience of the sacred is best indicated by evocation. The experience of the sacred is, like so many "special" experiences, familiar in shades and colors to everyone, but needs articulation through sympathetic evocation. Otto evokes religious experience by reference to the experience of the uncanny, the awesome, fearful and fascinating Mystery. Mircea Eliade in *The Sacred And the Profane*, discloses the sacred through considering how it is experienced through space, time, and natural cycles. We may also express the intuition of the sacred through the categories of relational life.

Who has not thrilled to the mystery of the stars? "But what is *sacred* about the mystery of the stars?" asks the secularist. Perhaps it is not the mystery of the stars which is sacred, but human life in the light of the mystery of the stars.

Who has not thrilled to the mystery of a human birth? "Yes, but what is *sacred* about the mystery of a human birth?" asks the secularist. Perhaps it is not what we don't know about the mystery of human birth which is sacred, but the joy of human life in the light of the mystery of what we don't know, and suspect we never will and never can know, about human birth.

Who has not been moved by the poignancy of marriage, a bride and groom setting out together on the journey of life? "But what is *sacred* about a wedding ceremony, a convention whereby two people contract obligations and privileges with respect to each other?" asks the secularist. Perhaps it is not the convention which is sacred, but the lives of people pledged to each other in the light of the fragility and poignancy of their commitment.

Each fundamental moment and each relation in life can be seen under the aspect of the sacred. Perhaps not everyone sees life under the aspect of the sacred. Perhaps, indeed, some people would rather not see life under the aspect of the sacred. The more resistance to seeing life under this concept, the more clear it becomes that the experience of the sacred *is* at least available. Whether it is a central value is another matter. But the first point merely asserts that there is an experience of the sacred which is different from that of moral obligation or sympathy. Accordingly it becomes clear that there is an opportunity for a particular form of moral theory which holds the cultivation of the experience of the sacred as a central value. The more some would criticize the valuation of the experience of the sacred as central to ethics, the clearer it becomes that there is a distinct religious ethic which holds that the strengthening of the experience of sacrality is a central value. Whether this is true or not, that is, the means by which such a religious ethic may be justified, is another matter. Indeed, it is the subject matter of the second point.

(2) The strongest argument for secular universalism, as we saw in chapter 2, relies on the understanding that I am not the only one in the universe having the objective property of being a self-reflective conscious agent, subject to pleasure and pain, happiness and suffering. Rather, that in virtue of which I have intrinsic value is had by others, and they, too, have what arises from that feature, namely, intrinsic value. In this way, from recognizing the objective difference between a rational conscious agent and a mere inert nonconscious, non agent, I realize commonality with all persons, and attribute intrinsic value to them on the same basis I attribute intrinsic value to myself. Thus far, the typical stance of the nonreligious ethical universalist.

To this the sacralist has no objection. The sacralist has something to add, however, to the particular picture of intrinsic valuation. For an ethical theory either founders in an abstraction so pure that it can never bring guidance to practical reason, or it yields, one way or another, a theory with particular content. And once it has such content, the content will either include or will not include a religious sacralism of this sort.

But how to justify the role a proponent of religious ethics would assign the experience of the sacred? Here, of necessity, one appeals to experience, breadth of reflection, and practice. Sacralism is a vital element in ethics because of its intensity and centrality.

How is it central? Consider the intuition of the pietist: human life is situated in the context of a fathomless and wondrous infinite, and it is the continual return, relating the finiteness of life to the wondrous infinite in which it is situated, that intensifies the experience of the preciousness of life. What is it, after all, which so gratifies when one goes out at night in the country and gazes up at the stars? Is it not the experience of the preciousness of life, a preciousness which constitutes a sacredness, intensified by the shift in frame of reference? Isn't it, indeed, our seeing with keen inner vision the unlimited domain open to the gaze of mind contrasted with the finitude and limitations of physical embodiment, which infuses our consciousness with the sense of the sacredness of that which lives, breathes, and has the capacity of mind?

And this intuition of life as a sacred trust, or gift, free and unbidden, which we first recognize in our own case, enables us to regard others under the same wondrous light of sacred preciousness. The manner of reasoning of the secular nonsacralist is then repeated by the sacralist: The secular humanist asks the egoist: Do you not value yourself intrinsically? And do you not see that that in virtue of which you properly value yourself is shared by all persons? Similarly, the sacralist asks the secular humanist: Do you not see your life within the light of the wondrously sacred? And do you not see that the capacity for experiencing human finitude immersed in cosmic infinitude in virtue of which you properly experience your sacredness is shared by all persons?

Does the intution of sacredness, then, make a difference to ethics? The sacralist can legitimately claim there is a difference, even though it's not a difference in specific delineation of interrelational obligations. The difference arises in two respects. First, there is the simple difference that so long as intensification of the experience of the sacredness of life is an intrinsic good, a contributor to the fulfillment and self-realization of the individual, a view of monadic fulfillment with this component recognized and articulated differs from one which does not recognize it. In practical terms, the life of the individual which is in some measure centered on the deepening of the sense of the sacredness differs from the life which is not so centered. The intuition of the sacred is a form of joy.

And second, the attitude of the secular humanist who recognizes obligation both intellectually and through the experience of sympathy differs from the attitude of the sacralist who, in addition, experiences the intensity of the recognition of sacredness of persons. This difference in attitude translates subtly into action. Like the difference between I-it and I-Thou, the difference may be subtle, but in this subtlety lies so much life, Mystery, and even outcomes in planning. One way in which the planning and the actions of the sacralist may differ from those of the secularist we will see through the next point.

(3) The thesis that human beings will not fulfill themselves willy nilly, but rather that training, discipline, and habituation is essential for the full realization of human potential is a trivial and uncontrovertible truth in one sense and a controversial matter in another sense. In the one sense, it is obvious that human beings need to learn all sorts of skills in order to fulfill themselves. Children throughout all time and in all cultures have been induced into the community, taught toiletries, eating mores, language, social niceties, food harvesting, cooking, healing, shelter making, clothes making, cultural mythologies, and so on. Children left to their own devices, before they've been weaned, will die. Thus, in one sense, the thesis is incontrovertible.

But in another sense, the thesis is controversial. If the thesis means people need to be disciplined in something that attaches to the very essence, the summum bonum of fulfillment, then there will be exceptions taken. "What?" says the critic of this third component of sacralism, "I need to be trained in my very mode of consciousness? Says who!" This response of the critic of this third component of sacralism, which component we might call "ritualist sacralism," is in many respects understandable and even fully justified. All too often, the training of consciousness through ritual and mythological tradition has been linked to a system of dogma which has rendered inseparable in pragmatic terms the two theoretically independent processes of specific sociopolitico-metaphysical indoctrination on the one hand, and training in the intuition of the sacred, on the other.

It is our task, then, both conceptually and practically, to separate these two processes. We know that the metaphysical imagination is highly subject to training. Human beings are indeed vulnerable to indoctrination. But what makes an indoctrination acceptable in one period of time and unacceptable in another is that in one period of time an education in the received wisdom, namely, the earth rests on an elephant and the elephant rests on a turtle, is education in the best teachings available to the educators. In another age, however, education in the received wisdom that the earth rests on an elephant and the elephant rests on a turtle, can only be done by suppressing interest in science. Nowadays, for instance, education of children and youth in literal revelatory theism of Jewish, Christian, Islamic, Hindu, or Buddhist, varieties can only be widely successful in a context which makes largely unavailable to teenage members of the community the relevant critical materials. Many adults educated in this narrow manner will characteristically find it too difficult, too psychologically stressful, to undertake midlife scientific and metaphysical adjustments. However, education which restricts access to the real issues does people a disservice.

We must distinguish, then, between humanist ritualist religiosity and dogmatic ritualist religiosity. Dogmatic ritualist religiosity, at its best, includes the two ingredients of training in consciousness of the sacred, and training of the metaphysical and scientific imagination. At its worst it only trains, by way of restricting, the metaphysical imagination, which is a disservice. In our time, unfortunately, dogmatic religiosity requires such restrictions. Humanist ritualist religiosity, on the other hand, only attempts to use ritual and myth to train people in the intuition of the sacred, and the intuition of bliss through the experience of Ultimacy. Because most religious systems of ritual have had elements of pure sacralism and elements of metaphysically and ideologically controversial doctrines combined, the modern enterprise of sacralist religiosity almost inevitably involves a reconstructive aspect. Mordecai Kaplan, Paul Tillich, Muhammed Iqbal, Agehananda Bharati, among others, have attempted reconstructions of Jewish, Christian, Islamic, and Hindu ritualist systems, respectively, in an explicitly humanist religious vein. It is religious neotraditionalism in something of this vein that we will be examining here.

Although many if not most people experience the sacredness of life in rare and special moments, the dimension of the sacred is universally accessible. The great interest in recent decades in mythological systems and pagan religious forms and concepts has undoubtedly to do with a desire on the part of many to develop again the orientation toward the world which sees everything as an embodiment of a mythic event, a mirror down here of an eternal event drawn from an *illud tempus*, as Eliade puts it in *The Sacred And The*

Profane. Of course every religious system of ritual presents an opportunity to do this. But the unacceptable literalism associated with so much religious ritual makes people turn elsewhere for their sources of ritualistic mythology.

Consider a ritual such as the Tibetan Buddhist practice of performing a hundred thousand deep prostrations. It takes a year or two of intensive work to complete this exercise. The teachers who assign this practice say that it is good for stabilizing the mind of the spiritual aspirant. Surely this ritual must sometimes have its desired effect. Having stabilized the mind of the aspirant, the teacher is ready to introduce new forms of meditation and contemplation. Or consider the Jewish Sabbath, the Christian Eucharist, Islamic recital of the creed, yoga *asanas*, or daily Buddhist recitations and contemplation. All of these, plainly, can have the desired effect of strengthening in the practitioner the experience of the sacredness of life, and the experience of the preciousness of consciousness. Through practicing religious discipline the religious aspirant has a living, active framework within which to establish the habits of thought and intention toward the hallowing of the everyday, and the accessing of the wellsprings of joy and bliss in the knowledge of Ultimacy, God, or the Divine Mystery. As Huston Smith emphasizes, although the intution of the sacred or of the mystical is available and familiar by glimpses to people, these intuitions cannot become definitive of our lives without our undertaking some hard work (Smith, *Forgotten Truth*, pp. 112-114). In addition to the capacity for ritual to provide the individual with a framework for the sacralization of consciousness, there is also the social efficacy of ritual to be considered. Tom Driver in *The Magic of Ritual*, for instance, suggests that ritual when properly conceived and implemented has a positive order-creating, community-building, and transformative effect.

A sacralist ethics, moreover, can be stated within the vocabulary of a theory of value, an ethics of virtue, an ethics of principle, and a relational ethics. Sacralism as a theory of value states that the experience of the precious, sacred, and blissful mystery of finitude in the context of the Unlimited is an ultimate intrinsic value. Sacralism as an ethics of virtue states that the ideal character is one who maintains the consciousness of blissfulness in sacred Ultimacy. Sacralism as an ethics of principle states that those actions which most conduce toward the accessibility and stabilization in everyone of the awareness of joy in sacred Ultimacy are the correct actions. Obviously this latter principle is not meant to contain any resolution of the problems of role conflict or role harmonization. Rather, the value of the sacred underlies the experience of both interrelational and monadic life.

In a relational ethics, sacralism is the view that each of the fundamental relations one occupies should be seen under the aspect of the sacred. Whether one is in dialogue, or experiencing in solitude, the aspect of the sacred can manifest itself. Therefore our ethical vision can encompass both monadic and interrelational emphases. It can encompass both emphases in the "different strokes for different folks" way, and it can encompass both emphases in that any one person can focus exclusively on the self-regarding monadic value in stillness and on both universal monadic value, and interrelational value in the life of community. Maintaining awareness of the sacred in all ways crystallizes and clarifies a point of constancy in monadic-polyadic dynamic.

We began by noticing an oddity. Enlightenment West is a tradition of secularism and the rejection of religiosity; Enlightenment East is a tradition of the sacred. Yet Enlightenment West, in some sense, would be expected to stress polyadic fulfillments, which is not the case with the dominant eudaimonian ethics of Enlightenment West, and only really clearly articulated within religious philosophical traditions. We can now see that by conceiving of itself as a liberation from religiosity, the Enlightenment West tradition has sold itself short. Enlightenment West needed to reject one point of connection between religiosity and ethics, namely, Divine Voluntarism. But in regarding Divine Voluntarism as the only point of connection between religious life and ethics, it has missed out on both theistic and nontheistic nonauthoritarian sacralism. It would not be quite right, however, to associate the missing sacralism with Enlightenment East. That would be simplistic, given that the mystical traditions, the traditions of Enlightenment East, have their share of authoritarian irrationalisms, and the nonmystical religions have their share of nonauthoritarian sacralism. The sacralism missing from Enlightenment West is a dimension of religious value which may be found either in mystical or nonmystical western religious traditions or eastern religious traditions, once the irrationalist authoritarianisms have been purged. Given the availability of this sacralism free and "enlightened" from the burden of irrationalist authoritarianism, Enlightenment West finds fulfillment and completion by rejoining with the roots of the experience of the sacred.

Having articulated a sacralism, which may infuse both monadic and polyadic values, we have provided the engagement ring for Enlightenment East and West. We are ready now to consider the

Enlightenment West critique of Enlightenment East on grounds that the latter's prioritizations are world devaluing, which will be the subject of chapter 7, and on the grounds that it is antiscientific, which will be discussed in chapter 8. In chapter 9, we will escort Enlightenment East and Enlightenment West down the long aisle of human history, and perform the marriage ceremony itself.

Seven

Mysticism and Social Philosophy:
A Hidden Connection

Ideally, one wants to combine Enlightenment East with Enlightenment West perspectives. One wants to say "Let us promote both values and practices. Let science, social justice, and mysticism all flourish." However, as we've seen, there are critiques of the Enlightenment East traditions based on Enlightenment West values. These critiques hold that mysticism inevitably creates an otherworldliness that devalues life. If nothing has ultimate identity, if the world is an illusion, then why bother with the intensely difficult task of improving it? Isn't one illusion, one nothingness, as good as another? Moreover, according to the critics of Enlightenment East values, social institutions associated with mystical practices are highly authoritarian and unduly hierarchical, robbing the individual of autonomy and independent judgment, and producing insensitive, cruel, and unjust social arrangements.

Thus, even if the views of chapter 3 are accepted, it still remains to be seen whether mystical practice tends toward distortion of social process. Even if we accept, that is, that the primary relevance of mysticism to moral theory is its articulation of mystical experience as the most important monadic value, still, the way in which the self-relation is to be prioritized against the other intimate and distant relationships needs to be looked at. Do mystics in fact encourage devaluation of intimate and distant social relationships in favor of arduous cultivation in hermitic retreat of mystical experience? Is mysticism too one-sided in its prioritization? Or, rather, is there a healthy interrelational moralism implicit in, or fostered by, the cultivation of mystical experience?

There are three sorts of theories currently being promoted in regard to these questions. The first, exemplified by Stace's theory in the final chapter of *Mysticism and Philosophy*, holds that there is a positive connection between mystical experience and moral consciousness. To put this in the relational vocabulary we have been employing, mystical experience conduces to sympathy, or interrelational moral feeling. The second theory, exemplified by Wainwright's theory in the final chapter of *Mysticism*, holds that although in certain ways mysticism may conduce to altruism, and in other ways hinder the development of moral consciousness, on the whole there is no interrelational moral value which requires mysticism theoretically or practically as its source. Mystical experience has no direct logical or epistemic bearing upon morality. An exponent of a similar view is Agehananda Bharati, who stresses the complete independence of mysticism and morality. According to Bharati, mystical experience only intensifies the moral, immoral, or amoral personality traits of the person prior to the mystical experience. The third theory, exemplified in Arthur Danto's work, holds that mystical theories, practices, and world views conduce to devaluation of the world, and hence hinder and are incompatible with interrelational moral consciousness.

In this chapter, I will begin by attempting to clarify the charges raised by proponents of the third theory, the view that mysticism detracts from moral consciousness. Then I will answer these charges both negatively and positively. I will reply to theories of the third sort, and provide a positive account of the connection between mysticism and morality which differs from the usual sort of positive account, as, for example, is found in Stace. In so doing, the account presented will counterbalance Bharati's and Wainwright's view that mysticism and interrelational morality are entirely, or at least largely, independent. However, the claim will not be made that to come to appreciate interrelational moral values one needs to appreciate mystical experience or to have it. Rather, mystical experience of a certain kind will be seen as a more or less extreme point on the scale of a certain kind of interrelational moral consciousness. Moral awareness may open the door to mystical experience. And mystical practice may itself be a training in moral consciousness when seen in a certain light. Finally, I will undertake to examine the question whether mysticism requires that interrelational value be demoted in favor of monadic value. I will conclude that this is not the case, and that one must recognize the openness of both the moral and the mystical approach to a wide variety of prioritizations, and a variety of valuational styles.

I.

Value-Based Criticisms Of Mystical Doctrine

We've already catalogued in chapter 1 the principal moral, social, and political charges against mystical teachings and doctrines. Here we will anchor these charges in specific versions of them actually found in the literature. For reasons of convenience we will select from the two most prominent western critics of Enlightenment East on moral grounds, namely, R. C. Zaehner in *Mysticism Sacred and Profane*, and Arthur Danto, in *Mysticism and Morality*.

(1) Mysticism often involves a devaluation of worldly pursuits. Instead of promoting a sense of the sacredness of life and the world, mysticism may promote a sense of the worthlessness of the multiplicitous order of things. ● worthlessness ≠ unattachment

Thus, for instance, Zaehner in *Mysticism Sacred and Profane* says of Hindu monistic mysticism, ". . . it will be seen that this doctrine reverses all our normal assumptions and values. . . . The phenomenal world is regarded as having less reality than has a dream, whereas deep dreamless sleep is seen as the nearest approximation to the fourth state which is final beatitude" (p. 154). And "The typical . . . message [of Sankara's hymns] is this: despise the world, for it is transitory; worship God and do good works. All this, however, is only for the spiritually immature, and can, of itself, lead nowhere. This is made quite clear in the last two stanzas where it is said that release from transmigratory existence can only come through *jnana*, 'knowledge' of the 'truth' of the non-dualist Vedanta, that is the atmabodha, the 'knowledge of the self' and not through good deeds or ✳ through any act of devotion" (p. 179). Similarly, Danto avers, "Moksha if no. [liberation] . . . is not a moral concept. It contrasts with moral con- isn't based cepts, and in pursuing moksha, we pursue a station beyond good and in morality evil, and so beyond morality" (*Mysticism and Morality*, p. 63). oppose does it Further: morals

(2) Mysticism encourages people to drop away from their plain moral obligations and relational lives in favor of renunciate hermit-like existence. Zaehner again (ibid., p. 169): ". . . Sankara maintains that the highest Brahman, the One without a second, can only be attained by *sannyasins*, men who renounce everything but their Selves, refuse to take part in religious ceremonies or to accept the grace of any God, and who abandon all works, whether good or evil. 'By ceasing to do good to one's friends or evil to one's enemies (the *sannyasin*) attains to the eternal Brahman by the yoga of meditation'" (*Narada Upanishad*, Schrader p. 145). Similarly, Danto writes, "In seeking to fulfill this end *[moksha]*, one turns one's back upon the world and upon the human scene. There is something inhuman in the concept of moksha" (*Narada*, p. 63). As a result:

(3) The social conditions in countries whose dominant ideology is highly colored by mysticism tend to be unjust and debased. Individual

lives are not highly valued. Life is cheap in countries in which the mystical influence is pronounced. India, for example, as we are frequently reminded by social critics of mysticism, has suffered greatly under a burdensome and oppressive caste system. Danto in chapter 2 of *Mysticism and Morality*, entitled "Karma and Caste," goes on at great length about how the "pessimistic cast of the Indian mind . . . is reinforced" (p. 33) by an elaborate series of superstitions concerning pollution, caste, and karma. And even worse:

(4) People are encouraged to believe that even the most heinous acts, such as murder, cannot really be accomplished. "Krishna utters these celebrated words: 'Thou hast mourned those who should not be mourned' (*Gita* II:ii). The wise do not mourn men, for men do not die: they but interchange one life for another. 'Not at any moment was I (ever) not, / Nor thou nor these kinds / And not at all shall we ever come not to be./. . . . The embodied soul is eternally unslayable / In the body of every one' (*Gita* II:12, 30). This is a radical teaching. It means, in effect, that if Arjuna wished to kill anyone he could not (really) succeed. This, of course, detaches one's homicidal acts from a certain chain of consequences" (Danto, *Mysticism*, p. 87). Mysticism, according to Danto, paves the way for a thoroughgoing amorality. Moreover:

(5) Mysticism aims to devalue the autonomy of the individual and attempts to thwart the development of the individual personality and individual will. Thus, Danto writes, "Taoism, like the Karma-Yoga of the *Gita*, is a teaching that aims at the stunning of the will, and I believe that generally the mechanism of the will is considered the enemy of ultimate happiness throughout the East" (ibid., p. 118). ". . . it is extremely difficult to derive a moral philosophy on the basis of this [being at one with the stream] if the very possibility of morality presupposes the mechanism of the will and the possibility of acting contrary to or deliberately in what one takes to be conformity with the world. Exactly that space that Taoism intends to collapse is what makes morality possible at all" (ibid., p. 119). The final result of this demolition of individuality and demotion of the autonomous will is the preparation of the way for the blind irrational following of guru figures who may or may not merit the attention they receive from their followers. Recent and contemporary Indian rationalists like Abraham Kovoor and B. Premanand espouse the latter viewpoint as well.

Responses to these criticisms

The responses to these criticisms are of two types: The first is to disarm them by showing that quotations have been taken out of context, and thus, the supposed criticisms have no genuine target. The second is to disarm them by accepting that there are things to be criticized in the institutions associated with mysticism, and that the points occasionally have merit. To admit that there are moral and social dangers associated with mysticism, however, is not to admit that mysticism is irredeemable. Rather, such admissions point out the need for the passion for justice to be brought to bear on the mystical social and institutional systems.

There are two levels of decontextualization which are found in the use of the quotations such as we have just seen. The first level is the decontextualization of the quote from surrounding textual materials. The second level is the decontextualization of the textual materials themselves from the psychosociological contexts in which they were first used and/or in which they continue to be used. It is easy to see how both levels of decontextualization *might* contribute to distortion in the commentary. It is only when one takes care to faithfully and accurately account for both contexts that one can hope to criticize fairly. I will undertake to show that there are relevantly connected textual materials and social contextual factors which reveal the other facet of the spiritual jewel Zaehner and Danto suggest is left out. It will not be my goal to demonstrate the point conclusively, but merely to show that enough has been left out of Danto and Zaehner's analyses as to establish the inadequacy of the criticisms. This paves the way for the second, stronger point, that by bringing Enlightenment West conceptions to bear on Enlightenment East traditions wherever moral and social imbalances are found to exist, a healthy reconstruction of Enlightenment East traditions is possible. Since such imbalances are found, integration of the two perspectives is required for healthy mystical and social practices to emerge.

Response to (1): Does mystical monism involve a devaluation of worldly pursuits?

Although it is true that many mystical texts contain references which on the face of it devalue worldliness, such textual references cannot be dissociated from the overall system in which they occur without serious distortion. For just as it is said that release from bondage of the world does not come "through good deeds or through any act of devotion," so, too, it will be said in many foundational texts not only of the same tradition, but also of the same author, that no knowledge of the Self is possible unless one is fulfilling one's moral relations and unless one is intensely involved in the practice of disciplined devotion. While Shankara's advice in the hymn quoted amounts to "despise the world for it is transitory," we must ask to what extent Shankara was addressing his remarks to people who were, in his view, in need of increasing their detachment. To what extent was Shankara concerned in that specific hymn to help people dissociate from the shackles, obsessions, and unbalanced slaveries of worldliness while remaining in the world, and fulfilling their obligations? When we reexamine the very text quoted by Zaehner, we see that Shankara is presenting a dynamic program of practice. Shankara says, "Chant (religious) songs more than a thousand times, think always of the form of Visnu, meditate in the company of good men, give your property to the afflicted, {refrain:} worship Govinda, worship Govinda, worship Govinda" (Zaehner, p. 178). This verse encapsulates some features of the moral foundation, namely, the performance of charitable deeds in a setting in which one is simultaneously worshipping and meditating. Thus, Shankara's hymn presupposes a vigorous moral practice as the context in which further instruction is being given! The final verse of the hymn states, "Though you perform pilgrimages to the Ganges, keep your vows and give alms, all this without 'knowledge' (is worthless); and no release can be obtained in a hundred births. Worship Govinda, etc. . . ." (ibid., p. 179). Once again, Shankara's teaching is only being addressed to those who are fulfilling the moral requirements, and is only meant to be comprehensible to one who has disciplined character through devotional acts and an ingrained moral practice. Shankara's teaching is that the moral practice is not enough. The moral practice must be transfigured through direct realization of the pure mystical monist teaching.

Now one might say that Shankara's philosophy is incoherent. Why bother with moral training and devotional activity if in the end multiplicity *is* all illusory? Why not just get on with the monist realization? The fact that Shankara, like so many other Indian mystical philosophers, sets forth a dynamic program of instruction in which sophisticated mystical insights are propounded for the benefit of the practitioner, who has been thoroughly imbued with moral practice and has a high degree of character training, shows precisely that the mystical teachings are not meant to be taken out of the overall pedagogical context. The monistic mysticism is meant to breathe within, or be in consonance with, a morally founded practice. And if one were to ask why the mystic should be concerned to insist on a moral foundation for the mystical aspirant, the mystic might well simply say, because it would lead to immorality to do otherwise. Why shouldn't Shankara's philosophy be as complex as it ought to be? Indeed, our articulation in chapter 4 of six non-ego placements of subject and object provides a systematic framework within which such dynamic systems of phenomenological training can be theoretically understood, even if Shankara's vocabulary is not as elaborate as ours in this regard. Of the six non-ego placements, two of them ("I am the Many"; and "Only the Many") provide a vision of the world in which the multiplicitous order is preserved. The moral relations are entirely preserved, as relations between persons are preserved. The other four require penetration in stillness, with social relations frozen. Standard criticisms of the moral nihilism of mysticism thus seem to be inappropriate in light of a comprehensive program of mysticism which includes both multiplicitous and non-multiplicitous non-ego based perspectives. Even if Shankara's program needs expansion, the tools are available for such expansion to take place.

In any case, Shankara's intention was to remain faithful to the foundational texts of his tradition, such as The *Gita*, the *Upanishads*, and the *Yogasutras.* In the *Gita*, again and again we find an emphasis on the importance of a person's following his or her own "law" or *dharma.* Yoga is defined variously as equaniminity in success or failure (ii; 48); skillful living among activities (ii; 50); serenity (vi; 3); non-attachment (vi; 4); and self-purification (vi; 12). Similarly, there is karma yoga, yoga through the path of action, in addition to sannyasa yoga, yoga through renunciation. When Shankara presents instructional material, which assumes the karma yoga and bhakti yoga practices, and then goes on to warn the individual that no true liberation is to be found except through *jnana* yoga, the yoga of knowledge, he is organizing the programs of practice into stages. This may or may not involve some significant degree of reformulation or departure from the original intent of the *Gita*, if there is any such identifiable original intent, but the important point is that the monistic realization is still supposed to occur within the context of moral and devotional practice. Only one who has fulfilled the moral and devotional practices is fit to become liberated from them. And liberation from them means nonattachment to them rather than violation of them.

Other texts of Shankara make the point equally clearly. Consider this, for instance, from Shankara's "Crest-Jewel of Discrimination": "He *alone* may be considered qualified to seek Brahman who has discrimination, whose mind is turned away from all enjoyments, *who possesses tranquility and the kindred virtues*, and who feels a longing for liberation" (Shankara 1963, p. 296; emphasis added).

It would seem that one qualified to seek Brahman is one who has genuine self-discipline, for only a self-disciplined and conventionally moral person is capable of tranquility and kindred virtues. Similarly, in the *Yogasutras*, the dynamic stages of practice are set out with admirable clarity. First one must practice the *yamas*, the external moral practices of non-harmfulness, non-theft, truthfulness, non-greediness, and continence. A deeper character training then involves the *niyamas*: cleanliness, cheerfulness-equanimity, energetic disciplined practices *(tapas)*, self-awareness, and surrender to Ishvara (God). With these two levels of practice established, one can undertake yoga *asanas*, or postural meditation practices. And once the body is flexible, one undertakes *pranayama* and *pratyahara*, or breath control, and sense withdrawal. Only then do the concentration and meditation practices of *dharani, samadhi,* and *dhyana* have a framework within which to take place. Thus, the tradition is a fundamentally moral tradition, and therefore, a tradition, which values the fulfillment of the worldly concerns, a tradition which supports mystical monist realization as the culmination of what we have been calling monadic fulfillment, leaving intact the interrelational fulfillments.

The relational approach developed in chapters 1 and 2, combined with the distinctions between multiplicitous and nonmultiplicitous mystical experiences, and between phenomenological and metaphysical approaches to mystical experience, developed in chapters 4 and 5, enable us to see easily and clearly how the overall structure of a mystical monist system can work. First the aspirant is instructed in interrelational moral practices and character training. Only in this context is the mystical monadic fulfillment undertaken. The psychological underpinnings of this dynamic are not hard to find. If one begins directly with the monadic fulfillment, there is a real danger that the person becomes a blissful solipsist, an egoist in society. The bliss-pleasure released through mystical meditation practice can be overpowering, leading the untrained individual to pathologically amoral expressions. Moreover, the Hindu mystic is perfectly capable of recognizing this danger. For example, Agehananda Bharati remarks, "To the mystic, temptation is desirable. . . . The mystic plays with temptation because all temptation reminds him of the zero-experience; the establishment must dissuade and warn from temptation, and hence discourage the zero-experience. . . . I would now say that most genuine mystics feel a lot but know very little. As a theologian, the mystic is just as good or bad as he was before he had his zero-encounter. As a prophet, he tends to make a mess of people and things. . . . As a person, he isn't very nice unless he happened to have been nice before. The mystical experience is neither noble nor ignoble, it is not powerfully this or that, just very powerful and absorbing" (1976, p. 59). Therefore the emphasis at the beginning must be on the moral practices so that a firm moral framework is in place within which the monadic mystical fulfillment can be undertaken.

The difficult moral challenge to mysticism based on its alleged denial of the importance of the world is in the first instance an intellectual or theoretical challenge, and not a practical one, and in any case it can only apply against a metaphysical interpretation of a nonmultiplicitous mysticism. The very worst that can be said, then, about nonmultiplicitous mystical systems given metaphysical interpretations of mystical experience, is that they require some theoretical reconstruction if moral practice is to be integrated in a fully intelligible manner. The analysis set out in chapter 4 provides us with the tools fully adequate for such a reconstruction.

Response to (2): Zaehner charges that mysticism encourages people to drop away from their plain moral obligations and relational lives. But once again Zaehner's interpretation of the text quoted, in this case the *Narada Upanishad*, is, or may well be, inaccurate. To cease to do good to one's friends or evil to one's enemies is not to cease to interact with others. The idea, rather, as it's put in the language of the *Gita*, is, or may be, to discover the capacity for actionless action *(naishkarmya karma)* (chap. 3). Actionless action is action which is freed from the desire for narrowly self-regarding benefit. Then one is not obsessed with benefiting one's friends and harming one's enemies. One has the wisdom which sees a whole, completely non-partisan picture, and actionless action flows from this wisdom. It would take a good deal more exegesis of the text and its context to determine the degree of misreading Zaehner has indulged in. But the very fact that there is a readily available alternate interpretation, relying on entirely standard conceptions within the tradition, which has not been raised by Zaehner and subjected to careful exegetical scrutiny, is a telling fact.

In general in our reading of mystical monist traditions, we must distinguish between periodically turning one's back on the world in order to experientially realize doctrines such as "I am the One," and turning one's back on the world altogether. In order to experientially realize the meaning of a doctrine such as "I am the One," it is necessary to practice rigorously disciplined meditation in stillness. But even the monastery or hermitage in which one may undertake such practices has a social dimension. Few people become true hermits to undertake the practices leading to the monistic realization. And whereas one is socially frozen while sitting in stillness, for example, one is also socially frozen when one sleeps, and no one remains, or needs to remain, socially frozen for more than a few hours at a time. How people clothe, shelter, nourish, heal, and mythologize, creates a community and a social process. The mystic community is a community undertaking like the community of farmers, or weavers, or any other community, for that matter. Shankara was not a hermit on a vow of isolation.

Similarly, to turn one's back on the world in the sense intended by the mystic, is not to cease to engage in any social activities; one engages in social activities, but the condition of one's being is freed from the activities in which one is engaging. The difference is subtle but fundamental. It would be a narrow, most unfree liberation, which *required* that everyone literally turn away from the world!

As for (3) and (4), life was cheap in ancient times more or less all over the world, and Western feudal arrangements were in many cases not a jot preferable to the Indian caste system. The link, then, between monistic mysticism and a climate of social injustice is by no means clear. Similarly, the standard form of mysticism is one which is supposed to take place within the context of a moral practice, thus leaving the specific social expressions open to reconstruction and evolution.

The same points can, and should be made in reference to Buddhist mysticism. The eightfold noble path is structured similarly to that of the *ashtanga yoga* of Patanjali. (The eightfold path of the Buddha, in fact, preceeded the *ashtanga yoga* system according to the standard datings.) The right meditation practices of the eightfold path can only be understood and undertaken in tandem with the cognitive and moral practices of right understanding, right thought, right speech, right action, and right livelihood. Only in the relatively marginal practices of left-handed Tantra can the amoral or immoral attitudes have an official framework within which to flourish.

As Peter Pardue shows in his study *Buddhism: A Historical Introduction to Buddhist Values and the Social and Political Forms They Have Assumed in Asia*, moral and social concerns constantly animate and catalyze theoretical speculations concerning the Buddhist teachings as well as the development of Buddhist institutions. Many elements of early Buddhism may have had a socially critical underpinning and appeal in their time (pp. 1-6). The teaching that the world is a place of suffering is counterbalanced by the teachings concerning the joys of the spiritual life (p. 21). The ideal of the arhat, the saint who comes to enlightenment through arduous effort, comes at a certain point to seem selfish, and so is displaced in many schools by the ideal of the bodhisattva; the ideal of the bodhisattva is a universally accessible ideal, and this "significantly undercut the rigidities of the class distinction between monk and layman" (pp. 35-37). Even the social amoralism of Buddhist Tantra may have had a social compo-

nent parallel to the Hindu Tantra of the same period. The popularity
of the latter, at least, may have been due in part to a reaction against
excessive state-controlled Brahmanism during the Gupta period
(p. 51). In China, some of the appeal of Buddhism to some groups
may have been its ability to counterbalance some excesses of
Confucian obligations: "the principle of 'filial piety' could be a form of
excruciating bondage in which deep hostilities evoked a longing for
social and spiritual freedom" (p. 58). In some contexts, Buddhism's
insistence on a spiritual focus provided a healthy counterforce against
an assertive temporalism. Thus, the military dictator, Huan Hsuan in
the early fifth century C.E. demanded that he be given complete
authority over the Sangha. "With remarkable courage, Hui-yuan [a
skilled Buddhist administrator whose temple on Mount Lu was a center of Buddhist and Confucian learning] refused. . . . In a superb,
quasi-prophetic treatise entitled *A Monk Does Not Bow Down Before
A King*, he argues that the monk does not lack loyalty or filial piety, ＊
but has a higher loyalty to the universal Buddhist law to which all *higher*
men are subject." According to Hui-yuan, the monk "understands *loyalty*
how one terminates woe. . . . This is why the monk refuses homage to
the emperor and keeps his own works sublime, and why he is not
ranked with kings or princes and yet basks in their kindness." Hui-
yuan was granted his wish to be free of having to bow to the military
dictator (p. 66). And on and on it goes, all the way to B. R. Ambedkar's
social crusade in the mid-twentieth century linking Buddhism with liberation from casteism in India (pp. 138-141). Currently we are witnessing a most interesting reversal of rhetorical style in the conflict
between the Chinese Communists and the exiled Tibetan Buddhists.
At the UN sponsored summer 1993 World Conference on Human
Rights in Vienna, the Dalai Lama was prevented from officially participating due to pressure from Beijing. However, he did address a
fringe meeting of the conference, at which he "attacked Beijing's
position that Asian and other Third World countries could not be
bound by western notions of human rights. 'It is the inherent nature
of all human beings to yearn for freedom, equality and dignity,' he
said. 'I do not see any contradiction between the need for economic
development and the need for respect of human rights'" (Quoted
from *Vancouver Sun*, June 16, 1993). In this case, the Buddhist is
insisting on Buddhism's inherent consonance with Enlightenment
West's articulation of rights and freedoms, and the Marxist-Leninist
Communists are resisting human rights theorizing! Thus, it is only
the most superficial, decontextualized account of Buddhism that can
hold it to have presented an antiworldly tradition with no positive

worldly connections, contributions, and effects. Any balanced assessment will surely agree with Rita Gross' conclusion that "Both interpretations of Buddhism as freedom from the world and freedom within the world are authentic and traditional" (*Buddhism After Patriarchy*, p. 150).

Point (5), that eastern monistic mysticism and Taoism tend to devalue the autonomy of the individual and lead to a dissolution of the individual will, is a good example of a charge arising, apparently, from decontextualization, or inadequate reading. Since it was raised by Danto largely in terms of Taoism, we will respond to it from within the Taoist literature. As with Zaehner and Hinduism, only an extensive exegesis can confirm the diagnosis. Here it is the superficiality of the charges which we want to establish. I will present an alternative account of the implications of Taoism for agency and interrelational life that seems on the face of it to be more in keeping with the Taoist spirit than Danto's.

It is hard to read Taoist literature without being struck again and again with the energy and dynamism attributed to the ideal individual posited by Taoism, that is, the Taoist sage, the one who is in conformity with the Way or the Tao. Far from being one who, in the literal, external sense, takes no action at all, the sage is one who is so in tune with the flow of events that it seems to everyone that the action taken by the sage is an entirely natural one. But for anyone other than the Taoist sage, it might be a real feat to accomplish!

The Taoist sage is not a spineless, will-less individual. As Roger Ames puts it in relation to the Chuang Tzu materials, ". . . the enlightened person is characterized by efficacy-in-action in virtually any capacity from high minister (Shun-shu Ao) to butcher (Cook Ting), from sage ruler (31/12/50) to brigand (Robber Chih), from military leader (15/6/11) to mutilated criminal" (1983 p. 44). The Chuang Tzu materials are a bit wilder than those of the *Tao Te Ching*. In the latter, it might be said, the ideal is for the politician's actions to be as deeply rooted in the natural Way as are a mother's actions in relation to the needs of her infant. Thus, for example, "Simply doing things for others, [the sage] feels he has all the more. Simply giving to others he feels all the richer. The Tao of the sage is to accomplish without competing" (No. 81).

Perhaps Danto wants to claim that no such actions are possible in the sphere of politics, and the relations between strangers in general. If such a claim is correct, then Taoism has a misguided theory of human nature and social interaction: Taoism posits an ideal practice which is unattainable. But one cannot properly criticize mothers' relations with their infants by saying that mothers have no individual autonomy, and do not exercise any will in responding to the needs of their infants.

In terms of the vocabulary of chapter 2, the Taoist holds that the naturalness and relatively unproblematic character of the intimate relations and of fulfillment in intimacy is appropriately imported into the distant relations, including, the citizenship relation. It is possible to argue against the Taoist that no such import can be successful. But just as there is a vigorous and dynamic sphere of autonomous voluntarism in the forging of one's intimate relations, so, too, when we consider the Taoist program, it is easy to see that there is at least supposed to be a vigorous and dynamic sphere of autonomous voluntarism in the forging of one's relations in general, all under the light of the ease and naturalness of the Way. Danto's confusion is to overlook the distinction between the ego/non-ego contrast and the contrast between autonomy/heteronomy. Consider stories of the Taoist sage's refusal of social status, titles, and honors. Here the sage is demonstrating autonomy, authenticity, lack of conventionality, and harmony with the Way, or egolessness, all at once. This account seems to be an obvious reading of Taoism, and is supported by much commentary and exposition, yet it is not considered by Danto, let alone eliminated from contention as the proper interpretation of the text.

II.

Assessing Mystical Institutions.

Does the examination of section "I" lead us to the result that monistic mysticism, Taoism, and the practices associated with them are invulnerable to moral criticism? Not at all. All we have seen so far is that the interpretations offered by the two most prominent moral critics of Enlightenment East traditions are unreliable, and they have not presented an analysis sufficient to establish grounds for moral criticism. For every quote suggesting mystical amorality or even immorality, we can find quotes, contextualizations, or plausible interpretations showing that the apparently amoral instructions or doctrines are being misread. This still leaves us, however, with the task of assessing the institutions and practices associated with Enlightenment East, as socially expressed in particular movements, to see whether or not, and to what degree, there are *in fact* moral dangers associated with the mystical practices. After all, if Arthur Danto can get what I'm suggesting is the wrong idea about the practices indicated in the texts, then surely, so can the practitioners themselves. It is important to raise, then, at least in general and theoretical terms, the sorts of issues that must be faced in the assessment of the actual institutional life centered on the practice of mysticism.

Criticisms of mystical institutions

Charges based on actual immoral practices or unhealthy practices, which, it is claimed, are encouraged by mystical institutional life are as follows:

(6) Mysticism, it is averred, encourages gullibility. Wherever there are mystical institutions, according to this charge, there are charlatans, sleight of hand and sleight of mind artists posing as genuine gurus, psychics, and so forth. According to this criticism, there are too many of these for one to be comfortable with assurances that the texts refer to the need for moral practice, truthfulness, and so forth, as a proper foundation on which to build one's mysticism. The facts belie these assurances, according to those who level this criticism. The pages of the journal, *The Indian Skeptic*, edited by B. Premanand, are full of charges of this kind.

A typical instance showing the astonishing nastiness reached in controversies over gullibility, is the following, taken from *The Vancouver Sun*, Nov 10, 1992, entitled, "Thousands cheer as yogi ends 5 days 'under water'": (*The Independent*, New Delhi).

> More than 5,000 people gathered in New Delhi last weekend to see a war hero turned yogi emerge from a pool where he had been roped to the bottom—unable to breathe—for five days. Among the onlookers was Sanal Edamaruku, the leader of the Indian Rationalists' Association, a group of skeptics, which has exposed many yogis as fakes. It was 1 P.M. and the tarpaulin covering the pool was about to be lifted—revealing whether the yogi, Pilot Babba, a former wing commander, was still alive.
>
> "Ssh," Edamaruku said. "If they recognize me, I'm sure these saffron goons will rough me up."
>
> The pool was covered. It had high sides that seemed to offer plenty of breathing room. Several suspicious pipes were visible.
>
> "I'm sure the pool has been empty until the last minute. He's probably been down there sleeping and reading magazines," Edamaruku said. "All the yogis we've met so far are either cheats or mental cases."

[handwritten margin note: "and so is true with Theism"]

The Rationalists, who have gone as far as filing a complaint with the local police, demanding a yogi's arrest for fraud, are extremely unpopular in Pilot Babba's camp. Babba, whose real name is Kapil Adwani, flew fighter planes until he almost crashed, when one of his engines conked out. He claims he was saved by an unseen force, that brought him down unharmed. As the tarpaulin was rolled back, the pandemonium was deafening. Photographers and devotees rushed the tank. Pilot Babba was on the surface, limp, and floating face down. Suddenly, the long-haired yogi flopped over like a walrus. The crowd roared. He was then dragged to the side of the pool where he removed his wet underwear in front of 5,000 people. With amazing bounce—for someone who has kept the lotus position for five days underwater—he sprinted up a ladder to a decorated altar. His skin was hardly wrinkled. Everyone was watching the yogi, except Edamaruku. He was examining several garden hoses in the pool. Suddenly, he was spotted.

"A rationalist," one of Pilot Babba's disciples said.

The tarpaulin was swiftly spread out again, hiding the pool and Edamaruku disappeared into the crowd. Edamaruku has since challenged Pilot Babba to perform the same stunt in a large aquarium—in open view.

"If he does it, I'll apologize and become one of his devotees," he said.

The gulf between the Rationalists and the devotees of the yogi here is enormous, demonstrating vividly, if nothing else, that there is an urgent social need for a proper forum for debate and open investigation. If, as the Rationalists claim, scientific investigation of yogic paranormal claims is often undertaken in the face of opposition, obstacles, and obfuscation from the mystical institutions, then this indicates an imbalance in the institutional arrangements.

(7) The mystical texts often encourage celibacy, and all too frequently the mystically realized, supposedly celibate male teacher turns out not to be celibate after all, and charges fly concerning the teacher's sexual relations with his disciples. In the last decade, some highly respected teachers have been at the center of such controversies. The charges include falsely claiming to be celibate and breach of trust; in some cases there are charges of sexual assault and rape. Reports of such problems in the cases of recent and contemporary gurus and teachers living in the west or with large followings in the

west are to be found in the following. (My citations here should not be taken to be an endorsation of facts alleged; I am merely citing them to establish that there are such controversies.) William Rodamor, "The Secret Life of Swami Muktananda" (1983); Katy Butler, "Events Are The Teacher" (1983); Rick Fields, "Perils of the Path" (1983); Sandy Boucher, *Conspiracy of Silence: The Male Teacher*, chapter 5, "Turning The Wheel" (1988); Don Lattin "The Cloud Over Indian guru's U.S. Tour" *San Francisco Chronicle*, Sat. July 23, (1988); Stephen Rae, "The Guru Scene" *Cosmopolitan*: Aug. 1991; Katherine Webster, "The Case Against Swami Rama of the Himalayas", *Yoga Journal* (Nov./Dec 1990); Katy Butler, "Encountering the Shadow In Buddhist America" (1991); Georg Feuerstein, *Holy Madness* (1992). Many of the charges listed here concern teachers within eastern mystical traditions. Of course similar charges are widespread amongst western religious traditions in which celibacy is featured.

(8) The mystical manuals encourage an absolute devotion to the teacher or guru who is thus placed in too tempting a position of authority. Consequently, there are, it is alleged, many gurus who abuse their authority, brainwash their disciples into elitist, authoritarian ideologies, and take advantage of their disciples's devotion and energies, sometimes for personal gain. Disaffection, disillusionment, and deconversion are often painful processes for disciples who, as they see it, wake up to the abuses and authoritarianisms of the charismatic leader and his organization. Janet Jacobs' *Divine Disenchantment* presents case histories and analyses. John Hubner and Lindsey Gruson's *Monkey On A Stick* presents a lurid account of gross abuses within the Hare Krishna Movement organization following the death of the founder. The abuses under the Rajneesh Osho regime in Oregon have been documented in many books as well, for example, Hugh Milne's *Bhagwan: The God That Failed* (1986).

My response to these charges is to embrace them in principle. In the cases in which charges of these kinds are brought, it is important to establish whether or not the facts, when seen in the light of common sense moral values, are such as to justify these charges. If the charges are justified in a given case, then the institution or individual in question is morally, civilly, or criminally liable, as the case may be. Those who have firsthand awareness of such problems are performing a service when they make the problems known so that the problems can be dealt with in a proper manner, corrected if possible, and so that the innocent can be warned. It's as simple as that.

Moreover, there are enough charges of these sorts floating around as to give the promoter of mysticism, such as myself, serious pause. In my opinion, no promoter of mysticism can afford to ignore or underplay these moral charges. Rather, it is incumbent upon promotors of philosophical mysticism and the meditation practices associated with it to emphasize the vulnerability of teachers to the temptations of authority, lust, and power to which so many other nonmystical charismatic figures are subject. To do so should not undermine legitimate mystical institutional life, but will rather encourage due care in mystical education, and reform of those institutions which do not exercise due care. Few exponents of Enlightenment West are shocked to hear that a secular politician has been caught with his hand in the public till, or that an admired writer or artist, say, has been charged with financial or sexual improprieties. There is no country so advanced that exposures of public corruption are unheard of. And the Roman Catholic Church is reeling under the charges of sexual improprieties levelled against a small, but much too large, percentage of its priests. It should hardly be a fatal blow against mysticism that its proponents are occasionally corrupt any more than it can be a fatal blow against secularism, rationalism, or nonmystical religion, that its exponents are occasionally corrupt (unless the latter makes claims to moral perfection right down the line).

In sum, the association between mysticism and abuse of authority has not been shown to be a direct, and certainly not a necessary one. Only if all the mystical institutions actually fall prey to this problem can we reject mysticism holus bolus on moral grounds. So long as there are many morally wholesome mystics and institutions revolving around the practice of meditation, we are justified in joining in with the critics in chucking out the bathwater, while rescuing the mystical baby, if we think there is a mystical baby to be rescued. We can and should remain true to the common sense moral foundations of the yoga system of Patanjali, and the eightfold path of the Buddha, for instance, and criticize what deserves to be criticized, while recognizing that there are entirely wholesome mystical teachers, and institutions whose raison d'etre is the promotion of mysticism.

As far as the important question of authority, obedience, irrationality, and mystical cultivation is concerned, it is often held to be the case that unless the disciple completely surrenders the ego, mystical progress will not occur. To this it may be responded that no one should have to do anything out of obedience to the guru or teacher which runs contrary to moral relations. And there is every reason to believe that complete surrender of the ego is possible without abandonment of common sense moral relations. The guru can request that the disciple engage in odd, even bizarre activities at the sym-

bolic level, but not at the moral level. For some disciples such surrender may be useful. For others, perhaps, less so. But in any case, surrender can take place without jeopardizing ethics. Any theory of mystical education, which denies such a distinction or requires not just
surrender of the ego, but, in particular, surrender of the ego through
surrender of common sense moral boundaries, is immediately suspect, and does not seem to tally with the facts surrounding healthy-
minded mysticism. As objective mysticism, avatar mysticism, and universal impersonal self mysticism show, one can simultaneously
express moral consciousness and mystical consciousness. Any attempt
to equate surrender of the ego and surrender of one's capacity to reason and make moral distinctions is bereft of what ought to be the
mystic's practical wisdom to use mystical stances in the appropriate
manner.

Georg Feuerstein's *Holy Madness* raises some very important
questions in this context, and we are in his debt for bringing forward
a good deal of information. We might want to go a touch further,
though, by way of engagement with the difficult issues. For example, Feuerstein agrees *in principle* that "[i]n some cases . . . a crazy-
wisdom teacher may well have been guilty of overzealousness and
misjudgment that caused harm to another human being. This raises
serious questions about the appropriateness and usefulness of crazy-
wisdom teachings in our time, and also about the moral and criminal
liability of teachers who work in this manner" (p. 229). And he is
willing to make references to atrocious moral failures involving "sexual abuse of disciples by unscrupulous or irresponsible mentors"
(p. 250). But when it comes time to actually treat questions such as
whether gurus should be making sexual advances to their disciples or
sexually initiating their devotees, he is vague, and, even, perhaps,
lacking in the ability to draw what one would think were obvious
moral implications from accepted factual premises. For instance,
Feuerstein belittles Dick Anthony and Bruce Ecker's apparently sensible view that sexual relations between guru and disciple tend to
create great psychological harm in enough cases so as to render inappropriate such encounters in general (*Spiritual Choices*, p. 90).
Feuerstein's response is that while it may be that most female disciples who have engaged in sexual relations with their guru end up
reporting no inner spiritual progress but rather deep psychological
wounds yet, nonetheless, Anthony and Ecker's rejection of sexual
relations as a means of conveying mystical teaching is "hasty and judg-
mental." Feuerstein fails to present any evidence that gurus can be
expected to be able to tell which of their disciples are likely to be psy-

chologically wounded and which will not. Thus, one is left with the impression that Feuerstein fails to recognize such elementary features of moral reasoning as that one should not engage in a practice which one can reasonably anticipate to create great psychological harm. Note also that Feuerstein's subsequent discussion sidesteps onto an irrelevant theoretical point: he accuses Anthony of subscribing to a dualistic philosophy that posits that enlightenment cancels out desires, and which cannot understand that desires continue to arise even after enlightenment. Feuerstein's praises of Tantrism's "great vision" which is, "to put it bluntly, that the Divine is not without genitals" is irrelevant to an assessment of the moral inference that sexual relations between guru and disciple tend to cause far more harm than good, and so they will not be found present in the practice of a teacher who is minimally competent in psychological grasp and consequent moral understanding (*Holy Madness*, pp. 250-254). Feuerstein concludes by stating that "Mysticism and morality must be spliced to form a spirituality that does not sink into the morass of a bottomless antinomianism, but that still has the vitality to effectively transmute our lives" (p. 254). Few will disagree with this; and the value that humor, eccentricity, unconventionality, and even some bizarre "crazy wisdom" behavior can have is important to be aware of. However, to discover the proper bottom below which is unacceptable antinomianism, requires an eagerness to keep one's eyes on the obvious moral issues such as the gross harm issues, to say nothing of subtler moral questions concerning consent and trust, the therapist and the guru, explicit and implicit conventions, and the like. The instability of Feuerstein's treatment when it comes to the specifics concerning sexual relations, hitting, obedience and so on, points to the need for an integration of the basic principles and methods of Enlightenment West moral analysis into mystical institutional theorizing.

Further, it should be possible to accomplish such an integration. In any religious system which survives thousands of years, and has evolved over many cultural stages, it is only to be expected that there will be enough strands of thought available within the tradition so that a vigorous reconstruction along one or another line of approach is always possible. Scientific practice is a self-critical practice. Social practice is, or can be, a self critical and reconstructive practice. Similarly, religious practice can be, and, perhaps, at its best always must be, a reconstructive practice. This should not surprise us. What would be surprising is a religious system thousands of years old which is either entirely free of failure, or wholly unaccommodating to vigorous reconstruction or reform, using traditional methods and materials in new ways, where such reconstruction or reform is required.

For example, the Buddhist traditional references to the obligations of husband to wife and wife to husband are obviously context bound. "The husband should always honor his wife and never be wanting in respect to her; he should love her and be faithful to her; should secure her position and comfort; and should please her by presenting her with clothing and jewellery. The wife in her turn should supervise and look after household affairs; should entertain guests, visitors, friends, relatives, and employees; should love and be faithful to her husband; should protect his earnings; should be clever and energetic in all activities" (quoted in Rahula 1974, p. 79). At the same time, "[L]ove between husband and wife is considered almost religious or sacred. It is called sadara-Brahmacariya, 'sacred family life.' Here, too, the significance of the term Brahma should be noted: the highest respect is given to this relationship" (ibid.). The contemporary Buddhist is free to update the details of the *Nigala-sutta* in ways that make sense within a modern perspective on gender relations. We may cite Sandy Boucher's *Turning The Wheel* and Rita Gross' *Buddhism after Patriarchy* as reconstructive efforts of this sort.

Similarly, the work relationship, the child parent, student teacher, citizen to citizen, relations all have ancient expressions and norms which can be updated without wrenching the monadic mysticism itself. The overall balance of interrelational practice can be altered. But the monadic core of the mystical traditions can be preserved.

III.

Mysticism and Justice: A Positive Connection

I'd like now to move forward, beyond defending the reconstructive enterprise, and point out what I believe is a fundamental positive connection between the practice of justice and the practice of mystical enlightenment. This connection is best got at with reference to the mysticism which in chapter 4 was called "Only the Many."

In chapter 4, we distinguished six non-ego images of the world: I am the One; only the One; I am the Many; Only the Many; I am the Void; only the Void. Of these six, four are limit images of the world, and are only barely accessible to rational conception since they altogether dispense with the representation of the world as a multiplicity. However, two of these six preserve the representation of the world as a multiplicity, while dissolving the ego perspective. They do so in one case by expanding the identified self to the world, yielding "I am the Many," and in the other case by contracting the identified self to nothing, leaving "Only the Many." Only the Many is the purely objective conception of the world, the conception of the world in which what Nagel (1979) calls the "objective stance" is taken to its furthest limits.

Let us review for a moment this purely objective conception of the world. In chapter 4, it was described in the section called, "The First Meditation: On the Silence Of The Subject." The key element of this meditation is the dropping away from language and the language of thought, all subject terms such as 'I,' 'me,' 'my,' in favor of proper names, objective descriptions or other objective designators, such as 'the speaker,' 'the only one in this room wearing a yellow sweater,' and 'Leonard Angel.' Thus, one conceives of everything as an objective element of the multiplicity which makes up the world, and nothing is distinguished as being me.

Now let us consider the basic intuition underlying dispute resolution which takes place under a system of procedural justice. Consider a paradigmatic dispute, such as may occur between two farmers fighting over the location of the border marking their respective lands. One says it is here, the other says it is there. Naturally, A says it is further towards B's side, and B says it is further toward's A's side. If they had a difference of opinion in which A says it is further towards A's side, and B says it is further towards B's side, then we have good grounds for forming the judgment that both are thinking objectively, which is to say, both are attempting to represent the truth in the matter of the location of the border, and neither is distorting his or her memory, consciously, or subconsciously, for self-interested reasons. (Though this is of course not *necessarily* the case: one or both may want to yield on a small dispute to gain psychological advantage on a bigger dispute.) On the other hand when A says the border marker is further towards B's property, and B says it is further towards A's property, we maintain that in all likelihood at least one of them is not thinking objectively. At least one of them has gotten some facts indicative of where the marker used to be garbled up, either deliberately, or through subconscious distortion of memory for self-interested reasons. A person who has gotten the facts distorted through self-interest has been thinking subjectively. The idea "I am A" has consciously, or subconsciously, crept into, and colored, the cognitive assessments.

What do we do in such cases? We appoint a judge. A judge is a person whose task is to embody the theoretical ideal objective perspective. A judge is a person who listens to statements made by both parties in the dispute and assesses them with regard only to the merits of the case. Moreover the judge is entrusted with the task of eliminating from her or his mind all factors having to do with the judge's placement in relation to the disputant. The judge is not to think, "How good looking A is; I would like to take A out on a date." The judge is not to think, "How able in business B appears to be; I'd like to propose to B after this is over that we do some business together." If such thoughts arise, they are to be abandoned. The judge is to understand the dispute based on knowledge of what it is to be human, but the particular placement of the judge in the situation is to be eliminated.

Now the strongest form of placement in a situation is expressed in the fundamental judgment of the ego-conscious standpoint: "There are many things in the world, and, interestingly enough, one of them happens to be me." Given this representation concerning the world, one is vulnerable to distortions in one's perception of facts such as the location of bordermarkers. Given one's judgment "That is A's farm, and I am A!" there is a vulnerability to distortion in one's memory as to where the border marker had previously been placed. Since I am A, I will tend to remember, or think I remember, or claim I remember, the border marker as having been further over towards B's property. If one is a stranger visiting the territory, one's memory as to where the border marker was the night before may be uncolored by personal interest, and, one supposes, one's memory is more likely to be objective and accurate. (It may have been more cursory, but that's another issue. We can assume the stranger was asked to take note of the location.)

Thus, a practice which requires that one abandon all self-reference in favor of entirely objective reference is at one and the same time a practice predisposing one to justice, and a practice predisposing one to the discovery of the no-self viewpoint. Further, the vocabulary of chapter 4 enables us to express this in perspicuous terms: whereas the ego-identified person thinks of the first person as constituting me, the no-self, non-ego-identified person thinks of the first person as merely the first person. The first person, moreover, stands as it were on a platform of equality with the second person or the third person. Thus, the non-ego identified person sees the first person from the standpoint of objectivity, that is, the standpoint of the judge.

The ego-identified person invests the first person with an aura of specialness, the specialness of being me, whereas the no-self identified person recognizes that the first person is the first person—this is, after all, a necessary truth—and the second person is the second person; and the third person is the third person. There is no specialness about the first person's being the first person. The specialness of being me, based on which special treatments may irrelevantly and unjustly be requested or expected is gone. The specialness of being me based on which the sparks of dispute are fanned is gone, and the tendency to disputation is minimized.

If A and B are no-self "only the many" mystic farmers, then their practice of mysticism expresses itself in objective terms: A says, "This person is A and this person is B." B says and thinks the same way. Both A and B are referred to and thought of as having the same footing in relation to the objective order. A thinks of A as a person, one of many persons in a vast objective order. A thinks of B as a person, one of many persons in a vast objective order. B thinks of B as a person, one of many persons in a vast objective order. B thinks of A as a person, one of many persons in a vast objective order. There is an intrinsic fairness in the conception of the world fostered by the no-self, "only the many" approach to mysticism. All persons are revealed in the light of a fundamental equality. The ego-perspective, which effectively exalts one person above others in virtue of this person being me, is gone. The no-self mystic thinks of all persons, including the first person, the way a judge thinks of the parties to a dispute which she or he is hearing.

Indeed, one might want to go further and suggest that an objective test of one's no-self mysticism is given in the degree to which one is given to subjective distortions in one's memory, claims in relation to others, perceptions and so on. If one is consistently given to such distortions, if one consistently recalls facts in an inaccurate manner, a manner, moreover, which gives one advantage, then this is powerful evidence that one has not accomplished the no-self meditation.

It may be objected, however, that it is impossible to practice objectivity of this kind; that one's self conception is inextricably bound to one's image of oneself as a member of a specific community with a specific tradition. In their various ways, Michael Sandel, in *Liberalism and the Limits of Justice*, Richard Rorty, in *Objectivity, Relativism, and Truth*, and Alisdair MacIntyre, in *After Virtue*, might be interpreted as presenting a critique of the sort of traditionless objectivity that the analysis I've just given seems to require.

In response to the charge that a traditionless objectivity is impossible, it might be said that the objectivity that's required for the demonstration of the connection between mysticism and ethics is not of the traditionless variety. Indeed, the very heart of the transition, for example, from a culture in which private vengeance is the conventionally approved response to acts of violence against one's kin, to a culture in which agents of violence are regarded as threats to the public and are tried and punished by the public, is precisely the transition from one tradition to another. Further, the ways in which the agents of violence are subsequently treated by the public must coalesce in traditions of treatment. Precedents must get created and followed to some degree, and so on. Expectations are woven into the fabric of moral intuitions, and expectations only exist in the context of practices and traditions, so that much of utilitarian, contractarian, and generalized deontological moral strategies are barren in the absence of a tradition. But equally barren are the notions of communities, virtues, practices, and traditions without the possibility in principle of striving for objectivity in the establishing of facts. So unless one's communitarianism and traditionalism amounts to a really radical relativism one will, one must, allow for the practices and traditions constitutive of procedural justice in the quest for facts. Rorty would, one suspects, make a good judge if he trained himself in that direction. Similarly, he would make as good a witness in a court trial as anyone else. In fulfilling such roles, he might well think of himself as R. Rorty, more than as Me. To the extent that he does so, he is thinking objectively in the sense required for our analysis. He is thinking objectively, and still operating within a tradition which is particularist in its social values, and which includes the notion of striving for objectivity, and neutrality in the sifting through of perspectives for facts. Thus, the objectivity we need is not a traditionless objectivity.

We will return to these themes in chapter 9. In the meantime, a second area needs clarification. In suggesting the link between no-self mysticism and justice, I do not wish to suggest that one who is scrupulously just and is extraordinarily attuned to objective thinking about the first person and others is ipso facto a no-self mystic. It would seem to be the case, rather, that one's basic image of the world can still be colored by ego-consciousness despite a high degree of attunement to objective thinking. It takes a very great effort indeed to pass from the objective thinking, within a moral and social tradition, to no-self realization. The fair people of this world one way or another have discovered objective thinking, and objective thinking, to some degree, involves acclimatization with objective first person reference instead of self-reference. But it is still possible for objective thinking to be an overlay upon a deeper level of ego-identified thinking, which is merely suppressed, as it were, when issues involving fairness arise.

Not every fair person is a mystic. But every genuine no-self mystic will think the way a fair person thinks.

In sum, mysticism is consistent with an overall stress either on interrelational or on monadic value. The line of balance between interrelational life and monadic life is not indicated by the mystic's theory of monadic value itself, and so it can be drawn in different places by different mystics. The empirical or philosophical claims that mysticism inevitably requires world devaluation or even simple unworldliness are without substance. Moreover, there is a strong connection between a form of mystical practice and the practice of a central social value, namely, the practice of justice.

In the final section of this chapter, we will discuss the general question of establishing priorities between monadic and interrelational values.

IV.

Mysticism, Monadic Ethics, and Interrelational Ethics

Having clarified the distinction in chapter 6 between monadic and interrelational ethical theories, we can now see that mysticism is sometimes criticized as an extreme form of monadic ethical theory. In effect the problem of evaluating monadic ethical theories against interrelational ethical theories is the problem of role prioritization. To what degree is it appropriate, permissible, or obligatory to assign such priorities? Can meaningful general remarks be made about such matters?

In chapter 2, we noted the fact that the problem of role prioritization raises the most difficult questions in ethical theory. If we are to be capable of establishing role prioritizations in a general and systematic way, now is the time for us to show this. On the other hand, if no such general or systematic approach to role prioritizations is possible, this, too, must be shown to be the case, and the implications drawn out for mysticism and value theory. Once again, then, we return to an exploration of the fundamental issues in moral theory including universalism and non-universalism, utilitarianism, deontology and complex moral theory, and the problems of role prioritization in a relational ethical schema.

The great divide in western ethical philosophical thinking over the entire range of its endeavor, beginning, that is with the Athenian golden age, is between universalistic and non-universalistic ethical standpoints. In chapter 2, we presented an argument whose conclusion was the principle of universalism, namely, that at the ultimate level of analysis, every sentient being should be counted in one's moral calculus. But in practice, how do I include everyone's interests as intrinsic interests in my moral reflections, and how does this affect the mystic's theory of the monadic summum bonum?

The first point is straightforward. Universalism alone implies that if there is a mysticism which is out and out egoist at the ultimate level, it can be rejected. The early Mahayana Buddhists seem to have taken it that the arahat ideal, the ideal of the individual who releases himself or herself from ego-consciousness, still was too individualistic, and, perhaps, amounted to a form of egoism. It was not clear to the Mahayanists that there was genuine universalism at the ultimate level of Buddhist doctrine as it had been formulated and was being practiced. Accordingly they posited the ideal of the bodhisattva, the individual who vows to enter final nirvana only after all other sentient beings have entered nirvana. The paradox of requiring that one become a bodhisattva before entering nirvana can be seen by imagining what would happen if two bodhisattvas are the last of all sentient beings to enter nirvana. Now who will enter nirvana? Both have vowed to let the other enter first. A perpetual "After you Alphonse" dance would occur. Perhaps for this reason, the bodhisattva's vow includes the reflection "sentient beings are infinite in number; I vow to save them all!" In any case, the Mahayanist criticism of the arahat ideal as they perceived it is a criticism of an allegedly non-universalistic mysticism. Thus, there is precedent for this sort of reconstructive criticism even within ancient materials, if any such precedent is required.

Now we want to distinguish between (a) bufferless universalism, in which I consider everyone's interests as intrinsic interests in my calculation; (b.i) buffered universalism, in which I have a "buffering" rule which enables me, for the purposes of the calculation, to ignore an entire class of sentient beings in this case; (b.ii) non-universalism, in which I do not recognize everyone's interests as intrinsic interests at the ultimate level of analysis. If I consider what's the best I can do with the ten dollars in my pocket, for everyone I could possibly affect by my use of the ten dollars, then I am adopting a bufferless universalism, in this case, a bufferless act utilitarianism. Indeed, bufferless utilitarianism often is act utilitarianism, the principle that I should try to bring about the maximum good calculated on the expected effects on all of each and every action. But there can also be a bufferless rule utilitarianism. For instance, the principle that I should try to maximize everyone's preferences (as opposed to trying to figure out if their preferences correspond to their true interests) is a buffer-less rule utilitarianism.

If in practice I am entitled to ignore vastly many of the billions of people and billions of higher animals on this planet in some given circumstance, for example, when I'm considering what to do with the ten dollars in my pocket, it could be for two quite different reasons. First, I could be entitled to ignore a large class of sentient beings in that circumstance given that I am acting out some role prioritization or other. Second, I could be entitled to ignore a large class of sentient beings because I am entitled under a utilitarian construal of the citizenship relation to do so. For instance, it may be that the greatest good in the long run is brought about by healthy competitiveness in circumstances such as these. Then citizenship fulfillment itself requires an egoist utilitarian component, or a "familialist" utilitarian component, or a "nationalist" utilitarian component. (The last mentioned is most implausible, but that's another issue.) It is a strength of the relational analysis that it can show how much buffer theory within traditional utilitarianism misconstrues the buffer as providing a comprehensive determination of obligation, when it should only be a buffer within an analysis of citizenship role fulfillment.

Next, we want to consider *(a)* bufferless universalism in relation to some form of *(b.i)* universalism with regard to the fulfillment of the monadic values of all citizens. It is doubtful that *(a)* universalism can be plausibly defended. For instance, an act utilitarian version of *(a)* bufferless universalism could require that I calculate the direct consequences of each particular action I am about to undertake. Act utilitarianism, as is well known, however, produces very counterintuitive results. For instance, consider a case posed by Bernard Williams: faced with a request from a dictator to kill an innocent person following which nineteen other innocents will be let go, on the understanding that if I decline, all twenty will be killed, act utilitarianism would assign me responsibility for the deaths of the twenty if I refuse. In this way, act utilitarianism fails to take account of fundamental moral intuitions such as those revolving around moral integrity and the assignments of responsibilities to individual moral agents. Also, it counterintuitively eliminates moral difficulties and dilemmas, suggesting that there is no dilemma at all, when our intuitions tell us that there are such dilemmas under such circumstances (Williams, 1973, pp. 96-117).

Bufferless rule utilitarianism fares no better, for it is especially vulnerable to the basic and most general criticisms of rule utilitarianism. For one thing, bufferless rule utilitarianism seems to share the features of act utilitarianism which produce profoundly counterintuitive results. If you expected that by torturing some innocent person everyone else's preferences were fulfilled, would that be the right thing to do? Second, bufferless rule utilitarianism seems to collapse into act utilitarianism: if the rule provides guidance toward the maximum good, then in any situation in which there's reason to believe the rule violated would maximize overall good, then the rule should be violated. But that seems to require that the rule is merely provisional, and the ultimate test of the right action is the act utilitarian test. Finally, the consequences of implementing a universalistic rule ripple out indefinitely into the future, since there are no restrictions whatever on the sentient beings being considered. My contemporaries and future generations's interests, preferences, or whatever, need to be taken account of now. This produces a dizzying fuzziness about how I'm to know when I can conclude that a strategy is working. For instance, what justifies the view that actions calculated on the greatest expected utility will in the indefinite future actually produce the greatest utility? It can't be our experience of the consequences of such choices in the past since it isn't clear that enough people have been basing their choices on the principle of expected utility for us to be able to judge. And even if it were, and if we could notice the short term utilities accomplished, we'd need to be able to predict that the consequences would continue to be good on into the indefinite future to be able to conclude what we need to conclude. If the problem is corrected by making action on expected or expectable utility the ultimate criterion of rightness, then the very objectivism of the principle of utility has been sacrificed, and an intentionalism introduced which seems at odds with the root utilitarian intuition.

Let us then consider the buffered forms of rule utilitarianism. One of the advantages of the relational ethical framework is that it enables one to separate out some layers which otherwise become conflated. Under the citizen relation there is, first, the layer at which I consider maximization of monadic interests, second, the layer at which I consider maximization of everyone's intimate interrelational interests, and then there is the layer at which I consider what sort of citizenship mutuality or citizenship interrelational value can occur.

With regard to the maximization of overall monadic and intimate interrelational fulfillments, it is doubtful that any simple buffering rule utilitarianism can be in fact justified. Is it plausible to think that by treating others as means toward one's own good, everyone's good, in general, would be served? Aren't there plenty of cases in which the maximum good of a group is served when people routinely consider each other's goods as ultimate intrinsic goods? For instance, families seem to be well served when their members often consider each other's intrinsic goods as intrinsic goods. And, inversely, if people only considered each other's goods as intrinsic ultimate goods, holding that one's own goods were to be regarded strictly as means toward the general good, everyone would regard himself as peculiarly debased. (If being fed is minimally more pleasant than feeding oneself, then I'd have to feed you at dinner, and you'd have to feed me! The buffer would quickly prove to be self-defeating.) Thus, only a mixed altruist, egoist utilitarian schema could possibly be correct. But once we have the mix of altruist and egoist rules of thumb, we have the equivalent of a relational ethical schema requiring an account of the prioritization problems even within the citizenship relation itself.

Another way to put this is to say that utilitarian systems tend to be relational ethical systems in which, rather surprisingly, only monadic citizenship fulfillments are recognized. Under utilitarian systems I am typically considering only the sort of goods which I might have if no other rational agent were around, or the goods of other rational agents of the same sort, and my obligations to maximize them. Typically left out of account, for instance, are the fulfillments consisting in the mutuality in intimate interrelationship. As soon as utilitarianism expands to include those intimate interrelational fulfillments as having a standing and character of their own, the prioritization problems articulated within a relational ethical schema are confronted, and the moral calculus has the fundamental characteristics of a complex moral theory. Each relationship has its own virtue, as the Confucians put it; and the virtues appear not to be particularly commensurable. The supposed strength of utilitarianism—the comprehensiveness of the principle, and the hope for commensurability of all values—has been lost.

Further, without acknowledging deontological reasoning, utilitarianism, however modified, is incomplete. One way or another, we must add in the deontological principles at least as factors in the moral calculation. Adding in the deontological principles as well, then, we find that the problems of incommensurability between deontological and utilitarian principles or factors, and of the incommensurability of the various deontological principles themselves, should they be in potential conflict, mirror the problems of role prioritization as well. If keeping a promise to one person requires that I lie to another, what am I to do? Similarly, if being a parent and being a worker and being a friend and being a citizen seems to require that I find twenty-seven hours in the day, what am I to do?

There are two sorts of responses. The first is to seek a systematic account of the resolution of such dilemmas, for example, by an elaborate analysis of case types and principles, so that one can articulate a learnable, yet comprehensive system of rules to guide one's prioritizations. The second is to give up on the systematization in favor of the cultivation of what amounts to the virtue of wisdom.

In the latter vein, Aristotle offers both methods for determining the mean, and the advice that one must gain what experience one can, and act with practical wisdom or insight *(phronesis)*. W. D. Ross holds that one must recognize the plurality of prima facie obligations and goods, and strive to make sense of each individual situation on its own terms. Ultimately, there are only three goods, says Ross, namely, pleasure, knowledge, and virtue. Resolving dilemmas in which fundamental or prima facie duties conflict can only be undertaken by the exercise of what amounts to intuitive wisdom *(The Right and The Good*, pp. 20-28; pp 134-141).

On the other hand, there are systems of elaborate casuistic (i.e., case by case) analysis. The *halacha* of Judaism, and the *sharia* of Islam, for instance, are elaborate legal and moral codes for the living of everyday life. They include not only prescriptions the violations of which are subject to public trials and penalties, but also prescriptions for moral and ritual conduct over and above the legally obligatory. In *The Abuse of Casuistry*, Albert Jonsen and Stephen Toulmin describe the history of casuistry in the Christian church, and discuss the prospects for the revival of a sort of casuistry, which seems to be underway in the latter half of the twentieth century. It seems doubtful, however, that traditionalistic casuistic systems could be more than vehicles of study by which people develop and cultivate wisdom. For how will one casuistic system justify itself against another?

This problem becomes even more acute when the moral dilemmas are articulated in an explicitly relational framework. How do I decide whether my priority is to myself, my family, or my country, in a time in which I am being conscripted for or requested to go on an extremely dangerous mission in what I consider to be a just war? Overall happiness is incalculable without a prioritization already given, for although at some level of theory, perhaps, the overall monadic good can be calculated, interrelational fulfillments are not monadic goods, and cannot be commensurated with the monadic goods by any nonarbitrary means. Moreover, the various relational fulfillments are all perceived by me as important. On what basis are these priorities to be assigned from the beginning? Are we to expect that there can be a general system for the resolution of such priorities? Why expect such neatness in life?

If intuitive wisdom is the best we can hope for to resolve our dilemmas such as arise within the complex ethical framework, what is the best we can hope for to resolve our prioritization problems such as arise within the relational ethical framework? I want to suggest that even the virtue of intuitive wisdom will not quite do for the relational prioritization problems. Further, although non-universalistic moral thinking, including radical existentialism, fails at the ultimate level, nonetheless the key experiential features of the radical existentialist vision are preserved and justified in consideration of the role prioritization and non-obligatory role occupation questions at the practical or immediate level. This results in what might be called "modified existentialism." Modified existentialism, I'll try to show, provides an indispensable element in any proper understanding of role prioritization theorizing.

According to existentialism under a *radical* interpretation, I must always remind myself of my complete openness and freedom. At any moment, I can decide to be a criminal. I can decide to be a saint. I can decide to sacrifice everything for love. I can decide to abandon society and live as a hermit. I can decide to plunge into political life in the hopes of relieving human suffering. I can decide to live my life under a strictly aesthetic attitude. And so on. In considering a future which is so open and unconstrained, there is no external source or calculus which I can rely on to provide me with essences. There are no such fixed essences governing me and my life. Rather existence precedes essence, and I constantly find myself in the position of what Sartre calls "*pour-soi*," or "for the self," that is, a condition in which I am open, and empty, and reaching forward into the future to define myself.

As a self-contained program of metaphysics, epistemology, and ethics, Sartrian radical existentialism leaves a great deal to be desired. Indeed, Sartre is by no means consistent in his position. On the one hand his epistemology is modernist, as when he grants in *Being and Nothingness* (p. 340) that our identification of other minds is "infinitely probable." On the other hand, if the modernist epistemology is to be taken seriously, then such identification of other minds gives us a system of essences within which we exist as one of these essences, and our moral attitudes, it would seem, ought to take cognizance of this feature. Our moral analyses are not as unconstrained as he often makes them out to be. Some suggest that Simone de Beauvoir in *The Ethics of Ambiguity* has found a way of reconciling the apparent inconsistencies. To my mind, she is not sufficiently explicit about them to have done so.

But to reject radical existentialism is not to reject the entire contents of existentialist thought. The greatness of existentialist thinkers such as Sartre and Simone de Beauvoir, is in their courageous willingness to remind us that above all else we make ourselves. Even if we allow that under healthy social conditions as well as under unhealthy social conditions there are constraints upon who we are and what we can be, even if we allow that there are nondefeasible relational activities and roles, still, the prioritization between our roles is sufficiently open as to preserve many of the most significant features of what the existentialist refers to as the existential condition. This means that within any proper Enlightenment West moral and social program there will be an important area within which moral and social calculus breaks down, and existential creativity takes over.

Every society has its own definition of the basic roles. Within each society at the same time, there will be areas of discretion for prioritization, and areas beyond which there is no discretion for prioritization. The significant point is that, even if one accepts the restrictions imposed within a given society and culture, even, that is, if one is highly traditionalistic in one's willingness to define oneself by the roles of the culture (an assumption far more traditionalistic than I am suggesting is generally obligatory or always permissible, I hasten to add), there will be areas in which the existentialist value of self-creation comes to the fore. And if there aren't such areas, then the social values are far too restrictive. A fortiori, then, existentialism in its modified form will correctly describe the moral situation of one who lives in any reasonably open society.

In a healthy society there is enough scope for self-determination that everyone can resonate to the existentialist characterization of life as a journey into uncharted seas on a boat whose design has never been tested. In a healthy society, there will be room for hermits, and saints, families, and larger collectivities. In a healthy society, there will be room for those who cultivate monadic interests intensively, and those who don't. In a healthy society, there will be room for tough minded utilitarian egoists and room for compassionately minded utilitarian altruists. In a healthy society, there will always be a tension between the self-willing, self-creating dynamism of individuals and the conservatism of traditional forms of life and traditionally patterned values. How, then, does this apply to the calls issued by mystics? Perhaps there are some mystics who think that all interrelational experience should be regarded as instrumental toward mystical bliss.

Perhaps there are mystics who issue calls for general renunciation in the literal sense. If so, they have unjustifiably separated off monadic experience from interrelational experience. Only if mysticism is confined to introvertive mysticism would a universalistic choice have to be made between interrelational and monadic values. But so long as self-altered releases from ego-consciousness are available, through no-self mysticism, and universal self mysticism, the mystical monadic intuitions can be cultivated even in extrovertive experience, and even together with interrelational experience.

Thus, even the most substantiated moral and social criticisms of Enlightenment East perspectives may be undercut by the development of an Enlightenment East moral and social tradition which is integrated fully with the Enlightenment West interrelational moral and social program. The fact that such a program must be tempered by what I've called "modified existentialism" does not tell against its essential adherence to the modernist vision. Undoubtedly some contemporary exponents of particular Enlightenment East traditions will claim that their tradition already has reached an adequate interrelational and mystic monadic value balance point. Spiritual communities such as the Radhasoami community at Dayalbagh may lay claims to have achieved such balance, for instance. (See "The Spiritual Socialism of 'Better-Worldly' Dayalbagh" in *Juergensmeyer* 1991, pp. 158-165). This may or may not be so. Once again, it is not our purpose here to make these specific assessments. Rather, our purpose is to acknowledge that specific integrations of Enlightenment West moral and social perspectives with Enlightenment East traditions are necessary to undertake in those mystical traditions whose social or moral expressions have failed in some basic way; and to show how such integrations are both possible and practical.

Eight

Mysticism and Science: A New Opportunity

There is a wonderful paradox associated with the topic of this chapter. Everywhere among New Age and Enlightenment East groups, we find an acknowledgment and endorsement of scientific values. Again and again we find contemporary proponents of mysticism using the language and vocabulary of scientism in the service of claims and methods which are, according to the proponents of Enlightenment West, not only unscientific, but also, in the end, antiscientific. In this chapter, we examine the accusation levelled by Enlightenment West proponents toward Enlightenment East practitioners that their world view is not only unscientific but antiscientific. We also raise the questions posed by the Enlightenment East critics of Enlightenment West vis à vis modern science: are the scientific rationalisms of Enlightenment West inadequate and incomplete without benefiting from the mysticism of Enlightenment East? More generally, then: What contribution, if any, does mysticism have to make to science by giving evidence of a sort which challenges existing physical paradigms? What contribution does science have to make to our understanding of mystical states? And finally, what contribution does science have to make to social theory and social practice by either confirming or disconfirming the sorts of paranormal reports that frequently form the basis of a mystical leader's social authority?

I

Enlightenment East groups promote sublime metaphysics and sublime meditation practices together, often, with extraordinary claims concerning the paranormal powers of the guru or the enlightened being. The connection between the social authority of the leader and his or her alleged demonstration of paranormal gifts is obvious, and not in principle different from the connection between the social authority of the theistic prophet and his or her alleged performance of miracles. But now if we are to practice social justice and the pursuit of scientific knowledge, if we are to unify the Enlightenment West values based on the two expressions of objectivity found in scientific investigation and social justice, with the mystical Enlightenment East values, then we must have a look at how the paranormal claims made by spiritual leaders provide the basis of their social authority, and whether the paranormal claims themselves have been established by methods consistent with the espoused value of scientific inquiry.

This is no easy task. It covers a vast field, and the research itself is dependent on the assessment of specific empirical claims of all sorts. What I hope to do here is, first, to present a reasonably comprehensive treatment, in outline form, of the philosophical problems and issues involved in such research; second, to present reflections on some of the research which has been undertaken over the years in fulfillment of the broad aims of the task; and third, to report on some pieces of research which I have undertaken in this line.

I hope it will not be taken amiss if I emphasize the importance of this chapter's inquiry within assessments of Enlightenment East and West in particular and in contemporary humanistic thinking in general. We find ourselves, in the world today, at a most exciting juncture in history. The practical values of scientific investigation have thoroughly impressed themselves throughout the world, and it is understood that these practical values cannot be divorced from theoretical interests. Similarly, the ideals of democratic, people-accountable social systems have, with some important exceptions, of course, diffused throughout the world. At the same time, there has been a gradual secularization associated with the pursuits of science and social justice. This secularization has the tendency to go along with a repudiation of the Enlightenment East project in many circles. Today, at last, the world is recognizing itself as a unity. But there is a real danger that this unity will be at the same time a victory for a de-sacralized, de-spiritualized scientific secularism. If the Enlightenment East project, as found in religious movements throughout the world, is to survive and integrate with Enlightenment West scientism and its associated push for social justice, it can only come about through the efforts of all women and men of spiritual intent, worldly common sense, and a basic scientific education, to ensure that social authority associated with groups promoting the Enlightenment East activities is founded in practices that are morally and scientifically of the highest calibre and standards.

Facts, causes, and miracles

I'll begin by describing in simple terms the position which I'll advance with regard to the relation between facts, causes, and miracles, since the assessment of any paranormal claims requires a theory of sorts concerning this relation.

The position is as follows: In order for the performance of a psychic or the occurrence of an apparently occult event to challenge a current scientific paradigm, two conditions must be fulfilled. (1) A set of facts must be convincingly and properly established; (2) It must be clear that the current paradigms of causal explanation are fundamentally inadequate with respect to accounting for these facts.

If these two conditions are fulfilled, then it is possible for one to go on to inquire whether some revised physicalistic causal paradigm can account for the facts better than the current physicalistic causal paradigm or not. There are two possible outcomes of this inquiry: (3a) If a revised physicalistic causal hypothesis is available, then one can devise tests which, one hopes, will confirm or disconfirm it. If the tests disconfirm it, one goes on searching for another physicalistic theory, and devises tests for the new theory. On the other hand, (3b) if it can be established that no plausible physicalistic causal hypothesis could account for the facts, then one is entitled to postulate that the events in question were miraculous. The position I am advancing, then, maintains that under some reasonably specifiable conditions, conditions which we determine to obtain by empirical means, we might be properly led to the conclusion that miracles have occurred.

Establishing facts

We begin by taking note of the fact that paranormal psychology, especially insofar as it is relevant to our project, concerns itself with what are taken to be powers or faculties which exist in some people, and, according to most defenders of the paranormal, can be cultivated in a large percentage of people, if not all people. Some people might hold that the cultivation of such powers is not without spiritual dangers. Others, that it's fine to cultivate the powers, but not to display them too much, and so on, but the claims as we find them are that there are such powers or faculties, and that they can to one degree or another be cultivated in many people.

What powers are we talking about? Perhaps the first systematic classifications are those found in early Buddhist texts (Cf. Kalupahana, 1992, p. 40, n. 20-23), and that of Patanjali in the Yoga Sutras (Section III, "Powers"). Patanjali's is elaborate. He says that the practice of yoga leads in the successful practitioner to: the knowledge of past and future, including the knowledge of past lives, and the time at which people will die; the ability to understand the language of animals, and the secret thoughts of people; the ability to make it impossible for others to see you by stopping the light from their eyes to you; having the strength of an elephant; knowledge of the world, the sun, the planets, the motion of the stars; being free from hunger and thirst; knowing everything; being comfortable in thorns; the ability to leave one's body at will; the ability to hear divine sounds; the ability to fly through the sky; and the ability to take any form whatever.

This is quite a list! A more typical modern list of types of paranormal powers might go something like this: telekinesis (the power to move an object external to the ordinarily identified body at will, without touching it); clairvoyance (the power to see contemporary events which are transpiring in locations beyond the range of one's normal sensory vision); clairaudience (the power to hear sounds out of the range of one's normal hearing); levitation (the ability to raise oneself off the ground without jumping or other normal means); precognition (the power to know the future other than by normal guessing or anticipation); postcognition (the ability to know past events without relying on normal information-gathering techniques or cues); telepathy (the power to know what another person is thinking without reliance on evident bodily cues); materialization (the power to create physical matter, usually in one's hands); and apportation (the power to cause an object to disappear in one location and reappear in proximity to one's body, or at some other location than the original location, at will).

How do we establish that somebody has such powers? In many cases, we can reasonably easily imagine what would be involved in confirming the genuineness of such powers. If we want to test telekinesis, materialization, or apportation, we ask a magician such as James Randi to devise the test. (See *Flim Flam*, for examples of the investigations Randi undertakes.) The tasks involved in these three types of cases are grossly physical and if there is a surface appearance of success our main concern is over whether such appearances have been created by normal means of the sort magicians the world over are familiar with.

Establishing the facts for clairvoyance, telepathy, precognition, postcognition, knowledge of past lives, and so on is a subtler business. Suppose the alleged or would-be psychic (henceforth, "the psychic," without prejudice to the issue whether there is some paranormal ability she or he has) is placed in one room, and a series of drawings is placed on a board in another room. The rate at which the drawings are changed is prearranged. The psychic is asked to draw what she "sees" on the board in the next room in the intervals as per the prearrangement. Here, too, we must check for means by which information can be transmitted from one room to the next without the experimenters knowing, or for means by which some prearranged sequence of images has been organized with the psychic's knowledge. But suppose expert magicians have done all the required checks. Still the question as to what is to count for paranormal performance is open. Imagine that a line drawing of a rowboat is placed on the board in the next room, and the psychic draws what the psychic considers to be a banana, but the viewers may think of as a rowboat on its side. Must we ask what the psychic meant by the drawing? If so, we'd judge that a banana is not a rowboat, and the psychic was off. Or should we just look at the outline of the banana, and judge that the outline is pretty much that of a rowboat, resulting in the judgment that the psychic was successful? Or again, if the psychic draws a rowboat now, and three figures later a rowboat appears, does this count in the psychic's favor in any way? Was there precognitive interference with clairvoyance? Obviously, there are so many correspondences to be found in any collection of events that we can easily fall into the trap of *overpatterning*, that is, attributing to causality, and in this case, agency, what is occurring in accordance with what ought to be expected by chance. There is so much information surrounding, or contained in, any given set of events that all we have to do is look for surprising connections and we'll find them. It is not surprising that we'll be surprised, for there is only a weak correlation between what the untrained intuition regards as improbable and what turns out to be improbable when precise methods are used.

This latter fact emerges in some striking ways. For example, most people who are randomly assigned a horoscope will judge the randomly assigned horoscope as being an accurate reading. This result has been well confirmed by simple experiments. (For a brief review of some of these, see Kurtz, *Transcendental Temptation*, p. 430.) And people's untutored intuitions concerning probability are notoriously off the mark. One well known example concerns the probability that in any arbitrary group of thirty people two people will have the same birthday, that is, same month and day of the month. The untutored intuition is that since there are only thirty people, and 365 days, there must be a low probability that two have the same birthday. In fact, however, there is roughly a 70 percent chance that in any given group of thirty, two will have the same birthday. When there are forty people in the group, there is roughly a 90 percent chance that two will share a birthday; and when there are are fifty people in the room, there is roughly a 97 percent chance that two will share a birthday.

(For an explanation of the probability calculation in such cases, see Robert Martin's *There Are Two Errors In The The Title Of This Book*, p. 28.)

The consequence of this is that it is doubly difficult to give credence to strictly post facto anecdotal accounts. If John says, "I had a vision of Aunt Mabel dead yesterday, and I haven't thought of her in years, and then I received the telegram that Aunt Mabel died," we have no way of confirming that John really hadn't thought of Aunt Mabel in years. Is it not equally likely that John thinks in passing of a great many people, and does not have any conscious recollection whatever of thinking of them unless some reason occurs for recall within say, twenty-four or forty-eight hours of the original thought? Similarly, we can question whether or not John's vision was of Aunt Mabel dying, or rather a more general one of her being in trouble, or being old, and hence near death, or of her being ill. We can't properly get to the bottom of John's claim, nor can we easily determine how probable it is that John's claim, although true, is not unexpected, in that given the millions, indeed, billions of people in the world, the odds are that some people will imagine things that do in fact occur. We are confronted with the cases reported, not the idle thoughts so many have which turn out not to correspond to subsequent events. Until we know a great deal more about thought processes, we can't make reliable determinations concerning the probabilities. And as has been decisively demonstrated we are not entitled to rely on untutored intuitions of likelihoods.

In a given incident of clairvoyance or telepathy, then, it is very difficult to determine whether or not the facts as presented have occurred, and even more difficult to determine whether or not the facts such as have been established constitute any challenge to current scientific paradigms. However, it is possible to set up a double blind experiment in order to test whether or not somebody has a true ability to gain information in a paranormal manner.

For if someone claims to have reliable clairvoyance, say, then it should be possible to set up a double blind experiment which tests this person's ability. This can be done with cards, so as to eliminate the element of subjective judgment as to whether a psychic's guess is accurate or not. But even in the case where there is subjective judgment, it is possible to set up double blind testing. The essential idea is that people judging the results would not know which target was the actual target of the guesses, and which target was not the actual target. If, after proper magic-proof elimination of the hypothesis of normal means of information-gathering, the guesses keep being judged closer to the actual target than to the non-target in a statistically significant manner, then one has some prima facie evidence that the psychic does have a paranormal ability. If a particular psychic, or better still, several individual psychics are individually able to confound the skeptics in a consistent manner over many trials, then one would take it that current scientific paradigms have been genuinely challenged.

Developing rival hypotheses

If a set of facts is properly established, the degree to which these facts challenge current scientific paradigms must then be assessed. Clairvoyance, clairaudience, and telepathy would challenge the current view in cognitive science that every thought which forms in a person's brain, forms as a result of information received by the normal sensory channels in combination with the current cognitive states of the person. While there are many differences of view currently held in philosophy and cognitive science circles concerning the relation of mind and brain, the physicalistic ingredient with regard to empirical information on which the cognition operates is standardly present. There are materialists, identity theorists, dualists, functionalists and non-functionalists, but all hold that whatever type of thing a mind-state is, the empirical information on which it works is received through physicalistic transduction along the sensory channels. (Even idealists, presumably, will agree with the concept, though they would put it differently.) This paradigm leaves no room for information to be received by other means. Nor does current physics lend itself to the view that there are other channels whereby information not within sensory reach might be transmitted. Accordingly, clairvoyance, clairaudience, and telepathy, if properly established, would challenge the current paradigm in cognitive science. Once a challenge of this sort is found to occur, however, one needs to see whether or not the facts might be explained on some physicalistic revision of the current scientific paradigm.

For convenience, we will simplify: suppose a psychic, A, performs tremendously well as a clairvoyant. Immediately, one would want to test A as to her ability in relation to distance. If A is able to be clairvoyant because there are subtle energy waves carrying information of all sorts washing over everyone, but A's brain has the capacity to tune into these waves, whereas most people's brains don't have the capacity to tune in, or aren't properly trained in tuning in, then one might suppose that the distance over which the waves have to travel has some effect on the integrity of the information. The longer the distance, the more noise in the message. This hypothesis could be tested.

If it was found that the clairvoyant has more trouble the further away the target image, then this would tend to support the hypothesis that there is a physical basis of the clairvoyance, a physical basis unknown to current science, but which is amenable to discovery and examination through hypothesis testing.

Einstein's correspondence shows that he viewed reports of telepathy and clairvoyance as implausible, since there appeared to be no relevance of distance in the claimed performance. Thus, Einstein was assuming that if telepathy and clairvoyance are genuine phenomena, there is a physicalistic basis of them. (Einstein's correspondence on this issue is found in Martin Gardner, *Science Good Bad and Bogus*, 1981, pp. 151-156.)

To be rigorously logical about these matters, however, we must canvas the possibility that that there is no physical basis for the phenomenon. That is, we must consider the possibility that each instance of clairvoyance is a mini-miracle. In order to clarify the difference between the view that clairvoyance is made possible by the reception of messages carried in some subtle and hitherto unknown physicalistic manner, on the one hand, and on the other hand, the view that clairvoyance is miraculous, we consider two rival views of agency.

On the first view of agency not only is every action the result of prior brain states, but also there is no cognitive state which is not embodied in a brain state. On the second view of agency (one held recently by Sir John Eccles and Karl Popper, for example, in *The Self And Its Brain*), there are cognitive states which are not embodied in brain states, and these unembodied cognitive states cause changes in the physical states of the brain, which then cause other alterations in the brain and in the nerves proceeding from the brain, leading to muscle contractions constituting basic action. The second view holds that there is a special kind of causation, which in a reasonably precise sense, is not physicalistic causation, since the antecedent state, the cause, is not embodied in a physical state, or does not correspond to a physical state, and so it is not the case that one physical state causes another. Rather, an unembodied mental state directly causes a physical change at some location of the brain.

Perhaps one might object on the grounds that it is inconceivable that an unembodied mental state might cause a physical change. By what means, it might be asked, can an unembodied, nonphysical mental state cause any sort of change in a physical system? What is its point of purchase?

The answer which the mind-brain interactionist theorist might give is that the connection between cause and effect is always mysterious, or in any case merely a matter of regularity of conjunction. Then it is no more inconceivable that an unembodied mental state is followed by a physical change than that an embodied mental state is followed by a physical change. On this point, the mind-brain interactionist is, I think, right. Mind-brain interactionism is a logically conceivable set-up. Moreover, we can conceive of empirical tests confirming it. Eccles has described what he took to be evidence suggestive of the truth of mind-brain interactionism. Elsewhere I've argued that Eccles has adopted an inconsistent attitude towards his own data, sometimes suggesting that it is merely indicative of the need for further research, sometimes suggesting that it is sufficient for his interactionist conclusion to be drawn (*How To Build A Conscious Machine*, pp. 92-94). And I've further argued that the latter suggestion is by no means warranted from the meagre data. But if a great deal more were known about the brain than is now known, and if sufficient data indicating mind-brain interactionism were consistently reported again and again, it might become plausible to conclude that the brain receives instructions from unembodied mental states, or that brain changes are caused by unembodied mental states. The mind-brain interactionist picture is a conceivable one.

We now wish to draw attention to a particular feature of the causal set up of mind-brain interactionism. If mind-brain interactionism were to turn out to be true, then not only would it be the case that unembodied mental states have direct physical effects, but also it would be the case that unembodied mental states, in some cases, overturn, or preempt the usual physical regularities. In order for an unembodied mental state to directly cause a physical change in the brain, then, there must be a violation of the conservation of energy law which (usually) operates in the neurochemical interchanges. After all, if it takes the expenditure of so much energy to get a neuron to fire normally, yet, as the mind-brain interactionist supposes, there is neuronal firing without any prior expenditure of energy or prior neurochemical triggering process, then the unembodied mental state, which directly causes a physical change in the brain, the firings of neurons, does so in violation of the ordinary mass-energy conservation principle. The x amount of energy is not supplied, and yet there is neuronal firing. Thus, mind-brain interactionism requires that there be what I have called "functional preemption" of physical laws (ibid., p. 85). A material arrangement is functionally preemptive just in case there are functional states which initiate physical changes without any corresponding prior physical causes occurring. If mind-brain interactionism is true, then there are functional states which preempt physical laws.

Let us apply this now to clairvoyance. Just as we can conceive of a functionally preemptive arrangement in which agency takes place, so, too, we can conceive of a functionally preemptive arrangement in which clairvoyance takes place. Information is embodied in some state of affairs. The state of affairs, say, is that a boat is moored in an island bay. The functional state directly causes a series of physical changes in the clairvoyant's brain, just as the unembodied mental state of the agent causes physical changes in the brain of the agent. The physical changes in the clairvoyant's brain are such as to cause the visual information of a boat moored in an island bay to register in the clairvoyant's consciousness. In both cases there must be functional preemption of the ordinary physical laws. It is because there is preemption of physical laws that we are entitled to import the traditional term 'miracle' to describe the nature of the clairvoyant's performance. It should be noted, however, that if we allow the term 'miracle' to be used in connection with functionally preemptive clairvoyance then we should also use it in connection with any functionally preemptive agency. And if functionally preemptive agency, or mind-brain interactionist agency is a standard feature of human agency, then we would be committed to a terminology that allows that human agency be described as routinely miraculous. 'The routinely miraculous' sounds somewhat odd, but the oddity, it should be conceded all around, is a merely verbal one. To say that there are routine miracles is only to say that when one makes a free choice some unembodied mental states directly cause physicalistic changes, which physicalistic changes occur in violation, or preemption, of the physical laws of nature. We note as well that the view of the human volitional system as routinely miraculous is essentially the prereflective view of voluntary agency for most people, who adopt a contracausal view of human choosing prior to being exposed to compatibilist and hard determinist arguments.

What isn't often realized, it might be added, is that the contracausal view of human freedom requires that an in principle confirmable and in principle refutable empirical thesis be true, namely, that the human brain is a functionally preemptive causal system. Assuming closure over implication for justification of beliefs (If I am justified to believe A, and I am justified to believe that A implies B, then I am justified to believe B) the proponent of contra-causal freedom is justified to believe in an empirical thesis which has not yet been confirmed. (And is very far indeed from being confirmed!) That is, the proponent of contra-causal freedom asserts that she is justified in believing that she is contra-causally free. However, if one is contra-causally free, then one has a functionally preemptive brain. Then one is justified in believing that one has a functionally preemptive brain. But one is only justified to believe an empirical thesis such as that one has a functionally preemptive brain through the appropriate empirical means. And this source of the belief is not appropriately empirical. Therefore it cannot be that the proponent of contra-causal freedom justifiably believes herself to be contra-causally free.

Returning, in any case, to the main line of discussion, there are two prima facie hypotheses concerning any verified occurrence of clairvoyance or telepathy. The first is that these phenomena occur through the operation of hitherto undiscovered physicalistic causal exchanges. The second is that these phenomena occur through functionally preemptive causal arrangements, causal arrangements which violate ordinary physical laws, and are therefore miraculous, however regular they may be. Furthermore, it is conceivable that we might empirically confirm the occurrence of miraculous events in this sense.

Supposing that clairvoyant and telepathic psychics were determined, to the best of our ability, to exist, then there would be three epistemic possibilities at any point subsequent to our research into the basis of the phenomena: (1) we are able to locate the subtle, hitherto undiscovered, physicalistic basis of the phenomena; (2) we are able to empirically confirm the non-physicalistic, and therefore, in our sense, miraculous, nature of these phenomena; (3) we are unable to empirically confirm any physicalistic basis for the phenomena, nor are we able to empirically confirm that these phenomena are, in the sense described, functionally preemptive, or miraculous.

It may be useful to compare the position taken here with Hume's position in the *Enquiry Concerning Human Understanding*. In the *Enquiry*, Hume suggests that miracles are, practically speaking, unverifiable. The evidence for humanly interesting contra-causal events, or miracles, is sure to be more dubious than the evidence for the causal regularities of which the miracles are in violation. By definition, a miracle involves a violation of a well established regularity; and since the evidence for an unusual, unrepeatable occurrence will always be subject to our doubts, we will never, in principle, find ourselves in a position to believe justifiably in a miracle on the evidence. There might be an unusual miracle-seeming occurrence which we might accept, and then seek a suitable hidden regularity to explain it. But then our investigation does not hold out the possibility that it is miraculous. Rather, our investigation proceeds on the assumption that there are features of regularity that we are missing, or facts concerning the situation of the seeming miracle which we are unaware of. The evidence for a true miracle, a suspension and, in our terms, a preemption of the laws or regularities of nature is in principle more dubious than the evidence establishing the regularity.

Thus, he writes, "It is experience only which gives authority to human testimony, and it is the same experience which assures us of the laws of nature. When, therefore, these two kinds of experience are contrary, we have nothing to do but to subtract the one from the other and embrace an opinion either on one side or the other with that assurance which arises from the remainder. But according to the principle here explained, this subtraction with regard to all popular religions amounts to an entire annihilation; and therefore we may establish it as a maxim that no human testimony can have such force as to prove a miracle and make it a just foundation for any such system of religion" (Hume, *Enquiry Concerning Human Understanding*, section X, part II).

There are two points we wish to make here. First, Hume was writing at a time when chemistry was still in its infancy, and there is a significant difference between a Humean causal analysis prior to the development of chemistry and a Humean causal analysis subsequent to the development of chemistry. Prior to the development of chemistry, the regularities observed are within the macroscale, and so the attuning of the cause to the effect is extremely rough. However, the regularities which constitute the laws of chemistry are microscopic and so it becomes possible to envision experiments designed to distinguish between a physicalistically ordinary sequence in the microscale, which constitutes an extraordinary sequence at the macroscale on the one hand, and the functionally preemptive or miraculous microscale extraordinary on the other hand, which might or might not be extraordinary at the macroscale.

So long as one's understanding of causal regularities is only rough, and strictly at the macroscale, one might be led to erroneously reject the miraculous, that is, the violation of physical law in the bringing about of humanly significant effects. One erroneously rejects the miraculous, say, because there is overwhelming evidence of macroscale constancy: all reports of macroscale physics-defying miracles such as loaves multiplying, fire from Heaven, and walking on water, are wishful thinking, mere myths, deceptions, and so forth. However, there might be miracles continuing to take place not at the macroscale but at the microscale. For instance, if Eccles's and Popper's picture of agency, and, indeed, the picture of agency held by the majority of people prior to exposure to the empirical and philosophical arguments, is correct, then there would still be microscale miracles. So Hume's rejection in principle of the miraculous based on macroscale regularities fails to take account of microscale possibilities. The absence of the macroscale miraculous is compatible with the presence of the microscale miraculous. And, although Hume does mention the possibility of what he calls secret causes (section IV, part II), he does not apply this possibility to the discussion of miracles at all, and certainly does not envision the possibility of macroscale regularities covering over and obscuring microscale miracles.

Suppose we were able to confirm some microscale miracles, such as routine functional preemption in voluntary agency. Would it not be possible, based on our experience of such miracles, to alter the balance of Hume's subtraction in the case of reports of telepathy and clairvoyance? I think it would. If we knew that physical laws were being routinely suspended in some part of the brains of self-conscious agents for the accomplishment of their voluntary acts, then we would at least have good reason to try to devise experiments to see whether or not further physical laws were being suspended in the psychics whose performance was good enough to be puzzling. Perhaps other parts of their brains are behaving functionally preemptively. Hume's maxim, then, is vulnerable in case microscale miracles show up.

The second point raises a stronger objection still. Hume suggests that in humanly neutral cases, cases which wouldn't tend to be religion building, or serving the interests of some special group of people, namely, the prophets of the miracles and their followers, we might have evidence of extraordinary miracle-like occurrences, and we could believe the testimony, and set about searching for the hidden causes of the extraordinary occurrences. The example he gives is of a report of a period of darkness extending for many days. He distinguishes such a report from the religion-building occurrences. But surely, in principle, there might be functionally describable circumstances regularly preceding macroscale wonders such that there is less room for doubt concerning the testimony of the wonders than there is room for doubt concerning the consistency of physicalistic natural law that had previously been justified by our experience. The more self-serving or religion-building a miracle story, the more cautious we are in regard to the testimony, and the more lightly we weigh the report. But there must be a point of unanimity or reliability of testimony beyond which we must begin to throw the burden of doubt onto our previously held views of consistency and uniformity of physical laws.

For instance, suppose ordinary subjects are placed in room A, and asked to guess concerning pictures simultaneously being shown in room B. Suppose it turns out that ordinary subjects succeed in an extraordinary way, but only if, and whenever, a sign bearing the word 'dog' is in room B along with the target pictures. Suppose we make repeated tests, and it doesn't matter what language the word for dog is a word of, so long as there is a natural language in which this word means dog. We test all other words, and there is no extraordinary performance on the part of the subjects when the other words are on the wall of room B. We bring in our most skeptical skeptics, and our most expert magicians, and all are confounded. This goes on for years and years, then generations and generations. Under such circumstances, surely, and even without microscale testing, we would be warranted in concluding that functional preemption is taking place. The reason is that there is no plausible physicalistic basis for a connection between the word for dog in any natural language being present in the room with the target pictures, and the ability of an ordinary subject, ignorant of whether the sign contains a word for dog or not, to be clairvoyant. Indeed, if a sign with the symbols for a combination of phonemes, which no experimenter recognized as the word for dog in any natural language, were up in the room, and the subjects performed phenomenally well, surely, one would be led to predict that those phonemes did indeed combine to make the word 'dog' in some natural language. Here, then, we would have a miracle regular enough to form the basis of a confirmable prediction! If a diligent search of the languages of the world finally revealed an obscure tribe for whom that concatenation of phonemes made the word for dog, we would have a striking confirmation of, or support for, the theory that there is functionally preemptive causation, and all special evidence is macroscale evidence.

Suppose further that one were to do microscale testing under such a circumstance. Again we note that there are two possible outcomes. The first is that there is a microscale miracle coinciding neatly with each macroscale miracle. The second is that there is a macroscale miracle, but we exhaustively confirm that each event in the brain accords with the physical regularities. Under the second possible outcome, the instance of clairvoyance would be something like a right mathematical sum wrongly achieved by double error whenever some arbitrary scent is in the air. A remarkable, and perhaps even inexplicable coincidence, unless one were moved to think that the whole business was planned to give evidence (of a subtle sort) of a super-person who'd previously arranged the whole thing, or to think that our universe is but one of infinitely many parallel universes, one universe for each logically possible sequence of events.

We need not try to adjudicate these three approaches to the second possible outcome, however, in order to see that Hume overstates his maxim. He says, "no human testimony can have such force as to prove a miracle and make it a just foundation for any such system of religion." But surely it is not that no human testimony *can have* such force, but rather that given our experience (Hume's experience, or the experience he assumes we share with him) *it is unlikely* that we will come upon human testimony with such force as to prove a miracle and make it a just foundation for a system of religion.

Against Hume, and in parallel with Paul Dietl, and Tai Wei Tan, I have argued that human testimony *can have* such force. But is there any such testimony which does have such force?

II

With this framework of approach in place, we are ready to consider:

A: the contribution mysticism has to make to the direction of our research in physics and neurochemistry;

B: the contribution science has to make to our understanding of enlightenment, or *satori*; and

C. the contribution science has to make to social practice in connection with mystical institutions.

A

It would be very exciting indeed if one were able to point to evidence challenging current scientific paradigms stemming from the activities of meditators, psychics, gurus, and yogis. Is there such evidence? The only way to get a sense of the range and problems is to overview the research that's been done and to undertake serious inquiries oneself wherever claims seem to arise. Here I can only point to some of the research and issues, and present summaries of investigations I've undertaken.

1. Telepathy, clairvoyance, precognition

The first problem to be encountered here is accuracy of reportage. It should be agreed all around, I hope, that no report about what a psychic purportedly revealed about a person's past or current situation, or future, can be considered seriously without an audiotape, and preferably a videotape (camera on the subject) of the psychic reading. People who receive psychic readings tend not to be sufficiently aware of the difference between information the psychic gives back to them in the form of a question and in the form of a statement. Nor are they likely to be aware of the degree to which information is suggested to them by the psychic only following a series of questions put by the psychic and willingly answered by them. Nor are subjects aware of the positive and negative indications subtly being communicated by them to the psychic with regard to a line of response being given by the psychic while the psychic is talking or pausing. Nor do subjects properly compare the questions answered by them in the negative with the questions answered by them in the positive. For instance, suppose the following exchange takes place between a psychic "P," and the subject, "S."

P asks, "Do you have an older brother?" S answers, "No, I have a younger brother, though." P replies, "Yes. I see you with your younger brother. Do you have a memory of sharing a room with your younger brother?" S says, "Yes, yes I do! We used to share a room in the cottage." P continues, "I see water, and you're swimming with your brother. There is an incident, confusion. This was causing you anxiety. You're feeling very anxious." S exclaims, "Yes! That must be my brother rescuing his friend Timmy. I was distraught because I had to call to my brother who was many yards away. I didn't know if Timmy would make it."

After the reading, the subject might well report this as follows: "She closed her eyes and said she saw my younger brother. She knew we shared a room at the cottage, and she saw the lake. She even got many of the details about the day my brother rescued Timmy from the lake."

Given that this sort of creative summarization takes place, the need for adequate recording of any psychic reading is an absolute requirement. (For a summary of some research into suggestibility, memory, and eyewitness reportage, see Reich Jr., 1993; and Kurtz, 1986, 138-140; also see Siegel, 1991, 319-321.)

Several years ago I offered as an assignment option to my students in an introduction to philosophy class the task of visiting a psychic, taping the reading, and analyzing the performance of the psychic. Each student opting for this assignment was to select his or her own psychic, and only two of the ten or so went to the same psychic. It seemed clear not only to me, but also to the students who undertook the assignment, that in these cases at least, the information supplied to the subject by the psychic was easily explained on the hypothesis that the psychic used all or some of the following practices:

(i) Gather impressions concerning the subject, sometimes directly, sometimes subtly before the official beginning of the reading.

(ii) Ask questions on matters of fact. The questions are put in such a way that there is likely to be a "yes" somewhere in the area of each question presented.

Psychics do a lot of question building, more or less in the twenty questions manner, during the course of a reading. Often the question is in the form of a first person statement, for example, the psychic says, "I'm receiving something about your situation at work," and then the psychic pauses so as to gauge reaction. Very frequently the psychic waits, subtly or overtly, (and the pause need be only ever so slight) for some kind of confirmation, again, either subtle or overt, from the subject before proceeding along a certain line of discussion.

(iii) Make direct statements in areas of personality and character, areas in which, as has been well confirmed, subjects overrate the fit between the reading and their own individual personality (Kurtz, *Transcendental Temptation*, p. 430).

(iv) Make the odd stab in the dark guess phrased openly with regard to the past or the future. If the answer is negative, the language of the guess is broadened somewhat, and it is suggested that the subject look out for something along these lines in the future. If the answer is positive, then the psychic takes credit for the guess.

(v) Relate to the subject as a concerned friend, genuinely interested in the subject's welfare, and so forth, and establish rapport with the subject.

(vi) Describe the subject as having a specific connection with certain specified symbols, these symbols being, in fact, a subset of a series of universal symbols or archetypes, so that more or less everyone can resonate positively to the messages or situations embodied in more or less any of these symbols, and in any combination of them.

For example, "The (ocean) (mountains) (plateau) (whale) (porpoise) (seal) (spear) (silver spoon) (gold key) (crown) (amethyst) (nose ring) . . . is a special symbol for you, has, or will have, a special significance for you." Often the reading revolves around a set of images yielded through some device such as a throw of yarrow sticks, or a dealing of cards. The specific throw or dealing produces a nexus of archetypal imagery to which anyone with imagination can respond positively. This may result in a highly beneficial psychological exchange between psychic and subject rather akin to the exchange between psychotherapist and client. But there is nothing, so far as one can see, paranormal about it, unless all psychological rapport is paranormal.

In general, the rapport established with the subject makes it hard for the subject to be objective about how much information was supplied by the subject and how much was supplied by the psychic.

If you, the reader, have any doubt about whether psychics have genuine paranormal abilities, by which we mean the ability to discover factual information without the use of normal sensory and cognitive channels, then why not go to one who knows nothing about you? In setting up the appointment give your first name only. (Check in advance as to cost of the visit.) Wear your ordinary "going downtown" clothing for the visit to the psychic. During the session, when the psychic asks you a question, simply hand the psychic a card on which is printed, "Please draw on your psychic abilities, and see if you can answer for me." Don't answer any questions, and don't react throughout the entire course of the visit. Better still, why not sit with your back to the psychic? If the psychic will not give you a reading unless he or she can see your face, then you have good grounds to conclude that the psychic relies on subtle cues in the form of changing facial impressions in response to leads initiated by the psychic. At home, analyze the reading (which you have taped) and see whether or not it is particularly impressive. If you continue to be impressed, then it might be appropriate to devise a properly controlled test of this psychic's ability.

For related discussions and summaries, see C. E. M. Hansel, *The Search For Psychic Power*, Parts I, II, and III; "Investigation of Psychics" James Randi, *Skeptical Inquirer*, 1981, vol. 5 no. 4; and "The Elusive Open Mind: Ten Years of Negative Research In Parapsychology," Susan Blackmore, *Skeptical Inquirer*, 1987, vol. 11 no. 3. Special attention should be paid to chapter 13 of Hansel's book. I don't know how many times I've been told that Russell Targ and Harold Puthoff have scientifically established the validity of remote viewing through their SRI research. Obviously, excited write ups of Targ and Puthoff's experiments have reached a lot of people. Unfortunately, far fewer people are aware of Marks and Kammens's review of these experiments. In particular, it turns out that in a supposedly careful experiment, the judges who were to determine which descriptions of the subject seemed to match which target locations, knew the order of the targets as originally presented, and the transcripts of the descriptions contained so many cues as to their order that Marks was able to match the five transcripts correctly solely on the basis of the cues without ever having even seen the target locations! (Hansel, p. 162). That Targ and Puthoff also have an amazing ability to pulverize their own credibility by either not keeping proper records, or not releasing them for scrutiny is made clear by Martin Gardner's "The Great SRI Die Mystery," chapter 20 in *The New Age*.

2. Postcognition

New Age practitioners frequently offer to give people "past life" readings. The question here is whether the information is imaginary, or factual. I have not come upon any reports which establish with even minimal credibility the accuracy of the information thus delivered. However, I have had an opportunity to follow up one such claim in detail. Several years ago, a student of mine named Donna Schmid received a reading putatively from a spirit entity named "Michael," (who has been written up in many books, for example, *Messages from Michael*, by C. Q. Yarbro) delivered through a Michael channeller, concerning her most recent past life incarnation.

According to the message, Donna Schmid's most recent previous incarnation was supposed to have been involved in academic life in England in the latter half of the nineteenth century. Some of the details I thought might be checkable, so I asked her if she would cooperate and we'd make a proper check of the information. She agreed. The plan was for her to ask three different Michael channellers for information concerning her most recent incarnation. She followed through, and the results were about as negative as one could imagine, both as far as the accuracy of any information revealed was concerned, and also for the hypothesis that each of the three channellers was genuinely revealing the mind of any coherent entity, Michael.

The channeller who originally told her that her most recent incarnation was an English academic who committed suicide in the latter half of the nineteenth century, speaking as Michael, refused to give any checkable information further to that of the original session, save to say that the death seemed to occur in the 1880s. The second channeler, speaking as Michael, refused to give any information concerning the subject's most recent incarnation at all, saying that it was not in the nature of Michael's relation with the subject to reveal such information. The third channeler channeled a Michael, who gave a host of specific information, claiming that the subject's most recent past life was as Thomas Scott, born in Ireland, in the year 1865 in Derry, christened in St. John's Church, January 12, 1866. Thomas Scott, according to Michael, channelled through the third channeller, moved to Montreal in 1882, worked for the Canadian Pacific Railway, met with an accident in Toronto, Ontario which led to infection and death in 1893, and was buried in the Mount Royal Cemetery in

Montreal, with the gravestone clearly marked "In the Beloved's Arms."

We noted that the third channeller contradicted the information of the first channeller as far as the decade of death went, and the career of an English academic was not that of a Canadian laborer. We further checked with the Mount Royal Cemetery in Montreal, which has complete records for that period. No individual fitting any of those particulars is buried there. Similarly, we asked the office of the Registration of Births, Deaths, and Marriages in Dublin to check the birth registration information for the years 1864 through 1867 inclusive, with entirely negative results. As far as death in Ontario in 1893 is concerned, the Ontario Registrar General Office searched the Ontario Index for 1891-1895 and there was no registration for the name indicated during that period. The entire framework of information supplied by the channeller was, we had to conclude, devoid of factual content. When the results of our investigation were reported to the channeller who provided the Thomas Scott information, his response was that channelling was not primarily concerned with providing factual information, and that such information when delivered through channelling might be, as he put, "a bunch of garbage." The full write up of this investigation may be found in *Rational Enquirer* vol. 2 no. 3, Jan. 1989.

Of course this is but a single alleged claim. Nonetheless, it is hard to account for such gross inconsistencies, failures, and so forth, and blithe responses to the inconsistencies, except by saying that these channellers are not much concerned with whether their entity constitutes an actual entity, as opposed to being merely a fictitious or conventional setting through which each channeller is given social permission to dip into his or her subconscious, and a format within which to do it. It further seems likely that these channellers are representative of at least a very large class of channellers who find what they do interesting at the personal level but have no curiosity about the sorts of experiments that can quite quickly give one a sense of the coherence of the entity supposedly being chanelled.

Is there empirical evidence for reincarnation?

This sort of investigation into a chanelled past life claim, however, does not address the cases of people who claim to remember past lives of their own. Probably the most important source of information concerning this phenomenon is a compendium of case studies by Ian Stevenson, originally published as volume 26 of the *Proceedings of the American Society for Psychical Research*, and then reissued under the more widely known title, *Twenty Cases Suggestive of*

Reincarnation (1974). In the 1950s, 1960s, and 1970s Dr. Stevenson went around the world investigating cases in which it was claimed not only that someone had remembered a past life of his or her own, but also that the memories had been verified, or were ripe for verification. Stevenson's aim was to write up the data he had thus far gathered in as objective a manner as possible, and check out the data to whatever extent possible. Stevenson's conclusion was that the stronger cases could not be accounted for plausibly except on one or another of these three hypotheses: reincarnation, spirit possession, or extra sensory perception plus personation (p. 382-383).

Reincarnationism is the theory that the mind at least sometimes survives the death of the body and continues to live, perhaps for a time without any body, or perhaps directly entering a fetus to become the mind of that fetus, so that the developing fetus is one and the same person as the person who lived before. Reincarnationists also hold that on at least some occasions a person remembers having lived before, and can remember significant details about one or another past life. The spirit possession theory is similar. It states that there is a soul, the soul lives on after the death of the body, but it also holds that on some occasions the soul of a departed person can take possession of an already existing child, entirely, or in a fragmentary way, so that the body of the child seems to be remembering some other life. The body of the child, however, according to the spirit possession hypothesis, now houses the other spirit, and the original child. ESP plus personation would account for apparent past life memories in this way: The past life memories are produced by the conjunction of two events. The child obtains information about the past through postcognitive, ESP, means, and then for one or another psychological reason, the child identifies with one person involved in the information picked up by extra sensory perception. According to the ESP plus personation theory, it's not that the child *is* that other person, but rather that the child adopts the persona of the other person whose information has been delivered to the child by ESP means.

What is important to us is that Stevenson's conclusion, that only these hypotheses singly or in combination can account for the richer cases, is a very strong one. For each of reincarnation, spirit possession and ESP plus personation includes an ingredient which is highly challenging to the current physicalistic paradigm in psychology. If reincarnation, spirit possession, or ESP, occurs then it would, very likely, occur through functional preemption. In particular one would expect there to be preemption or violation of the laws of conservation of mass energy, for neurons would apparently have to undergo changes without doing so in response to immediate physicalistic stimuli. For a summary of the reasons physicalism or organicism is the working hypothesis of neuropsychologists, see Barry Beyerstein (1987) "The Brain and Consciousness." Beyerstein outlines the compelling support for this view that mental and physical events are perfectly correlated, offered by split-brain experiments in which people in whom the two hemispheres of the brain are severed are asked to perform various tasks; by data gathered on patients, who have suffered brain damage of other sorts, including the fact that when function is restored the patients do not recall that they had a "free floating" competence which merely couldn't be acted on; by data concerning the psychology of perception, including hallucinatory perception; and by the apparent absence of any mechanism or medium whereby non-neuronally based function could integrate as it would have to with the neuronal activity. And so, although not impossible, it is nonetheless difficult to conceive of a plausible integration of a reincarnationist, possessionalist, or ESP, account with an organicist account of the mind. Hence, the potentially great significance of Stevenson's claim. Contrary to some popular myths, many if not most scientists would be delighted to find good evidence that some well entrenched theory, such as organicism, is in need of drastic revision. Stevenson seems to be claiming that he has such evidence.

To this, someone might respond by noting that Stevenson's title is "Twenty Cases *Suggestive* of Reincarnation." The term 'suggestive' is certainly a hedge of sorts. Perhaps Stevenson is not claiming that he has the evidence which would challenge the current scientific paradigm, only that he has evidence which suggests that the current scientific paradigm might be weaker than people think. What exactly is Stevenson claiming?

It turns out on careful reading that Stevenson's term 'suggestive' is only a hedge for him in relation to the reincarnation theory as opposed to the other two paranormal accounts, of spirit possession and ESP plus personation. He does claim to have found evidence which ought to challenge the current scientific paradigms. In the preface to the second edition, Stevenson states that he has nothing from the first edition to retract, and that, "I consider these cases *suggestive* of reincarnation and nothing more. All the cases have deficiencies as have all their reports. Neither any case individually nor all of them collectively offers anything like a proof of reincarnation" (p. x). He emphasizes the word 'suggestive,' but the entire remark is restricted by the demands of proving reincarnation. He also states in the introduction, "I argue that some of the cases do much more than suggest reincarnation; they seem to me to furnish considerable evidence for it" (2). Even allowing that "considerable evidence for reincarnation" falls short of a claim to have established it nonetheless we have to see to what extent any shortcomings of the evidence, according to Stevenson, are shortcomings in relation to reincarnation specifically.

In his general discussion of the twenty cases (chapter 8), Stevenson claims that fraud cannot account for the richer cases. "A consideration of the large number of witnesses for many of the cases and of the lack of apparent motivation and opportunities for fraud makes the hypothesis of fraud extremely unlikely for the cases here reported" (382). He also claims to eliminate cryptomnesia. Cryptomnesia is the hypothesis that the child somehow picked up the information by normal means, and subsequently forgot having picked it up. ". . . in the richer cases, cryptomnesia cannot account for the transmission of much intimate information about one family to a child of another family without supposing that much more contact had taken place between the families than either can remember" (p. 383). The only serious candidates left are the paranormal ones of reincarnation, spirit possession and ESP plus personation. Of these three, Stevenson further holds the likelihood of ESP plus personation to be much lower than reincarnation or spirit possession in the richer cases. Finally, he finds mild grounds to prefer the reincarnation hypothesis over that of spirit possession: the children exhibit fragmentary memory of the sort that is consistent with a progress of incarnations rather than a spirit possession (chap. 8, 372-386). Here is how he puts it: "The theory of extrasensory perception plus personation does not seem to me to account adequately for all the facts of the richer cases (p. 373), and "Extrasensory perception plus personation . . . can only be stretched with great strain to cover all the facts of the richer cases" (p. 383). His final conclusion is that "Most . . . features of the cases do not permit a firm decision between the hypotheses of possession and reincarnation" (p. 383). However, he adds that "The conformity of the apparent memories of many of the cases to the psychological 'law' that recognition exceeds recall favors somewhat the reincarnation over the possession hypothesis" (p. 383). This firmly establishes that Stevenson takes it he has presented a number of cases of spontaneous past life memory on the part of children, which can only be plausibly explained on a paranormal hypothesis, and that the data most supports the reincarnation hypothesis. Whatever qualifications are inherent in the term 'suggestive' pertain to reincarnation as opposed to spirit possession or

ESP plus personation. And since all three are paranormal and apparently inconsistent with organicism, a very strong claim indeed is being made. How has this claim been received?

Many investigators have emphatically endorsed Stevenson's assessment of the data. In fact it was my students in philosophy of religion classes quoting these ringing endorsations of Stevenson's data which prompted me to have a closer look at the Stevenson materials. Let's have a look at these endorsations: Pal and Linda Badham (1987) state that "Stevenson presents a strong case . . . for saying that at least some claimed 'memories of a former life' appear to be evidential for and suggestive of some theory of reincarnation or possession" (Clark, p. 269). Guy Lyon Playfair (1976) states that a study of the Imad Elawar case does not seem to lead to any probable explanation other than that of reincarnation (p. 165). Robert Almeder (1990) concludes that "there is good reason to suppose that the hypothesis of reincarnation is the best explanation of the cases documented by Ian Stevenson" (p. 50). Sylvia Fraser (1992), like Playfair, specifically cites the Imad Elawar case, and endorses Playfair's conclusion. Gunapala Dharmasiri (1989) states that "After scientifically ruling out the possibility of gaining such knowledge in their present lives, [Stevenson] objectively verified their claims and found them true" (p. 41).

Oddly enough, despite the length of time since publication of Stevenson's original work, it is hard to come by detailed critical reviews of it. Those who endorse his work state that they have been persuaded by the analysis, cite the fifty-one out of fifty-seven memories verified in a case such as the Imad Elawar case, and so on, but do not say much more than that. And skeptics tend to dismiss the work without a fully detailed analysis. For example, in Paul Kurtz' compendious *The Transcendental Temptation* a subsection is devoted to "Reincarnation: Past lives" (pp. 411-414), but there is only the briefest mention of Stevenson's data, analysis, and conclusions. Kurtz does not point to a single critical examination of Stevenson's research. He merely states that "The conscious and unconscious influences of the surrounding environment on the young child seem a more likely explanation of the tales he relates" (p. 411). Given that Stevenson attempted to consider as many alternative explanations as possible, and tabulated his data in the best way he could for independent inspection, and given that many investigators, upon supposedly detailed review of the Stevenson materials, have concluded that Stevenson's best cases can only be explained plausibly on the reincarnation hypothesis, or some other paranormal hypothesis, Kurtz's dismissal seems less than satisfactory.

Stevenson's claims concerning evidence for reincarnation from people who have been tested for their linguistic competence in the past-life's language have been critically scrutinized and found wanting by Sarah Thomason in an article called "Past Tongues Remembered" in the *Skeptical Inquirer* (1987). But, once again, it is the allegedly verified past-life memories summarized in *Twenty Cases Suggestive of Reincarnation* that have been most influential in creating an impression in various popular philosophical and scientific circles that reincarnation has been more or less established as the best hypothesis to account for a range of rigorously collected data.

Paul Edwards in a several part article called "The Case Against Reincarnation" (1987) has presented a wide variety of general arguments to support the view that the reincarnation hypothesis must be held to be highly improbable. He makes it plain that he regards the conclusions of Stevenson's work as lacking. But his analysis of the Stevenson materials is not sufficiently detailed to prevent the comeback that he sidesteps the issue of the specific content of the evidence. To put it in terms of an analogous case in the development of physics, the Michelson-Morley results seemed extremely unlikely at the time. But they were correct. Thus, one cannot simply insist that highly anomalous results are incorrect merely because they are inconsistent with current beliefs or the conclusions of apparently well established investigations. This, in effect, is Almeder's rejoinder to Edwards, and it seems to me to be reasonable: "Edwards's charge that all this is just too incredible for any rational person to believe is simply a blatant bit of question-begging" (p. 48). Similarly, John Beloff (1985) argues against a prioristic dismissals of the paranormal. Rather than pointing to inconsistencies with current beliefs as evidence of the incorrectness of the data on which a paranormal claim has been based, the skeptic must show that there is a plausible naturalistic explanation of the data at hand (p. 361). Beloff's point too seems well taken. To the extent that Edwards has relied on the inconsistency problems, he must expect the open-minded investigator to be less than satisfied with his evaluation of the data. What then of the specific criticisms of the data and analysis of Stevenson's best cases?

Ian Wilson (1981, 1987) criticizes Stevenson for being too light on the fraud issue. But suppose, as most reviewers of these materials hold, that outright deliberate deception on the part of all the participants is highly unlikely. Then how does one account for the data? Edwards quotes Chari's dismissal of many of the cases as cultural fabrications (Chari 1978). Unfortunately, though, Chari is not the right person for Edwards to rely on in dismissing the Stevenson cases, for Chari agrees with Stevenson that a combination of naturalistic and paranormal phenomena other than reincarnation suffices to explain the data. Chari disagrees with Stevenson on some of the specific Indian cases, and disagrees also on Stevenson's favoring of reincarnation against other paranormal accounts. He puts it this way: ". . . we cannot rule out some combination of the counter-hypotheses of hidden and disguised memories acquired in a normal fashion, extrasensorial selective tapping of the memories of others, and a psychometric or psychoscopic ESP achieving a strong empathic identification with deceased persons and an apparent 'resuscitation of memories' not belonging to the subjects in their normal lives. I have examined the hypotheses singly and jointly and conclude that a combination of them is not only feasible but actually illustrated by the empirical data of survival research" (Chari, p. 315). If a detailed review of the best case or cases seems only accounted for by a combination of natural and paranormal hypotheses, then Edwards's argument is incomplete. The question is, how difficult is it to account for the specific content of the best Stevenson cases on purely naturalistic hypotheses? Only a detailed review of the specific content and methods of Stevenson's cases will tell the story on whether or not the scientific community ought to feel the pinch and pressure of recalcitrant results.

Thus, it seems important, however belated, to undertake a more thorough critical examination of the *Twenty Cases* methods and materials than has been thus far been done. Further, I suggest that it is possible in a relatively short space to take the inquiry far enough so as to establish the presumptive unreliability of the Stevenson past-life memory case materials in general due to gross failures in his methods of research, write-up of data, and analysis of alternative hypotheses. In particular I'm going to suggest that Stevenson, Almeder, and others haven't even considered the most important sort of naturalistic account, which I'll call "subjective illusion of significance."

What proponents and opponents of the reincarnation hypothesis agree about

It is important to note at the outset that proponents and opponents of the reincarnation hypothesis as established or suggested by the Stevenson materials do not seem to be arguing at complete methodological cross purposes. Rather, Stevenson and those who concur with his conclusion, on the one hand, and, on the other hand, those who are skeptical of the reincarnation or possession hypothesis as established or suggested from these materials seem to agree about the criteria for successful theoretical accounts of alleged past life memories, namely: (1) simplicity, (2) scope of explanatory power, (3) depth or completeness of explanatory power, (4) predictive power and range, (5) internal consistency and coherence with other beliefs, and (6) capacity to render the data intelligible. When these criteria lead in different directions, then some method of weighing them must be sought. Where the proponents and opponents of the reincarnation hypothesis disagree is on the application of these criteria to the data.

Which case will we select for review?

Let us observe what case or cases have been found by Stevenson and the reviewers to be the most convincing. Stevenson himself singles out a number of cases as his most impressive (1974, p. 371, 377, 385), and among them is one which at least three investigators, who see themselves as open-minded researchers, seem to regard as the most important. The reason they regard it as being of singular importance is the fact that in this case alone among the twenty, Stevenson himself recorded the prior to verification memories, was present at the initial meetings between the boy who had the past life memories and the surviving family members of the apparent past life, and conducted the verifications of the memories. ". . . [Th]e most impressive in this respect is the case of a Lebanese boy called Imad, for in this case, Stevenson arrived before anyone had tried to verify any of his alleged memories" (Badhams, in Clark, ed., p. 261). Playfair also singles out the Imad Elawar case, emphasizing the fact that this is one case which Stevenson himself investigated. Playfair's reading of the case is summarized by the comment, "Imad produced fifty-seven pieces of information about his previous life as Ibrahim Bouhamzy, of which fifty-one proved to be correct or probable" (Playfair, 1976, p. 164). Playfair's explicit conclusion is that "a study of this case does not seem to lead to any probable explanation other than that of reincarnation" (ibid., p. 165). Fraser (1992) also selects the Imad Elawar case for presentation, and makes it clear that she finds it particularly convincing against the general skeptical objections that anecdotal accounts are unreliable (p. 327). Thus, the Imad Elawar case is an excellent case to choose for investigation: it reveals Stevenson's own methods of research, and is singled out by many, including Stevenson, as being a rich, and important case.

*Some expected features of a careful effort at recording,
investigating, and attempting to verify past life memories*

We'll now take note of some elements of proper data gathering procedure and of data presentation with respect to a case in which the
families had not yet met. (1) First and foremost is the need not only to
determine what the memories of the child are, but also to record and
report the the original, prior to verification memories in the very
form in which they were originally noted. (2) Second, any attempts on
the part of the investigator to distinguish between what the boy stated
and what the informant relatives of the boy interpreted him as stating
must be done before efforts at verification, and, assuming they are
done before verification, must be done in a realistic manner.
Obviously, it is a grossly unsatisfactory state of affairs if there is an
unexplained yawning gap between how the informants interpreted
the child's memories and how the investigator records the original
memories prior to verification. (3) Third, the data must not be presented in such a way as to obscure alternative hypotheses, making it
seem that memories are being confirmed when the data themselves
do not warrant such conclusions. Again, it is a grossly unsatisfactory
state of affairs if one cannot tell from the write up whether the boy
first stated a name, or whether the name was supplied by people
from their independent knowledge, when that name is tabulated as
having been verified subsequently. (4) Fourth, any attempt at tabulation of the data should not hide problems in comments. For instance,
any tabulation of memory as successfully verified cannot rely on the
boy's being capable of somehow identifying with two entirely different contemporary individuals. Significant misses should not be buried
in comments and left untabulated. A memory should not be tabulated
as verified when substantial reinterpretation of the content is necessary before the instance can be regarded as a verification. And so on.
(5) The specific methods of verification should be properly documented. (6) Finally, the analysis of the material should consider the
most plausible hypotheses other than reincarnation-possession.

The analysis of Stevenson's data and interpretation

Unfortunately, Stevenson's conduct of the Imad Elawar investigation
fails on all six of these points.

(1) Stevenson presents the original information he received con-
cerning the boy's memories, according to the parents, as follows:
"They believed that he was claiming to have been one Mahmoud
Bouhamzy of Khriby who had a wife called Jamileh and who had

been fatally injured by a truck after a quarrel with its driver" (p. 277).

Stevenson later tabulates fifty-seven items as constituting the original prior to verification memories. But the form in which they were originally recorded is not given. Inspection of the items of the tabulation makes clear the need for a record of just what the parents said, how Stevenson recorded their data prior to verification, and how it was or was not subsequently broken down or reorganized for presentation in tabular form. For the fact is that the boy's memories are in the end held to be good evidence for reincarnation in spite of the fact that the best past life candidate Stevenson found was not named Mahmoud Bouhamzy, did not have a wife named Jamilah, and did not die as a result of an accident at all, let alone one which followed after a quarrel with the driver! Yet Stevenson does not give sufficient information for the reader to know what exactly the parents or the boy himself said which entitled Stevenson to discount the original claims and present the very different claims given in the tabulation.

(2) When exactly did Stevenson formulate the memories as found in the tabulation itself? Let's look for a moment at the write up of the name 'Mahmoud' in the tabulation of data: "2. Mahmoud (name mentioned by Imad)" (p. 287).

Under Stevenson's "Comments" we find, "Mahmoud Bouhamzy was an uncle of Ibrahim Bouhamzy" (ibid.). (Ibrahim Bouhamzy is the apparent past life of the boy, according to Stevenson.) Thus, it is taken as verified that a name the boy mentioned corresponded to a real person in the past life's family, as though it is clear that the boy had been mentioning a name by way of referring to that uncle. What is not mentioned in the tabulation of data, nor even in the comments, is that the original information given by the parents of the boy was that they took their son to be claiming to have been Mahmoud Bouhamzy of Khriby. Presumably Stevenson doesn't mention this in the tabulation because he came to the conclusion that the parents had misunderstood the boy, or drew unwarranted conclusions from what the boy had said. But *when* did he come to that conclusion, and on what basis? There are several passages which might help us with this question: Stevenson says that prior to any visit to Khriby he was uneasy "about the accuracy of the details" he had recorded from the parents, (an ambiguous remark, given that he might be uneasy as to his recording accuracy, or uneasy as to the accuracy of their reports vis à vis what the boy had actually said), and that he therefore went over everything with them. "When we left for Khriby," Stevenson says, "I had a corrected version of everything the parents could then remember that Imad had said about the previous life" (277, 278). However, as noted earlier, Stevenson doesn't make explicit whether or not he continued to formulate the exact wording found in the tabulation as the verification effort continued, or whether, indeed, the exact formulation of the tabulation is what was recorded, in that form, prior to the first trip. In the tabulation, 'Mahmoud' is supposed to be merely a "name mentioned by Imad." Even accepting that Stevenson's revision of the parents' original inter-pretation occurred before the attempt at verification, by what inter-pretive process does Stevenson allow himself to refer to 'Mahmoud' as merely a name mentioned by the boy? Did the boy not distinguish in his remarks between his own previous name and those of others? Or did he simply go about mentioning names with no context? Are the parents likely to confuse a name merely mentioned by the boy with a self-reference? How did the parents make such a confusion? Was any effort made, prior to verification, to ask the boy what his past life's name was? Or who Mahmoud was? In all the tabulated facts of the case, Mahmoud, the uncle only comes up under item 2. Then how did the parents mistakenly conclude the boy thought he was Mahmoud? The boy probably used the name 'Mahmoud' frequently, but noth-ing is recorded in the tabulation about what was said by the boy about this Mahmoud. How can such a discrepancy occur? Finally, and most tellingly, Stevenson refers to his discovery that Mahmoud Bouhamzy was not killed as a result of an accident with a truck as a complication for interpretation of the data, and as "baffling" (p. 280). But if he had already clarified that Imad had not claimed to be Mahmoud prior to the first trip to Khriby, this discovery would not have been a complication, nor would it have been baffling. It would have accorded with the boy's claims as already recorded. The fact that Stevenson took it to be baffling, confirms that his formulation of the data to be verified followed the effort to verify and was not fixed prior to the verification! Without much clearer report as to the exact process whereby the original claims got reinterpreted, the entire framework of alleged correspondences has to be judged unsuccessful.

Moreover, examples of this sort of problem abound. Consider another. Item 20 reads: "A truck ran over a man, broke both his legs, and crushed his trunk" (p. 291). When exactly did Stevenson formu-late the wording "A truck ran over a man" thus leaving open whether the man run over was the past life or not? This memory is supposed to be verified in virtue of the fact that one Said Bouhamzy, a relative of Ibrahim Bouhamzy, the apparent past life, was killed as a result of an accident involving a truck. Yet in the body of the text, Stevenson notes that "His [the boy's] parents did quite certainly in their minds fuse the scenes of the death of Said Bouhamzy with other declarations of Imad and they assigned Said's violent death to the previous personality of Imad. Some similar fusion may have occurred in the mind of Imad himself" (pp. 303, 304). Since the parents certainly took it that Imad thought his past life was killed as a result of an accident, we have evidence that either *(a)* Stevenson, prior to the verification, changed the claim despite the parents apparent certainty that the violent death was according to the boy his own past life's violent death; or *(b)* Stevenson left the claim in his original notes as given by the parents, and changed it only subsequent to the discovery that the best apparent candidate for the past life did not die as a result of a traffic accident. If (a), then, Stevenson has withheld the precise information based on which he made such large changes. If *(b)*, the method used for the tabulation is clearly erroneous. Even worse, on another occasion Stevenson says, "This [muddling of images] had happened to some extent much earlier, especially in [the boy's] confusion of the death of Said Bouhamzy (in a truck accident) as if this had happened to Ibrahim" (p. 319). This shows Stevenson as understanding right to the end that the boy took it that the past life had died as a result of the accident! Then by what right did he alter the claim, and tabulate it as a memory about "a man," as though it had been presented about an unspecified man, any man, and hold it to be a verified memory? Finally, the very fact that we can't tell whether it's *(a)* or *(b)*, that is, the very fact that we cannot tell when Stevenson formulated the memory claims in tabular form, for instance, changing 'Mahmoud Bouhamzy' to 'Bouhamzy,' and changing the past life being killed as a result of an accident with a truck, to a memory held by that past life, and surviving into the present life, shows the inadequacy of the presentation of data. This is hardly rigorous reportage. In fact, it's grounds to dismiss the entire report, since Stevenson has obfuscated the prior claims.

(3) With regard to the third requirement, that the data as presented not obscure alternative naturalistic accounts, consider the identification of the town of Khriby. In the tabulation we find that the boy is presented as having remembered: "1. His name was Bouhamzy and he lived in the village of Khriby" (p. 287).

In the general account of the events, it is reported that Imad "had given the name of the village (Khriby)" (p. 276). Stevenson apparently made no effort to clarify *when* the boy began to refer to the name 'Khriby.' However, we are given to understand that the boy's claims were only taken seriously after the following incident: "One day a resident of the village of Khriby, where Imad claimed to have lived, came to Kornayel, and Imad, seeing him in the street, recognized him in the presence of his paternal grandmother. (For details of this recognition, see Tabulation 1 item 57). This unexpected recognition increased the credibility for his parents of Imad's declarations about the previous life" (p. 276). However, Stevenson does not clarify for us, nor, apparently, did he attempt to clarify for himself, whether or not the identification of the town by Imad *followed* the "recognition" of the lost friend in the street or *preceded* it. The clause "where Imad claimed to have lived" is ambiguous since it does not make clear whether the claim preceded or followed the encounter. The question is, did people infer from the recognition in the street that Imad's past life would have been in the town of the person recognized as a neighbor, which is to say, Khriby, and it was the fact of a recognition encounter that lent credibility to the past life memory? Or did Imad first state that his past life was in Khriby, and then recognize the visitor from Khriby as a neighbor of his past life? Nothing in item 57 clarifies the point either. Thus, the impression created in the tabulation of data that there was an original memory of the residence of that past life in a town named 'Khriby' is in very real doubt.

A similar question can be raised about Imad's identification of the name 'Bouhamzy.' Stevenson apparently made no effort to discover when the name 'Bouhamzy' began to be used by the boy. For instance, was it before or after the boy's father went to Khriby to attend the funeral of one Said Bouhamzy (a different Said Bouhamzy from the Said Bouhamzy who died as a result of the truck accident)? Here, too, there is a very real question as to whether the boy used the name 'Bouhamzy' prior to what we may presume to be naturalistic knowledge of a Bouhamzy family in Khriby. Stevenson's handling of this sort of issue, indeed, his failure to mention these questions, vividly demonstrates an unfortunate insensitivity to such central evidential matters as (i) the need to determine the process whereby Khriby was identified as the location of Imad's past life; and (ii) the existence of alternative naturalistic accounts for the impression created by Stevenson's tabulation, that the boy had, in effect, predicted, or claimed, that there would be a Bouhamzy family in Khriby.

(4) With regard to the fourth requirement, that difficulties should not be relegated unfairly to comments, Stevenson's tabulation of data constantly buries problems in comments, leaving the erroneous impression of clear verifications in the minds of those who do not read carefully. For instance, according to item 35, the boy referred to a full well and an empty well at the home of the past life. This is taken as confirmed by the fact that there were two vats used for stor-

ing grape juice. "During the rainy season one of these vats became filled with water, but the other shallower vat did not, because the water evaporated from it. Thus one would be empty while the other was full" (p. 293). Does a five year old Druse village boy not know the difference between a vat and a well?

(5) Stevenson's method of reporting on his verification standards is certainly inadequate and there is strong reason to believe that his verification standards themselves are inadequate. In any case, because he doesn't clearly report on his verification methods we see how insensitive he is to crucial issues. It is well known, both through common sense, and through careful research, that leading an informant is not the best way to obtain accurate testimony (See, again, Reich, Jr., 1993). In a setting such as this, where evidence has to be established to very high standards, if it is to be capable of challenging an immense quantity of scientific work on the intimacy of the mind-brain relation, it is inadequate to omit reference to the methods of seeking verification of original memories from informants. Stevenson, however, does not go into any details on the methods whereby he elicited verifications or rejections from informants concerning memories of the past life put forward by Imad or as narrated by his parents. But when we look at the surrounding material, we see that Stevenson on at least some occasions, gathered information by leading question, and we further find just how weak such information can be. Stevenson was at one point trying to understand why Imad had expressed such pleasure in being able to walk. His parents had taken it that he was referring to having broken his legs in an accident in the past life. But Ibrahim Bouhamzy had not had such an accident. "Ibrahim Bouhamzy . . . had, in fact, died of tuberculosis as a young man of about twenty-five after spending about a year in a sanatorium. Some mention having been made of a malady in the back of Ibrahim, *it occurred to me to ask the next day if Ibrahim had happened to have tuberculosis of the spine.* Mr. Haffez Bouhamzy then stated that Ibrahim had had tuberculosis of the spine and had experienced great difficulty in walking during his illness. He said that Ibrahim had not been able to walk at all for the last two months of his life. In this pitiful state Ibrahim complained of being ill, seeming to sense some injustice in the fact that one so young and formerly so strong should be thus disabled . . . Mr. Fuad Bouhamzy, brother of Ibrahim, when interviewed later, did not confirm Haffez' statement that Ibrahim had had tuberculosis of the spine or had been unable to walk. The tuberculosis affected his lungs and pericardium only, according to him. Ibrahim had been able to walk until shortly before his death, he said" (p. 281;

emphasis added). From this we see that Stevenson on at least this occasion phrased his question in such a way as to suggest a useful-to-the-genuine-memory-hypothesis answer. And, as well, Haffez Bouhamzy seems to have been willing to respond affirmatively to the question put. Given the discrepancy between Ibrahim's cousin Haffez, and Ibrahim's brother, Fuad, we learn that Haffez' testimony may not be reliable. According to the tabulation, however, the verification of data hinges very largely on Haffez's, remarks. Haffez's name appears as a verifier of twenty-eight items. All told, Stevenson's failure to document his methods of eliciting verification must count as a serious, even fatal, flaw in his work. '

(6) Finally, and most deeply problematic, is the fact that the most challenging rival account of the data to the reincarnation hypothesis has not been so much as raised, let alone assessed. There are several naturalistic hypotheses considered at the end of the book, namely, cryptomnesia, and fraud, (and the non-starter genetic memory), but these are not as threatening as the most important rival account, a rival account which was not considered at all. The reason that Stevenson does not consider the appropriate rival account is that his methods are inadequate to the task. The appropriate rival account has to do with the statistics of the informational nexus surrounding more or less any "psychically" delivered material.

Consider the names Imad used. Are the first names, 'Mahmoud,' 'Amin,' 'Said,' and so on, common names? Are they names Imad was likely to have heard in any case? Was it common for there to be wells in these villages? During the first few years of Imad's life were there any bad accidents in his village or surrounding villages, or would he be likely to have heard of accidents? How common were garages, sheds, gardens, and other items prominent in the tabulation of supposed verifications? In general, then, how difficult would it be to find someone in any large village in that general vicinity who matched more or less as many features as Ibrahim Bouhamzy is said to have matched, given an equal amount of post facto reinterpretation, and latitude allowed?

Stevenson never even *considers* the dominant alternative hypothesis to reincarnation or possession, namely, the hypothesis that the correspondence between the original memories and the supposedly best candidate are so loose as to be present in many possible candidates, allowing equal latitude in interpretation and reformulation of data. On the hypothesis that the identification of the village as Khriby *followed* the encounter with the visitor from Khriby, it is as plausible to search for any person in any village nearby for the correspondences in order to test for the significance of the correspondences found in Khriby. And even if the name Khriby (which, it turns out, when we read unrelated fine print, was originally pronounced "Tliby" in any case!) was mentioned by Imad prior to the encounter with the Khriby visitor, still these could have been excused. So many other misses are excused already. For instance, Imad couldn't recognize his own past life's mother, yet he "recognized" some person who lived in some unspecified proximity to the past life's family residence for some unspecified, possibly brief, period of time. If a better past life candidate had been found in another village, Stevenson could easily have speculated that the reincarnation produced odd distortions in the informational field, and that the recognition of the man from Khriby must have been in virtue of some resemblance to a man in the village with the better candidate.

When all's said and done, the correspondences are hardly impressive when tested against the original information given by the parents, and the information we find buried in the comments: The parents thought the boy thought he was Mahmoud Bouhamzy, but no Mahmoud Bouhamzy fitting other features could be found. The best candidate according to Stevenson and the family members was Ibrahim Bouhamzy. But Ibrahim Bouhamzy did not have a wife named Jamilah, did not have a daughter named Mehibeh, did not have a brother who was a judge in Tripoli, nor a son called "Adil," nor a son called "Talil or Talal," nor a son called "Salim," nor a son called "Kemal." He did not have an accident in which his legs were broken; neither did he go to the doctor's place where he had an operation as a result of the accident, nor was any accident connected with Ibrahim the result of a quarrel with the driver of a truck. People were not killed in such an accident; neither Ibrahim nor the driver of Ibrahim's truck died as a result of an accident. The driver of Ibrahim's truck was not a Christian, nor did Ibrahim have a hunting dog, nor did Ibrahim have two wells at his house, nor did he use a truck to haul stones to his garden (nor was the truck in the accident full of stones), nor was it correct that Ibrahim had enough money and land so as to enable him to be free of regular business. (Ibrahim used a truck commercially and was a bus driver.) The memory was not correct that he himself did not drive his truck (since Ibrahim was a truck driver), nor were there two garages in Ibrahim's house, nor was it true that Ibrahim had had one goat, (rather Ibrahim had a flock of goats when young), nor is it true that Ibrahim had a sheep (he had a flock of sheep when young), nor did he have five children (Ibrahim never married, and died at the age of 25, after spending the last year in a tuberculosis sanatorium), and finally Ibrahim could not speak English.

In virtue of what original claims, then, does Stevenson allow himself and the family to zero in on Ibrahim Bouhamzy? There were three informants who said Ibrahim had a mistress named Jamilah, and three who "gave discrepant testimony." Jamilah was beautiful, and Imad said Jamilah was beautiful. Jamilah wore red and dressed well; Ibrahim was a "friend" of the famous Druse politician Kemal Joumblatt; he had a farm; there was a sort of entrance with a round opening; Ibrahim was fond of hunting; Ibrahim had a hidden gun; Ibrahim once beat a dog; there was a slope near Ibrahim's house; Ibrahim had been rebuilding his garden; Ibrahim had a small yellow automobile, a bus, and a truck, (though they were owned by the family, and not as Imad had suggested, by the past life as an individual). That seems to be the sum total of the correspondences remaining from the original prior to verification memories. (That the garden had cherry and apple trees cannot be taken to verify the memory that the new garden had cherry and apple trees because Stevenson did not claim to establish when these trees were planted. If they were more recent than Ibrahim's death, for instance, it would not be verified that Imad had them as a memory from Ibrahim; and if they were too old they would disconfirm a memory of a change in the garden. So Stevenson has incorrectly claimed a verification on their account.)

All these correspondences are easily accounted for on naturalistic lines. The conflicting testimony about whether Ibrahim had any special relationship with Jamilah is accounted for by the hypothesis that Jamilah was a well-known beautiful young woman of this small village, and Ibrahim, like others, had some sort of attraction to her. The rest of the correspondences have not been shown to be particularly striking in the context of Druse village life. Perhaps it was not unusual for a woman to have a red item among her clothing. The small yellow car, like the bus and the truck, was owned by the family. Without information on how many other vehicles were owned one way or another, at one time or another, by the family or members of the family, there is no way to assess the significance of that supposed correspondence. The friendship with a famous politician is impossible to assess without a clearer exposition of what the friendship consisted of. Was Ibrahim really more of a friend than most others? Some famous politicians are awfully friendly people. As for the slope near the house, could it be that most of the houses in Druse villages have a slope somewhere near them? What remains is the fondness for hunting, having a hidden gun, improving the garden, having access to some vehicles, an entrance with a sort of round opening. Given all the failures, the uncertainties, and the unexplored contrary possibilities, and the evident unreliability of the supposed verifications, the case seems particularly unimpressive.

Most telling of all, the boy seemed to have in mind at the prior to verification stage that in his past life he was an important family man, wealthy enough not to have to work, with a beautiful wife and five children, moving in important circles, who met with a tragic accident in which his legs were broken, from which he died. This just doesn't seem to be Ibrahim Bouhamzy, a truck driver who used his family's cars, and died at twenty-five of tuberculosis, unmarried, and was either childless, or, if one credits some shaky testimony, had one illegitimate child. It's only the way in which the information is misleadingly tabulated that leads people to miss the problems. Once we factor in the problems in assessing correspondences with what Persi Diaconis (1978) calls "multiple end points," we see just how weak the Imad Elawar case is.

By far the majority of the details of the original claims attributed by the parents to their son were failures, but discounted on some ground or other, and the claims reformulated. One can't help but wonder what the boy would have done if he had been led to some other village altogether. If it is objected that the boy was not sufficiently suggestible as to follow the lead of the adults, and would not have merely gone along with the adult identification of the locale, then one only needs to read the following to realize just how suggestible, and how willing to play along with what the adults seemed to want of him, the boy indeed was: "Mr Abushdid [the translator] then turned to Imad and promised him a very large bottle of Coca-Cola if he would say that he had been in the village of Khriby before. To this Imad then replied that he had once before been there in an automobile with his mother and father" (p. 312). All in all the truly relevant rival hypothesis to reincarnation is that of distorted impression of significance of data. And it fits all the facts available far better than any paranormal hypothesis. Yet Stevenson never even considered it.

If a case which is alleged by Stevenson himself to be among the strongest of his cases, and has the special merit of having had its purported verifications conducted by Stevenson himself, falls apart under close scrutiny as badly as the Imad Elawar case does, it is reasonable to conclude that the Stevenson materials are presumptively unreliable. That is, we may presume that the impression of significance created by Stevenson's presentation of data concerning the verifications of past life memories first undertaken by untrained observers is even less reliable than the impression of significance created by Stevenson's tabulation of his own research in the Imad Elawar case. If anyone wishes to challenge this conclusion by pointing to another of the twenty cases, the presentation of which is held to be methodologically sound, I would be happy to scrutinize it.

Also it is worth noting here that Pasricha's work (1990) shows every sign of being similar to Stevenson's work not only in its format, but also in its insensitivities to crucial methodological issues.

3. Levitation

I have never witnessed an event at which a levitation was supposed to occur, but there are many reports of yogis performing levitation in India. Many Westerners and Indians take these reports at face value, and believe that levitations regularly occur. However, Agehananda Bharati's report on a supposed levitation event he witnessed supplies us with a very clear clue as to the unreliable nature of these claims, and, by implication, many other claims that might otherwise appear to be well established. Bharati describes how the followers of a guru claimed that he levitated annually. Bharati attended one year and found that there was nothing literally describable as a levitation. Some years later, Bharati asked the guru about this. The guru responded, "I never levitated, . . . nor do I do any of the feats told about me. It is the *bhaktas* [devotees] who say these things" (Bharati, 1976, pp. 106, 107). There are also some reports fostered by proponents of the meditation method established by Maharishi Mahesh Yogi that this method enables people to levitate. That there exists no minimally credible evidence of any gravity defying events taking place within the Maharishi's siddhi program is made clear by the analysis Randi provides in *Flim Flam*. A rather remarkable tale, though not a well documented one, is provided by A. L. Herman, in *A Brief Introduction To Hinduism*, pp.73-75. Herman says that a Harvard Professor filmed a performance of the Indian rope trick only to find that what appeared to be gravity-defying events were nothing but mimed actions indicating the activities which had been previously suggested verbally. The audience members had merely been hypnotized or lulled into an extreme form of suspension of disbelief. Until this story is better documented, though, one is not entitled to assume that it is accurate as told. It may include some skeptical folk mythology rather on a par with religious or occultist folk mythology, based, as usual, on some kernel of truth. On the other hand, the Canadian Swami Radha, of Kootenay Bay B.C., has on several occasions told of how she witnessed a performance of the Indian rope trick. During the performance, a mosquito landed on her, and instinctively responding to the mosquito with a swat, she woke herself up, as it were, to find that the performers were merely miming. Perhaps there is more than a kernel of truth to the story mentioned by Herman. For a thorough discussion both of the Indian Rope Trick and levitation methods from the conjuring point of view, see Lee Siegel, *Net of Magic*, pp. 197-221.

4. Materialization, Telekinesis, Mind Over Matter

A claim concerning the powers of a psychic to materialize objects from nowhere, and move matter at will is as easy as any paranormal claim to confirm or refute as a challenge to current scientific paradigms, because the only issue is the ability of the psychic to perform under as rigorous, magic-proof conditions as the best current magicians knowledgeable about the paranormal are capable of devising. The materialization and telekinesis claims I have come across have seemed to me to be very weak indeed. There are many investigations of materialization and telekinesis claims available, for example, those in Martin Gardner's *Science Good Bad And Bogus* and *The New Age; The Search For Psychic Power* by C. E. M. Hansel, Part IV; *The Transcendental Temptation* by Paul Kurtz, *Flim Flam* by James Randi, and the many articles of *The Skeptical Inquirer*, *The Indian Skeptic*, and similar journals.

An interesting but little known piece of evidence on materialization is provided by a rather unlikely source, namely, the Indian Yoga-Vedantist, Vivekananda. In a collection of his work entitled *Raja-Yoga* (1955 second edition), we find a lecture given by Vivekananda at Los Angeles, on January 8, 1900. An excerpt follows: "Another time I was in the city of Hyderabad in India, and I was told of a brahmin there who could produce numbers of things from nobody knew where. . . . He had only a strip of cloth about his loins; we took everything else off him. I had a blanket, which I gave him to wrap round himself because it was cold, and made him sit in a corner. Twenty-five pairs of eyes were looking at him. And he said, 'Now look here; write down anything you want.' We all wrote down the names of fruits that never grew in that locality—bunches of grapes, oranges, and so on. And we gave him those bits of paper. And there came from under his blanket bushels of grapes, oranges, and so on—so much that if all that fruit had been weighed it would have been twice as heavy as the man. He asked us to eat the fruit. Some of us objected, thinking it was hypnotism; but the man himself began eating; so we all ate. It was all right. He ended by producing a mass of roses. Each flower was perfect, with dew-drops on the petals, not one crushed, not one

injured. And masses of them!" (pp. 234-235). This description is typical of many apparently incredible materializations ascribed to Indian
holy men, even today. Vivekenanda continues, "When I asked the
man for an explanation, he said, 'It is all sleight-of-hand'." Vivekenanda
comments, "Whatever it was, it seemed to be impossible that it could
be sleight-of-hand merely. Where could he have got such large quan-
tities of things?" (ibid.).

From this account we observe two things: First, Vivekenanda was
incompetent in judging the likelihood of something's being sleight of
hand. Anybody familiar with methods of sleight of hand would know
how this effect may have been accomplished. And Vivekenanda's
ignorance was apparently matched only by his apparent lack of curiosity. Any moderately curious man in his position of access to information could surely have discovered the method by which the effect
was produced. Second, we note that the effect is identical to effects
described of Indian holy men through the ages, including the present. The only difference is that in most cases the holy man doesn't
say "It is done by sleight of hand." The holy man says "It is done by
supernatural power," or "science cannot explain the Divine process,"
or "there is a higher Science of Knowledge by means of which this is
done." In this way the holy man maintains the illusion beyond the
event itself, and the event becomes an act of religious inspiration,
evoking in the audience members a sense of awe concerning the
Creative Power underlying the world. Thus there is a justification in
the mind of the holy man who performs by sleight of hand to continue the illusion of his performance beyond the act itself. Some amus-
ing anecdotal material confirming the shady area dividing magicians
who announce themselves as magicians and magicians who maintain
the illusion beyond the performance itself is to be found in Paul
Brunton's book, *A Search In Secret India*, chapter 10. The remarkable
tales in Lee Siegel's *The Net Of Magic* show the degree to which conjuring can be woven into religious tradition.

There is one instance of a form of mind over matter which I have
had occasion to investigate. It is a case of alleged paranormal preservation of the body of a yogi, Paramahansa Yogananda, following his
death. The paranormal preservation of his body was claimed by his followers to be a miracle created by his yogic powers for the purpose of
demonstrating the power of the yogi, even after death. "For weeks
after the Master's passing, his unchanged face shone with the divine
luster of incorruptibility. This miracle appears to have taken place
through the grace of the Heavenly Father, that men might know the
goodness of Yoganandaji's mission on earth" (*Paramahansa*

Yogananda: In Memoriam, 1958 p. 10). I'll summarize here the results of my investigation to demonstrate just how careful one must be in considering descriptions of events on which paranormal claims are based.

Paramahansa Yogananda is an important figure in the story of the arrival of yoga institutions and practices in the west. Yogananda came to America in 1920, and is said to have personally initiated a hundred thousand disciples in Yoga and Vedantic philosophy. He was widely enough respected in India to have had a postage stamp issued in his honor, and bearing the image of his face. Many are familiar with Paramahansa Yogananda through his book, *Autobiography of a Yogi*. This book is chock-full of tales of the miraculous. The single independently attested miracle based on which other paranormal reports not similarly attested are supposed to be made plausible is described as follows:

AFTER DEATH THE BODY OF PARAMHANSA YOGANANDA MANIFESTED A PHENOMENAL STATE OF IMMUTABILITY

Paramahansa Yogananda entered mahasamadhi (a yogi's final conscious exit from the body) in Los Angeles, California, U.S.A. on March 7, 1952, after concluding his speech at a banquet held in honor of H. E. Binay R. Sen, Ambassador of India.

The great world teacher demonstrated the value of yoga (scientific techniques for God-realization) not only in life but in death. Weeks after his departure his unchanged face shone with the divine luster of incorruptibility.

Mr. Harry T. Rowe, Los Angeles Mortuary Director, Forest Lawn Memorial-Park (in which the body of the great master is temporarily placed) sent Self-Realization Fellowship a notarized letter from which the following extracts are taken:

The absence of any visual signs of decay in the dead body of Paramhansa Yogananda offers the most extraordinary case in our experience. . . . No physical disintegration was visible in his body even twenty days after death. . . . No indication of mold was visible on his skin, and no visible desiccation (drying up) took place in the bodily tissues. This state of perfect preservation of a body is, so far as we know from mortuary annals, an unparalleled one. . . . At the time of receiving Yogananda's body, the Mortuary personnel expected to observe, through the glass lid of the casket, the usual progressive signs of bodily decay. Our astonishment increased as day followed day without bringing any visible change in the body under observation. Yogananda's body was apparently in a phenomenal state of immutability. . . .

No odor of decay emanated from his body at any time. . . . The physical appearance of Yogananda on March 27th, just before the bronze cover of the casket was put into position, was the same as it had been on March 7th. He looked on March 27th as fresh and as unravaged by decay as he had looked on the night of his death. On March 27th there was no reason to say that his body had suffered any visible physical disintegration at all. For these reasons we state again that the case of Paramahansa Yogananda is unique in our experience" (*Autobiography Of A Yogi*, 1987 soft-cover, last page of text, p. 575). [The points of elision are in the original. This report including the extract from the Rowe letter is to be found in many of the major texts of Yogananda and the organization he founded, Self Realization Fellowship, or SRF.]

This sounded impressive enough, and as one of the aims of the SRF is "to unite science and religion" (ibid., p. 573), I proceeded to investigate. First, I obtained from the State of California a copy of the Death Certificate of Yogananda. It was not long before I realized that the information in the Yogananda Death Certificate was devastating to the miracle claim. In Box #23 of the Death Certificate, an embalmer had affixed his signature to certify that he had embalmed the body of Yogananda on or before March 11, 1952. Thus, Yogananda's body was embalmed within a couple of days of his death! I then obtained a copy of the full text of the Harry Rowe letter. If I had any uncertainties about whether I had read the information properly from Box No. 23 of the Death Certificate, these were quickly dispelled. The complete text of Harry Rowe's letter includes the following information in paragraph no. 5: "Paramhansa Yogananda's body was embalmed on the night of March 8, with that quantity of fluid which is customarily used in any body of similar size."

The question now remained as to what miracle, what extraordinary yogic power, was supposed to have "taken place through the grace of the Heavenly Father that men might know the goodness of Yoganadaji's mission on earth?" Everyone knows that embalming is a procedure which preserves the body of a corpse from decay. *The Concise Oxford Dictionary* defines 'embalm' as: "preserve (corpse) from decay orig. with spices, now by means of arterial injection" (p. 313, 1982). If Yogananda's body was embalmed at Forest Lawn, which was famous for its "memorialization" of the bodies of the beloved, using what we can presume was the best 1952 technology, would it be unusual that there was an "absence of any visual signs of decay in the dead body of Paramhansa Yogananda"? Is it miraculous that "no physical disintegration was visible in his body even twenty days after death"? Is it contrary to the laws of chemistry to find that "no indication of mold was visible on his skin, and no visible desiccation (drying up) took place in the bodily tissues"? Is it any cause for astonishment that "no odor of decay emanated from his body at any time"?

According to the full text of Harry Rowe's letter, the astonishment was only due to the fact that the funeral home staff had not used any creams in addition to the embalming fluid: "In cases of persons that are embalmed and exhibited to friends for a period of two or three weeks, it is necessary, to insure presentability, for the embalmer to apply, on the face and hands of the deceased, a creamy pore-sealing emulsion that temporarily prevents the outward appearance of mold. In Paramhansa Yogananda's case, however, no emulsions were used. They were superfluous, inasmuch as his tissues underwent no visible transformations" (*Yogi*, p. 122). This, it turns out, is the sum total of the miracle claim as far as Harry Rowe is concerned: no creams were used in addition to the embalming fluid to help preserve the body and skin tone.

To find out whether embalming fluid alone, that is, without the application of creams, could account for the preservation of a body without desiccation, for twenty days, I consulted two embalmers with local Vancouver funeral homes. The response of each was immediate and unambiguous: Ms. Crean, of Kearney Funeral Homes, Vancouver, an embalmer with many years experience, stated that she had seen bodies preserved well for two or three months, and that this was not unusual. She stated that creams are not necessary, and that the preservation of the body without creams all depends on the skill of the embalmer, the formula of the embalming fluid, the temperature at which the body is kept, and the medications given the person prior to death. And Ian Eliot, the Assistant Manager of Hamilton Mortuary Ltd., Vancouver, a qualified embalmer through the Saskatchewan Funeral Services Association, with a University of Saskatchewan certificate of Qualification, and Licensed from the Alberta Funeral Service Association was equally clear and emphatic: "Preservation for 20 days through embalming is not unusual," he said.

"We can keep a body a month or a month and a half without interral. We use an embalming fluid with lanolin base which will have humectant which prevents dehydration, which is the major concern. . . . The letter of Mr. Rowe is certainly misleading because of its failure to discuss the effects of the glass lid and makes no mention of the temperatures at which the body was being kept, and so on. Also if the person had been using creams on his skin prior to his death, this might have helped. There is nothing unusual about a body being embalmed with fluids in use in 1952 without creams and being preserved for 20 days in good condition."

Thus, the first two embalmers I spoke to flatly contradicted the claim made by Mr. Rowe that there was cause for astonishment in the fact that Yogananda's body was preserved by embalming fluid alone nineteen days after embalming in a good condition. There is no "demonstration of yogic powers" here at all, but only a misleadingly written letter by Mr. Rowe for his client, even more misleading selections of which were then used in publication after publication as a promotion for the organization with the crucial facts concerning the embalming of the body entirely left out! Full details of my investigation can be found in *The Rational Enquirer*, Vol. 4, No. 3, Apr. 1991, pp. 1-3, 8.

The moral of the story is that if one wants one's espousal of scientific values to be taken seriously, one has to be willing to practice these values. No responsible person can take seriously the descriptions made by proponents of the various religious groups concerning the paranormal powers of the guru they follow or the events the followers have witnessed without careful checks. If the reader knows of any individual who presents even minimally convincing evidence of the ability to have OBE's, or materialize objects, or demonstrate mind over matter effects, I would greatly appreciate hearing about it. Sadly, all the theorizing which one hears concerning the compatibility of quantum and relativity physics with the paranormal is empty until evidence can be found which merits a scientist's long-range attention.

Summary

The overview, then, has been rather disappointing. Despite many years of sincere searching I haven't found any minimally credible evidence of paranormal faculties. Of course this conclusion is only as good as the evidence I have come across and been able to investigate in a reasonably complete manner. It is hard, if not impossible, to claim exhaustiveness on this score.

B.

What of the contribution that science can make to our under-standing of mystical enlightenment? If science remains physicalistic, does this undermine the mystic's purported insights? Or, more pos-itively, can scientific studies of brain waves of meditators enhance our understanding of enlightenment, of non-ego states of identifi-cation?

Let us look at these questions in turn. There is a tendency for some rationalists and skeptics to assume that the rejection of para-normal phenomena based on the conclusion that the supposed facts have not been established warrants a rejection of mysticism. But this is misguided in several ways. Mysticism and physicalism, I suggest, are entirely compatible.

To show this, we first stipulate two senses of mysticism: *(a) Occultist mysticism* is the view that some telepathy, clairvoy-ance, precognition, postcognition, levitation, materialization, appor-tation, or telekinesis does in fact take place; *(b) philosophical mysti-cism* is either the genial mysticism of chapters two and three, or the view that the identification which is expressed in the statement "I am the first person" is not fixed as the only form of identification, and that one can come to discover other forms of identification, such as "I am the many things; the first person is a proper part of me," and "There is no me; there are only the many things."

I have already shown that *physicalism*, which, for our purposes, is the view that every mental or functional state is physically embod-ied, is consistent with occult mysticism. Anyone who believes that there is some subtle medium which carries information, and that the psychic's brain somehow manages to tune into the information car-ried by this subtle medium is presenting a physicalistic view of telepa-thy. Such a view entails a really drastic revision to current scientific paradigms, but it doesn't entail the elimination of physicalism. Only if evidence is presented which shows the functionally preemptive nature of the succession of functional states involved in telepathy, say, is the physicalist assumption called into question. Thus, physi-calism and occultist mysticism are compatible. Even if there were good evidence at the macroscale of telepathy or clairvoyance, this would not in and of itself negate physicalism. Materialization, too, might occur at the macroscale by physicalistic means: the psychic accesses some peculiar energy field which enables her to attract free floating atoms into her hands. This would seem to be extraordinarily improbable, but not logically incoherent.

As for philosophical mysticism, we recall the distinctions introduced earlier. *Ontological pluralism* is the view that there is more than one object. *Ontological monism* is the view that there is exactly one object. *Ontological nihilism* is the view that there is no object whatever. As we've seen, the ego perspective is committed to ontological pluralism: "The universe has many objects, and I am one of them, namely, this very person." However, there are two directions the mystic (henceforth, the metaphysically-minded philosophical mystic until otherwise noted) may take in negating the basis on which the ego perspective is formed. The mystic may deny ontological pluralism, in favor of either ontological monism or ontological nihilism. Or the mystic may deny the identification of self with the first person. The latter in turn may be done in two ways. The mystic may see self-referring terms as having the composite whole, the universe, as their referent. Or the mystic may deny that there is any extension to the self concept at all. In either of these two ways, expressed respectively in the statements, "I am the universe," and "There is no self, there are only the many objects," ontological pluralism is preserved, but the self placement is altered. The ego perspective vanishes, but the ordinary conception of the world as a multiplicity remains. Following our earlier usage, let us refer to mystics whose perspective is that of ontological pluralism as "self-altered mystics." Self-altered mystics, then, either are universal self mystics, or no-self mystics. If they are universal self mystics, they are either avatar mystics, or universal impersonal self mystics.

Now we can ask what the connection would be between self-altered mysticism and physicalism. In what way does self-altered mysticism undermine physicalism, or vice versa? We can see how one might argue that mystics who deny ontological pluralism ("object-altered mystics," to use parallel terminology) cannot be physicalists, since the physicalist conception requires ontological pluralism. But how is self-altered mysticism incompatible with physicalism?

I suggest that it is not incompatible with physicalism. To begin with, the onus is on the physicalist anti-mystic to show how self-altered mysticism is incompatible with physicalism. It is hard, moreover, to see where such an argument will come from. To be sure, an eliminative physicalist who believes not only that all folk psychological descriptions (states described in terms of desires, beliefs, perceptions, intentions and the like) are descriptions of physical states, but also that the folk psychological descriptions are strictly speaking false, or systematically misleading, or inadequate, might have grounds to reject the doctrinal expressions of self-altered mysticism, since they are still based, or may be still based, in the folk psychological language of the first person. ("I am the cosmos. The speaker is a proper part of me. The speaker *wants* a glass of water. The speaker *believes* there is water in that pitcher. The speaker *intends* to pour himself a glass of water.") But this, one suspects, is an insufficiently discriminating rejection of self-altered mysticism. Whatever language the eliminative physicalist wants to speak, presumably, can be adopted by the no-self mystic and possibly by the universal-self mystic as well. The critic of self-altered mysticism would prefer to be able to criticize it from a more focused basis.

More to the point perhaps would be the rejection of self-altered mysticism on the grounds that the supposed breakdown of the ego construct must be physicalistically realized, or chemically caused, to put it simplistically, and therefore self-altered mysticism is a delusion of sorts. However, grounds must be given for the view that the perspective gained through a series of chemical exchanges, in a given case, is less correct than the perspective originally had. Otherwise rank absurdity follows. If one sees an apple on the table and thereby comes to believe that an apple is on the table, there is a series of chemical exchanges underlying the sequence from absence of belief concerning an apple on the table, or belief that there is no apple on the table, to belief that there is an apple on the table. Does it follow from there being a physicalistic basis of belief formation that the belief is false or inadequate? Certainly not.

The critic of self-altered mysticism might have in mind an analogy with the rejection of a hallucination or delusion as drug induced in some appropriate case. But a very detailed argument indeed must be made out in order to place self-altered mysticism into the drug induced hallucination or delusion category rather than into a normal, non-pathological cognitive alteration category. And all indications are that such arguments will be hard to come by. It's only because we have consensus about hallucinatory errors and gross delusions that we can see whether introduction of certain chemicals into the brain creates hallucinations and delusions. But self-altered perspectives involve no alteration of the uncontroversial object placements. The self-altered mystic can still go to court and say, "Your Honor, the speaker pleads not guilty; the speaker has an alibi; the speaker was in Toronto on the day of the crime and so could not have been at the scene of the crime in Vancouver." Even the universal impersonal self mystic can teach the judge her language: "Your Honor, I am the cosmos. There are many parts of me. The speaker is one part of me. The speaker part of me hereby pleads not guilty; the speaker part of me has an alibi; the speaker part of me was in Toronto on the day of the crime. Undoubtedly the criminal is a part of me, too. But the task of the police is to arrest and charge the criminal part of me, not any of the billions of innocent parts of me, and the task of the judge is to convict the guilty as charged criminal part of me, and not any of the billions of innocent parts of me." Similarly, the avatar mystic can speak her language too: "Your Honor, I am the cosmos. There are many parts of me. There is a conscious volitional person at the center of me. All events are my subconscious doings; the conscious volitional personal body at the center of me was in Toronto on the day of the crime, and so could not have included the fingers that pulled the trigger. The pulling of the trigger must have been a subconscious action of mine in a body only weakly causally connected to the body which provides the perspectival center of my conscious agency." In these statements there are unusual perspectives and unusual ways of putting things, to put it mildly. But none of these perspectives requires or involves any form of change in the notion of the objects that form parts of the composite whole which is the universe as conceived under ontological pluralism. Then there should be no more difficulty reconciling physicalism and self-altered mysticism than reconciling physicalism and most any philosophical views concerning the universe so long as they are consistent with ontological pluralism. Physicalism in and of itself is compatible with self-altered mysticism.

What about the mystic who interprets mystical experience phenomenalistically? As such a mystic is speaking only as a phenomenologist, observing the degree of flexibility of the phenomenology of self-identification, no judgment is being made on possible grounds for the rejection of physicalism. The altered self-mystic does not speak as a neuro-physiologist, but rather produces more folk-psychological data, mystic-folk psychological data, as it happens, for the cognitive scientist to account for. The phenomenalistic altered self-mystic does not investigate whether functional preemption takes place in the mind-brain of the mystic, let alone find results one way or another on such questions, and so the phenomenalistic altered self-mystic has no quarrel with physicalism.

What of physicalism and object-altered mysticism? As has been already pointed out, the mystic regards the expressions of object-altered mysticism as limit expressions. They cannot be made fully intelligible, because they apparently deny ontological pluralism, whereas all descriptions, or, at least, many cognitively required descriptions, are expressed in a language that implies or seems to imply ontological pluralism. Thus, the quarrel between the physicalist and the object-altered mystic is an expression of the more fundamental quarrel between the physicalist qua ontological pluralist and the object-altered mystic qua ontological monist or ontological nihilist. The issues here are not empirical issues nor based primarily in empirical research. Rather they are issues of philosophy of language and metaphysics. Some mystics may declare "I am the One," or "There is no Object." Some philosophers will object that the mystic's very declarations presuppose ontological pluralism, and therefore their doctrines are inadequate. Perhaps some mystics will retreat into a defense of these forms of language based on the mystic's equivalent of the medieval philosopher's doctrine of analogy; perhaps others will retreat from the use of such forms of language. In this context, however, it is far more important for us to recognize the viability of a very rich vein of mysticism, namely, self-altered mysticism, which entirely sidesteps the issue of ontological pluralism *vs.* ontological monism or nihilism. We are concerned with the potential contribution of the scientist to our understanding of mysticism, and need not concern ourselves with a strictly philosophical controversy. (See also Wainwright, *Mysticism*, pp. 69-77 for an argument that physicalistic causes for mystical experience wouldn't undermine its noetic status. His arguments are plausible and the points offered here about phenomenalistic mysticism follow a fortiori.)

Science will not, then, contribute to our investigation of philosophical mysticism by giving us grounds for rejecting it. But might it aid in our understanding of the mystical perspectives by indicating the physical correlates of the mystical states? Can we learn about philosophical mysticism by studying rates of galvanic skin response of meditators, and duration of conscious theta wave activity in meditators?

To begin with, we note that there is some research into the physiology of meditation and perhaps even there are some results. Meditation induces relaxation, slows the heart rate, alters brain-states, and can refresh mental functioning (Behanan, 1937; Naranjo and Ornstein 1971; Ornstein 1972). These effects, of course, do not challenge current physical paradigms; nor, however, would this sort of research, even if taken much further, enhance our understanding of philosophical mysticism. It is naive to suppose that any neat and clean correlations will be discovered between theta wave durations and specific mystical claims, for example. We can't expect that no-self mystics will show one rudimentary pattern of EEG activity, and universal-self mystics another rudimentary pattern. It will take so much more understanding of cognitive science before we're in any position to correlate specific cognitive states with specific brain engrams that all we can say at this point is that the current research is at best preparatory for future research. We cannot anticipate what sort of fruits such future research will bear, if any, for our understanding of mysticism.

We may, however, be able to anticipate the sort of question which future empirical investigations may help us to resolve. Mystics the world over have reported the awakening of subtle energy circulating through the body. As mentioned earlier, the subtle energy is referred to as 'prana,' 'ki,' 'kundalini,' 'shakti,' 'interior light,' or 'hidden light.' It is described in kinesthetic terms as an energy or force that circulates through the body. It is often described as coalescing in bundles in various parts of the body, or as being particularly strong in various parts of the body. Some people report that it awakens in stages in the various parts of the body, others that it awakens all at once. People also report a strong link between the awakening of this subtle energy and the experience of bliss.

These reports give rise to two rival, equally physicalistic hypotheses. The first is that the experience of this subtle energy results from the reception in higher centers of the brain of signals from the nervous system of the body which in other people are not received by the brain at all or in any case not by the higher centers of the brain. The subtle energy experienced by the mystic is, on this hypothesis, as veridical as any proprioceptive experience. The second hypothesis is that there are link-ups entirely within the brain that are created by meditation practices, and that these link-ups result in the experience by the meditator of the phenomena reported. According to the second hypothesis, there are no impulses in the nervous system of the body corresponding to the experiences. The meditator who reports an explosion of subtle energy from the region of the solar plexus does not have anything unusual going on in the nerve bundles around the solar plexus. The kinesthetic experience would be somewhat akin to the phantom limb experience of an amputee. In this sense, if the second hypothesis is true, one could say that "the awakening of the subtle energy at the base of the spine" is a phenomenologically apt description but not a physiologically apt description. The question whether the first hypothesis or the second hypothesis, or some third hypothesis altogether, best accounts for the neurophysiology underlying the awakening of the blissful subtle energy phenomenon might well be answered one day through empirical research. Clearly, though, the phenomenology itself is not vulnerable to the results of such research, providing as it does the data for the research. Nor is the evaluation of the meditation practices which conduce to the phenomenology affected much by either result. By analogy, it matters little to the evaluation of sexual norms whether orgasmic experiences phenomenologically referring to the whole of the body or parts of it are linked to physiological changes throughout the corresponding parts of the body, or, are, rather, linked to physiological changes which are all in the brain.

Our general conclusion to the question of the contribution of neuroscience to our understanding of mysticism is that it is hard to foresee how empirical research will contribute centrally to an analysis or assessment of philosophical mysticism. This brings us to our third question:

C.

How may the scientist contribute to the moral and social practices surrounding mysticism?

It is here, I believe, that the contemporary scientist has an important, even central role to play. In modern times as in ancient times, institutions formed for the purpose of encouragement of philo-mystical practices often are associated with occult mystical claims. The occult mystical claims provide the basis on which the social authority of the institution rests. The Maharishi Mahesh Yogi's Siddhi program is a good case in point. Paramahansa Yogananda's Self-Realization Fellowship (SRF) is another case in point. In such cases, the integration of Enlightenment East and Enlightenment West values places an onus on both the scientist and the would-be mystic. The onus on the would-be mystic is to recognize that declarations of one's intent "to unite science and religion" ("Aims and Ideals of SRF," *Autobiography of a Yogi*, 1987 p. 573) are but preliminary steps. One must, in addition, be willing to find out what scientific values actually are. Scientific values presuppose the willingness to do experimental work in a serious manner, and the willingness to speak plainly, without doubletalk or doublethink, and without misleading or deceptive phrasing in the presentation of claims bearing on scientific matters. Once one has learnt something about scientific values and principles, one can then reflect on what it means to state that one wishes "to unite science and religion." If one has no intention of speaking plainly in one's literature in claims bearing on scientific matters then everyone is better off if one ceases from paying what amounts to mere lip service to the ideal "to unite science and religion."

Particularly objectionable in this regard is the practice of paying lip service to the unity of science and religion, making paranormal claims, but then refusing to allow scientists and magicians to check one's abilities, claiming that such investigations somehow draw too much focus on the *siddhis* or paranormal abilities, instead of the deep spiritual purposes for which the abilities are being drawn on. If I had a talking hamster from whose lips words of profound wisdom issued every 2:00 P.M., would it make sense for me to refuse to allow scientists to witness the hamster in the act of talking? It is, moreover, a moral failing to encourage people to rely on the authority of a teacher who actively prevents people from discovering what the fundamental order of nature is, and what its limits are.

And the onus on the scientist is to recognize that scientific values in no way preclude philosophical mysticism as an ethical position, and altered-self philosophical mysticism as a phenomenological or metaphysical position. As an ethical position, philosophical mysticism holds that the best thing an individual can strive for qua monadic individual is steady, blissful awareness of Ultimacy, moment by moment. As a phenomenological position, philosophical altered-self mysticism holds that *(a)* the steady, blissful awareness of Ultimacy is accompanied by the dissolution of the ego structure; *(b)* for the dissolution of the ego structure to be empirically possible, it must be the case that the intention of the self-concept held by a conscious being, namely, the entity present to consciousness with which the consciousness is extensionally identified, allows for the altered-self extensional judgments. Metaphysical mysticism holds one or another of the phenomenological descriptions to be the metaphysically correct description of how reality really is. Altered-self philosophical mysticism is, quite plainly, a matter for the philosopher to evaluate. The psychologist and cognitive scientist take an interest in the phenomenology of mystical states, but they do so not as potential critics of the phenomenon of mysticism, but as receivers of data to be accommodated and accounted for within their disciplines.

The philosophical mystic contributes to science by presenting the scientist with important phenomenological data. This contribution, true enough, is a sort of default contribution. After all we don't think of the tomato as contributing to science in virtue, merely, of its presenting the scientist with data for analysis. But it is, alas, the chief contribution mysticism seems to have to make to empirical science at the moment.

As has been mentioned in a slightly different context earlier in the chapter, much has been made in recent years of a supposed consonance between the metaphysics of Enlightenment East, and twentieth-century physics. I must confess to a certain bafflement about this supposed consonance. True enough, twentieth-century physics seems inconsistent with naive notions of individual object identity. And, true enough, mystical metaphysics also teaches us to question naive notions of individual object identity. However, so does Plato's theory of forms. So does Berkeleyian idealism. So does Hegelian idealism. So does Leibnizian monadology. And so, for that matter, does any position in metaphysics and the philosophy of perception other than that of naive realism! Second, it's hard to see how a broad brush stroke metaphysical position such as Berkeleyian idealism or ontological nihilism can either be supported or undermined by physical results. If the universe were Newtonian, not only at the macroscale, but also at the microscale, would this undermine Enlightenment East metaphysics? No, no more than any ordinary pluralistic description of events would, or does undermine Enlightenment East object-altered metaphysics. Since it wouldn't, or doesn't, then the supposed commonalities of physics and Enlightenment East are best regarded as analogies of the sort that can be drawn between modern physics and more or less any metaphysics which departs widely from common sense realism. (For two excellent discussions of the relations between quantum physics and mysticism, see Robert Crease and Charles Mann's "The Yogi and the Quantum," and Marshall Spector's "Mind, Matter, and Quantum Mechanics," both to be found in *Philosophy of Science and the Occult*, edited by Patrick Grim.)

In sum, then, the scientist contributes to mysticism by refining and purifying the mystic's own understanding of the paranormal effects which have been so long associated with their enterprise. And this contribution of the scientist has the most salutary contribution to social practice of facilitating the spiritual seeker in her or his efforts to discriminate wisely between mysticism-promoting institutions whose leaders appreciate scientific attitudes, values, and practices, and those whose leaders don't. In this way, the scientist contributes to social process as an expert witness, so to speak, advising the judges who sit on the court of reason and are charged with the task of evaluating religious and/or mystical institutions. There are many precedents within Enlightenment East traditions themselves indicating that such integration is welcome. In our own day, the monk and scholar Agehananda Bharati gives evidence of this in his autobiography, *The Ochre Robe*, and in his philosophical work, *The Light At The Centre*. Some strands within the Brahmo Samaj movement are integrative in this way. In ancient times, as well as modern times, one can find thinkers who insist on having a good look at things before jumping to conclusions. Mencius expressed healthy skepticism about some fabulous tales (*Mencius* V.A. 7, 8, 9), and yet seemed vigorously oriented to the Way of Heaven, referring to his skill in nourishing his "strong moving power" which is "difficult to describe" and, "if nourished by uprightness and not injured, will fill up all between heaven and earth. As power it is accompanied by righteousness and the Way" (*Mencius*, 2A.2.). One can also look to some passages in *Chuang Tzu* for hints of skepticism concerning the paranormal (e.g., the story of the encounter between the shaman Chi Hsien and the Taoist Hu Tsu, 1974, p. 154). More clearly, the explicitly Taoistic but naturalistic, skeptical works of Wang Ch'ung (27-100? c.e.) indicate that a spirit of mystical openness and naturalistic rigor combined with skepticism about the paranormal were possible in ancient times. Also the instructions to stay away from paranormal phenomena on the part of yogis and Buddhists often seem to be at least ambiguous with regard to the issue of the actuality of such occurrences.

In any case, in the relation of science and mysticism as well as that of social and moral expressions and mysticism, there is a need for the tools of Enlightenment West to be integrated with the practices of Enlightenment East if the latter is to complete its projects. In the final chapter, I hope to show that the need occurs in the reverse direction as well. Enlightenment West needs to absorb into itself the perspective of Enlightenment East in order to properly express its vision of the direction for progress in human history.

Nine

Mysticism and the Philosophy of History

To suggest, as I have in chapters 7 and 8, that the worldly no-self mystic must have practiced objective thinking sufficiently to have acquired an advanced sense of justice, that there are no obstacles within Enlightenment West moral and social theory for the existence or development of healthy expressions of mysticism, and that science has a salutary corrective role to play in some of the doctrinal, institutional, and authority patterns associated with mysticism, is not yet to link the values of mystical realization and the second of the two Enlightenment West values, namely, social progress. Nor have we thus far explicitly addressed the Enlightenment East critique of Enlightenment West on the grounds that it objectifies self, divorces mind from body, and falls prey to the myth of control. In this chapter, we pick up the thread linking mystical practices and doctrines with philosophies of history in which the idea of progress is espoused. I will defend the Enlightenment West view that it is reasonable to hope for progress. Science, technology, and the quest for justice have decisive contributing roles to play in the possibility of progress. Simultaneously, I will try to show the role that mysticism must eventually play in establishing the full criteria for progress. And I will address, along the way, the Enlightenment East critique of Enlightenment West's scientism and, as it sees it, Enlightenment West's excessive logic chopping, and control-mindedness. The vision of history which emerges indicates not only an opportunity for reconciliation of Enlightenment East and West, but also requires a full integration of the two perspectives.

Speculative versus critical history

In order to assess the idea of progress one immediately finds oneself undertaking grand-style history, the sort of history which attempts to look at human development over the last 6,000 years or so in a single overview, and to consider the future in the light of what is supposedly revealed by that overview. Obviously there are great dangers in such an interprise. As David King put it upon embarking on an investigation of this kind, there are many "risks involved in generalizing at the level of civilizational history. We know both too much and too little: too much about the parts, making difficult any attempt to pass through the domain of the specialists without getting it all wrong; and too little about how the parts relate to the whole. That is equally true whether we choose to look backward or forward" (*The Crisis Of Our Time*, p. 11). It is because of these enormous risks that historians and philosophers of history in recent decades have assiduously avoided the attempt to discern a grand pattern in history, which they call "speculative or philosophical history," preferring rather to engage in what they call "critical historical studies" and "critical philosophy of history" (See for example, William Dray, *Philosophy of History*, p. 1). Perhaps the most recent large scale exponent of the speculative historian's art is William H. McNeill's *The Rise of The West*, and that study was completed thirty years ago.

Yet although the risks are great, and although the enterprise is decidedly unfashionable, a full assessment of Enlightenment West and East cannot be undertaken without an attempt to examine what is, after all, one of the pillars of seventeenth- and eighteenth-century Enlightenment West thought, namely, the view that it is reasonable to think that there is progress in history, or that we can look forward to progress. Furthermore, however unfashionable and risky the enterprise, it is by no means clear that speculative history is to be ruled out of bounds a priori. Rather, the reluctance to engage in speculative history is born of many practical concerns and sociological influences. Finally, it may be that the more abstractly speculative and philosophical the historical enterprise, the fewer historical toes will be stepped on. That is, it may be that when one is not seeking detailed causal analyses, but rather investigating the conditions for happiness and the relation between such conditions on the one hand, and broad brush stroke social realities on the other hand, the enterprise is sufficiently philosophical and, in particular, sufficiently evaluative, that the relevant features of history on which the analysis trades are not dauntingly controversial. It *may* be so. Then again, it may not.

In our exploration, then, we will not assume at the outset that any one of the grand visions of history is or even might be coherent. Perhaps the very enterprise of grand history is mistaken. But neither will we, a priori, rule out the possibility that some form of grand history is coherent and insightful. Rather we will briefly consider each of the various grand theories of history on at least some of its apparent merits or demerits. We will undertake speculative history, then, despite its being out of fashion. But rather than defend the speculative approach to history in theory, we will assume only that it cannot be ruled out entirely, a priori, and attempt to locate at least some elements of it in practice.

Progressive, cyclical, and regressive views of history

One way to divide among grand philosophies of history is with respect to the attitude toward the idea of a progressive march through the ages. Sorted this way, we find three grand views: one which holds that there is, or will eventually be, progress through history, an evolution, however slow, painful, and two-steps-forward, one-step-back in local circumstances. Then there is the view that history witnesses changes without pattern, or, if there is pattern, that these patterns are more or less cyclical. Finally, there is the third type, a vision of steadily regressing history, beginning with an era of glory, and declining thereafter.

Let's look at the third type first. If history is to be regarded as a decline, then there is an apex within the epoch which includes humans, since it would be absurd to think of the evolution of homo sapiens itself as but another step in the decline from the glory of apes, and apes from the glory of lower mammals, and lower mammals from the glory of birds and so on to the ultimate fullness of inert gases. No. If history is declining, it is declining from some high point of human history which is not to be reexperienced. For if it is to be reexperienced, then the overall movement is not a decline, but a cycle, and the philosophy of history is of the second type, not the third.

This point eliminates many of the potential candidates for the decline theory of history. Hesiod's decline of the ages is cyclical rather than a pure decline, as we see from the fact that he wishes he had been born later than the then current age, presumably because he postulated a return after his own age to the glory of an earlier age (*Works and Days* 174-175; 180-181). Similarly, the Hindu image of the decline from the golden age to this corrupt Kali Yuga we live in now cannot properly be an example of the theory of pure decline, since the Kali Yuga, according to the myth, is the end of the decline and will reintroduce a new Satyayuga, a new age of glory after a conflagration and deluge. In the Hindu system, a thousand such groups of four ages makes for a single kalpa. And the kalpas keep on cycling!

Once we eliminate the cycle theories masquerading as declines, or focusing on the decline aspect we happen to be in, according to the theory, what true decline theories are we left with? In *The*

Technological Society (1964), Jacques Ellul argues a version of decline theory premised on the notion of a continued demotion of the realm of ends to the technological realm, the realm of means. But there is no apex to his historical vision, and we are left with an incomplete understanding of the historical sweep. It is as though there is a continuing decline, as the worship of means continues to take possession of the human race; yet at the same time, the worship of means is the very essence of the obscure origins of technique in the primitive notion of magic. Ellul writes, "It has not been sufficiently emphasized that technique has evolved along two distinct paths. There is the concrete technique of homo faber—man the maker—to which we are accustomed, and which poses the problems we have normally studied. There is also the technique, of a more or less spiritual order, which we call magic. It may seem questionable. Nevertheless magic is a technique in the strictest sense of the word, as has been clearly demonstrated by Marcel Mauss. Magic developed along with other techniques as an expression of man's will to obtain certain results of a spiritual order. To attain them, man made use of an aggregate of rites, formulas, and procedures which, once established, do not vary. . . . This fixity is a manifestation of the technical character of magic: when the best possible means of obtaining the desired result has been found, why change it? Every magical means, in the eyes of the person who uses it, is the most efficient one. In the spiritual realm, magic displays all the characteristics of a technique" (p. 24; paragraphing eliminated). Thus, according to Ellul, when our societies were most saturated with diffuse spirituality, they were, at the same time, most technological. For this reason, his vision of history taken as a whole is puzzling. And this, all the more so when we consider the peculiar balance between the pessimism of his vision of the future, and the Christianity of some of his other work. Ellul states again and again that he sees himself as describing facts, not as assessing them. Perhaps in this lies the key to the difficulty here. Progress and regress being essentially normative terms, if we take Ellul at face value as a descriptive theorist, he cannot properly be an exponent of a decline theory of history.

Consider, then, a decline theory of another type. The American poet, Gary Snyder, espouses a view of history which sees the neolithic revolution as ushering in the apex from which further revolutions and developments are regressions. As hunter-gatherers with a tad of agriculture, we were in the golden age. After that, it was all downhill. The image which permeates his essays and literary works is the campfire: "in the dark room, around the fire, children and old people, hearing and joying together . . ."; and the theme is that "the *indigenas* are bearers of the deepest insights into human nature, and have the best actual way to live, as well" (*He Who Hunted Birds In His Father's Village*, p. xi). And Snyder is representative of a large group governed by a studied and sophisticated nostalgia for simpler times. Marshall Sahlins's *Stone Age Economics* introduces us to a primitive, preagricultural society in which people are free from greed and blissfully unaware of obligations as per the work ethic. Snyder and those who share his views tend not to be explicitly concerned with the later connections between agriculture, property relations, and the development of large scale social conflict necessitating the development of militarism, of the sort that is discussed in Ernest Gellner's *Plough, Sword, And Book*. But then they must be prepared to think of the decline as inevitable if the apex, as they would see it, is ever reached— as it was, in the period, roughly, between ten to six thousand years ago.

However, even if we wish we had been born during some other period, which we view with romantic fondness, what counts is what we are prepared to do today to help lift ourselves out of the decline, and place ourselves, effectively, in the condition of that other period. In other words, even if the early agricultural period was an ideal period in human history, still we would want to find a way to reduplicate the psychological benefits of that period in our own day. It would be a narrow view of human nature indeed, which held that it was not in our capacity to work to create the psychological benefits of a period of history which had a somewhat different, less developed set of institutions. Thus, someone like Gary Snyder may live neolithically modernly, travelling both by canoe and airplane as appropriate. And this implies that an acceptable decline theory will describe a current decline, but will always leave open the real possibility of a return to the psychological conditions of the period of the apex.

The plausible contrast, then, is between cyclical views of history and the progressive views of history, if there is to be any grand view of history at all. And the difference between them is that the progressive view of history would hold that as we wend our way through various social and cultural experiments, we gradually make discoveries, some of which we justifiably keep. By contrast, the cyclical view would hold that whatever social benefits accrue during a given period are destined to disappear at a later period.

Now a cyclical view, which holds that history is destined to keep repeating itself in every detail, a cyclical view, in other words, such as finds its most extreme defenders in the Stoics (Cleanthes, Cicero,

Seneca, and others) during the ancient period, and in Nietzsche's theory of eternal recurrence in the modern period, can be grounded only in an arbitrary faith. In a world in which no one can predict the weather from one month to another, how can one say with any degree of assurance that every little event is destined to be repeated an infinity of times in an eternity of such repetitions of cycles of epochs? A mythically presented theory of eternal recurrence is, to be blunt, as occult a view of the world as any demonology, astrology, numerology, or what have you, ever was. Similarly, William Butler Yeats' vortex theory, however beautifully and intriguingly developed, is an occultist approach which is not sufficiently unified with empirical concerns to be of interest outside of the exclusively mythic domain.

Occult cyclical theories aside, cyclical theories of history are most plausible when they hold that happiness for a human being is not a function, or not very largely a function, of the organization of the society in which one has been born, and that there are phases of social structure which are loosely sequential and which societies will tend to go through. Hence, there are loose cycles in history, and the proponent of the cyclical view is not led to any evolutionary or progressivist view, since, as it claims, people can be more or less equally happy during any of these phases of social organization. The ongoing development of technology is mere icing on the cake and is not of substantial import in assessing the human impact of the changes in social organization from phase to phase.

The author of *Ecclesiastes* was perhaps a cyclical theorist of this kind. "There is nothing new under the sun," he said (I: 9), and: "To everything there is a season. . . . What is to be has already been" (III, 1-15), and so on. Human happiness, for *Ecclesiastes* consists in delighting with the spouse of one's youth, and living a full life in consciousness of the Divine process. As for society, "there is a time to set up and a time to tear down." (III: 3)

Aristotle and Polybius represent the ancient Greek exponents of this sort of cyclical view, both holding that the key features defining the phases are the forms of government. Polybius (*History*, BK. VI: 3) outlines the cyclic unit as consisting of monarchy, tyranny, aristocracy, oligarchy, democracy, and finally mob rule. This scheme draws on Plato's thinking for the categories, and something of Plato's historical sequence as well, but in Plato's thought, there is an ideal system of government, and no reason why we can't implement the plan of *The Republic*, institute, and presumably, maintain, the ideal. Plato's system, thus is essentially *normatively* progressivist, or potentially progressivist. Ludwig Edelstein, indeed, has argued that we can put the matter more strongly than that. Plato and Aristotle, according to Edelstein, were both thoroughly progressivist, and Plato introduced to antiquity the notion of endless scope for improvement, at least in the arts and sciences (*The Idea of Progress In Classical Antiquity*, 1964, pp. 85-118, citing *Laws* III, 667-678B; *Laws* XII, 951 B-C; 953 C-D; *Statesman* 299D, 300 C; *Timaeus* 22C, 23 A-B, 30 A etc.).

The evolutionary progressivisms of Greek and Roman antiquity soon gave way under the influence of monotheist and, indeed, theocratic evangelism, to the vision of a Divinely ordained progressive line. Thus, the philosophies of history of the Middle Ages are progressivist owing to their foundation in religious eschatology of Jewish, Christian, and Islamic stamps. It is from the seventeenth century and on that one returns to the possibility of cyclical theories of history, since the religious eschatology is often abandoned in favor either of a secular eschatology, or a non progressivist view. The cyclical theories of Oswald Spengler and Arnold Toynbee may be taken as representative of recent cyclical philosophies of history. According to Spengler in *The Decline of The West*, each people goes through a Dionysian phase in which the culture is expressed through mythic creativity, then an Apollonian phase in which abstract thinking and reason is emphasized, making for a rationalistic civilization, and finally, a phase of ossification in which the rationalism lacks the creative Dionysian spirit, and the civilization dies. Toynbee has a less Procrustean view of the phases, and is open to the possibility that some civilization will continue to evolve and change in responding to the challenges that face it. But failing to do so, and all civilizations in the past have failed, according to Toynbee, the civilization must eventually fossilize or die.

The greatest strength in the modern form of cyclical theory is its assumption, or observation, perhaps, that it needs to be shown how human happiness is dependent on particular systems of social organization or stages of technological development. In the absence of such a demonstration, our views of history are more or less bound to be cyclical. For, however much there may be linear progress in some dimension or other, and there certainly is a linear development (with some interruption for the Dark Age) in the development of technology in the West from the ancient period through the twentieth century, without a demonstration that human happiness is genuinely improved by all this technology and knowledge, all we are left with for a theory of history, is a description of patterns of change. And pattern observation being what it is, whatever polarities and variables one marks off for observation in one epoch will be usable in other epochs, and one will end up with cyclical patterns of uneven periodicity, which is all that theorists such as Spengler and Toynbee claim.

The challenge for any progressivist view of history is to mark the points of positive connection between human happiness, justice, and those aspects of social, political, and technological development which are plausibly argued to be linear in the long run. It will not do, in other words, merely to claim, as Hobbes does, for instance, that knowledge builds on knowledge, and thus there is technological progress. The key is to assess the impact of technological progress and similar cumulatively progressing elements for human happiness. This is the challenge which I wish to meet. The view of history to be presented is essentially neo-Hegelian in that history is regarded as the framework in which human beings endeavor to express consciousness of the Absolute in social forms. However, as it will be seen, although some of the shapes of Hegelian history are preserved, much of the content is replaced. Hegel's vision of the stages of religion is very much inverted, and the dynamics of the relationship between protection, science, and justice as developed here do not have exact correspondences in the Hegelian scheme. Most important of all, Hegel's theory of the state is largely abandoned. Rather than present point by point comparisons with Hegel's outline of history, however, the exposition will focus on the main themes themselves directly. Of course the account presented will be in the nature of a sketch, or a mere idea, and so will suffer the defects of such sketches or mere ideas: difficulties are too easy to ignore; too much data will be made to fit too few theoretical elements, and so on. But if there are at least some insights or possible lines of further research lurking in what follows, I will regard the effort to have been worthwhile.

Progress in justice

First, we will consider the basic functions of community, the tasks accomplished within the extended family, and, when it becomes politicized, within the community of citizens, as I've called the community which exists within authority patterns with a substantial element of conventionality. (There are many ways, of course, to see the functional constants of human organization. For some theories, see David Aberle *et al.*, "The Functional Prerequisites of a Society"; Clyde Kluckhohn, "Universal Values and Anthropological Relativism," *Modern Education and Human Values*; Kluckhohn, "Universal Categories of Culture," *Anthropology Today*; and Shia Moser's discussion "Panhuman Universals and Cultural Variants," in *Absolutism and Relativism in Ethics.*) For simplicity, we will conceive of the community as revolving around four fundamental tasks, tasks which even the least technologically developed communities must find ways to accomplish: nourishing, building-sheltering, healing, storytelling. Two further tasks, or functions, become necessary once the agricultural revolution has been introduced, and, consequently, surpluses of production begin to arise. There is some controversy as to the degree to which these functions arise even in preagricultural societies. But even if they don't arise in preagricultural societies, few societies have not undergone the agricultural revolution.

The fifth is the function of protecting the group from invaders. The protective function, indeed, may arise even prior to the development of the potential for surpluses, but we may associate it with the agricultural phase because it seems to be an unavoidable consequence of territoriality and surpluses, whereas warfare may be avoidable among small nomadic, loosely tribal, food-gathering groups.

Each of these tasks is associated with an authoritative agent. The parent nourishes, the engineer-craftsperson builds, the shaman heals, the priest-bard tells the mythic tales. Once the function of protection must be undertaken, it is the person who emerges as chief who supervises the function of protection. It is the chief's job to raise an army, repel the invaders, and restore security to the group. Although the chief function may be carried on by a group of people acting through consensus, there is a tendency in small groups for leaders to emerge, and when the leadership involves skill in force, there tends to be an association between the willingness of the person to use demonstrations of coercive capacity to establish competence in a group whose function is protection, and the means by which a leader emerges. Hence, there is a more or less inevitable drift, given a long enough period of time, toward the emergence of a single chief, and the organizational structure of the chiefdom.

The sixth function is internal dispute resolution. It is not hard to see why the agricultural revolution is linked with this function. Once again, although one has a potential need for a dispute resolution mechanism even in nomadic preterritorial groups, the emergence of the office of dispute resolver need not be fixed until farmlands create the institutions of real property, and the consequent potential for ongoing conflicts within the unit or group over which some chief has jurisdiction. This gives rise to the general question as to the relationship between protective authority, or the office of the chief, and the function of dispute resolution. There are clear reasons why the two offices become linked: it is natural for the chief, who has demonstrated supreme coercive authority to take control of dispute resolution, since effective dispute resolution often involves coercive implementation. There has been much discussion about the theory of the relations between loosely organized kin groups, formally organized chiefdoms, economics, and legal systematization. Leopold Pospisil has argued that any overly neat theory of such relationships is unlikely to be correct. (*Anthropology of Law*, especially chapters 3 and 5; for an overview of theories of legal evolution see Katherine Newman, *Law And Economic Organization*, chapter 1.) However, so long as we are interested in tendencies and patterns, useful analyses may be undertaken. In this case, we are concerned with the eventual convergence of the fifth and sixth functional roles in a single individual, the chief, or, still later on, the monarch.

To see how this works in some detail we need to distinguish three paths toward resolving a dispute among more or less private parties, rather than between large groups. Say two people are disputing the control of a well. Their dispute may be resolved *(a)* by force mustered by one of the disputants, or by force which is the implementation of the arbitrary or narrowly self-interested decree or will of a coercive authority; *(b)* by psychologically coercive means, including the credible threat of use of physical force, or the use of bribes, inducements, shamings, competitions, and so forth, on the part of the disputants or an authoritative third party, or instrument of a social authority such as a chief; and *(c)* by means of application of a system of procedural and substantial justice. These categories are obviously complex and full of gradations, and it is not intended that each ingredient of each instance of each category be necessarily sharply divided from those of other categories. (For instances of some of these shadings, see Adamson Hoebel's discussion of the Australian aborigines and various North American Indian groups in *The Law of Primitive Man*, pp. 293-311; Simon Roberts's *Order And Dispute*, pp. 53-79; P. H Gulliver, "On Mediators"; and Katherine Newman, 1983, chapter 2.) Another point which needs noting is that the arbitrary will of a coercive authority may establish positive law, which then serves (through the utility of expectation or custom) as a proper element in a system of substantial justice. As Lon Fuller implies in *The Anatomy of The Law*, (Part II, "Sources of Law"), the judge in the original position, that is, the judge who must use natural principles without any clearly established precedents for resolving a dispute, has available only custom, contract, and unspecified utility, upon which to base a decision. Anything entering this arena becomes a fit basis for the judicial resolution of a dispute. Thus, even the custom originally established by arbitrary will of a tyrant can become a proper basis for juridical reasoning. In any case, the distinction between physically coercive and judicial resolutions of dispute rests crucially on the presence of procedural justice in the latter.

These three paths to resolution of dispute we may simplistically, but conveniently, refer to as the paths of force, harmony, and justice, respectively. The office of one who resolves disputes within a group by *(a)* or *(b)* means we will call a "positive judge" since the resolution, or judgment is based entirely or to a large extent on factual or positive authority; the office of one who resolves disputes judicially we will call a "normative judge" since the resolution or judgment is based on how things ought to be in the light of what is fair and just.

In a loose tribal society in which no chief exists, our disputants over the control of the well are hardly likely to appoint a normative judge, or resolve the dispute in a procedurally just manner. The story in the book of *Genesis*, chapter 13, describing Abraham's use of procedural justice in the division of the land with Lot is surely meant as an ideal. The squabbling shepherds under them, like the shepherds in Exodus, who prevented Zipporah from watering her sheep, and others, are run of the mill tribalists who expect coercive threats to be the means for resolving disputes.

In the typical dispute resolution in a tribal society, one will establish status through use of or threats of force, or by shamings, symbolic competitions, or by inducements of one sort or another. These inducements may result in contractual or quasi-contractual arrangements. Thus, harmonious dispute resolutions have a tribal, quasi-contractual nature. These inducements, compromises, symbolic victories, or quasi-contracts eventually may result in customary usages. But one may not presuppose a substantially just outcome. The gap between harmonious and judicial resolutions of dispute is especially evident in the cases where a component of coercive potential is used. And where there is no procedural justice, there will tend to be such an element unless both disputants perceive themselves to be matched perfectly in coercive potential, a most unlikely state of affairs (until the development of nuclear warfare and mutual assured destruction strategies and capabilities).

Within chiefdoms, the situation is complex due to the vast range of methods possible. Disputants may attempt to link the dispute to the coercive authority of the chief. Given that a chief exists, so long as there is not a current war drawing on the full coercive resources of the chief, there will be a tendency for each disputant to link his or her claim, one way or another, and at one level or another, with the power or authority of the chief. It should be obvious how difficult it would be for a judicially minded disputant to rely on principle against a disputant who can successfully claim to have the coercive power of the chief on side. Of course it is also the case that the chief may wish to be above the fray, and so normative codes and methods may result under the authority of the chief, and these codes can be transmitted. Nonetheless, there is no guarantee of substantive justice here either. More importantly, for our purposes, the higher the level of the dispute, the less the system can cope with it, and there is a level, the top level, that is, the level at which one chief relates to another, in which there cannot be procedural justice.

Thus it happens that the office of chief and that of positive judge become fused. Tribal dispute resolutions typically occur through vengeance, other coercive forms, symbolic victories, or quasi-contracts. Agriculturalism leads to chiefdoms. And in chiefdoms dispute resolution will tend to occur in a wide variety of patterns ranging from despotic resolution to the maximal implementation of procedural fairness consistent with the chiefdom. But the chiefdom system cannot provide procedural justice between chiefs, nor will it allow for its growth.

Furthermore, I hope it is obvious, or if not obvious, at least uncontroversial, that the three paths of coercion, harmony, and justice are ordered inversely according to desirability. To hold otherwise, practically speaking, is to hold either that procedural justice has no overall utility, or that there is no intrinsic obligation to treat people fairly in resolving disputes between them. But once we allow that coercive, harmonious, and judicial paths to dispute resolution are ordered inversely by desirability, or at least that judicial dispute resolution is more desirable than either of the other two, then we have conceded a fundamental criterion for the evaluation of social progress. History is progressive to the extent that coercive and harmonious paths to dispute resolution are replaced by judicial dispute resolution.

Now when we examine legal history we find that there has been a gradual—as yet incomplete!—replacement of coercive and harmonious paths of dispute resolution by judicial dispute resolution. In the world today, there is no question but that the standard response to murder, rape, and theft is to attempt to bring the murderer, rapist or thief to a public trial. We most definitely do not leave it entirely up to the victim or the victim's family to determine guilt and retributive response. Moreover, we thoroughly disapprove of a system which allows the victim's family to establish a private price or restitution in the case of murder or rape, even if the restitution is by way of punishment rather than financial recompense. That is, we approve exclusively of a system in which victim's feelings vis à vis the criminal are processed through the public, as opposed to acted on privately. This is not to say that that the modern sensibility refuses to consider somewhat informal communal hearings rather than judicial hearings in the less weighty charges, but rather that some line is established such that offenses, which cross the line, are considered to be essentially public matters, and no longer private matters. It is this intuition of the public which brings with it procedural norms, and hence, the possibility, at least, for satisfaction of the basic demands of procedural justice.

We have, in short, become thoroughly permeated with attitudes of fairness and considerations of procedural justice within the identified group, extending out from the nuclear family through the kin group, the village, the region, and on to the sovereign state. This does not of course mean that we are without crime in the state. Far from it. There is a great deal of crime. But we disapprove of it, we consider it not a private but a public matter, and we do our best to improve our system of procedural and substantial justice in dealing with such crimes. Furthermore, we have created a network of states in which murder, theft, rape, and suchlike acts can be met with trials and punishments, deportations, and so on. Nor does this mean that the evolution of complexity in our legal systems has always or even generally tended to serve the interests in justice and fairness of the people regulated by the laws. Katherine Newman (1983) argues that legal complexity increases in proportion to increases in material production, social stratification, and exploitive social relations. Even accepting as strong a version of this thesis as one likes, the fact remains that the distinction between public and private resolution of dispute has become basic to our sensibility, and quite properly so. We not only accept that murder, rape, theft, and the like are to be dealt with by the public, but also we wouldn't have it any other way.

However, actions which are sanctioned by a sovereign power are still regarded differently. Privately motivated killings are regarded as murder. But publicly sanctioned killings, as in acts of war, are often considered justifiable killings so long as the war meets the conditions for a just war such as proportionality of response to provocation, reasonable prospect for victory, and observance of various rules of propriety in the conduct of the war. (For an examination of the just war concept, see Walzer, Michael, *Just and Unjust Wars*; see also Anthony Kenny's useful introductory chapter "The Ethics of War", in *The Logic of Deterrence*.) But there is something entirely left out of account in the just war tradition, and that is the requirement of procedural justice. Of course it is easy to see why the requirement of procedural justice is untreated. If the situation has become bad enough for disputants to consider, or be engaged in, armed response, conditions are certainly too bad for the parties to realistically consider a procedurally just solution, for a procedurally just solution involves the abandonment of sovereignty. Procedural justice in the undertaking of war has not been realistic to even consider, or so the situation has been until very recently. For we are now beginning to develop a political consciousness capable of recognizing that narrowly self-interested killing, even when the narrow interests are those of thousands, or millions of people, should be, and are capable of being, assessed in a procedurally just manner. We are only now beginning to create international institutions designed to apply principles of procedural and substantial justice to the so-called sovereign states.

After World War II, the creation of the United Nations, and the development of the Nürnburg laws, for the first time in human history, the human species had created an institutionalized system of objective coercion, a judicial body, which is expressive of the entire human community. To be sure, the vehicle which carries this responsibility, the U.N. Security Council, embodies as many characteristics of a council of chiefs as it embodies characteristics of objective normative judgment. It is as much a reflection of power balances at the end of World War II as it reflects the concept of justice implemented under a Rawlsian veil of ignorance. Nonetheless, just as the Magna Carta resulted from impure interest brokering and yet inaugurated the motion toward what became constitutional monarchy and parliamentary government, so, too, the United Nations as it is now constituted, namely, a *de jure* world government in the form of a Security Council, which is paralyzed when the permanent members are ideologically or pragmatically divided, and is procedurally unjust even when they are cooperating, is an enormously significant step in the development of the flower of justice, a world order that embodies the fundamental principles of procedural justice to which we have become so accustomed within the state itself.

Of course, many people regard the ideals of an international normative authority as unworkable. In my view, such responses are naive and shortsighted. Undoubtedly in the days when the establishment of cities of refuge were considered enlightened responses to the relentless overvengefulness of victim's families, some believed that entirely replacing the private retributive system by one of normative judges was unworkable. We now see how shortsighted those people were, or would have been had the issue been explicitly broached. Should we be equally shortsighted in our own time? In the vast openness of history, surely, we are capable of evolving from our pathetically inconsistent attitudes of today. Today we look back at systems in which private vengefulness and quasi-contractual arrangements were the approved methods of dispute resolution arising from murder, theft, and the like, thinking that in moving to the public approach, we have made progress. Yet we cannot imagine a substitute for the private cycles of vengefulness and political strongarming as means of resolving international disputes. If it had been put to a tribal council that the harmonious resolution is not always a just resolution, perhaps they would have objected that no judge can extricate himself or herself from a particular position and perspective within the tribe. We see clearly how far one can go in establishing systems of training in which one's identification is with a group and fairness for the members of the group rather than with one's position in a group. Surely we ought to recognize that over the next decades or hundreds of years, we will be able to train people to identify with fairness for the community of jurisdictions of the globe, and with fairness for each human, and, indeed, sentient member of the global community. I cannot agree with pessimists who hold that this is too much to expect.

The reader interested in a concise and, it seems to me, in the long run suitably optimistic review of the development of international law with an emphasis on recent developments, can do no better than to refer to Paul Sieghart's *The Lawful Rights of Mankind*. For an insightful discussion of the obstacles to international justice posed by political realism, there is Janna Thompson's skillful analysis *Justice and World Order*. Thompson first demonstrates that "Realists do not succeed in establishing that there is a logic of international relations which precludes perpetual peace, and Marxists do not show that there is a logic of capitalism which makes peace and justice impossible" (p. 73). She then goes on to "present a plausible story of how the international world could develop into a just world order" (p. 193). The key idea of Thompson's analysis lies in the view that "a society of interlocking communities . . . is predisposed to peaceful and co-operative relationships" (p. 171). Although a society of closed ethnic nations is not likely to provide fertile ground for the evolution of a just world order, a society of open interlocking groups does tend to create a society in which there is a strong sense of community despite the absence of a consensus of ideals and ways of life, for there are values implicit in the ways in which the interlocking groups interact, and these values provide the common ground. It is reasonable to both hope and expect that the world itself may become a society of inter-locking communities each of this kind. That is, it is plausible to think that the world will become a society composed of variegated levels of interlocking communities in which the communities themselves are comprised of interlocking groups. Large states, it may be expected, will downsize, and, quite probably will no longer be seen as, and, indeed, no longer be, the sole real players on the global interrela-tional scene. Finally, in light of the ways in which these interlocking groups function, it is plausible to think that habits of justice will be sufficiently practiced so as to allow us to "reasonably suppose that dis-putes and conflicts will be settled by procedures which all parties will recognize as fair" (p. 186). These procedures will enable the res-olution of disputes over harms done, over claims to fair share of resources from the regional communities, even if such resource claims are not possible to make on a global, one-world basis. As for world government itself, as opposed to variegated interlocking, regional systems, "[h]ow far the society of interlocking communities moves in the direction of world government is something for the people of the future to decide" (p. 187).

I think that it is possible to go a touch further than Thompson does. She holds, quite rightly, that intuitions and habits of justice will play a crucial role in the development of world peace, if we do indeed develop it. She also holds that the objectives of promoting freedom, the value of community, general well being, and the peaceful resolu-tion of disputes give rise to three principles of justice: "that people should be free to associate in accordance with their goals, interests, attachments, and needs; that communities determine for themselves their political and social arrangements; that communities develop and support mutually acceptable structures and institutions for the resolution of disputes" (p. 194). But one might also go a touch further than Thompson does in emphasizing the way in which habits of jus-tice create procedures which once instituted become ever more dif-ficult to dislodge. Thus, one country will, let us suppose, start flying the UN flag alongside its own flag wherever its flag is officially flown. Soon enough another emulates this practice. Gradually the con-sciousness begins to develop that states are jurisdictions of the global community. Then one country begins to inform the UN whenever its parliament is dissolved pending a general election. Soon enough others do. States with fragile democracies invite representatives of the UN to observe elections. If this becomes routine, it becomes increasingly difficult for coups to occur in conjunction with rigged elections. As the UN increases its intervention in civil wars as well as international threats to peace, norms and habits of procedural justice are brought into currency. Increasingly there may be a perception that criminal charges may be brought against state leaders acting in their official capacity, but in violation of fundamental international conventions and provisions of the UN charter. Although fragile at first, and subject to disappearance in the short run, nonetheless, in the long run, the drift is toward the procedurally just practice. The increase in interaction makes for an increase in protocols of interaction, and the more procedures and protocols of interaction there are, the more there will be a tendency for habits of justice, and perceived need to create the appearances of justice, to create new procedurally just standards. Application of these principles to the operations of the Security Council itself is, at the moment, and for the immediate future, unlikely, however. Rather it is much more likely that substantial reform of the Security Council will be forced upon it when all manner of procedures governing relations between smaller states will be so far in advance of those governing the Security Council that the members of the Security Council will have to catch up. Perhaps they will be shamed into catching up, but that is unlikely. More likely, there will be interests of individual members of the Security Council, which will be served by joining forces for reform of the Security Council initiated by states or NGO's outside the members of the Security Council. There is almost, one wants to say, a certain inevitability about such changes. The more interaction between states, the more procedural justice becomes necessary, generally desirable, and individual-interest-serving in the very long run.

Recently George Woodcock has argued in *A Monk And His Message* that determinist historical models are decidedly unreliable. According to Woodcock, the future has an openness and unpredictability about it that can be chagrining when the unexpected is catastrophic and refreshing when it is positive. Now, at the end of the twentieth century, after all the quick changes in Eastern Europe of 1990 and 1991, Woodcock asks us to take seriously the Dalai Lama's hope for the establishment of ecological oases of peacefulness, zones of gentleness and kindness. However, to believe that the Marxist and capitalist determinisms of the nineteenth and twentieth centuries aim for a tightness of pattern that has not been and probably could not have been fulfilled is not to imply that there cannot be conditionally inevitable outcomes. There do seem to be tendencies, structural drifts, and conditionally triggered patterns.

Also, we should remind ourselves that it is not only in matters of response to crimes such as murder theft and rape that we have identified with and implemented the values of procedural justice. There are many areas in which ideals of justice have been and are being implemented with enormous impact on the ability of the group to carry on its tasks effectively and properly. I will mention two of them: the avoidance of conflict of interest in the management of political affairs, and the handling of public meetings and public discussions.

During the last few decades many states and political jurisdictions in the western world have been developing means by which people in positions of trust not only will avoid acting in circumstances in which they have conflict of interest, but also will be seen to be prevented from acting in circumstances in which they have conflict of interest. These measures designed to guarantee conflict avoidance have the capacity to positively impact public life in a most significant way. In the not so distant past it was more or less taken for granted that people who went in for public life would find themselves profiting from their knowledge and contacts in a way beyond what was strictly sanctioned by those who entrusted them with their tasks. Fortunately, this is being changed. It is hard to see how anyone can prefer the system which, at its worst, creates an enormous underground economy of bribes, kickbacks, payoffs and the like, and at its best, creates distrust of politicians and cynicism about involvement in the public process.

Second, we have found through long historical experimentation that meetings are apt to be manipulated if there is no institutionalized procedure designed to minimize the muzzling of unpopular viewpoints and the suppressing of initiatives which might affect the interests of some powerful group or other. The systems whereby meetings are run have evolved over centuries. All of them involve rules for the setting of agendas, rules of recognition of speakers, rules for adopting resolutions, and the like. Naturally, we are not naive enough to suppose that every meeting is chaired fairly, any more than we are naive enough to suppose that no judge has ever been bribed or that all judges are paragons of creative wisdom. Nonetheless, a society whose meetings are managed by a chair, who must at least create a semblance of following a system such as that provided by Robert's Rules, for instance, is more likely to stave off partisan manipulation than one which is left to the unstructured whims of demagoguery and raw group dynamics. We haven't perfected the meeting process, but our ideals of fairness in giving people to be affected by decisions opportunities to speak and communicate their viewpoints are eminently practical.

These are but two further illustrations of many which could be given to show how the ideal of objectivity and impartiality in judgment and human communication is not a fantasy, but a practical, implementable ideal, and one which we have been busy implementing over the ages.

There is, then, an important element of social organization in which progress is a meaningful concept, and huge strides have been taken. Only one who rejects the ideals of procedural and substantial justice, or who rues the epoch in which we developed complex enough communities to require justice systems, or who has a peculiarly, and unjustifiably cynical view of the implementation of fundamental principles of justice can deny that there has been important progress in history on this score.

In the sphere of implementation of justice there has been progress, and in the international sphere where the ideal and the practice of procedural justice is only beginning to be considered, it is reasonable for one to expect the progress to continue. At least, it is reasonable to hold such expectations so long as the sociobiological arguments claiming the indelibly aggressive nature of human beings will always lead to unjust arrangements can be defused. Those arguments we will consider shortly. But first we will consider another possible line of progress in history, a line intimately related to progress in procedural justice. We will then subject that line of possible progress to critical scrutiny from the perspective of Enlightenment East. And then we will return to the sociobiological arguments holding aggression to constitute an obstacle to the sort of progress to perpetual justice and/or peace that Enlightenment West proponents are contemplating.

Justice and the scientific perspective

In one striking case, at least, there was a temporal proximity between the institution of a system of impartial judgment and the rise of abstract scientific curiosity. Thales began his first scientific or proto-scientific inquiries around the time of the introduction of the various judicial systems of the Greek peninsula. And these inquiries are usually identified with the launching of the scientific project in the western world.

It is not difficult, moreover, to indicate a possible connection between the development of a judicial system and the development of the scientific temperament and experimental attitude. The difference between a tribal resolution of dispute and a judicial resolution of dispute revolves precisely around the notion of a perspective of witness, and its concomitant requirement of the ideal of objectivity in the case of systems of judgment and the lack of such a perspective and concomitant ideal in the case of tribal resolutions of dispute.

In a tribal situation in which two members of the community are disputing, and the elder of the community hears about the dispute and asks to intervene, there may be a modicum of objectivity. On the other hand, there may not be even a modicum of objectivity. The elder may function ex officio as elder, as chief, in other words, and recommend or impose such resolution as he or she sees fit without particular regard to the independent perspectives of the disputing parties. It is at least partly out of the unsatisfactoriness of such situations, however, that the institution of justice develops.

Take the issues surrounding the identification of a criminal. A murder has been committed. The members of the victim's family point their fingers at a member of a family known to be having a feud with the victim's family. The elder may well want to use this opportunity to impose some sort of resolution of the feud. However, others in the community may have good reason for thinking that the murderer is a member of the elder's family. Here is a situation in which the demands of objectivity conflict with the tribal institutions of dispute resolution. If the elder hears of the charges against the member of his own family, and calls a council at which he effectively removes himself from the issues of identification of the murderer, then he is thinking in the manner of justice and objectivity. If he does not, then his capacity to think objectively and in the manner of justice is called into question.

Where there is a system, which recognizes itself as being concerned with the implementation of justice, there must be a concern for objectivity. That period in a civilization's history in which judges and the institutions of judgment are first set up is the period in which the concern for objectivity is first manifesting itself in social institution.

Let us continue our story of the murder in the village. Say there is now a council of elders representative of the whole village listening to the accusations. If they have the concept of justice in mind, they will want to establish facts. They will want not only to restore an outward appearance of harmony and cessation of hostility, but also to do so in a way which takes account of facts determined about who actually murdered the victim, what the motive was, whether there was provocation or extenuating circumstance, and so on. If the ideal of justice guides the community, the possibility that the murderer is from the family of the elder does not deter the inquiry into the facts.

But how does one determine the facts? One determines the facts, one hopes, by hearing everyone who has information to present.

Implicit in this procedure, an amazingly fundamental procedure, at that, is a theory about the world. The theory about the world is that the world exists in a unitary manner. If a body is found with a knife sticking out of its back, somebody put that knife there. And if somebody put that knife there, then anybody looking that way at that time, in normal circumstances, from nearby, will have seen the event, and seen who it was.

The human perspective is a perspective of witness. Underlying the shamming, the hidden agendas, the hypocrisy, the outright lies, and so on, which human beings sometimes bring to their public affairs, there is a fact of witness written into each and every human being. People may not bring their witness out. But they *are* witnesses. There is a human function, which is the function of witness. And a judicial inquiry relies on this perspective, the perspective of witness. For a judicial inquiry assumes *(a)* that there is a perspective of witness, and *(b)* that the perspective of witness can eventually be brought out by examination of all people who come forward as having a relevant perspective of witness. Indeed, it is sometimes a function of legislation to draw out the perspective of witness.

There is, then, a deep connection between the judicial process and the perspective sought in scientific inquiry, and assumed by the scientific method. Both scientific and judicial process revolve around the procedures of inquiry into a presumed objective world. Both justice and science seek to achieve in ever better ways reliable representation of an assumed objective world. The judicial process seeks to achieve reliable representation of particular sets of events involving people—who did what to whom, when—and so on. The scientific process seeks to achieve reliable representation of particular sets of events of all kinds not only those involving who did what to whom when, but also what happened first, second, and third, and what features can we abstract from the events we describe in order to better represent sequences of events in general.

In philosophical parlance, judicial inquiry, and scientific inquiry in large measure presume a metaphysics of objectivity: an objective world within which certain things happen. In addition to the metaphysics of objectivity there is a procedural epistemology common to both judicial process and scientific method. The role of corroboration of witness in judicial inquiry is paralleled by the requirement of repeatability in experimental science.

In the light of these profound connections between the perspective of one who seeks justice and the perspective of one who seeks scientific knowledge, it is easy to see why there is a connection between the development of the institutions of justice and the development of abstract scientific curiosity. It is the social dynamic of judgment and judicial trial which lays the basis for scientific thought.

Of course it may also be that it is the development of technology which gives rise to the perspective of objectivity which in turn feeds the social dynamic leading to institutions of judgment. Once metallurgy, engineering, meteorology, navigation, and so on, have reached certain stages of proficiency, the perspective of repeatability and objectivity is attained. The world is seen to have an order and regularity inherent in it. It becomes increasingly understood that the world is a unitary systematic phenomenon and not merely a capricious set of events each one of which is to be understood as the result of a capricious whim of a god, a personal power specifically willing, through the freedom of indifference, the tiniest movements of things. Rather, the realization is made, for example, that when a metal is heated till it glows white, it will be soft enough to fuse onto another metal, and so on. These events happen with complete regularity, and need not be attributed to the specific intervening will of some god. Nature works. The world is an objective system. And in addition, we humans have the perspective of witness and the capacity to represent our witness through thought and in language.

Given such an intuition of the world fostered by technological development, it is natural that the perspective on human affairs, which leads to implementation of institutions of justice and judgment, develops. Thus develop the extraordinarily powerful and mutually reinforcing practices: Technology, justice, abstract science. Given that we are so deeply imbued with the values of objectivity in scientific knowledge and justice in authoritative human relations it may be difficult for us to fully appreciate what great revolutions in human consciousness took place when we moved in these directions.

For there are contrasting ways of seeing the world. In the prescientific, prejudicial, and pretechnological ways of seeing nature and authority, within chiefdoms, nature is a series of events willed by gods and/or God, and justice is the favor of God or the gods, and is practiced through obeisance to the will of the authority instituted on earth by God or the gods, namely, the chief-monarch-priest. The power of the Divine Force(s) constitutes their legitimacy and authority. Thus, the pretechnological, prejudicial and prescientific way of thinking, within chiefdoms, includes a step of blind obeisance to what cannot be regarded except as a capricious order, unintelligible to us. Might makes right in the prejudicial chiefdom. And the will of the god—inaccessible to human discovery through experimentation—

makes what happens happen in the prescientific view of nature within the social chiefdom.

If we want to understand history, then, we may want to think in terms of the following main categories or phases: (1) nomadic food gathering and hunting families with mystic participation in nature and family life; (2) the emergence of technology, agriculturalism, large groups, disputes, wars, and the chiefdom; (3) the emergence of systems of justice; and finally, (4) the development of theoretical science, that is, abstract disciplines of knowledge, symbolized and embodied in the activities now associated with the university. But what is the connection between technological and scientific progress and human happiness?

Scientific progress and happiness

As I've tried to show, there is no greater happiness for an individual as monadic individual than the cultivation of blissful awareness of the ultimate gift of life in all normal circumstances. In familiar religious language, happiness consists in the constant realization of God, or the Sacred, permeating everyday life, and the experience of delight and pleasure in the Divine, or Sacred activity. In slightly less familiar religious language, happiness consists in the constant experience of the bliss of Ultimacy. As contemporary psychologists put it, happiness consists in the ability to maintain the "graceful flow" experience (See, for instance, Mihaly Csikszentmihalyi, 1991).

Most people experience the bliss of Ultimacy more through one sort of activity than another. Cultivation of happiness, then, comes through the diminishment of one's *reliance or dependence* on the particular touchstone setting or activity. Cultivation of happiness comes through the increase of the activities and settings that serve as touchstones for the experience of the bliss of Ultimacy. And this increase comes often by associating other activities with the familiar touchstone activity.

The actor cultivates happiness by thinking of the whole world as a stage and every act a command performance for a discerning audience. The one who thrills to hang gliding cultivates happiness by learning to see every setting as a metaphor for a thrilling free float. The one who is deeply satisfied through human fellowship cultivates happiness by developing an intuition of the fellowship even the hermit feels in nature. The one who thrills to interpersonal power cultivates happiness by developing the sense that the ultimate pleasure and the ultimate power is manifested in everyday agency: carrying water, chopping wood, moving the limbs at the direction of the mind.

One who can take deep pleasure in normal mundane experience, one who can experience the mountain climber's ultimate thrill by walking up the steps to the front stoop, one who can experience the pleasure of the recipient of the trophy of victory in the victory of awakening when one has been asleep, one who can experience the miracle of the birth of a child in the birth of each moment from the previous one, one who can experience the exultation of shaking off the oppressive yoke of some vicious tyrannical regime in the act of stretching out one's limbs in the morning—such a person is free. Such a person lives in God, or Ultimacy.

And everyone has the capacity for the cultivation of this, the deepest happiness, the experience of God, the sacred, the Holy One, the Ultimate, the Tao, the Absolute, the Way of Heaven, Atman, in everyday life. Moreover, this experience is our natural treasure, our birthright as it were, and our inheritance. Intrinsic in our psychophysical makeup is the capacity for the blissful experience of God, the sacred mystery manifest in the form of the world.

Our task in life, then, is twofold: to cultivate this deepest happiness, spiritual contentment, and spiritual realization in everyday life, whether we are mountain climbers, parents, entrepreneurs, teachers, entertainers, lawyers, doctors, farmers, engineers, police officers, scientists, or bankers, and to bring the sense of sacredness and blissful realization of Divine Life into our interrelational lives, our interactions and loving struggles with others: our siblings, our friends, our parents, teachers, and mentors, our fellow workers, our fellow citizens, and the community of sentient beings with whom we share existence.

The development of science is plainly an instrument with great potential for the increase of human happiness. The experience of the bliss of ultimacy is available to everyone in all normal circumstances. But what about abnormal circumstances? People had tooth abscesses hundreds of years ago. People caught bubonic plague. People died of cholera, diphtheria, tuberculosis, malaria, smallpox. People were subject to ravaging famines and droughts, without any possibility of importing refrigerated food. Women died in childbirth in calamitous percentages. However, it took the development of chemistry in the last few centuries to make possible antibiotics, anaesthetics, sophisticated surgery, and a proper understanding of the fundamentals of hygiene. Physics and chemistry were also required to be brought to roughly the same stage before refrigeration, canning, and rapid systems of transportation could be developed.

There are, then, two ways in which scientific and technological progress makes a positive contribution to human happiness: There is the contribution which science makes to those with a pure scientific temperament. The blissful experience of Ultimacy is enhanced for some people by the practice of scientific inquiry. As is well known, some physicists take the attitude toward their research that it is a way of contemplating God. Second, there is the contribution of science to the removal of extreme conditions of pain and suffering which prevent people from experiencing the blissful Ultimacy which is, as it were, every human being's birthright.

In our assessment of systems of private resolution of dispute versus systems of public, procedurally just, systems of dispute resolution, we saw that it takes an extreme cynicism or radical anarchism to deny that there is progress in regard to this strand at least. So, too, in regard to the assessment of the contribution of science to cure disease, it takes an extreme Luddism to deny that there has been progress.

It seems probable, moreover, that just as scientists labored in basic research for about a thousand years (including the hiatus of the Dark Age) before coming up with the foundational physical and chemical theories from which we have been able to develop the tools to ameliorate, routinely cure, and in some cases entirely eliminate, the diseases and noxious conditions mentioned, so, too, we will continue to learn the fundamentals of psychology so as to be able to eliminate in some distant future time many of the noxious conditions associated with living in groups.

For example, until recently it was taken for granted that children are best taught through a combination of rules and punishments for offenders. "Spare the rod and spoil the child" is Biblical advice (*Proverbs* 13:24, 29:15, etc.). Now, however, it is becoming increasingly clear that the hitting of children is an expression of parental frustration, and does not have a healthy role to play in either public or private education. It is, of course, sometimes, an understandable expression of parental frustration. But if, as is becoming increasingly clear, from the child's viewpoint, neutrality in limit settings, and positive reinforcements wherever possible, are the ideal vehicles for positive happy experiences in learning and living, then hitting children, and more generally, the use of negative reinforcements, punishments *qua* punishments, and so on, can be very largely eliminated. Is it not amazing that it has taken us thousands of years to distinguish clearly between such methods as setting of consequences, offering choices, and follow through with consequences, on the one hand, and punishment, on the other hand? What an enormous revolution in education and child rearing we are going through!

Alfred Adler launched this discussion in the modern setting by suggesting that the psychological effects of punishment were to isolate a child and convince the child that he does not belong to the community. At the same time, communal living requires understanding of consequences, and the capacity to implement such understanding (*Understanding Human Nature*, p. 30). Then Piaget distinguished between what he called "arbitrary punishment" and "punishment by reciprocity." Arbitrary punishment is punishment which is conventional in content, and bears no intrinsic or natural relation to the negative conduct which provoked the response. By contrast, punishment by reciprocity is intrinsically connected to the offense, and is proportioned to it (*Moral Judgement of the Child*, pp. 203-204). Rudolf Dreikurs and Loren Grey then picked up these distinctions and wrote *Logical Consequences* in which they distinguished between what they call "punishment" and "logical consequences," taking over Piaget's distinctions and Adler's assessment. The working through of logical consequences is friendly, oriented to group realities, goal related, flexible, and readiness-to-participate terminated. By contrast, punishment is connected with authority, anger, blame, retribution, and is focused on the past. We have also been coming to understand how any treatment of a problem which inflicts pain on the offender models aggressive behavior, and leads to cycles of aggression (N. H. Azrin, "Pain and Aggression"; for other references see Jeanne Ormrod, *Human Learning*, p. 110). More recently still, William Glasser shows how the educational system excels when it is more and more satisfaction driven and empowering, rather than manipulative and controlling by aversive means (*Control Theory in The Classroom*, and *The Quality School*).

For the sake of general overview of the problem, we will now recapitulate the dynamics of the noxious social and psychological conditions which might be removed by the application of further understanding of human psychology and psychophysiology. Some of the difficulties we have gotten ourselves into may never have occurred had we not inaugurated the agricultural and early technological revolutions. Had we never irrigated, never developed metallurgy, never built cities, and so forth, perhaps we would have been spared some of the psychological plagues we have inherited. Our overview will consider human history *given the drifts and tendencies*, including the drift and tendencies to farm, irrigate, consolidate control of water systems, develop metallurgy, defend against the new microbes released by new farming innovations, and so forth. (For the relevance of the consolidation of control of water systems to the development of despotic hierarchies, see Karl Wittfogel, *Oriental Despotism*; and for the relevance of agriculture to the need to control new diseases, and the emergence of various forms of "macroparisitism," see William McNeill, *The Human Condition*.)

Given a world in which agriculture, technology, and property do in fact emerge, there is a need for protection and coercive dispute resolution. This means that there is a permanent need for a chief and a judge. But in the long run, if the scourge of war is ever to be brought under control, the chief must become fully and decisively subservient to the judge. Moreover the function of judgment, which inaugurates, and for our purposes includes, the legislative process, must be coordinated with the popular will in some way, which inevitably necessitates a mix of technocratic meritocracy and democracy. One is not utopian enough to envision in any immediately forseeable future a total withering away of the internal coercive function which is the legacy of the chiefdom, though one would hope that in some future epoch, the educational process will have been so thoroughly refined and improved that crime and criminal tendencies are increasingly rare.

If such a withering away of the function of chief, the coercive power, is ever to be possible it would only be through the vast improvement of our understanding of human psychology and the educational process. It is here that we must see science as just beginning, if at all, to fulfill its promise. And it is here that the limitation of views such as those of Francis Fukuyama in *The End of History and the Last Man*, for example, are revealed. Fukuyama claims that in the contemporary social democracy we find the pinnacle of human progress reached. The end of history is upon us, he says. Such a view can only be maintained at the expense of the realm of the spirit. Social organization and spirit are not unconnected. Have we really reached the end of our communal spiritual evolution? Or is the case not rather more as Toynbee claimed, when he suggested that the great need for current civilization is the rediscovery of religion or spirituality, and that love is the true end of man? (Arnold Toynbee, quoted in Kenneth Winetrout's *Arnold Toynbee*, pp. 60, 69). If so, then it would be only reasonable to expect structural changes, and profound ones, in education, in city life, in commerce and its role in people's consciousness, in the relationship between community and the land, in the aesthetics and social tone of cities, and in the ways in which people are involved with their own basic sustenance, as social structures gradually come to be conducive to monadic fulfillment.

Mysticism and social progress

We have now developed and defended two lines for justification of the Enlightenment West view of history.

If agricultural and allied early technologies were inevitable, so were conflicts. If conflicts were inevitable, so was the chief's chair. If the chief's chair was inevitable, so was the *desirability* of replacing chiefdoms and monarchies with normative judges and legislative bodies. To the extent that we have acted on this ideal, we have an identifiable line of progress through history at the political level.

This line of progress through history parallels a second line of progress through history, the development of technologies of individual happiness which technologies address injustices of nature such as disease, lightening-caused fires, and drought, and the injustices arising from our drive to technologize food production and sheltering arrangements. To the extent that scientific progress has enabled large numbers of people to prevent abnormally painful circumstances from arising, there is an identifiable line of progress at the technological level.

The vision of Enlightenment West is to regard history in terms of these two lines of progress. Its standard message is that procedural justice grants individual autonomy, and that individual autonomy combined with the technological basis to prevent abnormally painful circumstances enables people to search for happiness, to define their happiness, and to achieve it. I want to suggest now that this vision is fundamentally incomplete. If all we had to go on in assessing progress is progress in procedural justice and progress in scientific knowledge, the postmodern critics of Enlightenment West would be right. The early individualistic postmoderns such as Kierkegaard, Schopenhauer, and Nietzsche, who recognized the social failings of their societies, the inability of their societies to provide the conditions for living in the depth dimension, and who anticipated the degree of conformity and irrationalism which animates the social process, have been vindicated by the cataclysms of the twentieth century and particularly by the fact that the nadir of technological barbarity was perpetrated by the society many had regarded as the most civilized in human history. If the only things we could ever point to in order to justify an Enlightenment West hope for progress are scientific advances and the implementation several thousand years ago of standards of procedural justice in dispute resolution, the critics of the idea of progress might well regard themselves as vindicated. And since Enlightenment West originally articulated its vision of progress in such terms, Enlightenment West as originally articulated fails.

The failure of Enlightenment West thinking is due to its failure, thus far, to consider the psychological and social fallout resulting from thousands of years of social arrangements in which the functions of justice and science were subordinated to the office of chief manager of coercive power. Since it is only recently that we have been able to concretely envision the subordination of international coercive authority to the normative judicial function, we are only now, at the turn of the twenty-first century, ready to recognize a possible third line of progress through history: the elimination of the ego-driven, patriarchal chief mentality in all social roles and relationships, and in its place the attitudes of sacralism and genial mysticism. The third line of progress begins when the normative judge and the scientist are being granted their maximal extensions, as has begun to take place in our century. Now that we see clearly how the normative judge and the scientist knit the world into a global village, we understand for the first time the way in which the Enlightenment West vision of science and social justice may be integrated with the mystical vision of Enlightenment East, expressed both in terms of monadic egolessness and interrelational sacralism and love.

Let us observe, then, the social and psychological effects of having lived for thousands of years under patriarchal chiefdoms. In a society which has a chief, the males emulate the chief. Thus, the chief mentality has created suspicion, fear, and competition between people even within the chiefdom. The chiefdom, that is, has created a society organized around little chiefs. It has created patriarchal social structures in which women have found it well nigh impossible to fulfill themselves through science, art, and social leadership. It has politicized the intimate family life, so that the father of the family in imitation of the chief, tries to rule the family, as the chief rules the community. In imitation of the chief's treatment given to criminals, it has introduced hitting children as a method of encouraging them to learn. It has distorted fellowships by fostering the political model of the community of fellows. It has inverted religious life, so that for thousands of years a dominant image of God has been that of a benevolent patriarchal chief who decrees by arbitrary freedom of indifference what others are to do in service of Him, using standards of reward and punishment unintelligible to his supposedly inadequate servants. It has created an economic system in which everyone wants to impress everyone else, since the chief has to impress everyone else with his power in order to stay chief. Thus, society becomes driven by materialistic, acquisitive, consumeristic, and power-centered foci. And what is the principal psychological condition of the chief considered as an individual? It is as ego-bound as a psychological condition can be, since the chief is aware of everyone else as a potential rival or enemy.

Thus, the legacy of thousands of years of living in patriarchal chiefdoms has been the deep entrenchment of ego-ridden modes of thought in each fundamental social role, affecting the relation of men and women, family life, teacher student relationship, work relationship, religious institution, and economic order. It is no wonder liberalism has not yet created paradise on earth, even in societies with material abundance. Indeed, the ongoing deterioration of the tone of city life is symptomatic of Enlightenment West's insufficient attention to the effects of the spread of chiefdom consciousness. If the Enlightenment West vision of progress in social justice, and scientific knowledge is to have direction, it must, at this stage in history, renew its interest in the spiritual condition of the human person. Without an articulation of the ways by which liberal modernity and a focus on spirituality can be joined, pervasive chiefdom attitudes will keep ruining social prospects.

Thus, Enlightenment West needs Enlightenment East to complete its project, and it is now our task to unite them. We do this by furthering the development of educational methods which result in young adults deeply imbued with interrelational values and experiences; we do this by furthering the development of a sacred family life in which we look both to the myth of the mother and to the myth of the father as myths of parental love; we do this by furthering the development of the vehicles of international justice, the international court, and the UN's institutions; we do this by furthering the development of the humanistic and pure scientific disciplines as practiced at universities and through international bodies of scientists such as Scientific Committee for Investigation of Claims Of the Paranormal; and we do this by furthering the practices of undogmatic sacred ritual, particularly, of meditation and contemplation of the blissful ultimacy of experience. But there are two objections to the possibility of such a unification, and to these objections we now turn.

Scientism, I-it attitudes, and alienation

It is frequently claimed that there exists a connection between objective I-it thinking and profane, materialistic, ego-bound consciousness. According to this view, once we technologized, we became bound to the profane experience of the world, and inevitably driven by materialistic control-minded quests. In my view, although the diagnosis of the contemporary problem is correct, for we have gotten ourselves into an unfortunately profane, acquisitive, materialistic, consumeristic, control-minded set of attitudes within the wealthy west, the causal analysis is incorrect, or badly skewered.

It was Martin Buber who popularized Pierce's earlier version of the distinction between I-Thou and I-it. It's not clear whether Buber arrived at his formulation entirely independently of Pierce. The I-thou, I-it contrast may actually have been suggested to Buber by James's incorporation of Pierce's idea into *The Will To Believe*, as suggested earlier. In any case, though, the distinction is now primarily associated with Buber's thought, and Buber certainly recognized the tremendous potential for the distinction. Accordingly, it may be useful to briefly consider Buber's thinking on the contrast, and through it to present the criticism of Enlightenment West, which holds that its rationalistic scientism amounts to a thoroughly alienating psychological takeover by the I-it stance.

Buber began his philosophical career as something of a mystic, but later adopted what he considered to be a worldly, as opposed to mystical, stance as a result of a tragic incident which highlighted to him the preciousness of each human being, and consequently, the importance of hallowing the everyday and the multiplicitous. It is evident from this progression that Buber restricted his conception of mysticism to what we have called "object-altered mysticism." Buber was unaware of the language of thought that enables one to preserve multiplicity and yet unpack the ego structure. Yet he was looking for such a language of thought, as we can see from his description of the difference between the I-thou stance and the I-it stance. However, lacking a distinction between self identification and first personal identification, Buber did not have the conceptual resources to articulate fully the potential for mysticism inherent in his notion of the I-thou stance. As it stands, then, he uses an interelational, indeed, interpersonal image for his view of successful monadic states, and is pressed to defend interpersonal imagery applied to how one sees, for example, a flower, or a stone, within the I-thou stance. Further, the I-it stance is, by and large, judged negatively. However, once we have the distinction between personal and impersonal modes of self-identification, as was developed earlier, we can see how the contrast between I-thou and I-it as expounded by Buber conflates a host of contrasts which would be tedious to enumerate. (For example, one contrasts any two of the following stances: *(a)* Personal-I/thou, *(b)* Impersonal-I/it, *(c)* selfless-first personal-this/second personal-this, *(d)* ego-identified first personal this/impersonal it, *(e)* ego-identified-first personal-this/third personal this, *(f)* universal personal self/thou, *(g)* universal personal self/it; etc.) Once we have articulated the distinctions in modes of self-identification and fully attended to the varieties of mystical phenomenology we can see how to avoid the simplistic demotion of the technological mode of thinking. The no-self mysticism is not necessarily a mysticism devoid of interpersonal relationship. Therefore, what Buber wants in the way of I-thou is preserved, as is the objectivity of thought of what would ambiguously and unsatisfactorily be assimilated to the I-it stance in Buber's system, lacking as it does, a rich articulation of fundamental subject-object images.

It is, then, the application of the ego-identified first personal-impersonal it stance which Buber aptly calls the I-it stance, to interpersonal dialogic life which may be judged negatively. However, the brain surgeon's application of either (i) an objective, no-self first personal–impersonal it stance, or (ii) Universal personal self–impersonal it stance, or (iii) an ego-identified first personal/impersonal it stance, to the activity of operating on someone's brain is appropriate. The last mentioned, i.e., (iii), Buber recognizes. What Buber does not recognize is the availability of the first two, i.e., (i), and (ii), and so he fails as well to realize that the no-self first person–second person stance, and universal personal self–second person stance, allow for the fullest interpersonal life, full release from ego-identified living, and, yet, in the case of (i), preservation of fully objective thinking all at once.

It is not objective modes of thinking per se which distort interpersonal life. Rather, it is objective modes of thinking which create surpluses and institutions of property, and thereby adventitiously affect social conditions so as to result in the ascendancy of the institution of patriarchal chiefdom. And the chiefdom then has a ripple effect right through society, entrenching not just ego-fixated modes of identification, but a particular psychic type, the chief, at so many levels.

Of course one does not want to exaggerate. There have always been loving families in which the natural unpoliticized relations have been preserved despite the ripple effect of the chiefdom. There have always been loving marriages, educations without beating of children, and religious understandings, in all traditions, in which Godhead is the center, or the God of Love, rather than God the arbitrary Chief. It is, rather, the fact that there are fathers who conduct themselves as chiefs, theologies in which God is conceived as unintelligible, benevolent, arbitrary dictator, classrooms, or homes in which children are hit for failure to learn or failure to follow orders, that indicates how entrenched are chief, and chief's henchmen attitudes. Given that there has been a ripple effect of the chief, and that the more enlight-ened, and dare one say, natural, educational methods, theological systems, familial systems, and relations of coercive authority to judicial systems, have had to struggle against the effects of chiefdom, all the more reason we have to look to the contemplative methods associ-ated with Enlightenment East.

Objectivity and scientific rigor are not in the slightest degree undermining of mystical intuition. On the contrary, pure objectivity conduces directly to no-self mysticism. It is only when objectivity is subordinated to chiefdom consciousness, that is, when objectivity is subordinated to materialistic power, that ego-identified conscious-ness is reinforced. Similarly, trust in the expressive power of language is not inimical to mysticism except when in the service of ego-identi-fied modes of thought. One of the more useful features of the analysis of mysticism provided in chapter 4, I hope, is the demonstration that the self-altered mysticisms, namely, no-self or purely objective mysti-cism, avatar mysticism, and universal impersonal-self mysticism, are all amenable to full expression in language. There is no thought at the practical, ordinary level of daily functioning which cannot be expressed in a form of discourse appropriate to the altered self mys-ticism in question. This, I hope, should put to rest the notion that mysticism is especially connected with ineffability in the sense that the mystic is incapable of expressing ordinary ideas while enjoying mystical experience, or in the sense that mystical experience is nec-essarily ineffable in a way that non-mystical experience of qualia is not ineffable. (See the author's *The Silence Of The Mystic*, chapters 1 & 2, on this point as well.) The distinctions between ego-bound and ego-released states can be precisely described even if the quality of such differences needs to be experienced directly. And the fact that the quality of such differences needs to be experienced directly does not entail that ordinary mental states and ordinary agency cannot be expe-rienced in conjunction with the ego-released experience of the world.

As for the idea that Enlightenment West has set us on a path so control-minded as to be threatening our very survival, unfortunately, we have hovered close to the brink of nuclear destruction, and have used upon ourselves weapons of abominable mass destruction as instruments of war. But because war only obtains between states as chiefdoms in which the values of procedural justice have not been fully brought to bear, it is unreasonable to associate the instruments of war specifically with Enlightenment West. Since patriarchy and chief-dom consciousness has developed, apparently independently, in most areas of the globe, and certainly in India, China, Japan, and the Middle East, as well as in Europe, along with agriculture, and technology, warfare and chiefdom consciousness do not arise because of Enlightenment West values of science, social progress, and justice. One cannot blame Enlightenment West for a problem it inherited. Indeed, one of the main thrusts of Enlightenment West has been the effort to subordinate monarchical chiefdoms to systems of procedural justice! Thus, efforts to lay the account for the aberrations of Nazism and Pol Pot's slaughter of innocents, for instance, on the excessive rationality of Enlightenment West, as John Ralston Saul most recently has in *Voltaire's Bastards* (1992), are in vain. Hitler was no product of Enlightenment West, even if his henchmen proceeded technologically.

Are human societies doomed to make war against each other?

This brings us to the pessimistic psychological and sociobiological criticisms of Enlightenment West, even when it attempts to fuse with various forms of mysticism from the genial to the arcane. We've already noted that if Enlightenment West depends only on science and justice for its vision of progress, it fails. We've noted what additional value must be supplied at the conceptual level. But is it reasonable to hold out hopes that such a value will indeed prove practical? Isn't it perhaps enough to point to the holocaust, and, various campaigns of ethnic cleansing to prove the bankruptcy of the Enlightenment West hopes that collective irrationalist barbarities can be overcome?

I realize that to some theorists the sort of Enlightenment West, justice driven account presented in these pages will seem out of touch. Thus, for instance, the following remark, "[T]he tradition of liberal theorizing [Rawls' *A Theory Of Justice*] inaugurated has done little more than articulate the prejudices of an Anglo-American academic class that lacks any understanding of political life in our age, an age distinguished by the collapse of the Enlightenment project on a world-historical scale" (John Gray, 1992, p. 13). It is understandable that the high hopes of the eighteenth century have been dashed. But it is shortsightedness to think that genocidal irrationalism is an invention of the twentieth century, as though designed by an antirationalist puppeteer to prove the hopelessness of rationalistic human prospects. For such a lesson cannot be drawn from the holocaust and contemporary ethnic cleansings and similar atrocities. From the earliest days of our history we have records of genocidal intentions and campaigns. The Hebrew Bible records explicitly genocidal practices in many places (e.g., Numbers 21; Deut. 7; Deut 25:19; I *Samuel* 27:8-12).

Even if some of these materials are historical retrojections from somewhat later periods, they do reflect what was held, during those later periods, to be, or to have been, proper conduct. Nor should we think that the Israelites were unique in these practices. The earliest known reference to the Israelites in ancient Egyptian materials is a boast of genocide against the Israelites inscribed on the Merneptah Stele roughly thirty-two hundred years ago: "Israel is not; his seed is destroyed" (Wilson, 1985, p. 25). Indeed it is possible in the ancient context to present genocidal instructions side by side with the injunction: "Justice, justice shalt thou pursue" (Deut. 16: 20). So it must be said that our shock and outrage at the abominations of the twentieth century must be taken as indications of disappointment at the collective failure of the human race to meet *raised* expectations, more than as proof of any absolute limits on the capacity of the human species to live harmoniously. If the Hebrew Bible can take for granted the acceptability of genocidal campaigns *and* the pursuit of justice, then our collective horror at the Holocaust shows the degree of moral progress we have made collectively over the last several thousand years. And the fact that there was no system of just international order in place which prevented the Holocaust, or Pol Pot's murder of a million of his countrymen, can't be taken as proof that no such system can ever be developed. We know how collectively irrational and antagonistic we can be as communities. We've seen it over and over again in history. The question, rather, is whether there is an indelibly irrationalistic, aggressive, antagonistic, human nature which *must* manifest destructively in collectivity. And this question, it would seem, is answered favorably (i.e., negatively) by several considerations.

First, there are the studies of gentle collectivities. When we take cognizance of the gentleness of societies such as the Arapesh society Margaret Mead wrote about *(From The South Seas)*, the Semangs, (E. R. Service, *The Hunters*), the Zunis (Ruth Benedict, *Patterns of Culture*), or the Canadian Inuit (Jean Briggs, 1970), we realize that the human is an amazingly flexible, open, unfixed being. It is as wrong to insist on the impossibility of progress as to insist on a naive, overly neat set of stages constituting progress and held to be inevitable. Erich Fromm calls these societies "life-affirmative societies," and describes them this way: "[T]he main emphasis of ideals, customs and institutions is that they serve the preservation and growth of life in all its forms. There is a minimum of hostility, violence, or cruelty among people, no harsh punishment, hardly any crime, and the institution of war is absent or plays an exceedingly small role. Children are treated with kindness, there is no severe corporal punishment; women are in general considered equal to men, or at least not exploited or humiliated; there is a generally permissive and affirmative attitude toward sex. There is little envy, covetousness, greed, and exploitativeness. There is also little competition and individualism and a great deal of cooperation; personal property is only in things that are used. There is a general attitude of trust and confidence, not only in others but particularly in nature; a general prevalence of good humor, and a relative absence of depressive moods" (*The Anatomy Of Human Destructiveness*, p. 194).

The problem with this path toward refutation of sociobiologists and others who would hold human aggression and collective irrationalism to be endemic, and that large scale wars between collectivities are inevitable, is that the data are controversial in the first place, and, in the second, hard to apply to large, complex industrial or postindustrial collectivities. For instance, Margaret Mead's picture in *Coming Of Age In Samoa* of the peaceful Samoans was vigorously challenged by Derek Freeman, who claimed that the same peoples Margaret Mead held to be peaceable, sexually liberated, and universally loving, were in fact aggressive, sexually conservative, prone to rape, war, and acts of violence (*Margaret Mead and Samoa, The Making and Unmaking of An Anthropological Myth*). Lowell Holmes attempted to adjudicate the controversy, and held that although Mead overgeneralized, her main conclusions were correct. On the other hand, Holmes criticized the quality and accuracy of the Freeman research (*Quest For The Real Samoa*, pp. 172-175). But evidence since Holmes's evaluation has emerged from an elderly informant for Mead's original research to the effect that the informants simply hoaxed the anthropologist! (Derek Freeman, "Fa'apua'a Fa'amu and Margaret Mead"; other references in Martin Gardner, "The Great Samoan Hoax"). Suggestions that Freeman is being biased and somewhat credulous in his assessment of the information given by the informant can be found in Cole (1993) and Schwartz (1993).

One interesting point about this controversy is that Derek Freeman attributes what he considers to be Mead's errors to a blinding belief in cultural determinism and relative lack of biological constraints on cultural diversity. "In the case of Mead's Samoan researches, certainly, there is the clearest evidence that it was her deeply convinced belief in the doctrine of extreme cultural determinism, for which she was prepared to fight with the whole battery at her command, that led her to construct an account of Samoa that appeared to substantiate this very doctrine" (Freeman, 1983, p. 292).

On the other hand, Holmes quotes anthropologist Jerry Gold's observation that Freeman does not actually argue from a biological position in opposing Mead's environmental, or cultural determinism. He opposes her, rather, by "arguing . . . that his knowledge of Samoan culture is superior to hers" (Holmes, p. 174, quoting *Samoan News*, Aug. 26, 1983: 22).

This points to a difficulty in the sociobiological argument for the permanence of the human collective tendency to aggression even if it could be established that no peoples have in the past been as gentle as Mead, Benedict, Service, Fromm, and others, have made out. Unless one can marshall evidence directly linking the social and the biological, there will always be the possibility that it is specific cultural factors which have been the operating causes of tendencies toward collective aggression.

But perhaps such evidence can be marshalled. Lionel Tiger and Robin Fox, in *The Imperial Animal*, contrast what they call "the medieval view" that man has a vicious and lascivious beastly element which needs constantly to be controlled and managed, with the opposing view that man is innately good and that wars can be eliminated by social tinkering: "Two world wars, hundreds of local wars, and millions upon millions of deaths by violence later, many of us stubbornly cling to this view: that we can end violence by changing circumstances. Since violence is learned, we can simply stop teaching it—remove all the provocations to it—and men will then be the good and peaceful beings that they are by nature. Those who still cling to the medieval notion are likely to find themselves condemned as evil men who argue that violence is inevitable and thus encourage it. At the risk of joining the ranks of the condemned, we argue that the medieval view is intellectually more satisfactory, scientifically more accurate, and pragmatically more sensible" (1989, p. 205).

Tiger and Fox are willing to concede that violence is learned. "But," they say, "it is learned as language is learned—easily. In our terms, violence and love are learned easily because we are wired to learn them; because they have both been essential to survival, and so mutation and natural selection have produced a creature which will readily learn both in the same way as it will readily learn languages and rules" (p. 206). The link between biology and aggression, indeed, according to Tiger and Fox is the competitiveness associated with reproduction. "Aggression in the human species is the same as aggression in any other animal species. It springs from the same causes and subserves the same functions. It is a necessary force in the evolutionary processes taking place in any sexually reproducing species. There has to be competition in order for natural selection to occur. One animal has to strive to outdo another for nest sites, territory, food, mates, dominance, so that selection can take place" (pp. 208, 209). Then human beings have no special killer instinct. Rather, "wars and organized killing, with the imperial component of conquest, arrive on the scene when the tool was perfected into the weapon, and the expanding and convoluting brain was able to cope with organization, on the one hand, and with categories of friend and foe on the other" (p. 211).

However, to recognize this is not to require a complete pessimism about human prospects. Sociobiology of this sort is perfectly compatible with optimism about the elimination of large scale wars, because having biological drives toward aggressive competitiveness does not constrain the forms of expression of these drives, and the degree of symbolic sublimation consistent with their satisfaction. Sociobiology of this sort allows for the recognition as well that entire communities can function adaptively within the biological pressures without making war so long as there are the appropriately counterbalancing factors. Thus, for instance, sociobiologist David Barash in *The Whispering Within* refers not only to the conclusions favored by some including William Durham (1976) to the effect that aggression is adaptive when resources are scarce (Durham, 1976), but also to the adaptive function of nonaggression in differing circumstances: "The Bushmen of Africa's Kalahari Desert are often cited as a peaceful, non-warlike society, and it is true that the Bushmen do not fight over hunting territories. . . . Individuals seem free to wander or hunt where they please in an idyllic, if rather dry, Garden of Eden, in which jealous concern over mine versus yours appears, at first sight, to be nonexistent. But, it happens, there are other resources [clumps of berries, fruit trees, and the like] which are defendable and in short supply. These are the objects of much aggressive dispute. . . . The Eskimo, another frequently mentioned example of a society that does not wage war, also fit within evolutionary predictions. The opportunities for Eskimos to find food vary dramatically from one period to the next and, given the harshness of their environment they are forced to migrate when resources become scarce, most notably during the Arctic winter. Not surprisingly, these people do not make war. Instead they make haste—to go where food is available. People living on the razor edge of starvation gain little from warring with each other" (Barash, p. 195).

Moreover, so long as there are millions of people who have lived lives in technologically advanced civilization without having had to go off to war, we have all the evidence we need that people can live out their lives without manifesting the potential for the irrational collective aggressions of large scale wars. In short, we have all the evidence we need that both in small scale societies and in large scale technologically advanced collectivities there is no overwhelming need for wars. Any neat sociobiological or psychological argument for pessimism is too neat for its own good. At very worst, our question as to the degree to which war is eliminable is wide open for further investigation in theory, and in the catch-as-catch-can practical efforts to forge our destiny.

Conclusions

Although it is fashionable to suggest an inevitable link between scientism and ego-driven alienation from nature, theorists who subscribe to the inevitability of the link seem to be confusing a correlation with a causal relation. Scientism and objective thinking have led to social arrangements which have resulted for reasons unrelated to the objectivity of scientism in the spread of patriarchal chiefdom consciousness. Patriarchal chiefdom consciousness has taken a terrible toll on social arrangements. But to abandon Enlightenment West scientism and objectivity in order to rediscover attitudes of mystic participation in the general sense (not Levy-Bruhl's specific sense) would be to compound whatever current difficulties we now face. Without objective thinking we are led into parochial nationalisms, and subtle chauvinisms. The correct target of current feminist, pessimist, radical ecophilosophical, postmodernist, and Enlightenment East critiques of control-minded approaches to nature, is the ego-driven, patriarchal chiefdom structure manifested in all its forms, and not the objective thinking which underlies scientific ideals, democratic ideals, and the ideals of social justice. After all, it is objective thinking which enables one to understand that someone else's family is a family just like one's own.

Enlightenment West has always been an enlightenment which is an unburdening and a lamplighting. Now, too, it must continue to be an unburdening and a lamplighting. We must unburden ourselves of chiefdom consciousness and its effects. And we must learn to relight the lamp of mystic participation. Enlightenment East must integrate with Enlightenment West or it will be missing crucial social values. Enlightenment West must integrate with Enlightenment East or it will have an incomplete vision of human prospects. There is more to fulfillment than can be achieved by positing fulfillment as the goal, and setting forth a just framework to achieve it. It is our burden and our fortune to be living in the epoch in which the third line of progress in history, the dismantling of indiscriminate chiefdom consciousness, so that scientific knowledge and social justice can be joined with warm familiality, and joyous consciousness of the sacred, is finally beginning to emerge. The supremacy of the chief over the judge, and the judge over the mystic, has begun to play itself out. Now that the function of the judge is in the course of establishing a full and permanent political supremacy over the function of the chief, we must undo the damage that chiefdom consciousness has perpetrated in rippling through our social institutions and entrenching ego-consciousness. There is no better way of accomplishing this, than by our collective reeducation in the intuition of the sacred, in science, in international justice, and the art of meditation. In this collective reeducation, we begin with sacralism, infuse monadic ethics with mysticism, and subject all social and religious institutions to the canons of science and justice. This constitutes the marriage of Enlightenment East and West.

Bibliography

Aberle, David, et al. 1950. "The Functional Prerequisites of a Society," *Ethics*, 60: 100-111.

Adams, Robert M. 1973. "A Modified Theory of Ethical Wrongness," in *Religion and Morality: A Collection of Essays*. Edited by Gene Outka and J. Reader. NY: Doubleday.

Adler, Alfred. 1927. *Understanding Human Nature*. Translated by Walter Beran Wolfe. NY: Greenberg.

Almeder, Robert. 1990. "On Reincarnation." Edited by Gary Doore. *What Survives?* Los Angeles: J. P. Tarcher, pp. 34-50.

Althusser, Louis. 1977. *For Marx*. Translated by Ben Brewster. London: NLB.

———. 1984. *Essays on Ideology*. London: Verso.

———. 1990. *Philosophy and the Spontaneous Philosophy of the Scientists & Other Essays*. Edited by Gregory Elliott and translated by Ben Brewster. London: Verso.

Ames, Roger. 1983. *The Art of Rulership*. Honolulu: University of Hawaii Press.

Ames, Roger T., and David L. Hall. 1987. *Thinking Through Confucius*. Albany: SUNY Press.

Angel, Leonard. 1983. *The Silence of the Mystic*. Toronto: Philosophy In Canada Monographs.

———. 1989. *How to Build a Conscious Machine*. Boulder: Westview.

———. 1989a. "Two Hypotheses About Channeling." *Rational Enquirer*, Vol. 2, No. 3 (Jan.). Vancouver: BC Skeptics, pp. 1-3, 10.

———. 1991. "Paramahansa Yogananda's 'Scientifically Attested Miracle,'" *Rational Enquirer*, Vol. 4, No. 3 (April). Vancouver: BC Skeptics, pp. 1-3, 8.

Anselm. 1962. *Anselm's Basic Writings*. Translated by S. W. Deane, 2nd edition. LaSalle, Ill.: Open Court Publishing Company.

Aristotle. 1941. *The Basic Works of Aristotle*. Edited by Richard McKeon. NY: Random House.

Augustine, St. 1958. *The City of God*. Garden City: Doubleday.

Austin, John L. 1962. *Sense and Sensibilia*. Edited by G. J. Warnock. Oxford: Clarendon Press.

Azrin, N. H. 1967. "Pain and Aggression." *Psychology Today* (May), pp. 27-33.

Badham, Paul, and Linda Badham. 1982. *Immortality or Extinction?* London: Macmillan. (Note: Page references are to Paul Badham and Linda Badham, "Claimed Memories of Former Lives," in Clark, Ralph, Ed., *Introduction to Philosophical Thinking*. St. Paul: West Publishing, 1987, pp. 260-270).

Barash, David. 1979. *The Whispering Within*. NY: Harper & Row.

Barnes, Jonathan. 1979. "Parmenides and the Eleatic One." *Archiv Fur Geschichte der Philosophie* 61: 1-21.

Basham, A. L. 1969. "The 'Greater Vehicle' of Mahayana Buddhism." Chap. 3 of *The Buddhist Tradition*. Edited by William T. de Bary. NY: Random House Vintage, pp. 73-81.

de Beauvoir, Simone. 1948. *The Ethics of Ambiguity*. NY: Philosophical Library.

Beehler, Rodger. 1978. *Moral Life*. Oxford: Basil Blackwell.

Behanan, Kovoor T. 1937. *Yoga: A Scientific Evaluation*. NY: Dover.

Beloff, John. 1985. "What is Your Counter-Explanation? A Plea to Skeptics to Think Again," *A Skeptic's Handbook of Parapsychology*. Edited by Kurtz, Paul. Buffalo: Prometheus Books, pp. 359-377.

Benedict, Ruth. 1934. *Patterns of Culture*. NY: Houghton Mifflin Co.

Berkeley, George. 1961. *Three Dialogues Between Hylas and Philonous*. Garden City: Doubleday.

Berman, Morris. 1984. *The Reenchantment of the World*. NY: Bantam.

Beyerstein, Barry. 1991. "The Brain and Consciousness." In *The Hundredth Monkey*. Edited by Kendrick Frazier. Buffalo: Prometheus Books, pp. 43-53.

Bharati, Agehananda. 1976. *The Light at the Centre*. Santa Barbara: Ross-Erikson.

———. 1980. *The Ochre Robe*. Santa Barbara: Ross-Erikson.

Blackmore, Susan. 1987. "The Elusive Open Mind: Ten years of negative research in parapsychology." *Skeptical Inquirer*, Vol. 11, No. 4.

Bolen, Jean Shinoda. 1989. *Gods in Everyman*. San Francisco: Harper & Row.

———. 1984. *Gods in Everywoman*. San Francisco: Harper & Row.

Boucher, Sandy. 1988. "Conspiracy of Silence: The Male Teacher." In *Turning the Wheel: American Women Creating the New Buddhism*. San Francisco: Harper & Row, pp. 211-257.

Bouquet, A. C. 1956. *Hinduism*. London: Hutchison University Library.

Briggs, Jean L. 1970. *Never in Anger*. Cambridge: Harvard University Press.

Brody, Baruch A. 1974. "Morality and Religion Reconsidered." In *Readings in the Philosophy of Religion*. Edited by Brody, Baruch. Englewood Cliffs, Prentice Hall, pp. 491-502.

Brunton, Paul. 1935. *A Search in Secret India*. Philadelphia: McKay.

Buber Martin. 1970. *I and Thou*. Translated by Walter Kaufmann. NY: Scribners & Sons.

Butler, Katy. 1991. "Encountering the Shadow in Buddhist America." *Common Ground* (Summer). Vancouver, Canada: Box 34090, V6J 4M1, pp. 12, 13, 16, 17, 19, 71.

———. 1983. "Events are the Teacher." *Co-Evolution Quarterly* (Winter). Sausalito, Cal.: Box 428, 94966, pp. 112-123.

Campbell, Joseph. 1973. *The Hero with a Thousand Faces*. Princeton: Princeton University Press.

Caputo, John D. 1987. *Radical Hermeneutics*. Bloomington: Indiana University Press.

Capra, Fritjof. 1982. *The Turning Point*. NY: Simon & Schuster.

Cardozo, Benjamin Nathan. 1946. *Growth of the Law*. New Haven: Yale University Press.

Carter, Robert E. 1992. *Becoming Bamboo*. Montreal & Kingston: McGill-Queens University Press.

Chari, C. T. K. 1978. "Reincarnation and Research: Method and Interpretation." Edited by Martin Ebon. *The Signet Handbook of Parapsychology*. NY: Signet, pp. 313-324.

Chuang Tsu. 1974. The Inner Chapters. Translated by Gia-Fu Feng and Jane English. NY: Random House.

———. 1981. Translated by A. C. Graham. London: George Allen & Unwin.

Chung Yung. 1928. Translated by Ezra Pound. NY: New Directions.

———. 1963. Translated by Wing-Tsit Chan. "Doctrine of the Mean" excerpts, in *Sourcebook in Chinese Philosophy*. Princeton: Princeton University Press.

Chinmayananda, Swami. n.d. *Talks on Sankara's Vivekachoodemani (Crest Jewel of Discrimination)*. Bombay: Shri Ram Batra.

———. 1982. *Atma-Bodha by Bhagawan Sri Sankaracharya*. Bombay: Central Chinmaya Mission Trust.

Clark, Ralph. 1987. *Philosophical Thinking*. St. Paul: West Publishing.

Clifford, W. K. 1879. "The Ethics of Belief." In *Lectures and Essays*, Vol. 2. London: Macmillan, pp. 163-176.

Cole, John. "Follow-up: Samoan Hoax." *Skeptical Inquirer*, Vol. 17 (Summer 1993): 435-436.

Confucius. 1979. *The Analects*. Translated with an introduction by D. C. Lau. Harmondsworth: Penguin.

———. 1951. *Confucius*. Translated by Ezra Pound. NY: New Directions [includes *The Analects* and other Confucian materials].

Crease, Robert, and Charles Mann. 1990. "The Yogi and the Quantum." In *Philosophy of Science and the Occult*. Edited by Patrick Grim, 2nd ed. Albany: SUNY Press, pp. 302-314.

Cudworth, Ralph. 1976. *A Treatise Concerning Eternal and Immutable Morality*. NY: Garland Publishing.

Curd, Patricia Kenig. 1991. "Parmenidean Monism." *Phronesis* 36.3: 241-264.

Csikszentmihalyi, Mihaly. 1991. *Flow*. NY: Harper.

Dancy, Jonathan. 1985. *An Introduction to Contemporary Epistemology*. Oxford: Basil Blackwell.

Danto, Arthur. 1972. *Mysticism and Morality*. NY: Harper & Row.

Daly, Mary. 1978. *Gyn/Ecology*. Boston: Beacon Press.

Descartes, Rene. 1934. *Philosophical Works*. Translated by Haldane & Ross, Cambridge.

de Sousa, Ronald. 1987. *The Rationality of Emotion*. Cambridge: MIT Press.

Dharmasiri, Gunapala. 1989. *Buddhist Ethics*. Antioch: Golden Leaves.

Diaconis, Persi. 1978. "Statistical Problems in ESP Research." *Science*, no. 201: 131-136.

Dietl, Paul. 1958. "On Miracles." *American Philosophical Quarterly*, 1958: 5.

Dray, William H. 1964. *Philosophy of History*. Englewood Cliffs: Prentice Hall.

Dreikurs, Rudolf, and Loren Grey. 1969. *Logical Consequences*. NY: E. P. Dutton.

Drengson, Alan R. 1989. *Beyond Environmental Crisis*. NY: Peter Lang.

Driver, Tom F. 1991. *The Magic of Ritual*. San Francisco: Harper.

Durham, William H. 1976. "Resource Competition and Human Aggression: A Review of Primitive Wars." *Quarterly Review of Biology*, 51: 385-415.

Earle, William. 1980. *Mystical Reason*. Chicago: Regnery Gateway.

Eccles, John C., and Karl Popper. 1977. *The Self and its Brain*. NY: SPringer International.

Eckhart, Meister. 1941. *Meister Eckhart, A Modern Translation*. Translated by Raymond Blakney. NY: Harper & Row.

Edelstein, Ludwig. 1964. *The Idea of Progress in Classical Antiquity*. Baltimore: John Hopkins Press.

Edwards, Paul. 1986-1987. "The Case Against Reincarnation." *Free Inquiry*, Vol. 6, No. 4 (Fall 1986); Vol. 7, No. 1 (Winter 1987); Vol. 7, No. 2 (Spring 1987); Vol. 7, No. 3 (Summer 1987). Buffalo: Codesh Inc.

Einstein, Albert. 1981. "Letter to Dr. Jan Ehrenwald." Quoted in *Science, Good Bad and Bogus*. Martin Gardner. NY: Avon, p. 152.

Eliade, Mircea. 1959. *The Sacred and the Profane*. NY: Harcourt Brace.

Ellul, Jacques. 1964. *The Technological Society*. Translated by John Wilkinson. NY: Knopf.

Feinberg, Joel. 1989. *Reason and Responsibility*, 7th edition. Belmont: Wadsworth.

Feuerstein, Georg. 1990. *Holy Madness*. NY: Viking Penguin Arkana.

Fields, Rick. 1983. "Perils of the Path," *Co-Evolution Quarterly* (Winter), pp. 124-129.

Fingarette, Herbert. 1972. *Confucius, the Secular as Sacred*. NY: Harper & Row.

Forman, Robert. 1990. Ed. *The Problem of Pure Consciousness*. NY: Oxford University Press.

Foucault, Michel. 1972. *Archaeology of Knowledge*. NY: Pantheon.

————. 1970. *The Order of Things*. NY: Pantheon.

Fox, Robin, and Lionel Tiger. 1971. *The Imperial Animal*. NY: Holt, Rinehart & Winston.

Fraser, Sylvia. 1992. *The Book of Strange*. Toronto: Doubleday.

Freeman, Derek. 1983. *Margaret Mead and Samoa: The Making and Unmaking of an Anthropological Myth*. Cambridge: Harvard University Press.

———. 1989. "Fa'apua'a Fa'amu and Margaret Mead." *American Anthropology*, Dec.

Fromm, Erich. 1973. *The Anatomy of Human Destructiveness*. NY: Holt, Rinehart & Winston.

Fukuyama, Francis. 1992. *The End of History and the Last Man*. NY: Free Press.

Fuller, Lon L. 1968. *Anatomy of the Law*. NY: New American Library.

Gale, Richard. 1960. "Mysticism and Philosophy." *Journal of Philosophy*, 57.

Gardner, Martin, 1981. *Science, Good Bad and Bogus*. NY: Avon.

———. 1988. *The New Age*. Buffalo: Prometheus.

———. 1993. "The Great Samoan Hoax." *The Skeptical Inquirer*, Vol. 17, No. 2 (Winter 1993): 131-135.

Gatens, Moira. 1991. *Feminism and Philosophy*. Bloomington: Indiana University Press.

Geach, Peter T. 1969. *God and the Soul*. NY: Schocken Books.

Gellner, Ernest. 1988. *Plough, Sword and Book: The Structure of Human History*. Chicago: University of Chicago Press.

Geras, Norman. 1983. *Marx and Human Nature*. London: Verso.

Glasser, William. 1986. *Control Theory in the Classroom*. NY: Harper & Row.

———. 1990. *The Quality School: Managing Students Without Coercion*. NY: Perennial Library.

Gold, Jerry. 1983. "Review." *Samoan News*, 26 (Aug.): 22.

Goldman, Alvin. 1986. *Epistemology and Cognition*. Cambridge, Mass: Harvard University Press.

Gray, John. 1992. "Against the New Liberalism." *Times Literary Supplement*, July 3, No. 4657: 13-15

Gross, Rita M. 1993. *Buddhism After Patriarchy*. Albany: SUNY Press.

Gruson, Lindsay, and John Hubner. 1988. *Monkey on a Stick: Murder, Madness and the Hare Krishnas*. San Diego: Harcourt Brace Jovanovich.

Grim, Patrick. 1990. *Philosophy of Science and the Occult*, 2nd ed. Albany: SUNY Press.

Gulliver, P. H. 1977. "On Mediators." *Social Anthropology and Law*. Edited by Ian Hammett. NY: Academic Press.

Hall, David L., and Roger T. Ames. 1987. *Thinking Through Confucius*. Albany: SUNY Press.

Hansel, C. E. M. 1989. *The Search for Psychic Power*. Buffalo: Prometheus Books.

Harris, Marvin. "Margaret and the Giant-Killer." *The Sciences*, 23(4): 20-21.

Hatab, Lawrence J. 1990. *Myth and Philosophy*. Lasalle: Open Court.

Hoebel, E. Adamson. 1954. *The Law of Primitive Man: A Study in Comparative Legal Dynamics*. Cambridge: Harvard University Press.

Hegel, Georg Wilhelm Friedrich. 1955. *Lectures on the Philosophy of History*. Translated by E. S. Haldane, and F. H. Simson. Reprint. London (1892-1896).

Herman, A. L. 1991. *A Brief Introduction to Hinduism*. Boulder: Westview Press.

Hesiod. *Works and Days*.

Hobbes, Thomas. 1988. *Leviathan*. Buffalo, NY: Prometheus Books.

Holmes, Lowell Don. 1987. *Quest for the Real Samoa*. South Hadley: Bergin & Garvey Publishers.

Horne, James R. 1983. *The Moral Mystic*. Waterloo: Wilfrid Laurier University Press.

Hume, David. 1975. *Enquiry Concerning Human Understanding*. Oxford: Oxford University Press.

Indian Skeptic. See Premanand, B.

Iqbal, Muhammed. 1963. *The Reconstruction of Religious Thought in Islam*. Lahore.

Islam, Kazi Nurul. 1988. *Sankara's Philosophy of Appearance: A Critique*. Allahabad: Vohra Publishers.

Izutso, Toshihiko. 1982. *Towards a Philosophy of Zen Buddhism*. Boulder, CO: Prajna Press.

Jacobs, Janet Liebman. 1989. *Divine Disenchantment: Deconverting from New Religions*. Bloomington, IN: Indiana University Press.

James, William. 1897. *The Will to Believe*. NY: Longman Green & Co.

———. 1961. *The Varieties of Religious Experience*. NY: Macmillan.

Jaspers, Karl. 1951. *The Way to Wisdom*. Translated by Ralph Manheim. New Haven: Yale University Press.

Juergensmeyer, Mark. 1991. *Radhasoami Reality*. Princeton: Princeton University Press.

Jonsen, Albert R., and Stephen E. Toulmin. 1988. *The Abuse of Casuistry*. Berkeley: University of California Press.

Kalupahana, David. 1992. *A History of Buddhist Philosophy*. Honolulu: University of Hawaii Press.

Kalupahana, David, and Indrani. 1982. *The Way of Siddhartha*. Boulder, CO: Shambhala.

Kant, Immanuel. 1964. *Groundwork of the Metaphysics of Morals*. Translated by H. J. Paton. NY: Harper & Row.

Kaplan, Mordecai. 1985. *Dynamic Judaism*. NY: Schocken Books.

Katz, Steven. 1978. "Language, Epistemology, and Mysticism." In *Mysticism and Philosophical Analysis*. Edited by Steven Katz. Oxford: Oxford University Press, 1978.

Kaufmann, Walter. 1976. *Religions in Four Dimensions*. NY: Reader's Digest Press.

Kenny, Anthony. 1985. "The Ethics of War." In *The Logic of Deterrence*. Chicago: University of Chicago Press.

King, David Burnett. 1988. *The Crisis of Our Times: Reflections on the Course of Western Civilization, Past, Present, and Future*. Selinsgrove: Susquehanna University Press.

Kluckhohn, Clyde. 1952. "Universal Values and Anthropological Relativism." In *Modern Education and Human Values*. Pittcairn-Crabbe Foundation Lecture Series. Pittsburgh: University of Pittsburgh Press, pp. 87-112.

———. 1958. "Universal Categories of Culture." *Anthropology Today*. Chicago: University of Chicago Press, pp. 507-523.

Kovoor, Abraham. 1976. *Begone Godmen*. Bombay: Jaico Press.

Kuhn, Thomas. 1976. *The Structure of Scientific Revolutions*, 2nd ed. Chicago: University of Chicago Press.

Kurtz, Paul. 1986. *The Transcendental Temptation: A Critique of Religion and the Paranormal*. Buffalo: Prometheus.

Lao Tsu. See *Tao Te Ching*.

Lattin, Don. 1988. "The Cloud Over Indian Guru's U.S. Tour." *San Francisco Chronicle*, Sat. July 23, 1988.

Lemesurier, Peter. 1988. *The Healing of the Gods*. Dorset: Element Books.

Levy-Bruhl, Lucien. 1923. *Primitive Mentality*. London: Allen & Unwin.

Lewis, David. 1986. *On the Plurality of Worlds*. Oxford: Basil Blackwell.

Leibnitz, Baron Gottfried. 1956. *Philosophical Papers and Letters*. Chicago: University of Chicago Press.

Locke, John. 1961. *An Essay Concerning Human Understanding*. Edited by J. W. Yolton. NY: Dutton.

MacIntyre, Alisdair. 1984. *After Virtue*, 2nd edition. Ind: Notre Dame University Press.

McNeill, William Hardy. 1980. *Human Condition*. Princeton: Princeton University Press.

———. 1963. *The Rise of the West: A History of the Human Community*. NY: New American Library.

Maimonides, Moses. 1981. *The Book of Knowledge (Mishneh Torah*, Vol. 1). Edited by Moses Hyamson. NY: Feldheim.

———. 1956. *The Guide for the Perplexed*. Translated by M. Friedlander. NY: Dover.

Mann, Charles, and Robert Crease. 1990. "The Yogi and the Quantum." In *Philosophy of Science and the Occult*. Edited by Patrick Grim. 2nd ed. Albany: SUNY Press, pp. 302-314.

Marcuse, Herbert. 1964. *One Dimensional Man*. Boston: Beacon Press.

Marshall, Howard. 1979. "The Genealogy of Jesus." *Commentary on Luke*. Michigan: Eerdmans, pp. 157-165.

Martin, Robert. 1992. *There are Two Errors in the the Title of this Book*. Guelph: Broadview.

Maslow, Abraham. 1962. *Toward a Psychology of Being*. Princeton, NJ: D. van Nostrand Co.

———. 1964. *Religions, Values, and Peak Experiences*. NY: Viking Press.

Mayeda, Sengaku. 1979. *A Thousand Teachings*. Tokyo: University of Tokyo Press.

Mead, Margaret. 1939. *From the South Seas*. NY: W. Morrow & Co.

—–—. 1961. *Coming of Age in Samoa: A Psychological Study of Primitive Youth for Western Civilization*. NY: W. Morrow & Co.

Meister Eckhart. 1941. *Meister Eckhart*. Translated by Raymond Blakeney. NY: Harper & Row.

Mencius, Book of. 1963. (excerpts). Translated by Wing-Tsit Chan. Chap. 3. *Sourcebook of Chinese Philosophy*. Princeton: Princeton University Press. Also, D. C. Lau, ed., Penguin, 1970.

Mill, John Stuart. 1987. *Utilitarianism*. Buffalo: Prometheus Books.

Milne, Hugh. 1986. *Bhagwan: The God that Failed*. NY: St. Martin's Press.

Moore, G. E. 1912. *Ethics*. London.

Morris, Lois B., and John M. Oldham. 1990. *The Personality Self-Portrait*. NY: Bantam.

Moser, Paul K. 1989. *Knowledge and Evidence*. Cambridge: Cambridge University Press.

Moser, Shia. 1968. *Absolutism and Relativism in Ethics*. Springfield: Charles C. Thomas.

Mourelatos, P. D. 1979. "Some Alternatives in Interpreting Parmenides." *Monist*, 62: 3-14.

Munitz, Milton K. 1986. *Cosmic Understanding*. Princeton: Princeton University Press.

Murty, T. R. V. 1960. *The Central Philosophy of Buddhism*. London: George Allen & Unwin.

Naess, Arne. 1988. *Ecology, Community, and Life Styles*. Cambridge: Cambridge University Press.

Nagel, Thomas. 1979. *Mortal Questions*. Cambridge: Cambridge University Press.

Naranjo, Claudio, and Robert E. Ornstein. 1971. *On Psychology of Meditation*. NY: Viking.

Neville, Robert C. 1987. *The Puritan Smile*. Albany: SUNY Press.

Newman, Katherine. 1983. *Law and Economic Organization*. Cambridge: University Press.

Nielsen, Kai. 1973. *Ethics Without God*. Buffalo: Prometheus Books.

Nietzsche, Friedrich W. 1954. *The Portable Nietzsche*. Translated by W. Kaufmann. NY: Viking.

Nikhilananda, Swami. 1968. *Hinduism*. Mylapore: Sri Ramakrishna Math.

Noddings, Nel. 1989. *Women and Evil*. Berkeley: University of California Press.

————. 1984. *Caring: A Feminine Approach to Ethics and Moral Education*. Berkeley: University of California Press.

Oldham, John M., and Lois B. Morris. 1990. *The Personality Self-Portrait*. NY: Bantam.

O'Neill, Onora. 1989. "A Simplified Account of Kant's Ethics . . ." In *Introduction to Philosophy*. Edited by James E. White. St. Paul: West Publishing.

Ormrod, Jeanne Ellis. 1990. *Human Learning*. Columbus: Merrill.

Ornstein, Robert E. 1972. *The Psychology of Consciousness*. San Francisco: W. H. Freeman & Co.

Ornstein, Robert E., and Claudio Naranjo. 1971. *On Psychology of Meditation*. NY: Viking.

Otto, Rudolf. 1957. *The Idea of the Holy*. Translated by John W. Harvey. London: Oxford University Press.

Paramahansa Yogananda: In Memoriam (no author listed). 1958. L.A.: SRF.

Pardue, Peter. 1968. *Buddhism: A Historical Introduction to Buddhist Values*. NY: Macmillan.

Parfit, Derek. 1984. *Reasons and Persons*. Oxford: Oxford University Press.

Parmenides. 1965. *Parmenides*. Translated & commentary by Leonardo Tara'n. Princeton: Princeton University Press.

Parrinder, Geoffrey. 1971. *World Religions*. NY: Hamlyn Publishing Group.

Pasricha, Satwant. 1990. *Claims of Reincarnation*. New Delhi: Harman Publishing House.

Patanjali. 1938. *Yoga Aphorisms*. Translated by Shri Purohit Swami. London: Faber & Faber.

Piaget, Jean. 1932. *The Moral Judgement of the Child*. NY: Harcourt & Brace Co.

Pierce, C. S. 1934. *Colleged Papers*. Edited by C. Hartshorne, and P. Weiss. Cambridge: Harvard University Press.

Plato. 1937. *The Dialogues*. Translated by Benjamin Jowett. NY: Random House.

Playfair, Guy Lyon. 1976. *The Indefinite Boundary*. NY: St. Martin's Press.

Pojman, Louis P. 1986. *Religious Belief and the Will*. NY: Routledge & Kegan Paul.

Polybius. 1962. *The Histories*. 2 vols. Translated from the text of F. Hultsch by E. Shuckburgh. Bloomington: Indiana University Press.

Popper, Sir Karl Raimund, and John C. Eccles. 1977. *The Self and its Brain*. NY: Springer International.

Pospisil, Leopold. 1971. *Anthropology of Law: A Comparative Study*. NY: Harper & Row.

Premanand, B. Ed. 1988–. *The Indian Skeptic*. (serial) Podanur. India: B. Premanand-Indian CSICOP.

Proudfoot, Wayne. 1985. *Religious Experience*. Berkeley: University of California Press.

Quine, W. V. O. 1960. *Word and Object*. Cambridge, Mass: MIT Press.

Rae, Stephen. 1991. "The Guru Scene." *Cosmopolitan Magazine* (August). NY: Hearst Corp., pp. 176-179, 238.

Rahula, Walpola. 1974. *What the Buddha Taught*. NY: Grove Press.

Raju, P. T. 1985. *Structural Depths of Indian Thought*. Albany: SUNY Press.

Randi, James. 1982. *Flim-Flam! Psychics, ESP, Unicorns, and Other Delusions*. Buffalo: Prometheus Books.

———. 1981. "Investigation of Psychics." *Skeptical Inquirer*. Vol. 5, No. 4.

Rawls, John. 1971. *A Theory of Justice*. Cambridge: Belknap Harvard University Press.

Reich, James R. Jr. 1993. "The Eyewitness: Imperfect Interface Between Stimuli and Story." *Skeptical Inquirer*. Vol. 17, No. 4 (Summer 1993): 394-399.

Rifkin, Jeremy. 1991. *Biosphere Politics*. NY: Crown.

Roberts, Simon. 1979. *Order and Dispute*. Oxford: Martin Robinson.

Rodamor, William. 1983. "The Secret Life of Swami Muktananda." *Co-Evolution Quarterly* (Winter): 104-111.

Roll, William G. 1982. "The Changing Perspectives on Life after Death." *Advances in Parapsychological Research*. Edited by Stanley Krippner. Vol. 3. NY: Plenum Press.

Rorty, Richard. 1991. *Objectivity, Relativism, and Truth*. Cambridge: Cambridge University Press.

————. 1987. "Pragmatism and Philosophy." In *After Philosophy: End or Transformation*. Edited by Kenneth Baynes, James Bohman, and Thomas McCarthy. Cambridge: MIT Press.

Ross, W. D. 1930. *The Right and the Good*. Oxford: Clarendon Press.

Rothberg, Donald. 1990. "Contemporary Epistemology and the Study of Mysticism." In *The Problem of Pure Consciousness*. Edited by Robert Forman. NY: Oxford University Press.

Roy, S. S. 1965. *The Heritage of Sankara*. Allahabad: Udayana Publications.

Russell, Bertrand. 1959. *Mysticism and Logic*. London: Allen and Unwin.

————. 1961. *Religion and Science*. NY: Oxford University Press.

Ryle, Gilbert. 1931-1932. "Systematically Misleading Expressions." *Proceedings of the Aristotelian Society* 32: 139-152, 157-163, 165-169.

Sahlins, Marshall David. 1972. *Stone Age Economics*. Chicago: Aldine-Atherton.

Sandel, Michael J. 1982. *Liberalism and the Limits of Justice*. Cambridge: Cambridge University Press.

Sanjana, J. E. 1954. *Dogma of Reincarnation, A Critical Inquiry*. Bombay: New Book Co.

Santina, Peter Della. 1986. *Madhyamika Schools in India*. Delhi: Motilal Banarsidass.

Sartre, Jean Paul. 1956. *Being and Nothingness*. Translated by Hazel Barnes. NY: Philosophical Library.

Saul, John Ralston. 1992. *Voltaire's Bastards*. Toronto: Viking Canada.

Sangharakshita, Sthavira. 1985. *The Eternal Legacy*. London: Tharpa.

Shankara, 1963. "Crest Jewel of Discrimination." In Swami Prabhavananda, *The Spiritual Heritage of India*. Hollywood: Vedanta Press.

Scharfstein, Ben-Ami. 1973. *Mystical Experience*. Baltimore: Penguin.

Schopenhauer, Arthur. 1958. *The World as Will and Representation*. Translated by E. F. J. Payne. NY: Dover.

Schwartz, Theodore. "Follow-up: Samoan Hoax." *Skeptical Inquirer*, Vol. 17 (Summer 1993): 436-438.

Service, Elman Rogers. 1966. *The Hunters*. Englewood Cliffs: Prentice Hall.

Siegel, Lee. 1991. *The Net of Magic*. Chicago: University of Chicago Press.

Sieghart, Paul. 1985. *The Lawful Rights of Mankind: An Introduction to the International Legal Code of Human Rights*. NY: Oxford University Press; Opus.

Singer, Peter. 1979. *Practical Ethics*. Cambridge: Cambridge University Press.

Singh, Kirpal. 1961. *The Crown of Life*, 4th ed. Anaheim: Ruhani Satsang.

Sivananda, Swami. 1985. *Life and Works*. Vol. 2, Sivanandanagar: Divine Life Society.

Skeptical Inquirer. 1976-. Edited by Kendrick Frazier (1993). Buffalo: CSI-COP.

Skolimowski, Henryk. 1992. *Living Philosophy*. London: Arkana.

Smart, J. J. C., and Bernard Williams. 1973. *Utilitarianism: For and Against*. Cambridge: Cambridge University Press.

Smart, Ninian. 1964. *Philosophers and Religious Truth*. London: SCM.

————. 1958. *Reasons and Faiths*. London: Routledge & Kegan Paul.

————. 1968. *The Yogi and the Devotee*. London: George Allen & Unwin.

Smart, N., and R. Hecht. Eds. 1982. *Sacred Texts of the World*. NY: Crossroad.

Smith, Huston. 1958. *The Religions of Man*. NY: Harper & Row.

————. 1976. *Forgotten Truth*. San Francisco: Harper San Francisco.

Snyder, Gary. 1979. *He Who Hunted Birds in His Father's Village*. San Francisco: Grey Fox Press.

Solomon, Robert C. 1976. *The Passions*. Garden City: Doubleday.

Sowerby, Eileen. 1993. *Nel Noddings' Caring: A Critical Analysis*. Master's thesis, University of British Columbia.

Spector, Marshall. 1990. "Mind, Matter, and Quantum Mechanics." In *Philosophy of Science and the Occult*, 2nd ed. Edited by Patrick Grim. Albany: SUNY Press.

Spengler, Oswald. 1926-1928. *The Decline of the West*. Translated by Charles Francis Atkinson, 2 vols. NY: A. A. Knopf.

Spinoza. 1982. *The Ethics and Selected Letters*. Translated by Samuel Shirley. Indianapolis: Hackett Publishing Co.

Spretnak, Charlene. 1991. *States of Grace: The Recovery of Meaning in the Postmodern Age*. San Francisco: Harper.

Staal, Frits. 1975. *Exploring Mysticism: A Methodological Essay*. Harmondsworth: Penguin.

Stace, Walter. 1960. *Mysticism and Philosophy*. London: Macmillan.

Stevenson, Ian. 1974. *Twenty Cases Suggestive of Reincarnation*. Charlottesville: University Press of Virginia.

Stevens, Anthony. 1982. *Archetypes, A Natural History of the Self*. London: Routledge & Kegan Paul Ltd.

Strawson, P. F. 1965. *Individuals: An Essay in Descriptive Metaphysics*. London: Methuen & Co. Ltd.

Tao Te Ching. 1972. English & Fu-Feng trans. NY: Vantage.

———. 1963. Translated by D. C. Lau. Harmondsworth: Penguin.

Tan, Tai Wei. 1972. "Recent Discussions on Miracles." *Sophia* (Oct. 1972): 24.

Taylor, Charles. 1991. *The Ethics of Authenticity*. Cambridge: Harvard University Press.

Taylor, Rodney. 1988. *The Confucian Way of Contemplation*. Columbia: University of South Carolina Press.

———. 1990. *The Religious Dimensions of Confucianism*. Albany: SUNY Press.

Tiger, Lionel, and Robin Fox. 1989. *The Imperial Animal*. NY: Holt, Rinehart and Winston.

Tillich, Paul. 1952. *The Courage to Be*. Glasgow: William Collins Sons.

Thomason, Sarah. 1987. "Past Tongues Remembered." *Skeptical Inquirer* (Summer 1987): 367-375.

Thompson, Janna. 1992. *Justice and World Order*. London: Routledge.

Toulmin, Stephen E., and Albert Jonsen. 1988. *The Abuse of Casuistry*. Berkeley: University of California Press.

Unger, Peter. 1975. *Ignorance: A Case for Skepticism*. Oxford: Clarendon Press.

————. 1984. *Philosophical Relativity*. Minneapolis: University of Minnesota Press.

————. 1984a. "Minimizing Arbitrariness: Toward a Metaphysics of Infinitely Many Isolated Concrete Worlds." *Midwest Studies in Philosophy* 9 (1984): 30-51.

van Buren, Paul M. 1972. *The Edges of Language: An Essay in the Logic of a Religion*. NY: Macmillan.

Vivekananda, Swami. 1955. *Raja-Yoga*, 2nd ed. India: Ramakrishna-Vivekananda Centre.

Wainwright, William. 1981. *Mysticism*. Brighton: Harvester.

Walzer, Michael. 1977. *Just and Unjust Wars*. NY: Basic Books.

Webster, Katherine. 1990. "The Case Against Swami Rama of the Himalayas." In *Yoga Journal* (Nov./Dec. 1990): 60-69, 92.

Weedon, Chris. 1987. *Feminist Practice and Poststructuralist Theory*. Oxford: Basil Blackwell.

West, Robin. "Jurisprudence and Gender." University of Chicago Law Review, Vol. 55, No. 1 (Winter 1988).

Williams, Bernard. 1973. *The Problems of the Self*. Cambridge: Cambridge University Press.

Williams, Bernard, and J. J. C. Smart. 1973. *Utilitarianism for and Against*. Cambridge: Cambridge University Press.

Wilson, Ian. 1981. *Mind Out of Time*. (Cited by P. Edwards, 1987, as a British publication.)

————. 1985. *Exodus*. NY: Harper & Row.

————. 1987. *The After Death Experience*. NY: William Morrow.

Winetrout, Kenneth. 1975. *Arnold Toynbee: The Ecumenical Vision*. Boston: Twayne.

Wittfogel, Karl. 1957. *Oriental Despotism*. Yale University Press: New Haven.

Woodcock, George. 1992. *The Monk and His Message: Undermining the Myth of History*. Vancouver: Douglas & McIntyre.

Wu, Kuang-ming. 1990. *The Butterfly as Companion*. Albany: SUNY Press.

Yeats, William Butler. 1962. *A Vision*. London: Macmillan.

Yarbro, Chelsea Quinn. 1980. *Messages from Michael*. NY: Berkley Books.

Yogananda, Paramahansa. 1946. *The Autobiography of a Yogi*. Los Angeles: SRF.

Zaehner, Robert C. 1957. *Mysticism Sacred and Profane*. Oxford: Clarendon Press.

Index

A

Aberle, David, 315
Abraham, 318
Absolutism and Relativism in Ethics (Moser), 315
Abuse of Casuistry, The (Toulmin and Jonsen), 250
Actionless action (*Naishkarmya karma*), 229
Adam, 202
Adams, Robert M., 188
Adler, Alfred, 333
Advaita Vedanta, 2, 100, 155, 171, 182, 223
After Death Experience, The (Wilson), 278
After Virtue (MacIntyre), 79-80, 244
Agape, agapism, 49, 57, 184
Agency, 86, 126, 261, 263, 265–266, 340
    as monadic good, 85-86, 87, 90
Agriculture, 333, 334
al-Ghazali, 102
Alienation, and scientism, 337-341
Almeder, Robert, 277, 278, 279
Altered-self mysticism, 118-132, 149, 241-243, 253, 299-301, 305, 340
Althusser, Louis, 23
Ambedkar, B. R., 231
American Society for Psychical Research, 273
Ames, Roger T., 41, 210, 232
Amoralism, amorality, 10, 100, 224, 239
Analects (Confucius), 41-42

Ananda, 97, 100
Anatman doctrine, 152, 156-157
Anatomy of Human Destructiveness, The (Fromm), 342, 354
Angel, Leonard
    How to Build a Conscious Machine, 262
    investigations of paranormal claims, 295-297
    "Paramahansa Yogananda's "Scientifically Attested Miracle," 297
    The Silence of the Mystic, 340
    "Two Hypotheses about Channelling," 273
Animals, 46, 95
Anselm, Saint, 169
Anthony, Dick, 238-239
Anthropology of Law, The (Pospisil), 317
Anti-modernist approach to values, 22ff
Antinomianism, 10, 100, 224, 239
Apportation, 257, 298
Arapesh society, 342
Archaeology of Knowledge, The (Foucault), 25, 353
Archetypes, 47-48
Archetypes, A Natural History of the Self (Stevens), 47
Arhat, 230, 246
Aristotle, 15, 39, 73, 90, 250, 313
    on friendship, 42-43
    on virtues, 42-43, 73
Arnold Toynbee: The Ecumenical Vision (Winetrout), 334
Art of Rulership, The (Ames), 232

367